THE CHRONICLES OF

The Wars
of the Roses

ur moost goode and graciouse. Queue Elisabeth
Soster vnto this oure ffraternite. Of oure blissed
ladi. And modr of merci. Sanct Mary Virgyn the
modr of God

THE CHRONICLES OF

The Wars of the Roses

General Editor
Elizabeth Hallam

Preface by
Hugh Trevor-Roper

CLB

4733 The Chronicles of the Wars of the Roses
This edition published in 1997 by CLB
Distributed in the USA by BHB International, Inc.,
30 Edison Drive, Wayne, New Jersey 07470
© 1988 CLB International
All rights reserved
Printed and bound in Spain
ISBN 1-85833-588-4

Above *Seal of the mayors of London, 1381.*

Frontispiece *Elizabeth Woodville, wife of
Edward IV, who rose to the throne from
minor gentry origins in the chaos of the Wars
of the Roses.*

Created and Produced by Phoebe Phillips Editions
Editorial Director: Tessa Clark

Editorial:
Editor: Cecilia Walters
Richard Bird
Fred Gill
Yvonne Ibazebo
Paul Mackintosh
Sheila Mortimer
Jenny Overton
Timothy Probart
Picture Research:
Dr Margaret M. Condon
Ancilla Antonini
Agnès Viterbi

Design and Production:
Rachael Foster
Phil Kay
Rebecca Bone
Keith Ireland

Specially commissioned photographs:
Marianne Majerus

Maps:
Jeff Edwards

General Editor:
Dr Elizabeth Hallam, *Assistant Keeper of Public Records,*
  Public Record Office, London

Preface:
Hugh Trevor-Roper

Translators:
Editor: Dr Richard Mortimer, *Keeper of Muniments,*
  Westminster Abbey
Catharine Edwards
Dr Meryl Foster
Avril Powell
Janet Shirley
David Smallwood
Emily Thomas
Geoffrey West

Contributors to illustrated spreads:
Dr Trevor Chalmers, *Assistant Keeper, Public Record*
  Office
Anne Crawford, *Assistant Keeper, Public Record Office*
Dr Lindy Grant, *Conway Library, Courtauld Institute*
  of Art
Professor Ralph Griffiths, *Head of Medieval History,*
  University College, Swansea
Dr Gerald Harris, *Fellow and Lecturer, Magdalen College,*
  Oxford
Dr Jennifer Harris, *Honorary Lecturer, Whitworth Art*
  Gallery, University of Manchester
Geoffrey Hindley, *Writer*
Nicholas Hooper, *Master, Bradford Grammar School*
Dr Frances Horgan, *Fellow, Fitzwilliam College,*
  Cambridge
Dr Rosemary Horrox, *University of Cambridge*
Dr Charles Kightly, *Writer*
Dr Pamela King, *Lecturer in English, Westfield College,*
  University of London
John Kirby, *Historian*
Dr Simone C. MacDougall, *Lecturer in Medieval History,*
  University of St. Andrews
Dr A. K. McHardy, *Lecturer in History, University of*
  Aberdeen
Dr William Mark Ormrod, *Fellow, St. Catherine's*
  College, Cambridge
Dr Carole Rawcliffe, *History of Parliament Trust*
Dr Colin Richmond, *Reader in History, University of*
  Keele

Special help from:
J. Conway, *British Library*
Carol Morris, *British Museum*
The London Library
R. Edwards, *The Itinerary of Richard III, 1483–85,*
  Richard III Society, 1983
The Dean and Chapter, *Chester Cathedral*

Ly commence le anquieme
liure de Rusticam parlant
des arbres. Et de la nature
et prouffits de leurs fruis
Et premierment
Le prologue de ce liure ·

J ay dit par
dessus ou se
cond liure en
general plu
seurs choses des arbres
quant ie parloy de la na

ture des plantes et des cho
ses communes appertenans
a labouraige et de chascune
maniere de champs · Mais
a present en ce quint liure
ie vueil traittier de chascu
liure par soy. Et pour
ce que aulcunes choses sont
communes a tous arbres et
aulcunes propres ie vueil
parler ou premier en sermon
general du labouraige de

Editor's Note

England hath long been mad, and scarred herself;
The brother blindly shed the brother's blood,
The father rashly slaughtered his own son,
The son, compelled, been butcher to the sire:
All this divided York and Lancaster.

SHAKESPEARE, in *Richard III*, thus sums up the Tudor propagandists' horror and revulsion at the carnage of the Wars of the Roses. For many centuries his view of these conflicts – which spanned more than three decades, from 1455 to 1487 – has been widely accepted. In contrast modern interpretations of the struggle tend to play down its effects on society at large, and to view it as a savage and bloody but intermittent contest between noble factions with the crown as the prize: fighting was sporadic, there was no general and prolonged breakdown of law and order, and damage to people and crops was relatively minor.

In political and dynastic terms, however, the Wars of the Roses were of singular importance. They mark the climax in the struggle of the Lancastrian and Yorkist offshoots of the Plantagenet house – a struggle which ended in the final destruction of Henry II's male descent. Richard II was the last of the direct line of eldest surviving royal sons; the Lancastrians and Yorkists were both cadet branches, the offshoots of Edward III's third son, John of Gaunt, duke of Lancaster, and of his fourth son, Edmund of Langley, duke of York. The surname Plantagenet was adopted by Richard of York in the 1460s and used by his family to emphasise the superiority of their claim over the Lancastrians; and Shakespeare applied it to both the doomed and warring families. It is his usage that we here follow.

This volume covers the final century of Plantagenet rule in England, from 1377 to 1485, beginning with the troubled reign of Richard II, and tracing the triumphs and downfall of Lancaster and York. The story is, as in previous volumes in this series, narrated by contemporary or near-contemporary chroniclers, ranging from cloistered monastic writers such as Thomas Walsingham to Italian humanists like Dominic Mancini. Until 1453 England's French possessions were a major preoccupation, and the voices of her enemies in France and in Scotland can also be heard. So too can those of more parochial Englishmen, such as the London-based author of John Benet's chronicle, and indignant critics of inadequate governance, such as John Hardyng.

Selections from the works of this diverse and lively collection of chroniclers have here been translated into modern English and linked with explanatory text. Where necessary names, titles, dates and places have been added, as have a few comments in square brackets. The aim of these editorial interventions is to elucidate the text, but they have been kept to a minimum in order to allow readers to make direct contact with the sources from which history is made, so that they may interpret the words of the chroniclers for themselves.

To help in this process our team of scholars has written a series of notes commenting on events and people in the main narrative, and exploring the artistic and literary as well as the social and economic context. The notes and chronicles are complemented with illustrations from manuscripts, and with photographs of objects and of places. In all these ways are the dramas, triumphs and tragedies of the last century of Plantagenet rule brought to life.

*Left **The white rose, badge of the house of York, appears with the royal arms in the margin of a book produced for Edward IV, first of the Yorkist kings.***

Contents

Preface

THE later Middle Ages in England – the period from Richard II to Richard III which is covered in this volume – is a tragic period in our history: tragic in a real sense because it supplies the material of Shakespeare's historical plays which, as a series, illustrate a classical tragic theme. That theme is *hubris* leading to *nemesis*: a fatal process, uncontrollable by man, launched by the weakness, not the wickedness, of one man. This tragedy of the house of Plantagenet, like the tragedy of the house of Atreus, took three generations to unfold. The man who, by his infirmity, set the process in motion was Richard II.

How winningly Richard II steps into history! Grandson of Edward III, son of the Black Prince who had died before his father, he is king at the age of ten and is projected at once into the political jungle. An ambitious and powerful uncle, John of Gaunt, towers over him, jealous of his succession. Such an uncle had murdered the young prince Arthur to secure the crown for himself two centuries ago, and another such would imitate him a century hence: no wonder if those around the boy king exalted his authority, and its legitimacy, the only guarantee of order in troubled times. Four years later he was called to the test. The great Peasants Revolt of 1381 was the most serious challenge to social order in medieval England: its leaders, Wat Tyler and Jack Straw, would be bogeymen for the next three centuries. But the young king was undismayed. He rode out to meet the huge and violent mob which had forced its way into the terrorised city, and by his natural authority and presence of mind dispersed it. Thereby he began to feel his power: to suppose that it could be exercised absolutely.

Today, after six centuries, we can look back on Richard II as a man of culture and taste, a royal aesthete, whose court was a splendid centre of the arts, who patronised Froissart, Chaucer and Gower and rebuilt Westminster Hall in its present magnificent form. Of course these arts and these buildings ministered also to his sense of power. They were the advertisement of royalty. Charles I too would be a royal aesthete to whom, for that reason, we forgive his questionable politics. Contemporaries, naturally, had different priorities. Hence the tragic end of each reign.

'Old John of Gaunt, time-honoured Lancaster', the overpowering uncle whom Richard II sought to keep at arm's length, died seven months before his nephew's deposition; but he obtained a posthumous victory in the succession of his son. Indeed all subsequent monarchs of England descend from him; yet to many Henry IV was a usurper who had dethroned and murdered his legitimate king. He lacked the aura of divine right, and the magnates who had raised him up because they resented the absolutism of Richard II were determined also to keep him down, lest he imitate it. For several years the ghost of Richard II haunted the royal palace. It was supposed that Richard was still alive, in Scotland, and discontent could be mobilised in his name. Between the taint of usurpation, the poverty of the new court, and the power of the great lords to whom he owed his throne, Henry IV had an uncomfortable reign. Then his brilliant son, Henry V, seeking to strengthen the dynasty by a victorious war, launched the cascade of disasters which brought it, instead, to ruin.

Perhaps it would have been different if Henry V had lived longer. Who can tell what might then have happened? But in fact, by renewing the long war with France, and by giving to that war the spurious glamour of the great initial victory of Agincourt, he set England on a fatal course. Under his son, Henry VI, at first an infant at the mercy of ambitious uncles, then the helpless observer of total defeat abroad, finally an imbecile *dévot* in the midst of anarchy and civil war, men could reflect on the folly of that adventure and the need not only of peace but also of strong undisputed central government: a government able to control those 'over-mighty subjects' who now abused the authority of a feeble king.

The civil wars were the Wars of the Roses between the rival heirs of Edward III: the house of Lancaster, defending its usurped rights, now validated by three generations of power, and the house of York, seeking to replace it, not because it was despotic or illegitimate but because it was weak, unfit to rule. They were horrible wars, marked by savagery and treachery: cannibal orgies of an inflated high aristocracy – never had there been so many dukes in England, or so little of aristocratic honour or feudal loyalty: an aristocracy which finally, by mutual slaughter, would destroy itself, leaving the country ready to accept any ruler who could give it peace and stability.

Such a rule was provided, for a time, by the most unlikely of statesmen, the debonair, indolent, pleasure-loving Edward of York. In 1460, at the age of nineteen, he inherited the claims of his father killed at Wakefield, and the following year he managed to depose the wretched Henry VI and make himself king as Edward IV. Nine years later, the struggle would be resumed when a successful revolt brought Henry VI from the Tower and replaced him on the throne; but it was a brief success, soon reversed: within a year Edward would be back in power, Henry back in prison, there, like Richard II, to be quietly murdered. After that, Edward would rule till his death, ruthless but effective and, because effective, popular: who now cared whether the heads of another batch of aristocratic bullies rolled? The confiscation of their estates enriched the Crown; skilful diplomacy and profitable peace encouraged trade. After the horrors of civil war, these bourgeois virtues would be appreciated.

Meanwhile Edward IV himself lived and ruled, as his subjects wished him to do, like a real king: nobly, grandly, with authority. He was not an aesthete like Richard II: there was nothing effeminate about him. Having married his sister to the duke of Burgundy, he imitated the splendour of that grandest, most ceremonious of European courts. He was a great builder who enlarged his numerous palaces and built St George's chapel at Windsor, one of the triumphs of late English Gothic architecture; he established a royal library and stocked it with fine illuminated manuscripts; and he delighted in rich jewellery and costly clothes. It was a far cry from the necessary parsimony of Henry IV, the threadbare monastic austerity of Henry VI.

Unfortunately Edward IV, like so many of his contemporaries, died young; and so, once again, a child was king and an overbearing uncle his 'Protector'. This time the Protector was not content to overbear: he destroyed. The young Edward V and his brother, 'the Princes in the Tower', were first declared illegitimate, then murdered; and the Protector stepped forward as king.

So began the brief, notorious reign of Richard III. Perhaps, if he had lasted, he would have overcome his sanguinary beginnings and continued his brother's policies. After all, he was no more ruthless than Edward IV who cut off heads as liberally as any, murdered his inconvenient predecessor, and had his own brother, the duke of Clarence, drowned in the famous butt of malmsey. And were the early Tudors much better? But the taint of usurpation and the callous murder of the innocent young princes could not be immediately digested. It split his own party and multiplied his enemies, who were already numerous enough; and so, before he could establish himself, he too was overthrown, killed in battle, and it was left to the new Tudor dynasty to continue, more successfully, because they lasted, the frustrated policies of the house of York.

Thus the period of Lancastrian and Yorkist rule passed into history, to be seen in retrospect as an illegitimate interlude between the great successful dynasties of Plantagenet and Tudor. Sir Thomas More would draw the classic portrait of the tyrannical monster Richard III, and Shakespeare would incorporate it in his series, in the last and most shocking act of the great morality drama which began with Richard II. The thesis served the Tudors well, for a time. In the end it could be turned against them. When Queen Elizabeth, at the end of her reign, saw the plots thicken about her, she saw herself as Richard II. 'I am Richard II, know ye not that?' she said; and a performance of Shakespeare's *Richard II* was banned.

But perhaps, in viewing the period as a whole, we should not see it in parochial, English terms. This continuing royal drama was played out against a European background: a background of general economic contraction and political disintegration. It was not only in England that feudal monarchies seemed to dissolve in civil war. At the head of Christendom the papacy too fell apart: the Great Schism, which divided the whole church between Rome and Avignon, began in 1378, the first year of Richard II, and was not healed till 1414. The French monarchy, once so stable, crumbled under Charles VI and was torn apart between 'Armagnacs' and 'Burgundians' – the French equivalent of the Wars of the Roses. The effects of the Black Death were felt throughout Europe. The Peasants Revolt confronted by the young Richard II was paralleled by the Jacqueries of France. We read of 'the turbulent London of Richard II', but similar 'turbulence' shook other European cities at the same time: Florence, Ghent, the German cities of the Rhine. The hardening of orthodoxy and the decline of the monastic orders was general throughout Europe. So was the response – the rise of heresy and the resort to private mysticism. The Lollard heresy of Wycliffe in England was matched by the Hussite movement in Bohemia, the mysticism of Rolle and Hampole by that of Suso and Tauler in Germany and the Brethren of the Common Life in the Netherlands. If the history of England from Richard II to Richard III makes melancholy reading, at least the long crisis was not particular but general.

Nor was the age without its achievements. In spite of anarchy and civil war, economic life continued. English wool was exported to the Staple in the Burgundian Netherlands and great 'wool churches' were built on the proceeds, in the Cotswolds and East Anglia. A new style of gothic architecture, peculiarly English, was developed. The Carthusian monks and Brigittine nuns, patronised by the Lancastrian kings, preserved the credit of the church. Great educational institutions were founded: Winchester and New College, Oxford, by William of Wykeham under Richard II, Eton and King's College, Cambridge, by Henry VI, and other colleges in both universities. They were set up as citadels of orthodoxy but would acquire a life of their own. Examples of literacy were given by the Lancastrian kings: Henry IV and his sons

were all bibliophiles. One of them, Humphrey duke of Gloucester, a great patron of literature, effectively created the university library at Oxford by his gifts of books. Some of the most ruthless and cruel noblemen in the Wars of the Roses – such as John Tiptoft, earl of Worcester – were famous as patrons of the new Italian humanism. Under Edward IV Caxton brought the new art of printing to England.

Finally, it was in this century that the English language replaced Norman French and Latin as the language of literature and the court. For three centuries since the Conquest it had been little better than a peasant *patois*, but in the last century it had gained ground. Now, thanks especially to Chaucer, the final barrier was broken. Wycliffe's Bible was in English. The Pastons wrote to each other in English. Malory's *Morte d'Arthur* was written in English. The books which Caxton printed were mostly in English. So were some of the chronicles from which this book is compiled.

The Chroniclers

With the monasteries there declined also the monastic chronicles. St Albans indeed, the great Benedictine abbey which had employed the talents of Roger of Wendover and Matthew Paris, still sought to keep up its old tradition. Its last great chronicler was Thomas Walsingham: as precentor and head of its *scriptorium* he continued the story down to the death of Henry V in 1422. Other monastic chronicles also had their continuators. The *Eulogium Historiarum*, compiled by a monk of Malmesbury, was carried on by a later scribe as far as the death of Henry IV in 1413. Many continuations were tacked on to an immensely popular 14th century work, the *Brut*, a French history of England, from legendary beginnings until 1377. It was translated into English and then continued in English in stages. The text up to 1461 was printed by Caxton in 1480. A furthur manuscript continuation has been ascribed to John Warkworth, who became Master of Peterhouse, Cambridge, in 1473, and presented the work to his college. The monastery of Crowland found an even later continuator who carried its chronicle down to 1486. He was not a monk but a sophisticated and active man of the world – a civil lawyer perhaps – who lodged for a time in the monastery. Some think he may have been John Russell, bishop of Lincoln and chancellor of Oxford University, who was employed on government business by Edward IV, Richard III

and Henry VII. Whoever he was, he suddenly and usefully invigorated the dim, sour chronicle of a dim, sour Fenland abbey.

Beside the dwindling band of monastic chroniclers we now find a growing crop of freelance writers, who however show no more independence of mind; but in those treacherous times, who can blame them for that? Even Walsingham, protected by a great Order, had to toe the changing line: his *Chronicle of England*, written under Richard II, was critical of John of Gaunt, but when Gaunt's son became king, the abbey insisted that he supply a new text more appropriate to the time. John Capgrave, a learned Augustinian Hermit friar at Lynn, Norfolk, wrote enthusiastically about the Lancastrian kings in the works which he dedicated to Henry VI, but in the later chronicle which he dedicated to Edward IV he changed his tune: he then described his former hero, Henry IV, as an 'intruder'. 'It is impossible', says his 19th century editor sadly, 'to defend our author from the charge of sycophancy'. John Hardyng, a north-country squire who fought in many a battle, including Agincourt, turned to chronicling in his retirement. His chronicle, written in English, in deplorable doggerel verse, was constantly revised to flatter changing patrons. As he was still writing at the age of 86, there was room for such revision. He was a resourceful old rogue: sent by Henry V to Scotland to collect proof that Scotland

Henry V to Scotland to collect proof that Scotland was a subject nation, he returned with a most satisfactory haul of documents, obtained, he said, at great cost and danger; for which he was well rewarded. The documents, it has since been shown, were all forged by himself. Another freelance was the Warwickshire antiquary John Rous who nestled, for most of his life, in a chantry at Guy's Cliff, Warwick. He too changed with the times. A strong Yorkist until 1485, he then turned about and described Richard III as a deformed monster, an Antichrist.

A third and new group of chronicles is provided by the towns: evidence of a new civic replacing an old monastic spirit. The most important of these ruban chronicles (which are written in English) are the London chronicles, mostly compiled by John Fabyan, clothier, alderman and sheriff of London. Like his monastic predecessors, he went in for 'universal history', beginning in legendary times, for which he relied on that old stand-by, *the Brut*. But gradually he found himself concentrating on the history of London, and for his own time he is original. The most ambitious of these London chronicles is *the Great Chronicle of London*, an important source for the reign of Edward IV. Londoners were partial to Edward IV, who encouraged trade and courted the City, as the clergy were to the devout and orthodox Henry VI.

Another less official London chronicle is that ascribed to (but in fact merely copied by) John Benet, vicar of Harlington in Bedfordshire. The author was clearly a learned man, perhaps a civil lawyer, who had been in Oxford during the great irot of 1440, but lived in London and could give first-hand accounts of its turbulent life under Henry VI.

Finally, there are the historical accounts written by foreigners, particularly by Netherlanders, subjects of the dukes of Burgundy. The dukes, who held their splendid court at Bruges, had regular political and economic relations with England and watched events closely. They were also great patrons of chroniclers. After Froissart, who revisited England under Richard II, and was received by the king at Leeds Castle in Kent (where perhaps he obtained his graphic but prejudiced account of the great Peasants Revolt), there is Jean de Wavrin, a soldier who fought on the French side at Agincourt and compiled a huge 'universal' history of England; Olivier de la Marche, the famous Burgundian master of ceremonies; and, greatest of all, Philippe de Commynes, who deserted to the court of Louis XI of France, and wrote his memoirs there. He too visited England and wrote about it. Less politically involved were the Italians who came in search of scholarly employment. Two of them feature here. The first is Tito Livio Frulovisi, a humanist poet whom Duke Humphrey fetched to be his secretary and employed to write a Latin life of his brother Henry V. The second is Domenico Mancini, also a poet, sent over from the court of Louis XI to report on English affairs. He did his job well and presented to his patron, and to us, a valuable account of the last episode in this mounting tragedy of the English royal house, *The Usurpation of Richard III*.

Hugh Trevor-Roper

Europe in 1377

In the later Middle Ages Europe was still very much on the peripheries of the civilised world. The most powerful, advanced and wealthy state was ruled by the Chinese emperors, and Islam was making great gains in the Middle and Near East, often at the expense of Christianity. Devastated by plague earlier in the century, Europe was also, from 1378, riven by the religious and political divisions consequent on the Great Schism in the Church.

NORWAY

SWEDEN

RUSSIAN STAT

Moscow

SCOTLAND

○Edinburgh

North
Sea

DENMARK

Baltic
Sea

TEUTONIC

KNIGHTS

IRELAND

Dublin ○

○Copenhagen

ENGLAND

○Lübeck
○Hamburg

Elbe

LITHUANIA

London

Thames

○Utrecht

Warsaw ○

POLAND

○Kiev

Calais

○Cologne

○Leipzig

Vistula

Atlantic
Ocean

Rhine

HOLY

○Rouen

○Frankfurt

○Prague

Paris

Seine

Brétigny ○

○Orléans

Troyes

ROMAN

○Vienna

Loire

FRANCE

BURGUNDY

○Constance

○Budapest

HUNGARY

EMPIRE

Rhône

Bordeaux

Guyenne

Milan ○

○Trent

Armagnac

Venice

Bayonne

○Avignon

Ferrara

REPUBLIC OF VENICE

Danube

NAVARRE

Garonne

○Marseilles

○Genoa

PAPAL

Black
Sea

PORTUGAL

Douro

ARAGON

Pisa ○

Florence

STATES

Adriatic
Sea

SERBIA

BULGARIA

Siena ○

Tiber

Ebro

○Lisbon

Tagus

Madrid

Barcelona

Corsica

○Rome

EASTERN

CASTILE

Sardinia

EMPIRE

Constantinople

Naples ○

OTTOMAN TURKS

NAPLES

Balearic
Islands

GRANADA

○Granada

SICILY

Rhodes

Crete

Mediterranean Sea

○ **Paris**   Main cities

English possessions in 1377

0		200		400	Miles
0	300		600 Km		

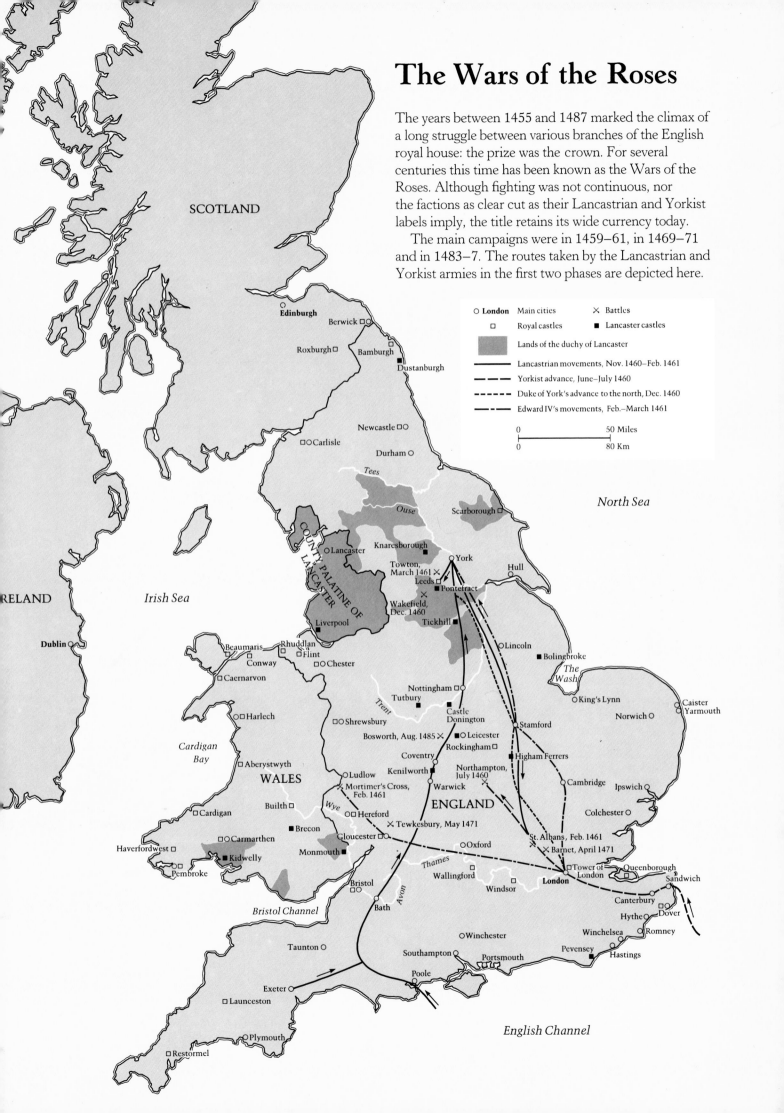

The Wars of the Roses

The years between 1455 and 1487 marked the climax of a long struggle between various branches of the English royal house: the prize was the crown. For several centuries this time has been known as the Wars of the Roses. Although fighting was not continuous, nor the factions as clear cut as their Lancastrian and Yorkist labels imply, the title retains its wide currency today.

The main campaigns were in 1459–61, in 1469–71 and in 1483–7. The routes taken by the Lancastrian and Yorkist armies in the first two phases are depicted here.

○ **London** Main cities	×	Battles
□ Royal castles	■	Lancaster castles

Lands of the duchy of Lancaster

—————— Lancastrian movements, Nov. 1460–Feb. 1461

– – – – Yorkist advance, June–July 1460

· · · · · Duke of York's advance to the north, Dec. 1460

–·–·–· Edward IV's movements, Feb.–March 1461

0	50 Miles
0	80 Km

SCOTLAND

Edinburgh
Berwick □
Roxburgh □
Bamburgh
Dustanburgh ■

Newcastle □○
□○ Carlisle
Durham ○

Tees

Ouse
Scarborough □

North Sea

Knaresborough ■
○ Lancaster
Towton, March 1461 ×
York
Leeds □
Pontefract ■
Hull

IRELAND

Irish Sea

COUNTY PALATINE OF LANCASTER

Wakefield, Dec. 1460 ×
Tickhill ■
Liverpool ■

○ Lincoln
Bolingbroke ■

Dublin ○

Beaumaris □
Rhuddlan □
Conway □
Flint □
□○ Chester
Caernarvon □

The Wash

Nottingham □
Tutbury ■
Castle Donington ■○
Stamford

King's Lynn ○

Caister
Yarmouth

Harlech □

Cardigan Bay

WALES

Aberystwyth ■

Shrewsbury □
Bosworth, Aug. 1485 ×
■○ Leicester
Rockingham □
Higham Ferrers ■

Norwich ○

Cambridge ○

Ipswich ○

Colchester ○

Coventry ○
Kenilworth ○
Warwick ○
Northampton, July 1460 ×

Cardigan □
Builth □

Ludlow ○
Mortimer's Cross, Feb. 1461 ×

ENGLAND

Wye

□○ Hereford

Tewkesbury, May 1471 ×

St. Albans, Feb. 1461 ×
× Barnet, April 1471

Tower of London □
Queenborough ○
Sandwich

Carmarthen □○
Kidwelly ■
Haverfordwest □
Pembroke □○

Brecon ■
Monmouth

Gloucester □○

Thames

○ Oxford
Wallingford □

London

Bristol □○

Bath ○

Avon

Windsor □

Canterbury ○
Hythe ○ Dover
Winchelsea ○ Romney ○

Bristol Channel

Taunton ○

Southampton ○
Poole ○
Portsmouth ○

Winchester ○
Pevensey ○
Hastings ■

Exeter ○
Launceston □

Plymouth ○
Restormel □

English Channel

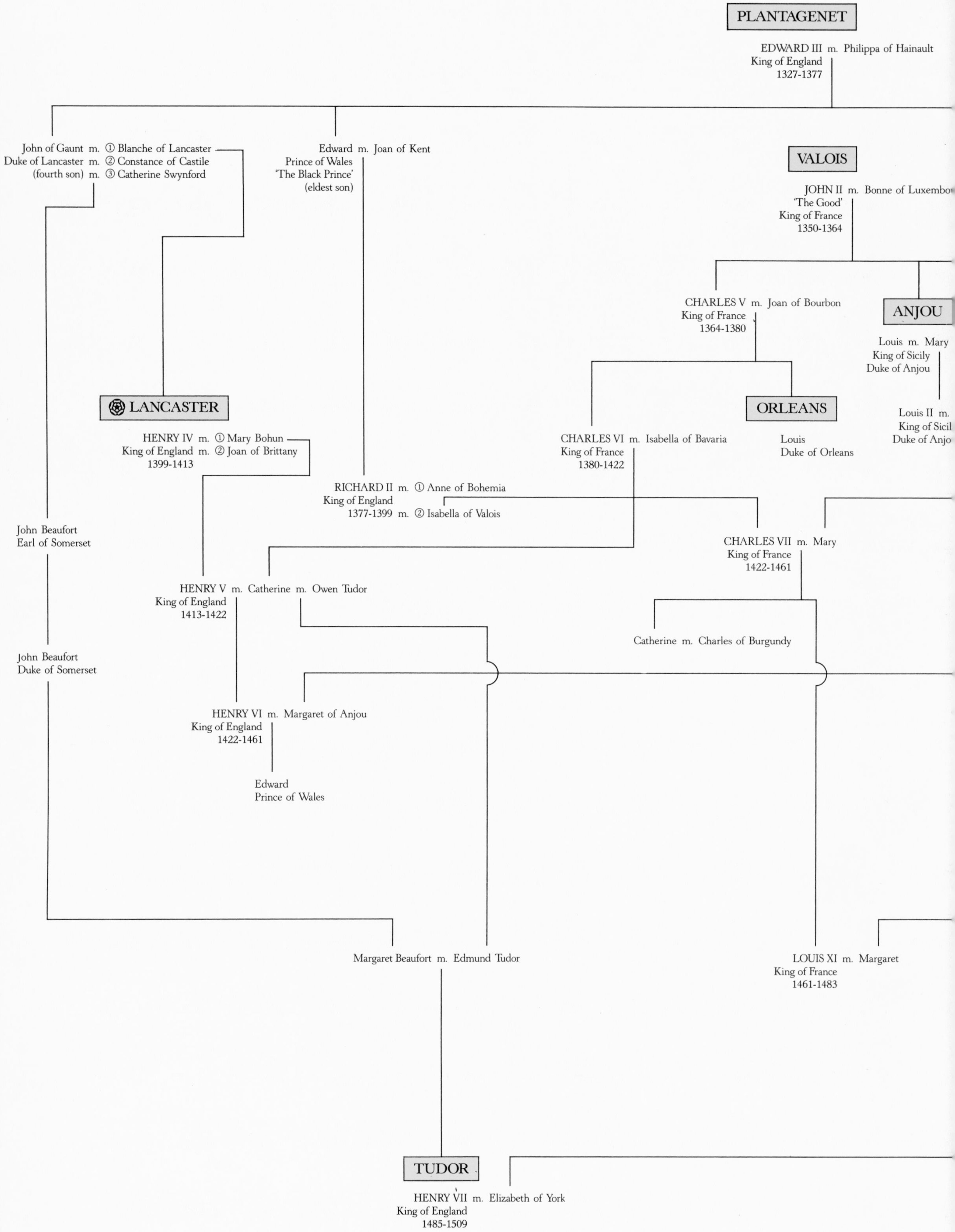

PLANTAGENET

EDWARD III m. Philippa of Hainault
King of England
1327-1377

John of Gaunt m. ① Blanche of Lancaster
Duke of Lancaster m. ② Constance of Castile
(fourth son) m. ③ Catherine Swynford

Edward m. Joan of Kent
Prince of Wales
'The Black Prince'
(eldest son)

VALOIS

JOHN II m. Bonne of Luxembo·
'The Good'
King of France
1350-1364

CHARLES V m. Joan of Bourbon
King of France
1364-1380

ANJOU

Louis m. Mary
King of Sicily
Duke of Anjou

LANCASTER

HENRY IV m. ① Mary Bohun
King of England m. ② Joan of Brittany
1399-1413

CHARLES VI m. Isabella of Bavaria
King of France
1380-1422

ORLEANS

Louis
Duke of Orleans

Louis II m.
King of Sicil
Duke of Anjo

RICHARD II m. ① Anne of Bohemia
King of England
1377-1399 m. ② Isabella of Valois

John Beaufort
Earl of Somerset

CHARLES VII m. Mary
King of France
1422-1461

HENRY V m. Catherine m. Owen Tudor
King of England
1413-1422

Catherine m. Charles of Burgundy

John Beaufort
Duke of Somerset

HENRY VI m. Margaret of Anjou
King of England
1422-1461

Edward
Prince of Wales

Margaret Beaufort m. Edmund Tudor

LOUIS XI m. Margaret
King of France
1461-1483

TUDOR

HENRY VII m. Elizabeth of York
King of England
1485-1509

Kings of England, France and Scotland

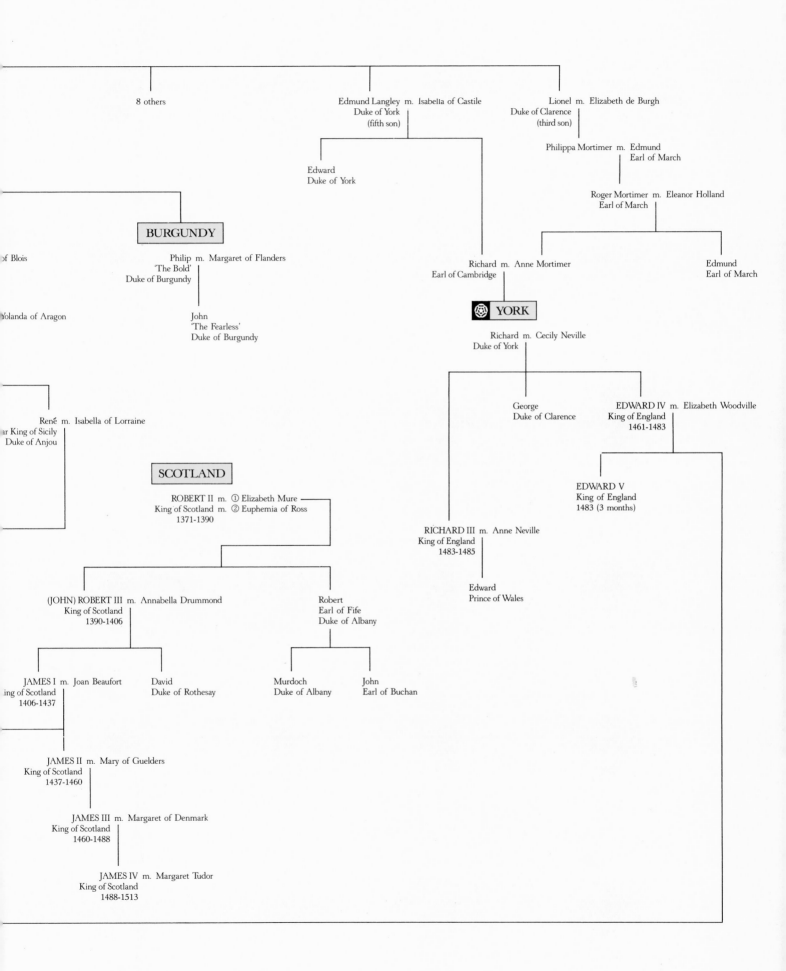

8 others

Edmund Langley m. Isabella of Castile
Duke of York
(fifth son)

Lionel m. Elizabeth de Burgh
Duke of Clarence
(third son)

Edward
Duke of York

Philippa Mortimer m. Edmund
Earl of March

Roger Mortimer m. Eleanor Holland
Earl of March

BURGUNDY

of Blois

Philip m. Margaret of Flanders
'The Bold'
Duke of Burgundy

Yolanda of Aragon

John
'The Fearless'
Duke of Burgundy

Richard m. Anne Mortimer
Earl of Cambridge

Edmund
Earl of March

YORK

Richard m. Cecily Neville
Duke of York

René m. Isabella of Lorraine
ar King of Sicily
Duke of Anjou

George
Duke of Clarence

EDWARD IV m. Elizabeth Woodville
King of England
1461-1483

SCOTLAND

ROBERT II m. ① Elizabeth Mure
King of Scotland m. ② Euphemia of Ross
1371-1390

EDWARD V
King of England
1483 (3 months)

RICHARD III m. Anne Neville
King of England
1483-1485

(JOHN) ROBERT III m. Annabella Drummond
King of Scotland
1390-1406

Robert
Earl of Fife
Duke of Albany

Edward
Prince of Wales

JAMES I m. Joan Beaufort
King of Scotland
1406-1437

David
Duke of Rothesay

Murdoch
Duke of Albany

John
Earl of Buchan

JAMES II m. Mary of Guelders
King of Scotland
1437-1460

JAMES III m. Margaret of Denmark
King of Scotland
1460-1488

JAMES IV m. Margaret Tudor
King of Scotland
1488-1513

Part I

Richard II
1377–1399

Only ten years old at the time of his coronation, Richard II first emerged into the limelight in 1381, when he dealt bravely with the leaders of the Peasants Revolt. This promising start was not, however, sustained: the king's political and administrative incapacity, coupled with his marked partiality for his favourites, aroused bitter opposition, which was strengthened by Richard's uncle, John of Gaunt, duke of Lancaster. Eventually, Richard was deposed by his cousin, Henry Bolingbroke, John of Gaunt's son. This unhappy reign is well served by the chroniclers. The dangers of the Peasants Revolt are vividly described by Jean Froissart; Thomas Favent gives a chilling account of the aptly named 'Merciless Parliament'; and a melodramatic treatment of Richard II's deposition is provided by an anonymous Burgundian writer. However, the main source for the events of the reign is Thomas Walsingham, a well-informed monk of St Albans Abbey. He shows, as the reign begins, the repercussions of the recent quarrel between John of Gaunt and the citizens of London over legal rights.

(Opposite: Richard II)

In 1377, when it became known that the noble king of England, Edward III, had died on 21 June, the Londoners sent some of the most powerful of their number to Kennington, where Prince Richard and the princess his mother were then staying, to commend to their goodwill the city and citizens of London. Once they had received this pledge, the citizens proceeded to the royal manor of Sheen, where they found the new king, Richard II, and his mother, together with the duke of Lancaster, John of Gaunt, and his brothers, sons of the late king, and several bishops, all gathered around the body of the deceased monarch.

When King Richard heard of the arrival of the Londoners, he ordered that they be brought into his presence. Whereupon they, as before, begged him to apply all his energy to peacemaking between John of Gaunt and the citizens, assuring him that they were ready to submit to the royal will in everything.

On the following Friday 26 June, at a gathering attended by the duke and the commons of London and Westminster, a herald proclaimed aloud the concord and peace now established between the duke and the citizens, after which everyone returned home rejoicing.

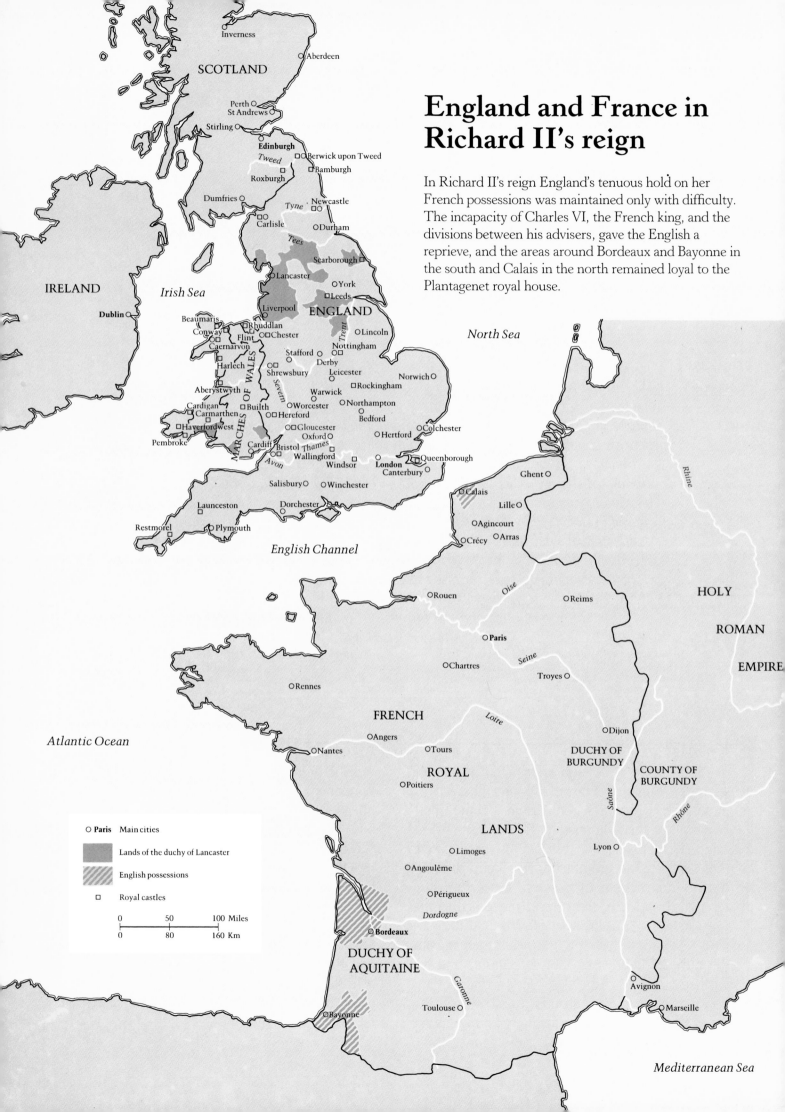

England and France in Richard II's reign

In Richard II's reign England's tenuous hold on her French possessions was maintained only with difficulty. The incapacity of Charles VI, the French king, and the divisions between his advisers, gave the English a reprieve, and the areas around Bordeaux and Bayonne in the south and Calais in the north remained loyal to the Plantagenet royal house.

Inverness
Aberdeen
SCOTLAND
Perth
St Andrews
Stirling
Edinburgh
Berwick upon Tweed
Tweed
Bamburgh
Roxburgh
Dumfries
Tyne
Newcastle
Carlisle
Durham
Tees
IRELAND
Irish Sea
Scarborough
Lancaster
York
Dublin
Leeds
Liverpool
ENGLAND
Beaumaris
Rhuddlan
Conway
Chester
Lincoln
Flint
Caernarvon
Nottingham
Stafford
Harlech
Derby
Shrewsbury
Leicester
Norwich
Aberystwyth
MARCHES OF WALES
Warwick
Rockingham
Severn
Worcester
Northampton
Cardigan
Builth
Bedford
Carmarthen
Hereford
Haverfordwest
Gloucester
Colchester
Pembroke
Oxford
Hertford
Cardiff
Bristol
Thames
Wallingford
Avon
Windsor
London
Queenborough
Salisbury
Winchester
Canterbury
Launceston
Dorchester
Restmorel
Plymouth
English Channel

North Sea
Ghent
Calais
Lille
Agincourt
Crécy
Arras
Rhine
HOLY
ROMAN
EMPIRE
Rouen
Oise
Reims
Atlantic Ocean
Paris
Chartres
Seine
Troyes
Rennes
FRENCH
Loire
Dijon
Angers
DUCHY OF
BURGUNDY
Nantes
Tours
COUNTY OF
BURGUNDY
ROYAL
Poitiers
Saône
LANDS
Rhône
Limoges
Lyon
Angoulême
Périgueux
Dordogne
Bordeaux
DUCHY OF
AQUITAINE
Garonne
Avignon
Toulouse
Marseille
Bayonne
Mediterranean Sea

○ **Paris**   Main cities

Lands of the duchy of Lancaster

English possessions

□   Royal castles

| 0 | 50 | 100 Miles |
| 0 | 80 | 160 Km |

Richard II and Ireland

Ever since its conquest by Henry II in the 1170s, Ireland had proved a problem to the Plantagenets; in the 1390s matters reached crisis point. Attempts three decades earlier to consolidate English power had succeeded only in the areas around Dublin, and the rest of Ireland was dominated by the native chieftains under the leadership of Art McMurrough. Richard II led an expedition to Ireland in 1394–5: he was the first English king to set foot there since 1210. The Irish leaders submitted to him and did homage, McMurrough even undertaking to allow English settlement in his Leinster lands. The principal Irish lordships accepting English rule are here depicted.

The show of loyalty had no real substance, however, and after unrest broke out in 1398, Richard hurried back to Ireland to restore order. The expedition was unsuccessful – and his absence from England at a crucial time was a major factor in his downfall.

The young king, from his own innate goodness, desired peace among all his subjects everywhere. On his accession Richard II brought the duke of Lancaster and William of Wykeham, bishop of Winchester, to an agreement for peace and unity. Also, when he learned that discord had arisen anywhere within his kingdom, he took the quarrels into his own hand, promising that he would bring them to a conclusion suitable and profitable to both sides. A happy omen, that a boy of the tender age of ten should, under no compulsion, concern himself in peacemaking, and, with no instruction, understand that peace is beneficial to his people!

Nor should one overlook how, as soon as Richard had assumed the name of king, he undertook to free Peter de la Mare, who was still held in strict custody in Nottingham Castle. He had been imprisoned there as punishment for his fidelity to the king and the realm when, having been chosen as speaker in the parliament held at Westminster in the last year of the reign of Edward III, he had refused assent to the taxes demanded on that occasion. In order that de la Mare might be completely safe from his enemies, the king issued letters patent remitting and relaxing any demands or penalties which might be imposed upon him in the king's name. De la Mare, for his part, soon hastened to the king, to express his thanks in person.

You might then have seen the people of the cities and towns coming out to greet de la Mare's arrival with great jubilation, and saying, with no less acclaim than was given long ago to St Thomas Becket on his return from exile: 'Blessed is he that cometh in the name of the Lord.' The Londoners themselves, welcoming him, paid their respects eagerly with a variety of gifts and presents.

At dawn on 29 June, five thousand Frenchmen in fifty boats, both large and small, attacked the town of Rye, which they captured with ease, although the townspeople, confident of their own strength, had decided and had given a strict undertaking that no one should take his movable possessions away from the town, the idea being that love of worldly goods would encourage everyone to hold out more vigorously in battle. Yet

The boy king

EDWARD III was 64 when he died on 21 June 1377, and had been on the throne of England for over 50 years. His death allowed an opportunity for a new start. But along with eager anticipation, there was also a sense of unease: the continuity had gone, and no one knew what the future might bring.

Edward's eldest son, the Black Prince, had died in 1376, and the king was succeeded by his grandson, the ten year old Richard II. Richard's mother Joan, a granddaughter of Edward I, and countess of Kent in her own right, had had a colourful past: she had been involved in a famous love triangle with the earl of Salisbury and Sir Thomas Holland. The 'fair maid of Kent' was a great beauty, and after the death of her first husband, Sir Thomas Holland, had been snatched up as the bride of the Black Prince in 1361.

The couple spent much of the first ten years of their marriage in Gascony, where the prince ruled on behalf of his father, and it was here that their two sons, Edward and Richard, were born. Edward died in infancy, and Richard was brought home to England in 1371 to be groomed for eventual kingship. The deaths of his father and grandfather brought him the crown unexpectedly early.

A minority was always a problem, particularly when, as in 1377, there were rifts within the royal family. The natural candidate for regent was the new king's uncle, John of Gaunt, but he was widely suspected of having ambitions for the throne and was opposed by his young brothers, Edmund of Langley, earl of Cambridge, and Thomas of Woodstock. As a result, a compromise was worked out. No regent was appointed, but a 'continual council' of 12 men was set up to decide policy and advise the king's ministers. The committee, led by the earls of

March and Arundel, included representatives of all the political groupings which had emerged during Edward's dotage. But far from producing consensus, this uneasy coalition simply sank into paralysis. England had no effective government during Richard's early years.

Meanwhile there was the question of the young king's education. His principal tutor was Sir Simon Burley, an old friend of the Black Prince. Burley possessed a number of books on the art of kingship, and is supposed to have encouraged his pupil to restore the glory of the throne by exerting his personal authority. Richard did this in dramatic fashion during the Peasants Revolt of 1381. While his advisers prevaricated, the 14 year old king exhibited considerable bravery and decisiveness, meeting the rebel leaders and helping to calm the excessive zeal of their followers. The revolt had a considerable influence on Richard and convinced him – wrongly as it turned out – that he was a strong and capable leader of men.

For all his privileges, Richard was a solitary and sad youth. With no father and no brothers, he depended on the company of women – the strong-minded Princess Joan and later his own Queen Anne. His one close friendship, with the young earl of Oxford, was ruinous to his political career.

In his isolation, Richard sought solace from the arts; surviving portraits of the king, done when he was still only in his late twenties, reveal the delicate fingers and finely chiselled features of a true connoisseur. The great tragedy and irony of Richard's life was that he combined this artistic sensitivity with a political ineptitude the like of which had rarely been seen in medieval England.

Opposite Richard II's coat of arms, from the celebrated Wilton Diptych, commissioned by Richard and taken with him on campaigns.

Below The young king, surrounded and overwhelmed perhaps by older and more forceful advisers. John of Gaunt, his uncle, is the figure wearing the ermine hat.

in the event they were as the sons of Ephraim, for 'being armed and carrying bows [they] turned back in the day of battle' [Ps. 78⁹]. Because of their foolishness, the town was taken, and all their possessions with it.

Early in July, mindful of his promise, King Richard II appeared before the Londoners. It was fitting that the citizens who welcomed him generously with gifts should be addressed by him with respect. Shortly afterwards, the lords and magnates decreed that the king's coronation would take place on 16 July. Both churchmen and laymen were summoned to attend, in order that so great a ceremony should be conducted with due solemnity.

Meanwhile, the great lords sought a formal declaration of the various duties which by ancient right pertain to them at coronations. The judges, having regard to the hereditary right of everyone concerned, lest any lawsuit should arise on a day of such great solemnity, set out carefully the privileges of each lord.

When the Londoners demanded the office of the butlery, which belonged to them, Robert Belknap, Chief Justice of the King's Bench, replied most ill-advisedly, 'My good sirs, butlers have many duties. It falls to some to draw the wine, to others to carry it in, to others to pour it, to others to serve those seated around the hall, and to others to wash the vessels, namely the ewers, pots and goblets. There is no point in asking that a duty be assigned to you, unless you specify precisely what it is.'

Hearing this, the citizens were incensed. They replied promptly that it was no duty of theirs to wash pots, but that they had some better pots than he did, and they would be happy to prove this by clouting him on the head with them. Uttering such threats against the Chief Justice, they departed in great anger, and they would have killed him if they had caught him in the city subsequently. Since they could not capture him, they insulted him by setting up on the conduit in Cheapside an effigy with a face resembling his, which spewed wine from its mouth when the king and people arrived there.

The magnates and crowds of the common people had flocked into London on the day before coronation day. On that day, at the ninth hour, the great lords of the realm, together with the Londoners and many others who had come thither for love of the king, rode on magnificent horses to the Tower of London, where Richard was waiting.

When those who were to ride in front and those who were to follow had been drawn up in procession, they rode towards Westminster through the crowded streets of the city of London, which were so bedecked with cloth of gold and silver, with silken hangings, and with other conceits to entertain the onlookers, that you might suppose you were seeing a triumph of the Caesars or ancient Rome in all its grandeur.

At the head of this great procession were the citizens of Bayeux, dressed in matching livery, who led the way with pipes, trumpets, drums and other carefully selected musical instruments.

Behind them followed the men of one of the divisions of the city of London, which are called 'wards', wearing livery likewise, and producing beautiful music. They were succeeded by Gascons, resplendent in robes of a different colour from those who had gone before.

The earls and barons of the realm followed, accompanied by their knights and squires, wearing hoods which matched the one worn by the king; they were all dressed in white, the colour chosen to represent the king's innocence.

The king came after them, mounted on a mighty destrier fit for so great a personage, and royally caparisoned. Richard's knights and contemporaries, and the members of the royal household, followed him.

In the king's honour, the citizens had arranged for wine to flow freely from the pipes of the conduit, which it did throughout the duration of the procession, a period of three hours or more. At the upper end of Cheapside, a castle with four towers had been constructed, from two sides of which wine poured out abundantly. Four beautiful

The making of a monarch

LIKE his forebears, the young Richard II, last in the direct line of the Plantagenet kings, was crowned in Westminster Abbey. The ceremony, devised for the coronation of Edward II 70 years earlier in 1307, was a modified version of a far earlier form. But it included an entirely new element: a magnificent, colourful procession from the Tower of London to Westminster on the day before the crowning, an idea introduced by John of Gaunt, duke of Lancaster. As lord high steward of England, the duke was responsible for master-minding this coronation. Richard was the first king to be crowned in England since Edward III in 1328, and Gaunt, with his eyes on the ever fickle populace, was determined to stage a memorable event. The exchequer would later bear the cost.

After the pageantry and spectacle of the procession, the boy king spent the night at the palace of Westminster. The next morning he was escorted to Westminster Hall, where he was installed in the marble chair on the King's Bench. Then, with his regalia, he proceeded in state into the abbey.

The ceremonies which set the ten year old monarch apart from his people and gave him a semi-priestly character then began. Richard ascended a platform, and, after a sermon preached by a senior prelate, swore his coronation oath, in which he promised to keep and maintain the laws and liberties of England. A litany was sung and the king's hands, chest, back, shoulders, elbows and head were anointed with holy oil. The chrism, the miraculous oil which gave the sovereign the power to touch for scrofula, was also applied to his head.

Once blessed, Richard was robed in his dalmatic (a long vestment), tunic, sandals and spurs, his sword with its belt, his stole and finally his great mantle woven with royal eagles. The crown was set on his head, the ring on his wedding finger, and gloves on his hands. Finally the sceptre was put in his right hand and the golden rod in his left. He was now ready to be enthroned on the coronation chair by the bishops and nobles, while the *Te Deum* was sung. The leading men of the kingdom did homage to their new lord and, lastly, mass was celebrated.

As was customary, the coronation was immediately followed by a banquet in Westminster Hall, during which the royal champion rode into the hall on horseback and, according to ancient practice, challenged to personal combat anyone who denied the king's right to his throne. Sir John Dymoke, lord of the manor of Scrivelsby, held the office as part of his feudal duties; but he was uncertain of his prescribed role. He had first appeared unexpectedly at the west door of the abbey during the coronation service, and been sent ignominiously away.

Above *Written and illuminated in the early years of Richard II's reign, the* Liber Regalis *gives a detailed description of the ritual and ceremony of the coronation. Depicted here is the moment when the king is crowned.*

Richard was so exhausted by the impressive and elaborate ritual of his coronation that he had to be carried from the abbey to Westminster Hall on the shoulders of his tutor, Sir Simon Burley – despite the abbot's protests that this was contrary to ancient custom. One of the child king's red velvet shoes fell off and was never recovered – perhaps an ominous portent for the future.

girls, of the same stature and age as King Richard and likewise dressed in white, stood, one on each of the four towers. As the king approached, they wafted down golden leaves before him, then, as he drew nearer, they scattered imitation golden florins upon him and his horse. When he reached the castle, the girls took up golden goblets, which they filled with wine from the pipes in the castle. These they then offered to the king and the lords.

At the very top of the castle, which was built up high between the four towers, stood a gilded angel carrying a golden crown; so cleverly was it constructed that it could lean down as the king approached, to present the crown to him. It would be a long task to list all the many other displays which were set up in the city that day in the king's honour, for the people in the streets and squares vied with one another to offer him the greatest reverence. Thus, amid the revelling of the common people and the citizens, and the rejoicing of the lords and magnates, the king was conducted to the royal palace next to the abbey of Westminster, where he rested that night.

On Thursday 16 July, in the abbey church of St Peter's, Westminster, the king swore his coronation oath before Simon, archbishop of Canterbury, and the magnates there present. After these ceremonies had been completed, King Richard II went up to the banqueting table, and there the bishops, earls and barons feasted splendidly with him.

Innumerable people had gathered there from all corners of the realm, and so many had crowded into Westminster Hall that if the duke of Lancaster, who was the steward of England, the earl of Buckingham, the constable, and Lord Henry Percy, the marshal, with several others, all mounted on their great horses, had not cleared a way through the hall, those who were serving at table would scarcely have managed to reach the guests with the dishes which they were carrying.

If I were to attempt to recount the preparations, the splendour of the tableware and the variety of dishes, the reader, struck as much by the value as by the quantity of such fine things, would perhaps hesitate to believe me. I consider, however, that

Gothic fashions

A new style of dress first made its appearance in Europe at the time of Richard's coronation. Known now as 'international Gothic', like the architecture and painting with which it was contemporary, it was initially flamboyant and whimsical – but within 20 years it had come to border on foppishness.

Men's dress was characterized by collars mounting to the ears and either short, closely fitting tunics, or voluminous gowns called 'houppelandes' with sleeves that swept almost to the ground. Shoes had pointed toes, so long that, according to legend, the points sometimes had to be chained up to the knee before the wearer could walk. Two-coloured hose were commonly worn with the short tunic. The parson in Chaucer's *Canterbury Tales* denounced the red and white variant for making men look as though they had hernias, and had had half their 'shameful privee membres . . . flayne'.

Women's dresses resembled the 'houppelande' but were longer, covering their feet, and had trains. By the end of the century their head-dresses had developed into towering, complex edifices composed of false hair or of a horseshoe-shaped roll stuffed with wool, above which a linen veil might be suspended. Their reassembly each morning took a great deal of time. Said to be a breeding-ground for mice and rats, they were much reviled by contemporary commentators, some of whom compared them to the horns of snails, others to those of the devil.

Underwear for the wealthy of both sexes consisted of a long shirt and, for men, a pair of drawers, both made of fine linen. People bathed infrequently, but linen was easily washed and laundered and underwear was probably changed regularly. Most household accounts list many shirts and record the purchase of large quantities of linen; that from Paris and Reims was especially prized.

The author of *The Goodman of Paris* (about 1393), a treatise on domestic management, gives recipes for

removing stains, but, otherwise, outer garments seem to have remained unwashed.

Fashionable dress represented a considerable capital investment, and clothing was often bequeathed in people's wills. The clothes of the aristocracy found their way into the hands of the wealthier middle classes, who sold them to secondhand dealers – and once-fashionable garments ended up on the backs of the poor. Clothes were left to religious houses to be made into vestments, or used as security on loans. In 1387, and again in 1388, Sir Simon Burley, Richard's tutor, borrowed from six London citizens offering his clothes and his beds as security.

Although distinctions between the dress of the leisured and the labouring classes had always existed, they became much more obvious during Richard's reign. The gowns with trains, and wide, hanging sleeves and the impractical footwear worn by the rich prevented even modest physical exercise. Nevertheless, moralists lamented that, higher up the social scale, great nobles were failing to stop their squires and servants from wearing rich and extravagant dress, which they saw as a factor contributing to the development of political instability.

Opposite *Fashionably dressed courtiers.*

Above *The height of fashion as worn at the Burgundian court in 1430.*

Below *The knight parts from his lady. Elaborate head-dresses and trains were worn in the mid 15th century.*

(leaving all else aside) one thing is worth mentioning, which was devised in order to emphasize the king's magnificence. In the middle of the royal palace, a carved marble column had been set up on a few steps; at its very top was a large gilded eagle, beneath whose feet, from the capital of the column, wines of various kinds flowed down on four sides, throughout the day of the king's coronation. No man, not even the humblest, was prevented from drinking there. The coronation took place when the king, Richard II, was in the eleventh year of his age.

The following day, a public procession took place, to honour the king and the peace of the realm. The archbishop of Canterbury, together with the bishops and abbots who had participated in the coronation ceremony, all robed in their vestments, took part in the procession, as did the duke of Lancaster himself, with the magnates and a great throng of the people.

Within a few days, the duke of Lancaster, John of Gaunt, came to realize that a completely new situation would prevail in the kingdom, now that his father, Edward III, was dead and the new king, Richard II, established, and that his diligence would be thought of no account by the new regime. He was afraid that he would be held to blame if any ill were to befall Richard II or the kingdom, but would receive little or no thanks for anything that turned out well. So he obtained from the king licence to depart, and left for his own estates, promising that if the king were ever in need of assistance, he would come at once with a greater retinue than that of any other lord in England, in order to help the king or to do anything else for the king's advantage or honour.

The duke retired from the court to his castle at Kenilworth, but before leaving he was instrumental in the selection of those who were to be members of the king's council or who were in any way to have the young monarch in their charge. Various good, wise and well-known men were appointed to the council, among them William Courteney, bishop of London, Edmund Mortimer, earl of March, and many others who were held in the highest esteem by the people. There was disquiet among the populace, however, because the bishop of Salisbury and Lord Latimer were among the councillors.

At the same time, the marshal of England, Henry Percy, earl of Northumberland, surrendered his wand of office and returned to his estates. Lord John Arundel, brother of the earl of Arundel, was appointed in his place. This man put up vigorous resistance to the French when they attacked Southampton; he prevented them from entering the town and forced them back to the sea.

Lest, however, the English should revel in joys unclouded by grief, that same year the French, more by cunning than by courage, seized the supposedly impregnable Isle of Wight, which no force of men could have taken if a proper defence had been maintained. It was the careless over-confidence of the islanders which led to their own downfall, to unexpected triumph for the French and to disgrace and disaster for the English.

Meanwhile, a disaster for the whole of England was taking place in Aquitaine. The noble knight Thomas Felton, to whose sole care the defence of the province of Aquitaine had been committed, made a most ill-judged attack on a large French force with only a few men of his own. Overcome by the enemy's superior numbers, he was taken prisoner along with many of the local lords who supported the English. This calamity occurred near the town of La Réole.

A parliament was summoned to London, which sat from 29 October until the end of November. Almost all the knights there had been with Peter de la Mare in the assembly in 1376 which had earned the title 'the Good Parliament', when they had been so steadfast in their work, nobly undertaken for the good of the land and the kingdom.

Now they brought up once more the petitions which they had put aside in that very place on the previous occasion: they pressed for the banishment of Alice Perrers [mistress of Edward III], who, in contempt of the statute passed by the Good Parliament and of the oath which she had taken, had dared to enter the king's court, in order to

The unwinnable war

Above Mortagne in central France, held by the English, was besieged by the French in 1377. The English defenders succeeded in killing Owen of Wales, a mercenary fighting for the French.

WHEN Richard II became king, the military and diplomatic situation was verging on catastrophe. Rarely has England been as friendless and vulnerable as she was in 1377.

Richard's problems were a legacy from his grandfather Edward III, who had first gone to war against France in 1337 to defend his claim to the duchy of Aquitaine – thereby starting the Hundred Years War. The treaty of Brétigny (1360) had brought its first stage to a conclusion, allowing Edward full control over Calais and a much-enlarged duchy of Aquitaine in return for his renunciation of the French royal title. But after the death of John II (the Good) of France in 1364, the kingdom had been transformed by his son, the able and energetic Charles V. The political factions and financial instability which had crippled the Valois regime were eradicated and he turned his army from a disorganized rabble into an effective fighting force. By a series of diplomatic manoeuvres he also managed to create and foster a powerful network of political alliances.

When Edward III died, a two-year truce with France, negotiated in an attempt to buy time, was about to expire. Enemy forces were already making raids on England's south coast, and rumours flew about an impending French invasion. All that was now left of the once enormous Plantagenet possessions in France was the town of Calais and a small strip of coastline in Gascony stretching from Bordeaux to Bayonne.

Yet England refused to surrender, for, although peace seemed the obvious recourse, if the English crown was to salvage any land in France, and any prestige, it was essential to carry on fighting. Gascony was not only a symbol of national pride, it was also an essential link in the English economy: earlier in the fourteenth century it had been estimated that the duchy was worth £13,000 a year to the crown. Much of the wine consumed in England came from this region of southern France; and in turn, Gascony was a market for the high-quality woollen cloth produced in England.

Many commercial interests depended on preserving English lands in southern France. Richard II's government therefore faced the grim prospect of an unwinnable but unavoidable war.

It was unfortunate for England that none of the commanders of the 1370s had the tactical flair or good luck which had attended Edward III in his earlier campaigns.

wheedle and demand from him whatever she wanted. Although she had bribed several of the lords and all the lawyers in England, who spoke not secretly but openly on her behalf, nevertheless, thanks to the diligence and wisdom of the knights in parliament, she was now convicted and all her goods, movable and immovable, were judged forfeit to the king's exchequer.

A few days before Christmas, Pope Gregory XI despatched a bull to Oxford University, by the hand of Master Edmund Stafford. In it, as their holy father, he reprimanded the masters for their slothfulness, because they had for so long allowed the erroneous opinions of that disciple of Antichrist, Master John Wycliffe, to take root among them, while not one of them would strive to take up the sword of Catholic doctrine in order to eradicate this poisonous and harmful plant which flourished so evilly.

It is a clear sign of how far today's proctors and regents of that university have fallen from the standards of discretion and wisdom set by those of former days, that after they had learned the reason for the visit of the papal envoy, they remained long undecided whether they should receive the bull with due honour, or reject it disgracefully. University of Oxford, you have indeed suffered a mighty fall from your peak of wisdom and learning, you, who were once accustomed to clarify complex or doubtful subjects for the whole world, but now do not fear to waver, wrapped in a cloud of ignorance, in a manner unfitting for any Christians, even mere laymen. It is shameful to recall such great stupidity, and so I shall not dwell upon it, lest I should seem to be biting the breast of the mother who used to offer the milk of knowledge.

The papacy itself was, however, in dire straits with the outbreak of the great schism. As Walsingham recounts, papal envoys from both sides attended parliament to seek support.

1378

A parliament was held at Gloucester; to it, from Italy, came solemn envoys seeking a strict agreement with King Richard II and the magnates for the provision of assistance to Pope Urban VI. They told of the insults and injuries which the pope was enduring from the wickedness of the apostate cardinals, who were attempting to undermine and weaken not only the pope himself, but the whole Church with him. Envoys from these same cardinals came there also, bringing letters bearing ten seals to seek support for the cardinals and to urge their case strongly. But by the will of God, who settles all things rightly, the apostates were turned away, and Pope Urban's envoys were welcomed and given a promise of help for the pope as soon as a suitable opportunity should arise.

One of the cardinals was absent, namely the former bishop of Amiens, who had been sent by order of Pope Gregory XI of blessed memory to settle some dissension which had arisen at Pisa between the pope and the citizens. On hearing of the death of Pope Gregory and of the election [of Urban VI] which had just taken place, the cardinal had decided to remain in Pisa until he received word either from his brother cardinals or from the new pope. Soon afterwards, however, he was summoned by letters from Urban VI, and he hastened to the Curia, in obedience to the pope's commands. After the bishop's arrival, the new pope entered the consistory and began to deliver a homily. He spoke out at length against the avarice of those cardinals who, corrupted by gold and blinded by money, love pieces of metal more than peace among men, that peace which they had been sent to renew between nations.

The pope went on to denounce and condemn publicly the bad faith of the bishop of Amiens, with an accusation that although on several occasions the bishop had been sent by the late Pope Gregory to bring about a peace settlement between the kingdoms of England and France, and had indeed, on the pope's orders, extracted large sums of gold and silver from both realms as recompense for the toil of his travels, nevertheless, neglecting his duty, he had not worked for peace, but had in fact promoted further discord and hatred between the kings. His purpose in this had been that while he was making frequent visits to them on the pretext of negotiating for peace, he might, by returning often and by keeping the

The birth of heresy

IN the late 14th century, the English Church was threatened by heresy for the first time in its history. The progenitor of this threat was John Wycliffe (c. 1330–84), an Oxford don and philosopher who, during Edward III's last years, was employed by the government as a propagandist for its policies of curbing papal demands and extracting heavier taxes from the clergy.

As Richard II's reign opened, however, the English bishops counterattacked with full papal support. By condemning errors in the Church, they declared, Wycliffe had himself committed grievous errors; he must either recant or suffer imprisonment. He did neither. Powerful supporters prevented his arrest and he retired in 1378 to Oxford, where he carried his assault on the Church still further. Previously he had criticized its actions: now he struck at its most vital doctrines.

First, he proclaimed the Bible to be the only true source of Christian doctrine. The many non-biblical teachings and practices of the Church were therefore heretical, and so was the official view that the Scriptures were too dangerously obscure to be read by laymen in their own language. During the closing years of his life, Wycliffe supervised the production of the first Bible in English. Next he argued that only those souls predestined by God for salvation could be members of the true Church. Because nobody knew who these were, it was quite possible that the pope was not among them.

Still more momentous was Wycliffe's attack on the Church's central doctrine of transubstantiation: that the bread and wine at mass literally became the body and blood of Christ at the priest's words of consecration. Wycliffe denounced it as philosophically absurd and idolatrous. The dispute which he initiated on this matter ultimately culminated in the Protestant Reformation.

Revolutionary pronouncements like these rapidly frightened off Wycliffe's highly placed sympathizers – a process completed by the shock of the Peasants Revolt of 1381, which orthodox chroniclers, wrongly, blamed on his heresies. At Oxford, however, his theories attracted enthusiastic support from a group of young intellectuals, who continued to preach them after Wycliffe had retired to Lutterworth in Leicestershire (where he died in 1384). At first protected by Oxford's dislike of interference with its academic freedoms, these disciples were eventually brought to heel by increasing church pressure; by the end of 1382 all had recanted or fled the country.

Heresy spread rapidly through the rest of England after 1382, however, and although there is little evidence for the chroniclers' tale that Wycliffe formally commissioned an order of heretical 'poor priests', wandering preachers undoubtedly played a crucial part in the growth of the 'Lollard' movement. The name means 'mumblers' and was applied to any kind of heretic.

Many Lollard preachers were not strictly Wycliffites; the doctrines they taught were simplified, often more extreme versions of his theories, generally with their own touches added. Some condemned the mass, while others denounced images and pilgrimages, or confession to priests. Some proclaimed that all good men (and, said one, all good women) automatically possessed priestly powers; others upheld pacifism, while another – William Ramsbury – preached and practised free love. All were united in opposition to the existing Church.

If not the founder, Wycliffe was the essential catalyst of the Lollard movement. Men like William Swynderby were, perhaps, more ultimately influential. Between 1382 and 1393, this poor, unbeneficed priest preached in Leicester, Coventry, the West Midlands and the Welsh borders, pursued by the ecclesiastical authorities. He was protected by locally important men like Leicester merchants and Herefordshire knights, and it was this kind of support that most alarmed the bishops.

In 1395, a Lollard petition was nailed to the doors of parliament, an action that provoked stronger measures against heresy. In 1401 William Sawtry was burned alive at Smithfield, the first Lollard to die for his faith.

business unfinished, fill his purse wickedly with the ill-gotten wealth which he had taken from the Church, despoiling both realms with his deceit.

Hearing all this, the bishop of Amiens was enraged. He rose to his feet and there in open court, with indescribable arrogance, he pointed his finger at the pope, replying with these wrathful words: 'Archbishop of Bari, you are lying!' Then he swept out of the consistory and departed insolently from the pope's presence. A number of the cardinals followed him, some because they agreed with him, others because they were guilty of similar misdeeds. The pope immediately stripped them of their offices, and appointed others to take their place, twenty-nine in all, men of great excellence from various realms, archbishops, bishops and archdeacons.

After these events, the apostate cardinals dared to stir up open war against the pope, and they determined to pursue him and his supporters to the death. To strengthen their cause, they chose as Pope Clement VII a well-born Frenchman, who was related by blood to the king of France.

1379

In parliament at London, with the connivance of certain persons who were always working out some harmful scheme, a new tax [the poll tax] was decreed for the use of King Richard. The house of lords forbore to bring this proposal before the commons, who had been almost overcome by earlier exactions. The dukes of Lancaster and Brittany were to pay twenty marks, that is ten marks apiece, and the archbishops the same. The earls were each to pay six marks, as were the bishops and the mitred abbots, and what is more the abbots were obliged to pay forty pence per head for their monks.

The regulations for the collection of the tax showed clearly that those who had devised them lacked good judgement, for the poorest abbot was bound to contribute as much by reason of his headgear as the richest of the earls and bishops, and more on top of that for his monks, so that his total liability would exceed that of the dukes.

The great schism

THE great schism lasted for 39 years, from 1378 to 1417, during which there was no one universally recognized pope. For the previous seven decades, since 1309, the papacy had been based at Avignon, despite many appeals to return to Rome: it was widely believed that the Avignon popes, living close to France and mostly French-born, were under the thumb of the French monarchy. But not until 1376 did Gregory XI move the papal court back to the Eternal City.

When Gregory died in 1378, the college of cardinals that met to elect his successor was split into three parties: unable to elect a pope with the required two-thirds majority, the cardinals selected an outsider – Bartolomeo Prignano, archbishop of Bari, Italian by nationality but French in education and outlook. The mob broke in, however, clamouring for a Roman pope, and to pacify them, the cardinals pretended to have elected the aged Roman Cardinal Tibaldeschi. Once the crowd had departed, and after the college had moved to the fortified papal palace at Anagni, a place of greater safety, they proclaimed Archbishop Prignano as Pope Urban VI.

Severe and ascetic, Urban VI detested clerical luxury and its attendant sins, and was determined to reform the Church – starting with the cardinals. He also possessed a violent temper, a tendency to sadism, and an obscene vocabulary, and before long the combination of his shocking behaviour and his plans for reform convinced the cardinals they had made a disastrous choice. They withdrew to Anagni, where they deposed Urban, declaring that, because he had been chosen only through fear of the mob, his election was invalid. The college proclaimed the French cardinal, Robert of Geneva, as Pope Clement

VII and re-established the papal court at Avignon. Urban VI remained alone in Rome, 'like a sparrow on a housetop'. The great schism had begun.

The European monarchs exploited the split in their own interests, dividing along strictly nationalist lines in their support for the popes. As a Frenchman, Clement VII was backed by France, her allies Scotland and Spain, and the French kingdom of Naples, whose queen Urban had insulted. Urban was upheld by Hungary, the Holy Roman Emperor – and England, whose rulers at first regarded the schism as merely an episode in the war with France. Richard II's marriage to Anne of Bohemia was part of a plan to create a pro-Urbanist (and anti-French) alliance.

The schism took its toll of the papacy and the Church. Deprived of revenue they would otherwise have received from dissenting nations, both popes were forced to make greater and greater concessions to the monarchs who supported them. In addition, respect for the papacy diminished as the pontiffs thundered out denunciation and excommunication, each proclaiming the other to be Antichrist. They also appointed bishops to dioceses under their opponent's control, so that there were rival English Urbanist claims for the sees of many Scottish Clementist bishops.

The split did not end with the deaths of Urban (1389) and Clement (1394): both sides elected successors to perpetuate the dispute, and an attempted reconciliation in 1409 resulted in yet a third papal line.

The 'Conciliar Movement' gradually gained ground among clerics and laity of all factions. It held that the pope did not possess supreme power, but was subject to the rulings of a general council of the whole Church.

However, only the pope could summon such a council – and there was no universally recognized pontiff. The General Council of Constance, called in 1414, was therefore technically illegal. Nevertheless, in 1417 it finally deposed all existing popes by general agreement, and elected Martin V as undisputed pontiff.

Above left Portrait believed to be of Robert of Geneva, later Pope Clement VII

Above The coronation of Pope Boniface IX, a successor of Urban in Rome.

Below Sarcophagus of Urban VI: the great schism began during his pontificate.

No one could avoid this tax: not one judge, sheriff, knight or squire, nor any rector, vicar or mere chaplain. If good can come of such spoliation, God alone knows.

The heavy and unequal burden of the poll tax helped to swell popular resistance to the royal administration, and within two years opposition erupted in the Peasants Revolt. Its violent and dramatic course is vividly charted by the chivalrous chronicler Jean Froissart, whose bias against the peasants is immediately apparent.

1381

In 1381 there was a most dangerous rebellion in England, an uprising of the common people which brought the country to the brink of ruin. No other land or kingdom has ever been in such peril.

In England, as in other countries, it is usual for the nobles to exercise great authority over their men and to hold them in a state of serfdom; that is to say, as serfs they are compelled by law and custom to plough their lords' fields, harvest the grain and bring it home, store it in the barns, thrash and winnow it, make and carry the hay, cut wood and bring it in, and all such work; they owe all these servile duties to their lords.

There are very many such people in England, more than elsewhere, especially in the counties of Kent, Essex, Sussex and Bedford, where they are more numerous than in the whole of the rest of England.

These evil creatures in the counties I have mentioned became presumptuous. They said their servitude was too harsh, and that there were no serfs when the world began.

They had been much stirred up and encouraged in these lunatic ideas by a mad priest, an Englishman of the county of Kent called John Ball, who had often been detained in the prison of the archbishop of Canterbury on account of his impassioned preaching in the villages after mass on Sundays, just when the people were all coming out of church.

The first socialist revolution

FOR a few short weeks in June and July 1381, many parts of England were threatened by riots and demonstrations: it was the start of the Peasants Revolt.

The immediate cause was the poll tax, which parliament had granted to the king in 1380. Every man and woman over the age of 15 was to pay a standard levy of one shilling to the crown. This was the third such levy in as many years, and was deeply resented in a society not conditioned to regular taxation. In some parts of the country, there was a virtual tax strike.

The government responded by sending out special commissioners to enforce payment. By all accounts the men chosen for this job were unsavoury and unscrupulous. One of these, John Bampton, infuriated the people of Essex to such an extent that certain local communities decided to take matters into their own hands. In the last week of May 1381 the villagers of Fobbing joined with their neighbours to attack the commissioners at Brentwood. The Peasants Revolt had begun.

The real centre of the unrest was London, where rebel bands from Essex united with men from Kent on 13 June to form a force conservatively estimated at 10,000. The population of London was only about 40,000, so the insurgents represented a major threat to national security. For two days the rebels wandered around the city, burning buildings, pillaging property, and executing their enemies.

Events in London brought a number of remarkable rebel leaders to the fore, among them John Ball, Wat Tyler and Jack Straw. Ball was an itinerant preacher who for years had been embarrassing the establishment by his controversial sermons and Tyler was an Essex man, possibly a tiler by trade, who had done service in the French wars. Jack Straw, however, is an enigma and, indeed, it is possible that he and Tyler were one and the

same man: medieval rebels often assumed nicknames.

The nature of medieval society normally prevented men of this class from exercising their latent political talents. The Peasants Revolt created a rare opportunity for popular demagogues; but their moment was brief, and the rebellion failed because of the naïvety of its supporters and the radicalism of their demands: the abolition of the poll taxes, the removal of the king's evil councillors, and a guarantee of their own personal freedom. The young Richard II – he was only 14 – assented verbally at Mile End on 14 June, and most men returned home, unaware that the crown had no real intention of keeping its promises. Wat Tyler and a hard core of supporters stayed on, and secured a second meeting with the king at Smithfield on 15 June. Here they demanded a complete reform of the law, the abolition of all lordship (except that of the king), and disestablishment of the Church.

Wat Tyler shocked the royal party by the boisterous and familiar way in which he met and addressed the king; and, in a fit of rage, the mayor of London, William Walworth, drew his dagger and knocked him down. Tyler was killed, and his murder marked the end of any effective resistance.

Contemporary chroniclers were deeply prejudiced against the rebels for daring to challenge political and social convention. Today, many historians see 1381 as a time of violence which produced few tangible results. Others, however, view the revolt as the beginning of an heroic struggle between labour and capital, and hail Wat Tyler and his men as medieval Socialists.

Above left Meeting between Wat Tyler (on the left), John Ball and their forces.

Above Tyler is struck down by William Walworth while the king addresses the peasants.

Below Walworth's dagger, said to have been used to strike down Tyler. Froissart's description of it as a 'cutlass' was probably artistic licence.

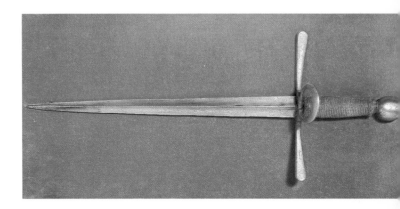

'Good people,' he would say, 'nothing can go well in England, nor ever will do, until all goods are held in common, until there is neither villein nor nobleman, until we are all one. The men we call lords, what makes them our masters? They wear silks and velvet furred with squirrel and ermine while we wear poor cloth. They have wine, spices and good bread but we eat rye and chaff and straw and have water to drink. They live in fine manors and dwelling houses, we sweat and toil in the fields in the wind and rain; and it is from us and from our labour that all their pomp must come. They call us "serf" and beat us if we do not hasten to serve them, and we have no overlord to complain to, no one to listen to us or do us justice. Let us go to the king, he is young; let us explain our condition to him and tell him that we want it changed, or else we will change it ourselves.'

John Ball's teaching was well known to many of the common people in the city of London, who were envious of wealthy and aristocratic men and were beginning to say among themselves that the kingdom of England was badly governed and that it was being robbed of its silver and gold by those who called themselves noble.

They spread the word to the men of Kent, Essex, Sussex, Bedford and the neighbouring districts, who rose and began to make for London. There were a good sixty thousand of them under one principal captain, a man called Wat Tyler, together with his comrades Jack Straw and also John Ball. These three were the commanders of all the rest, and Wat Tyler was the leader of the three. He was a roof tiler by trade, a young man of bad character, full of venom and hatred.

On Monday 10 June, in the year 1381, these people left their homes and set out to go to London to talk to King Richard and be made free.

Everyone came out to join them from the villages to the left and right as they travelled on. They cut off several men's heads on their journey, and in due course reached a height four leagues out of London known as Blackheath, where they halted. When the rulers of London learned how near they were, they closed the gate of the bridge over the Thames and put guards there. But the mob rose and poured down upon the capital. Entering its suburbs, which are beautiful and extensive, they tore down a number of fine buildings and in particular they demolished the king's prison known as the Marshalsea and released all the prisoners; and they committed many other outrages.

At last perforce the gates of London had to be opened and the hungry mob burst in and at once rushed into the well-provisioned houses and fell upon the food and drink. No one refused them anything; on the contrary they did their utmost to make them welcome in order to pacify them.

Then the leaders, John Ball, Jack Straw and Wat Tyler, and thirty thousand of their men went straight across London to the duke of Lancaster's noble palace of the Savoy, which stands by the Thames on the way to the royal palace at Westminster. They rushed in, killed the guards and sent the building up in flames. Nor did they stop at that outrage but went on to the dwelling of the Hospitallers of Rhodes called St John of Clerkenwell and burned house, hospital, church and all. Thus they behaved, these wicked men, like creatures out of their minds, and did untold harm that Thursday 13 June, all over London.

In the morning on Friday those of the mob who were lodged in St Katherine's square near the Tower took up their arms and began to shout and clamour saying that if the king did not come and speak with them they would assault the castle and take it by force and kill everyone inside it. These threats caused much anxiety, and Richard II made up his mind to go and speak to them. He sent word to them to leave London and go to a place called Mile End, a most beautiful meadow where people go to amuse themselves in summer time. Here King Richard and his barons found more than sixty thousand men from different counties. He went right in amongst them and said to them with all kindness, 'Good people, I am your king and your lord. I grant you the freedom you ask of me. Go back peacefully to your own homes, go as you came and leave two or three representatives from each village. I will have letters written for

The rebel serfs

IN the 30 years between the Black Death and the Peasants Revolt, England experienced some of the most profound social and economic changes in the whole of the Middle Ages. The plague of 1348–9 swept away between a quarter and a third of the population, and after further epidemics in the 1360s and 1370s England's population stood at just over half its level in 1300. Ultimately, this decline brought about an enormous improvement in the lot of the peasant, who in the 15th century entered upon his 'golden age'. In 1381, however, it was unclear how the new economic trends would affect the lower classes; and this sense of uncertainty does much to explain both the timing and the motivation of the Peasants Revolt.

The most obvious result of the Black Death had been a sudden decline in the number of mouths that needed feeding, and an equally dramatic drop in the number of men available to produce the food. The value of arable land and the price of grain fell, while wage costs increased. Landholders had to take stock of these adverse conditions; and their solutions fell into three broad categories.

First, some lords of manors consciously reduced the amount of land under the plough. This helped to keep grain prices high, and cut down on labour costs. The untilled fields were usually put over to sheep-farming, which was less labour-intensive and still highly profitable. In the long term, whole communities were thrown out of their homes by grasping landlords eager to create new grazing. And although there was little compulsory eviction in the period immediately before the Peasants Revolt, there was a good deal of migration from the countryside into the towns; urban crafts and industries were attractive alternatives to peasants disillusioned by working conditions and prospects in agriculture.

The second option open to landholders after the Black Death was to give up farming their estates for profit, and to lease them out for fixed rents. That way, they were guaranteed an income without worrying about fluctuations in the market. In 1359 the scholars of Merton College, Oxford, put their manor at Cuxham out to lease, and within a few years many major landholders were following suit. The new leaseholders were often drawn from the more substantial peasantry, who were eager to take on the best available lands. By the 1370s, however, when agricultural prices plummeted, many of them were finding it difficult to make ends meet.

The third possible response was to ignore new economic conditions and carry on as though nothing had happened. This ostrich-like approach was doomed to failure, but in the decades immediately after the Black Death many major landholders were remarkably success-

Above *Peasants at their traditional tasks. After the Black Death, fewer were prepared to accept their lot passively.*

ful in holding back the forces of change. Determined to keep their costs down, they persuaded the government to fix a ceiling on wages. The justices of the peace, who enforced the new regulations, became unpopular for allowing local landholders to pursue personal vendettas against workers.

Most controversial of all, however, were attempts by some great lords to reimpose certain compulsory unpaid services on their peasants. In the past, these had been performed by serfs or villeins who had no legal status and were bound forever to the manor and its lord. In formal terms, serfdom had been on the wane before the Black Death, and was to become an irrelevance in the new socio-economic environment of the later Middle Ages. But in the uneasy atmosphere of the 1370s, many peasants believed that reviving these antiquated services was the first step towards formally reimposing villeinage.

them and have them sealed with my own seal, and for further comfort and reassurance, you shall receive my banners.'

These words pacified the commons there, that is to say the simple, ignorant and honest folk who had gathered there but did not know what they were asking, and who shouted out, 'Well said, well said, that is all we want.' And so they were appeased and began to go back into London.

On the Saturday morning, 15 June, King Richard went to hear mass at Westminster Abbey and set off about nine in the morning to ride back to London.

On that same morning all the wicked men commanded by Wat Tyler, Jack Straw and John Ball met together to hold discussions in a large place called Smithfield, where the horse fair is held on Fridays. There were more than twenty thousand of them all in the one fellowship, and as many more in the town breaking their fast and drinking sweet *grenace* wine and malmsey in the taverns and in the Lombards' houses without paying a penny.

Suddenly the king arrived with sixty mounted men. He was not thinking about the rebels but intended to pass on and continue his journey. Reaching the abbey of St Bartholomew, he saw them all assembled and he drew rein and stopped, saying that he would not go any further without finding out what they wanted. If they were troubled, he would pacify them.

When Wat Tyler saw the king halted there, he spurred his horse and rode forward alone, coming straight up to Richard II, so close that his horse's tail brushed over the head of the king's mount. And the first word he spoke was to Richard, saying, 'King, tell me, do you think it right for those men there, and as many again in London, all under my command, to go away and leave you without having your letters? No indeed, we shall take them all with us.' 'The order has been given,' said the young King Richard. 'It is our intention that each of your villages and boroughs shall have its letter, as has been agreed.'

Just then a dozen men rode up, led by William Walworth, the mayor of London. They were fully armed under their coats, and forced their way through the crowd. 'Well!' said the mayor, who had formerly been a king's advocate, 'you stinking wretch, do you speak like that in front of my own natural lord? May I die the death if you do not pay for it!' With that he drew a great cutlass he was wearing and let fly with such a blow at Tyler's head that he knocked him down among his horse's hooves. [Soon after that Tyler was killed by John Standish, one of the king's squires.]

When those madmen saw that their leader was dead, they began to exclaim among themselves, 'They have killed our captain, come on, come on, let's kill them all!'

Meanwhile a panic cry spread about London, 'They are killing the king! They are killing the mayor!' and so all sorts of honest men of the king's party sallied out well armed and equipped and made their way to Smithfield and the king. There were about seven or eight thousand men, all armed and ranked in battle array beside the king.

Richard II knighted three men there: Sir William Walworth, mayor of London, Sir John Standish and Sir Nicholas Brembre, and sent them to the insurgents. When they were near enough to be heard, they said, 'Listen. The king sends to tell you to return his banners and, on pain of death, to return all letters granted by him.'

As soon as the royal banners had been returned these evil men lost all semblance of order. They broke ranks, flung away almost all their bows and straggled off to go and conceal themselves in London. Sir Robert Knollys was furious that they had not been all of them attacked and slaughtered on the spot, but the king refused to allow this and said that he would take ample vengeance later, as indeed he did.

When calm had been restored, the leaders were all executed. The king then decided to inspect his kingdom, to ride through all the boroughs, sheriffdoms, castellanies and borders of England in order to punish the evildoers, to recover the letters

The gentle Bohemian queen

ANNE of Bohemia and Richard II were both 15 at the time of their marriage in 1382, Anne the elder by a few months. The social prestige of the match was high – Anne was the eldest daughter of Charles of Luxemburg, king of Bohemia, later the Holy Roman Emperor, Charles IV. Diplomatically, it was an opportunity to detach Luxemburg from Valois influence, and to strengthen a web of anti-French alliances. But the new queen brought no dowry, and that, together with her large train of Bohemians, did not augur too well for her future popularity. Fortunately, her mother-in-law, Joan, princess of Wales, who was both popular and generous, prompted her to ask for a pardon for Wat Tyler's followers at her coronation. This had the desired effect. Anne's prestige with the people was enhanced by her mediation during the king's quarrel with London in 1392.

The queen became an effective moderating influence on Richard, who loved her dearly; and particularly after the death of his mother in 1385, Anne provided a strong, stable core to his life.

Anne had been brought up in the highly cultured court of Prague. Her father Charles was one of the chief patrons of German Gothic art, and at least one Bohemian artist may have come to England with her. None the less, French influence at Prague was strong, and what is believed to be the crown made for Anne, one of the finest examples of the 14th-century goldsmith's art, was produced either in Paris or by a French craftsmen in Prague.

The Bohemian members of the queen's household may also have been responsible for connections between the Bohemian religious reformer, John Hus, and his English counterpart, John Wycliffe.

Anne made only one political blunder during her years as queen, when she intervened on behalf of one of her Bohemian ladies, Agnes Launcecrona, who had become the mistress of the king's favourite, Robert de Vere, earl of Oxford. The earl wished to marry her, but to do so he had first to obtain a divorce from his countess. Queen Anne pressed the pope to sanction the divorce, but in doing so she provoked a hostile reaction at the English court: the countess was Philippa de Coucy, granddaughter of Edward III, and the king's first cousin.

The English grew to value Anne for her beneficial moderating influence on Richard and her willingness to act as a mediator between the king and his subjects. She begged on her knees for the life of Sir Simon Burley, the king's former tutor, to whom he was much attached and who had helped to negotiate their marriage, when he was impeached by the Merciless Parliament for his malign influence on the king.

Richard never forgave Gloucester and the lords appellant for the humiliation they inflicted on the queen by spurning her pleas.

Above *Anne of Bohemia's crown.*

Below *A queen's coronation of the period.*

he had been forced to grant in several places, and to restore the kingdom to order. More than fifteen hundred peasants were beheaded, hanged and put to death.

Despite these disturbances, courtly pageants re-sumed the following year, as Walsingham relates.

1382

In January, after the feast of Epiphany, the nobility of the whole realm of England assembled in London, to attend King Richard's marriage ceremony and to perform their duty according to the custom observed since ancient times. At Westminster, the Holy Roman Emperor's daugh-ter, Anne of Bohemia, was hallowed as the king of England's bride, and crowned queen with glory and honour by the archbishop of Canterbury.

To enhance the splendour of this great oc-casion, a tournament was held lasting several days, at which the English displayed their valour and the queen's fellow-countrymen demonstrated their worth. In the lists, praise and acclaim were won for knightly achievements, but not without losses on both sides.

During that year, the mayor of London, John of Northampton, with the help and support of the common people, brought the city's fishmongers to such a wretched state that year that any fishmonger outside London was better situated than one who had inherited or purchased citizen-ship in the city. Indeed, any outsider was permitted to sell his fish himself within the city, whereas the right to sell such fish had been taken away from the fishmongers of London, on penalty of a heavy fine and imprisonment if they attempted to defy this ban.

Consequently, the common people, seeing this improvement in market conditions, praised the mayor to the skies; full of hatred for the fishmon-gers who were their fellow-citizens, they were ready to kill them, if that seemed right and proper to the mayor. Sea fish now became so cheap as to be worthless in London, while it became both dear and scarce elsewhere in the country, since

the Londoners prevented free passage. But these measures, which gained for the mayor the favour of the men of the city, also brought upon him the hatred and wrath of everyone dwelling round about.

That summer, on 21 May, about the ninth hour, there was a massive earthquake in England, where such things are rarely felt or heard. The tremor, which brought terror to many people, was of such great force in Kent that it shook several churches and caused them to collapse. Another quake followed on 24 May, just before sunrise, but this was not as alarming as the previous one.

The bishop of Norwich, Henry Despenser, had recently received a bull addressed to him by Pope Urban VI, empowering him to treat as a crusader anyone who would volunteer to accompany him on an expedition to France to destroy the antipope who called himself 'Clement VII', and to dedicate as a holy war the campaign against Clement's supporters. Because the bull gave him such great powers, the bishop made sure that it was pro-claimed in parliament, and he arranged for copies to be sent around the country, with orders that they were to be hung up for public display on church doors and monastery gates.

This 'crusade' aroused intense popular fervour, but although a large army was to cross to France in 1383 to chastise the Clementists, it achieved nothing beyond the short-lived capture of Dun-kerque, Gravelines and other ports on the coast of northern France. Neither its overt religious objec-tives nor its covert political and economic aims were accomplished, and it served only to swell the growing tide of cynicism against the crusading movement.

Edmund, earl of Cambridge, the king's uncle, arrived back in England with the force which had been sent with him to Portugal. On their return voyage they had suffered misfortune at sea, and had lost some of their possessions. They had been sent to assist the king of Portugal, Ferdinand I, against the bastard of Spain who styled himself King John I. This man had inflicted many injuries on the king of Portugal, and would have worn him

White herrings

JOHN of Northampton began a two-year term as mayor of London in the autumn of 1391. A member of the Drapers Company, with political ambitions and connections with John of Gaunt, he had built up a party among the lesser craft guilds opposed to London's controlling oligarchy. Northampton's programme, dismantled after he left office, called for one-year terms for older men, city government by a common council that met at least eight times yearly, and abolition of the monopoly enjoyed by the Fishmongers Company.

This last point was enthusiastically welcomed by Londoners. Wednesdays, Fridays and Saturdays, as well as the 40 days of Lent, were fish days and the fishmongers, the city's most powerful company, exploited their position to the full. Northampton's election was followed by civic ordinances against the company and, within the month, a parliamentary statute that permitted 'foreign' (non-London) fishmongers to deal in the city and virtually excluded the company.

The fish – none of it fresh – was supplied by English and foreign fisheries. The cured 'white' herring of Skania, together with high-quality fish oil, came from regions controlled by the Hanseatic League. Good, white herring was also imported from the Netherlands.

English fishermen had become increasingly adventurous during the 14th century. Codfish from Norwegian waters was bought by English merchants to be salted down, but, increasingly, boats from east coast ports such as Hull, Cromer and Yarmouth fished around Norway. In the next century, many switched to Iceland, because of the swingeing export duty boats had to pay at the Staple in Bergen before leaving Norwegian waters.

Some of the adventurers may have adopted innovations like the triangular lateen sail from the Mediterranean, but most fishing 'doggers' were small and simple boats, often less valuable than their cargo. In Bristol, for example, a vessel worth £40 carried a cargo worth £100. Petitioning to be spared royal naval service, the men of Cromer claimed none of their boats was above 12 tuns and all were too small to carry horses.

Large seine nets that hung vertically in the water were used for trawling from a single boat, or from two working together. Smaller drag nets with wooden floats on the upper edge might be handled by teams of men working from the shore. Single fishermen along the rivers used a line, a floating fish-trap or perhaps a small hand net. Ropes and nets were tarred for greater durability.

Monasteries and many large houses had their own fish ponds; sometimes two or three were dug along the bed of a hillside stream, often with elaborate engineering works to ensure a steady flow of water and to allow different chambers for different types of fish: carp, trout, and even, perhaps, pike. This was considered a great luxury – a single fish might cost as much as two pigs. The best lamprey were thought to come from the Severn.

For the average household, salted stockfish or herring was the staple, red (smoked) herring a pleasant change and fresh fish of any kind a luxury. Each year, Norwich in the east rendered the king 24 pies of the first fresh herring – each pie containing five fish, spiced with ginger, pepper and cinnamon. In the west, the king had fresh fish rights at Bristol: for example, 12 fish from every boat with 30 or more fresh haddock, whiting, bream, mackerel or plaice.

Whale and sturgeon were technically royal, though the former was available at Bristol for two shillings the barrel. Bristol men were also licensed to buy or catch Irish salmon from the Shannon at Limerick in southern Ireland and the Bann in the north. The Irish sold great quantities of salt fish, and fish pickled with soured wine in barrels of Irish oak, to English west coast ports.

Above A man fishes with rod and line. Detail from a wall-painting in Horley Church, Oxfordshire.

Below A lively illustration of a 15th-century fish market.

down completely, if Ferdinand's position had not been strengthened by help from England.

After our men had been in Portugal for a year, during which time they had made several incursions into Spain and had captured various strongholds, the Spanish decided to take the field against the king of Portugal and the English force. Ferdinand I was not slow to meet them, accompanied by our men, to fight as fortune permitted and, as he hoped, to emerge victorious.

Fearing both Portuguese resistance and our men's courage, the Spanish sought to parley with King Ferdinand, their one condition being that neither the earl of Cambridge nor any other Englishman should participate in the negotiations. The king agreed to this, and went to the meeting. Since both sides were eager to make peace, they soon reached agreement.

Once the Spanish had conceded what was required to the king of Portugal, and the Portuguese had made concessions also, the peace was concluded secretly. By its terms, the king of Portugal was to clear his realm of Englishmen; lest any of them should claim that there was no shipping available, the king of Spain would provide them with some of his own ships, and the king of Portugal pay for their passage and make any other provision which seemed necessary.

There is no doubt that the Spaniards were afraid of the English, but by now the English had become burdensome to the Portuguese also for, having been brought in as protectors against the enemy, they had subjected the Portuguese to an even worse oppression, not only seizing their property, but treating their wives and daughters abominably, so that they became hateful to their hosts.

The king of Portugal, returning from the negotiations, ordered both his own men and ours to lay down their arms and to return home. He then proclaimed publicly the terms of the settlement with the Spaniards. Our men were obliged to obey his commands, whether they wished to or not; thus, they left the field, bitter at heart because they had not been allowed to join battle with the

A Spanish interlude

JOHN of Gaunt's second wife, Constance, was one of the two daughters of Peter I the Cruel, king of Castile. Her father had been murdered in 1369 by his illegitimate half-brother Henry of Trastamara, who took over the kingdom as Henry II, and she married John in 1371. A year later, in 1372, John laid claim to the Castilian throne in his wife's right, declaring himself king. For the next 16 years he struggled to make good that title by a mixture of military might and diplomatic double-dealing.

To make any headway against Henry II of Castile, it was essential to have the backing of Portugal. This powerful Iberian kingdom had close commercial links with England, and its king, Ferdinand I, seemed more than willing to support John of Gaunt's claims. At the last moment, however, Ferdinand married his daughter Beatrice to Henry of Trastamara's son and successor, John I of Castile. When King Ferdinand died in 1383, this same John I tried to claim the throne of Portugal through Beatrice. But the citizens of Lisbon set up Ferdinand's half-brother, John, as their king. Three Johns – John of Gaunt, John of Castile, and John of Portugal – were now embroiled in the same dispute.

John of Portugal soon realized that the interests of his realm would best be served by an English alliance, and in 1386 he came to terms with the government of Richard II. The treaty of Windsor created a perpetual alliance between the two realms, and guaranteed their mutual defence in times of war. This meant that Portugal would supply troops for John of Gaunt's attack on Castile. In 1387 yet another royal wedding took place when the king of Portugal married Gaunt's daughter Philippa. He promptly joined his new father-in-law in an ambitious campaign in northern Castile.

But Gaunt's hopes of capturing the throne shrivelled under the hot Spanish sun. The Castilian defences were more than a match for the Anglo-Portuguese army, and Gaunt was forced to come to terms. He agreed to give up the title of king of Castile and to recognize John I as the legitimate ruler, in return for an indemnity of £100,000 and an annual pension of £6,600; his daughter Catherine would marry the future Henry III of Castile.

John of Gaunt's campaigns created considerable animosity in Castile and aroused suspicion in England. The Iberian connection itself, however, proved much more positive and enduring. With the kings of Castile and Portugal married to cousins of Richard II, personal and political connections abounded. The Portuguese alliance opened up new trade links. Exotic equatorial fruits graced English dinner tables, and the broadcloths of England were paraded on the streets of Lisbon.

Six hundred years later the treaty of Windsor is still in force, the most ancient and one of the most highly respected foundations of English diplomacy.

Opposite *John of Gaunt leaves for Lisbon.*

Above *He and his ships arrive at the port.*

Below *John is feasted by the king of Portugal, with musicians in the gallery.*

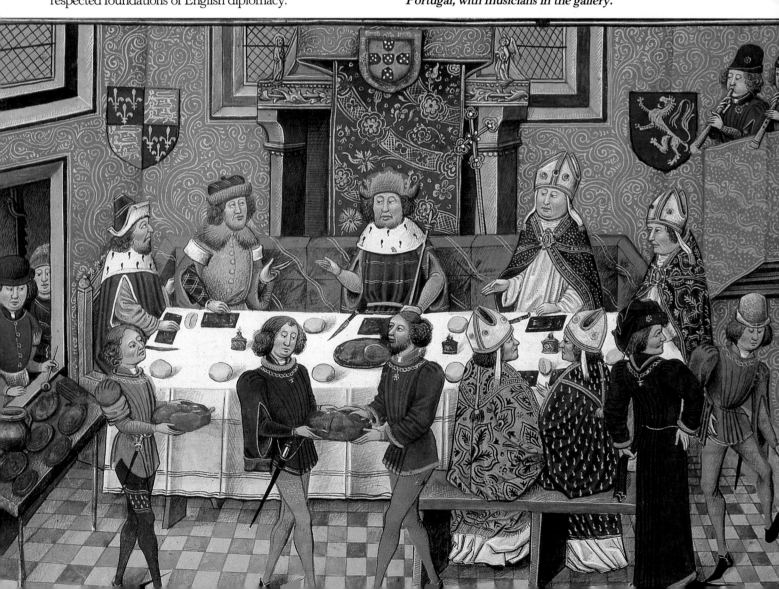

Spaniards. From that day, they were not so much made ready for their return voyage as forced into it, until Portugal should be entirely free of Englishmen.

Thus, the earl of Cambridge came home with his men. He brought with him his wife Isabella, the younger daughter of Peter I the Cruel, late king of Castile, and their son, born some years before the earl had left England. During their stay in Portugal, this son had married the daughter of the king of Portugal with due ceremonial; but because the earl doubted the good faith of the Portuguese, he would not leave the young man there when the English forces departed, despite the entreaty of the king of Portugal. Nor did the king wish to send his daughter to England with the earl. This was the state of affairs in Portugal at that time.

1383

King Richard II and his queen, Anne of Bohemia, with the queen's Bohemian attendants, made a tour of the abbeys of the kingdom. Their arrival brought to these houses sadness in proportion to the burden it caused, because the royal party came with an enormous company, not to make offerings but to take what they could get.

The abbey of Bury St Edmunds felt the weight of their presence especially heavily: the house spent eight hundred marks on the king and queen and their household during the ten days of their visit, as if it had not suffered already, with a four-year vacancy in the office of abbot, the irreparable damage done during the peasants' revolt, and the massive expenditure necessary to recover its rights both at the papal Curia and in this country.

When he had completed this damaging visit to Bury, King Richard moved on to Thetford, and thence to Norwich, where he cleverly obtained 'gifts' from both the monastic and the secular clergy, thus committing two evil deeds at once.

Great offerings were not sufficient for the king unless they were matched by gifts of equal value to the queen. In fact, the people would not have felt it burdensome to make such extravagant presentations out of consideration for the king's honour, if these offerings had been devoted wisely to the maintenance of the royal household. But whatever the king's grasping hand grabbed from them was soon wasted on the queen's foreign attendants, the Bohemians, with the result that the royal party returned from this progress shorter of funds than when they had set out. The truth of the words of the Book of Wisdom was clear to all: 'Woe to thee, O land, when thy king is a child' [Ecclesiastes 10[16]].

This year the produce of the fruit trees was very dangerous to eat, because the fruits themselves, apples, pears and suchlike, were contaminated by foul-smelling mists, vapours and a variety of poisons in the air. As a result of eating the fruit, some people contracted a lethal sickness, others developed serious and debilitating illnesses.

It was a grievous year for the English, of whom many perished, both in Flanders and at home. For the Flemings it was deadly: they and their homeland suffered devastation at the hands of their own people as well as foreigners. To the French it was a year at the same time terrifying and burdensome: terrifying because never before had they feared any English duke as they now feared the bishop of Norwich, and burdensome because the king of France assembled a great army, the cost of which fell heavily upon them all.

1385

On 29 December, the death occurred of John Wycliffe, that agent of the devil, that enemy of the Church, that misleader of the common people, that idol of heretics, that mirror for hypocrites, that provoker of schisms, that sower of hatred, that fabricator of falsehood.

Just as he was getting ready to spew out the blasphemous prayers which he had prepared to accompany his sermon that day, the feast of St Thomas Becket, he was stricken suddenly by the vengeance of God, and felt numbness spreading through all his limbs. His mouth, which had spoken so wickedly against God, His saints and His Church, became dreadfully distorted, a frightful

Medieval health foods

THE royal household accounts show that the medieval court consumed a large variety of meats and fresh and salted fish. Cheese, bread and eggs were staple foods but there is little mention of vegetables or fruits, other than peas, beans and imported figs, dates, raisins and almonds. However, recipe and regimen books, and herbals, refer to home-grown apples, cherries, plums, strawberries and pears; and add onions, leeks, garlic, pumpkins, shallots, fennel, celery, radish and rhubarb.

Food was seldom fresh, with the exception of produce grown in gardens. Fish was preserved by being salted down, and meat made into pies and pastes. Seasoning with herbs and spices made dishes more palatable.

Medical texts expressed deep mistrust of fresh fruits: Galen believed them to be the 'cause of purified fevers', while the popular *Regimen of Salerno* advised that certain fruits affected digestion or bred bad humours. Such beliefs were integral to medieval preventive medicine.

The body's four humours – blood, yellow bile, phlegm and black bile – corresponded respectively to the qualities – hot and wet, hot and dry, cold and wet, cold and dry – which determined a man's temperament (sanguine, choleric, phlegmatic or melancholic) – and food and drink shared the four qualities. Food of hot and dry quality would exacerbate a choleric man's temperament, while food with an opposing quality would maintain essential harmony and ensure his good health. The *Regimen* states:

'If unto choller men be much inclined
'Tis thought that *Onyons* are not good for those,
But if a man be flegmatique (by kind)
It does his stomach good as some suppose.'

Certain fruits (generally raw rather than cooked) were believed to possess qualities likely to cause an excess of black bile, melancholy, poisoning and, consequently, illness. The cure was a different diet, or blood-letting, purgatives and laxatives that would release the noxious humours and redress bodily harmony. The *Regimen* counterposes approval and warning:

'Some *Nut* 'gainst poyson is preservative;
Peares wanting wine, are poyson from the tree,
But bak't peares counted are restorative,
Raw peares a poyson, bak't a medicine be,
Bak't peares a weak dead stomach do revive,
Raw peares are heavie to digest we see,
Drink after peares take, after *Apples* order
To have a place to purge yourself of ordure.
Ripe *cherries* breed good bloud and help the stone.

Coole *Damsons* are a good for health by reason
They make your intrailes soluble and slacke,
Let *peaches* steepe in wine of newest season,
Nuts hurt the teeth that with their teethe crack,
With every Nut 'tis good to eate a *Raison*
For though they hurt the spleen, they help the back.'

Rhubarb was considered a most effective purgative, especially of phlegm, while herbs soothed stomach disorders and counteracted poisons; rue and horehound were particularly efficacious against hidden toxins.

Above *Leeks, thought to influence coitus.*

Below *A fruit and vegetable market.*

sight for those who saw it. His tongue became dumb, denying him the opportunity to make his confession or to testify to his faith. The shaking movements of his head showed clearly that he had been smitten by the same palsy with which the Lord blasted Cain.

And that no one might be in any doubt but that he was destined to keep company with Cain in Hell, those who were present as he lay dying reported that his outward behaviour showed that he had expired in a state of despair. Such was the end of all his wickedness.

Walsingham tells of the growing antagonism between Richard II and his most powerful subject, which brought danger to the realm.

In England at this time great trouble arose for John of Gaunt, the duke of Lancaster, as the young king and his youthful companions conspired to bring about the duke's death. They plotted together to arrest him without warning, and to send him for trial before Justice Robert Tresilian, who had given a bold undertaking to pass upon the duke a sentence appropriate to his alleged crimes. But the duke, warned by a member of the council, and mindful of his own well-being, sensibly took himself off as quickly as possible to his castle at Pontefract, which he stocked well with arms and provisions.

As a result, the mutual hatred of king and duke increased, nourished by grievances both personal and public. There was real danger that what the commons had sought for so long would now come about, namely open war between the two, giving licence for people to roam about and rampage around with impunity, as in the past when the common people had no rulers, but raged out of control.

The Lady Joan, the king's mother, was not prepared to allow such evil to afflict the kingdom. Although she was easy-going and devoted to pleasure, and so fat from over-eating that she could scarcely walk, she set aside thoughts of her personal comfort, and voluntarily undertook to travel, first to the king, then to the duke, sparing neither expense nor entreaties, until by her wearisome journeying she had fulfilled her intention of bringing about peace and harmony between them.

1386

At Easter John of Gaunt, duke of Lancaster, made preparations to set out for Spain, with a great host of knights, squires and captains. That kingdom belonged to him in hereditary right of his wife Constance, elder daughter of Peter the Cruel, late king of Castile, and the purpose of his expedition was either to gain control there by a peaceful settlement with the inhabitants, or to make good his claim by right of conquest. Pope Urban VI gave the support of his authority to this enterprise, granting pardon of their sins to all who set out on the campaign or who donated funds towards it; indeed, he seemed to have turned from a prince to a treasurer.

That summer, rumours began to multiply that the king of France, Charles VI, intended to lay siege to Calais, and was gathering an army for that purpose. To withstand or rather to repel his attacks, several valiant knights, well provisioned, were despatched from England, among them Henry Percy the younger, son of the earl of Northumberland, a shining example of honesty and skill in arms. After this force had waited in idleness at Calais for a long time, Henry Percy declared angrily that he hated such inactivity. Indeed, on an earlier occasion, while he had been guardian of Berwick upon Tweed, he had forced the Scots, that restless race, to remain quiescent, tormenting them from time to time with his own zealous activity. For that reason they nicknamed him, in their own tongue, 'Hotspur'.

This Henry, having assembled his forces, now led raids against the men of the Pas-de-Calais and of Picardy, took booty, and generally performed knightly actions worthy of praise. After he had led a number of such raids, and had encountered no resistance, he came to realize that the king of France was not planning to besiege Calais, but in fact intended to invade England. So Hotspur returned home, hoping to find in England the battle with the French for which he longed.

Time-honoured Lancaster

JOHN of Gaunt was a major influence in English and European affairs in the later 14th century. The third surviving son of Edward III, he was born at Ghent (hence the corruption 'of Gaunt') in 1340, and grew up during the glorious years of the French and Scottish wars. In 1359 he married his distant cousin Blanche, daughter of Henry, duke of Lancaster, and through her inherited the vast Lancastrian estates in northern England, the Midlands, and the Welsh Marches. With the deaths of his elder brothers, the Black Prince and Lionel of Antwerp, the new duke of Lancaster became the natural representative of the crown during Edward III's dotage and Richard II's minority.

John epitomized the contradictions inherent in any great medieval prince. He was ambitious but honourable, proud but fair, pious but promiscuous. He grieved deeply for Lady Blanche, who died in 1368; but he carried on a scandalous affair with Katherine Swynford. He laid claim to Castile in 1372 but had no designs on the English throne, and was always loyal to Richard II.

This was not the popular impression. The nobility mistrusted Gaunt, and prevented him from taking on the title of regent during Richard's early years. The loss of many of England's French possessions in the early 1370s was laid at his door, and in 1381 rebels sacked and burned his town house, the Savoy Palace. Gaunt reacted to this hostility by building up a powerful following, and by absenting himself from the court on military and diplomatic missions. His great wealth allowed him to support a military retinue of up to 500 men, and in the early 1380s he was backed by powerful aristocrats like the earls of Warwick, Arundel and Stafford.

As the 1380s progressed, and unease increased about the young king's favourites, Gaunt attempted to mediate between the political factions that sprang up as a result. In 1386–7, however, when his own son, Henry Bolingbroke, joined the appellants – a group of powerful nobles attempting to curb royal excesses – in their stand against the king, John was away in Spain. He returned to England late in 1389, and for a while succeeded in healing the rift between Richard and his opponents. In 1390, however, the king gave his uncle one of his own titles – duke of Aquitaine – for life. Richard's subjects in England and Gascony reacted sharply, claiming that the duchy should not be alienated from the English crown in this way, and casting further suspicion on Gaunt and his family. Not even this, however, could dent the close and trusting relationship between king and duke in the early 1390s.

By 1397, however, as the king became increasingly tyrannical, Gaunt was too old and too weak to take sides

Above *Though he never reigned as king, John of Gaunt's fame is attested by this fine oil portrait attributed to Luca Cornelli, a Dutch painter at Henry VIII's court over 100 years after Gaunt's death.*

or carry out his former role as mediator and in 1398 Bolingbroke was sent into exile. Gaunt's death the following year, and the king's refusal to allow the Lancastrian estates to pass to Bolingbroke, precipitated Richard's enforced abdication in 1399.

Relations between the deranged Richard and the dying Gaunt were strained. The king is said to have left bills on his uncle's deathbed; while Gaunt, in helpless anger, exposed his pox-ridden genitals to the royal visitor.

No sinister uncle scheming behind the throne, John of Gaunt tried to save Richard II from his own foolishness. Had the king heeded Gaunt's advice, he might have saved his own life.

When the Londoners knew for certain that the king of France had assembled a fleet and made ready an army, and had taken a definite decision to attack England, they, being as timid as hares and as fearful as mice, sought ways of escape and looked for hiding-places. As if the city was already on the point of being taken, they began to lose faith in their own strength and to despair of putting up any resistance.

In times of peace these people had made inflated boasts that they would blow all the Frenchmen out of England, but on hearing a mere empty rumour of the arrival of the enemy they thought that the whole land of England could scarcely afford them protection. So, as if drunk with wine, they rushed to the city walls, tore down the houses built up against them, and in their terror did all the things which defenders are accustomed to do as a last resort. At this point, not one single Frenchman had set foot on a ship, let alone had the enemy fleet put to sea, and yet the Londoners were behaving as though the whole realm lay conquered: they were as fearful and as agitated as if they were even now seeing the French in front of the city gates.

Thus these men who are accustomed to proclaim themselves as fine figures, and who are valiant in times of quiet and fierce in times of peace, showed what they would really do if they thought that battle was imminent and danger at hand. It was an example which should not be followed.

King Charles VI of France, as he prepared to invade England, did not believe that victory would be gained by arms alone, but put his trust in wooden walls. He called in a large number of joiners, whom he ordered to construct a wall of wooden planks, thick and closely joined. It was to be twenty feet high, with a tower every twelve yards, to hold ten men, the towers being higher than the wall itself by ten feet.

The king of France intended to set up this wall at the place where he landed, so that it would shield him from arrows and provide protection for his gunners while they launched terrible destruction upon our men. When need arose, he would be able to call his army back within the circuit of the wall, where the weary could rest and the wounded recuperate. According to reports, the wall was three thousand yards long, with many strong towers set along it.

While this work was in progress, some of our naval forces encountered two ships belonging to the king of France, which were on their way towards Sluys. In the ensuing engagement, the two French ships were captured and taken back to Sandwich, where they were found to contain part of the wall and some of the towers. The man in charge of the construction work was also taken prisoner. He was an Englishman, who had long ago been banished from the realm. The master gunner was taken as well; he had at one time lived among the English at Calais.

Besides these, our men captured various machines for hurling stones and for battering walls, and a number of guns, as well as a large quantity of powder, the value of which outweighed that of all the machines put together. The captured section of the wall was erected at Sandwich, thus setting up against our foes that which they had constructed to use against us.

Countless forces of common soldiers and captains were gathered from the various counties of the kingdom. They then waited within a twenty-mile circuit of London, as if to hold the castles. There seemed to be little difference between them and an enemy force of occupation, for the common soldiers, who were short of both food and money, were compelled to despoil the local populace in a search for subsistence, and to perpetrate in their homeland all the deeds which are normally done between enemies, with this one exception: they refrained from burning the neighbourhood.

After they had waited for a long time, achieving nothing worthwhile for themselves or for their fellow-countrymen, they were ordered to return home, and to hold themselves ready to reassemble when King Richard II should decide to recall them. Many of them, from want of any resources for daily subsistence, were obliged on returning home

The fight for peace

THE Hundred Years War with France was not going well for the English when Richard became king. Although fighting had been renewed in 1369, it had not been possible to recapture the success which attended English arms before the peace of Brétigny (1360). The domestic tranquillity that had resulted from Edward III's victories vanished, as military failure in the 1370s and 1380s compounded political disharmony in England.

Charles V, king of France, had since his accession in 1364 proved himself an able leader. He and his advisers realized that meeting the English in combat only invited another crushing defeat like Crécy and Poitiers, and adopted a new and more successful approach. They refused battle – and undermined the only strategy the English government was able to devise: the plundering raid or *chevauchée*. Several were launched during the 1370s and 1380s, but as they did not culminate with victory in battle there were no ransoms from captured French nobles to balance very heavy expenditure of English money.

While funds and men were diverted to futile *chevauchées*, French armies under commanders like Bertrand du Guesclin laid siege to English-held towns in Brittany and Gascony. During the 1370s the English were driven back upon Calais and Bordeaux.

Charles's other great advantage was the Castilian fleet, western Europe's leading naval force, which operated from the Biscay ports of Spain. It soon gained control of the Channel and disrupted England's commerce with Flanders and Gascony. The French, advised by Castilian admirals, established a naval base at Rouen, and the problems faced by the English government were vastly increased.

Merchant shipping became prey to French and Spanish pirates and the south coast was raided from Cornwall to the Thames. The Isle of Wight was occupied, and in 1380 Winchelsea and Gravesend were burned.

In 1380 Charles V died and was succeeded by the 12 year old Charles VI. Weak and vacillating by nature, he was dominated by his uncles, whose quarrels did much to lessen the pressure on Richard's armies. In 1385, however, a large French fleet was assembled and in 1386 England was in real danger of invasion by France. However, the expedition was called off at the last moment as the great French nobles resumed their wranglings – and Richard's realm was saved.

None the less, the cost to England was immense, yet with no tangible return. Enormous sums were raised in taxation to pay for armies, garrisons and shipping. Coastal counties bore additional financial burdens at a time when their livelihoods were at risk: merchant ships had to be diverted from their proper uses and town walls improved at great expense. The most impressive evidence of English fears is the castle built by Sir Edward Dallingrigge in about 1385 at Bodiam, in Sussex, 'in defence of the adjacent country against the king's enemies'.

One reaction to these events was to blame government. Another was to seek peace. Richard II and the French both wearied of the strains and distractions of war, and fighting died down after the late 1380s – although many in England still favoured continuing the struggle and opposed Richard's pacific inclinations.

A solution was almost reached by diplomatic means in 1394, but peace foundered on Gascon opposition to severing their ties with the English crown. Instead, in 1396 a truce was agreed – which was to run for 28 years.

Above *English soldiers on their way to France on a* chevauchée.

Below *Bodiam Castle.*

to sell their horses or weapons; others turned to looting and rapine in their search for provisions.

The parliament had not yet been formally dismissed, but the commons went home, although the lords stayed in London, awaiting reports of the arrival of the French, who were expected daily.

King Richard, lest he should appear to be idle, now elevated Robert de Vere, lately earl of Oxford but created marquis of Dublin in the recent parliament, to the rank of duke of Ireland, to be raised later from duke to king if fortune favoured him. This action demonstrated the depth of King Richard's affection for this man, whom he cultivated and loved, not without a degree of improper intimacy, or so it was rumoured. It also provoked discontent among the other lords and barons, who were angry that a man of such mediocrity should receive such great promotion, for he was not superior to the rest of them in either nobility of birth or gifts of character.

At King Richard's insistence, it was provided that the English would let the French ransom the heirs of Charles of Blois, late claimant of the dukedom of Brittany, for thirty thousand marks, so that, with the help of this money, de Vere might find the strength to win control of the lordship which the king had granted to him in Ireland. One condition was attached, namely that he should sail to Ireland before next Easter. Indeed, both lords and commons were so anxious that he should leave the land, that they preferred to see the kingdom lose this great sum of money, rather than suffer any longer the presence of the man who had seduced and captivated King Richard.

In the mean time, the king of France, with dukes, counts and a host of magnates, was waiting in Flanders, ready to seize the kingdom of England. Yet God frustrated his efforts, for during the entire period from 1 August to 31 October, no wind that was favourable to King Charles blew even for a few hours.

On 31 October, however, a strong wind did arise, which he considered suitable; he moved his ships from the moorings at which they had lain for

The rise and fall of a favourite

MOST of Richard II's favourites were unpopular, but none was so hated or despised as Robert de Vere, ninth earl of Oxford. Born in January 1362, he was five years older than Richard, with whom he spent much of his boyhood. Married to Edward III's granddaughter, Philippa de Coucy, while still a teenager, he exploited to the full his strong connections at court. As the young king's closest friend, his influence was out of all proportion to his ability. This was the cause of his downfall. Richard was too inexperienced, too headstrong – and probably too infatuated – to curb the earl's relentless ambition. It was commonly believed that 'if de Vere said black was white Richard would not contradict him'.

Richard's reckless generosity towards his favourite (who was sometimes compared to Edward II's lover, Piers Gaveston) became little short of a national scandal. In creating de Vere marquis of Dublin, for example, Richard introduced a foreign title hitherto unused in England, and also bestowed an almost unprecedented amount of authority upon him. When the marquisate was converted into a dukedom, in 1386, rumours that Richard intended eventually to make de Vere king of Ireland seemed to be more than idle speculation.

Almost all the rewards lavished upon the earl (including such prizes as the castles and lordships of Oakham and Queenborough, the castle of Berkhamsted and the office of Chief Justice of both Chester and North Wales) were slights to the aristocracy, whose ancestral titles were brushed aside. Far worse, however, was Richard's failure to punish de Vere for repudiating his wife, Philippa, and abducting one of the queen's Bohemian attendants, whom he married after obtaining a divorce by fraudulent means. This blatant affront to the royal family brought down on the earl's head the blind fury of Edward III's many kinsmen.

In the long run, it was de Vere's general contempt for the aristocracy, as much as the prominent part he played in helping Richard to undermine the authority of parliament, that in 1387 led the lords appellant to demand his execution for treason, along with four other crown servants.

Although de Vere was ready enough to take up arms, he showed little aptitude as a commander. He was trapped by the rebel lords at Radcot Bridge, Oxfordshire, in 1387 and then deserted his men by swimming the Thames under cover of fog; and after a last interview with Richard in London he fled abroad, never to return alive.

Not surprisingly, the earl was one of the first victims

claimed by the Merciless Parliament of 1388. His estates and titles were confiscated, and he was sentenced in his absence to be hanged, drawn and quartered. He died, apparently in great penury, in 1392, after being savaged by a wild boar while out hunting.

Three years later, after the de Veres had been rehabilitated, Richard had Robert's embalmed body exhumed from its burial place at Louvain, in Flanders, and interred beside his ancestors at Earls Colne Priory in Essex. Many distinguished clerics were present to see

Above Hunting *was a dangerous occupation; the wild animals of the forest could retaliate when sufficiently aroused. De Vere's death, gored by the boar, could be seen as providing a moral ending to a nasty story of greed and arrogance.*

the king throw open the coffin, gaze upon his friend's face and clasp his hand, but the nobility boycotted the ceremony in disgust.

so long, and left the port of Sluys precipitately. But when all the vessels had set sail and were out at sea about twenty miles from port, a contrary wind suddenly struck them and forced them all back again. It did not merely drive the ships along, but buffeted them against each other and battered them, to the extent that some of them were broken against the entrance of Sluys harbour. By these events England was freed from fear, and the king of France returned to his own land.

1387

At this time Robert de Vere, puffed up by the honours which King Richard had bestowed upon him, suddenly repudiated his wife, Philippa de Coucy, a beautiful young noblewoman, who was the daughter of Edward III's daughter Isabella. He took up instead with a woman who had come to England from Bohemia with Queen Anne. Her name was Agnes Launcecrona; she was reputed to be the daughter of a saddler, and was certainly low-born and of no honourable estate. This provoked a great scandal. The king supported de Vere whole-heartedly, not wishing to give his friend any cause for grief, or rather, as was widely believed, being unable to oppose de Vere's wishes in any way, because through the evil machinations of a certain friar who was in the earl's household, King Richard was rendered incapable of discerning or doing what was good or right.

The magnates were enraged, especially Thomas, duke of Gloucester, who was Philippa's uncle. Although at that time he was not in a position to avenge the insults to his niece, the duke kept them all in mind, for a time of reckoning in the future. This was not unnoticed by de Vere, who determined to take care for his own safety, and formulated plans to do away with the duke of Gloucester and all his supporters.

Eastertide passed, and with it the date at which de Vere should have set sail for his dukedom in Ireland, yet he was still in England, seemingly with no thought of departure. In order to prevent great upheaval among the magnates of the realm, the king journeyed to Wales with de Vere, as if he were accompanying him to his ships.

However, Richard II was not about to see de Vere on his way, but intended to keep him there in that remote region in order that they could discuss, with fewer interruptions, how they might use trickery to capture and then kill the duke of Gloucester and his allies, the earls of Arundel, Warwick, Derby and Nottingham, and other faithful men of the realm. With the king and de Vere were Michael de la Pole, earl of Suffolk, Chief Justice Robert Tresilian, and various others who, scared for their own skins, joined in this conspiracy.

Some time later, King Richard, acting as if everyone in England had forgotten about the duke's obligation to set out for Ireland, returned from Wales with de Vere and his treacherous accomplices, and went to Nottingham Castle, there to make final plans for the deaths of Gloucester and the other nobles. They summoned thither a number of Londoners, who were known to be ready to give their support to either faction, together with all the sheriffs and judges of the kingdom.

These Londoners were as restless as swallows, found at one time with the lords, at another with the king, never settled, and untrustworthy. Many of them had recently confessed to treason against the king, but they had been received back into his grace, and freely they repaid him, bringing against Gloucester and the other lords a variety of criminal charges which the king had taken the precaution of fabricating while he was lurking far away in Wales.

Meanwhile, King Richard's opponents had not been idle. Thomas Favent takes up the story.

The duke of Gloucester, the earl of Arundel and the earl of Warwick gathered their forces on 14 November 1387, at Waltham Cross in Hertfordshire; and they sent letters to the other members of the council, who were with the king in the palace of Westminster. They also sent a written appeal accusing the archbishop of York, the duke of Ireland, the earl of Suffolk, Robert Tresilian and Nicholas Brembre of treason; they offered to prosecute them and to prove the charge lawfully, if they were given the task; and they offered as a pledge their possessions and competent guarantors. They made all the other commissioners subscribe to their appeal, as fellow-prosecutors and parties to it, and asked them to refer the matter to the king.

When this news reached King Richard's ears, he sent to them asking what their proposal was and what they wished to do. They replied: 'It is in the interest of the state that any traitors who cluster around you deserve to be thrown out and punished, since it is better for some men to die for the country than for the whole nation to perish.' They also asked to have the freedom to come and go quite safely to confer with him.

The king considered their wishes, and sent back asking them to come. When they arrived at Westminster, where the king was sitting on a throne in the great hall among his commissioners, the three prosecuting peers entered the hall with a large crowd of their kinsmen, and greeted the king on bended knee, bowing three times. They explained their reason for coming, just as they had done previously at Waltham Cross, and they accused the archbishop of York, the duke, the earl, Tresilian and Brembre of treason. These men were at the time lurking and concealing themselves in secret corners and hiding-places in the palace, like Adam and Eve hiding from God in the beginning, for they did not have the courage to be discovered.

The king then accepted the appeal so that it could be proved and prosecuted, and fixed a date for the next parliament, 3 February 1388.

In the mean time the king took both parties, with their men and possessions, under his special protection, so that neither of them might harass the other until the next parliament. This was publicly proclaimed throughout England, and they went away feeling consoled.

From this 'appeal' for treason, Richard's opponents are known as the 'lords appellant'. But they were not quite as consoled as Favent claims. Events moved rapidly to a climax, at Radcot Bridge on the Thames in Oxfordshire, as Walsingham relates.

After returning from the meeting, the lords appellant concluded that it would not be safe for them to separate from one another just yet, because of the king's unreliability and the notorious dishonesty of his treacherous favourites. Subsequent events proved the lords' wisdom on this point, for with the king's connivance de Vere, the duke of Ireland, assembled a large band of fighting men in Cheshire and the Welsh Marches. Their captain in the field was the constable of Chester, Thomas Molyneux, a wealthy and daring man who commanded the obedience of the whole region.

De Vere's wicked plans could not long be kept hidden from the appellants. Forewarned of all these preparations, and knowing that the duke of Ireland was setting out for London with his troops to join forces with the Londoners and to unite the two armies in a single invincible host, the lords armed their own men forthwith and encouraged each other not to neglect their own safety, but rather to hasten to forestall and eliminate those who had conspired deceitfully to destroy them.

They set out in secret to meet the duke of Ireland, sending parties of their men to block every path by which he might be expected to approach. De Vere rode along with the army which he had raised, lofty and arrogant in his belief that no one would dare to oppose him.

Suddenly, however, he glanced sideways and saw the army of the lords stationed in a valley not far distant, awaiting his arrival. This struck fear into his heart, and he said: 'My friends, I see that I must now take flight, because the enemy's forces appear to be far stronger than our own. So, before battle is joined, I shall slip away and save myself, if I can; for they are seeking me, and me alone; they have no quarrel with you. When I am gone, you may slip away easily.'

One of his soldiers replied: 'You made us leave our homes, you persuaded us to give you our allegiance, you brought us on this expedition: we are ready, therefore, to fight at your side and; with you, to obtain victory, if that is the outcome, or, if fortune does not favour us, to die bravely with you.' 'I am not so ready to die as you are,' replied de Vere, and spurring on his horse he fled in haste. Seeing this, many of those who had come with him reviled his cowardice, and prepared to give battle to the lords.

Thomas Molyneux, who was there, made ready to fight, since only one member of the lords' party had yet arrived: Henry Bolingbroke, earl of Derby, son of the duke of Lancaster. After Molyneux had fought for some while, tired and dispirited he plunged into the river. Many people, including Sir Thomas Mortimer, urged him to come out, saying that if he did not he would certainly be pierced by arrows while in the water. 'If I come out,' said Molyneux, 'are you willing to spare my life?' 'I will not promise that,' said the knight, 'but you must either come out or fall where you are.' 'If that is the case,' answered Molyneux, 'allow me to climb out, and I will fight you or any of your men, so that I may die like a man.' But as he was climbing out, Mortimer grabbed him by the helmet, and dragged him out head first, then, drawing a dagger, plunged it into Molyneux's brains.

Meanwhile, in his flight, the duke of Ireland had reached the river, but when he tried to cross it he found that the bridge had been broken down. He went on to another bridge, but found his passage there blocked by enemy captains. Turning in another direction, he found a ford and forced his horse into the river. Changing himself from a horseman to a swimmer, he reached the opposite bank.

Night had now fallen, and the lords' men were not pursuing the fugitive, largely because they were not familiar with the local byways. De Vere's horse, however, along with his helmet, his gauntlets and his breastplate, fell into the hands of the lords, who for a long time thereafter supposed him to have drowned. They found his wagon and baggage as well, containing many interesting things, among them letters from the king telling him to hurry to London with a large army, where he would find the king ready to devote himself wholeheartedly to living or dying with the duke. These words offered the lords written proof of Richard's untrustworthy and inconsistent character.

Women in the age of Chaucer

AROUND 1393 the author of *The Goodman of Paris*, in his treatise on domestic management, advised his young wife to emulate the behaviour of a faithful dog in order to please her husband. Freedom was limited for women in Chaucer's time, despite the law of jointure which provided that the bridegroom's family must make formal provision for the bride's possible widowhood – with the practical result that she would hold estates in her own right if she outlived her husband.

Marriage was a contract arranged by men for social and financial advantage; the woman was an accessory, and the higher her social rank the smaller her hope of being free to act as she wished. Further down the social scale women appear to have had more freedom. The widow of a craftsman or tradesman could effectively carry on his business in her own right, whereas a male heir was essential to secure landed estates. Many women of all ranks died early, either in childbirth or exhausted by childbearing.

One obvious way to view the aristocratic literature of love is as an escape from these economic facts, which governed the real relationships between the sexes. Romances conventionally relate how the man's suit is rebuffed until he has performed deeds of altruistic valour in the service of a lady, who may nevertheless choose to remain chaste. In *The Canterbury Tales*, Chaucer contributes to this convention, notably in the Knight's Tale. On the other hand, the heroine of his *Troilus and Criseyde* is a fascinating and elusive love-object, a widow of dubious pedigree, shrinking and vacillating. In accepting her lot as a political pawn, and her need for male protection, she demonstrates both the romance ideal and the real plight of women in a patriarchal military society.

In *Epistre au Dieu d'Amours* (1399) Christine de Pisan

drew attention to the discrepancy between the status of women in romance and in society, asking why a woman's seduction is a matter of such effort in literature, if women are as pliant, in real life, as men would have them believe: books written by women would tell a different story.

Chaucer used 'middle-class', mercantile settings to illustrate the cash base of contemporary marriage, exposing many of the shortcomings of being born a woman. However, he is no champion of womanhood. His work is full of conventional, self-sacrificing women, elevated for

Above *Spinning in the home: the traditional image of women.*

Above left *The distaff put to a different use. Wife beating husband; a misericord in Chester Cathedral.*

their conformity to the ideals of an unreflecting patriarchal society. Even the woman's voice which laments the death of a child in *The Canterbury Tales* is that of the prioress, a nun.

When the parliament assembled, as arranged, and the lords appellant arrived to prosecute their appeal, Richard was in no position to defend his allies, most of whom fled. The result was a foregone conclusion, and the occasion came to be known as the Merciless Parliament. This is Thomas Favent's account of it.

1388

Since Lent was thought to be a suitable and acceptable time to punish and correct the criminals according to their deserts, a great parliament was held on 2 February as follows: all the men of both estates, the nobles and distinguished men of the kingdom, met in the White Hall at Westminster.

The five prosecuting peers, whose integrity was justly famed throughout the land, and who had been endowed with constant good fortune, entered the hall with a large crowd of followers, clothed in gold and linking their arms together; and when they saw the king they bowed in unison and greeted him. The hall was so crowded with people that even the corners were full. But how many of the conspirators do you think could be found at the time? Only Nicholas Brembre had been caught earlier and ordered to be thrown into prison at Gloucester.

Following the ancient traditions of parliament, the laity sat on the king's left and the clergy on his right; then the chancellor stood immediately behind the king, and explained how the business of parliament traditionally proceeded. When this had been done, the five peers stood up and nominated Robert Plesington, a wise knight, as their speaker. Then he said: 'Behold the duke of Gloucester come to purge himself of the treasons laid to his charge by these conspirators.'

The chancellor, Thomas Arundel, bishop of Ely, then spoke for the king to excuse the duke: 'My lord duke, the king could not suspect that any such thing could be imagined of you, seeing that you were born of such noble royal stock, and in a collateral line to himself.' At these words the duke of Gloucester and his four companions knelt and thanked the king.

Then, after silence had been ordered, these peers put forward written articles of accusation on the subject of the act of treason. Geoffrey Martin, the crown clerk, stood in the middle of parliament and for two hours hurriedly read through these articles. Many people's hearts were stirred by the horrific content of the articles. Many had faces swollen with weeping, and tears were rolling down their cheeks.

After the articles had been read, the prosecutors appealed to the king to pass sentence of a just and appropriate kind, on the evidence of their allegations and proofs, so that the execution of the defendants could take place. King Richard promised to do this. This was what happened on the first day. The second day they spent in council, and nothing was achieved; so I shall not proceed according to days, but deal only with the more important actions of this parliament.

When, on the third day, they came to prosecute the said defendants, the chancellor of England, Thomas Arundel, in the name of the clergy, declared in front of a full house that it was impossible for the clergy to be present at these proceedings or take part in any trial where a verdict of death was involved. To confirm this he read a written claim from the clergy in which they said in their own defence that it was not for any reason of bias or fear of hatred or expectation of any reward that they were absenting themselves, but because they wished to observe the sanctions of canon law and all other laws which forbade them to enter into this sort of base business. The knights of the various counties used to sit in the chapter house of Westminster Abbey to do their business, and they sent them the appeal to notify them of it.

Meanwhile, despite the claims of the clergy, the five peers did not cease to press for the conviction of these criminals. The clergy got up, and went temporarily into the king's chamber next door. Richard II, moved by his conscience or by charity, and seeing that in all things it is wise to remember the end, and, within the confines of the law, being inclined to favour the defendants rather than the prosecutors, continued to delay the trial in case any new evidence could be alleged or proved on

King versus parliament

THE Merciless Parliament of 1388 is undoubtedly the most famous – or notorious – of the 24 parliaments which met during Richard II's reign. In it the bitter political struggle between Richard II and his advisers on the one hand, and the majority of the lords and commons on the other, was fought out.

This had begun in earnest two years earlier, during the Wonderful Parliament of 1386, when Richard had suffered the humiliation of seeing his chancellor, the earl of Suffolk, deprived of office and impeached, and of having to accept the supervision of a group of councillors appointed by parliament to curtail the worst excesses of his rule. The question was how far parliament could, or should, assume an active role in directing government; and Richard was determined to reassert his authority at the first opportunity.

His rehabilitation of Suffolk in 1387, his refusal to co-operate with the new council, his reliance upon unpopular favourites, and, above all, his manipulation of the judiciary to deny the legality of the proceedings of the Wonderful Parliament, provoked a strong reaction.

In November 1387, Richard's uncle, the duke of Gloucester, and the earls of Warwick and Arundel 'appealed' (accused) five of the king's closest intimates of treason. These lords appellant were later joined by Henry Bolingbroke, earl of Derby, and by the earl marshal. Richard was threatened with deposition and, after a feeble show of resistance, had to summon parliament.

The assembly which gathered at Westminster on 4 February 1388 was truculent. Many of the shire knights were enthusiastic supporters of the appellants, and the commons as a whole wanted a sweeping purge of the royal household. The five so-called traitors (the earls of Suffolk and Oxford, Sir Robert Tresilian, Chief Justice of the King's Bench, the archbishop of York, and Sir Nicholas Brembre) were summarily convicted; Brembre and Tresilian lost their lives; the others fled overseas.

In early March, the commons demanded the impeachment of the judges who had endorsed Richard's attempt to undermine the authority of parliament. They clamoured for the death penalty, but a sentence of banishment to Ireland was adopted as a compromise.

Many members of the upper house believed that the lords appellant threatened to outdo the king in vindictiveness. While the commons pressed for the further impeachment of Richard's confessor and four knights of his chamber, the more moderate peers believed it was time to call a halt. By having the knights condemned to death without a hearing the lords appellant and their supporters were vulnerable to charges of despotism.

The trial and execution of one of the knights, Sir Simon Burley – once the young king's tutor – caused particular ill-feeling. This distinguished soldier had many friends, including the duke of York, and the queen spent three hours on her knees before the earl of Arundel, pleading in vain for Sir Simon's life – which explains Richard's intense hatred of the earl, whom he subsequently executed.

Although they were successful in the short term, the lords appellant failed to impose lasting restraints upon the king. They removed his friends, and temporarily curbed his despotism by placing him once again – as in his minority – under the control of a council. But their intransigence merely fuelled Richard's desire for revenge.

57

behalf of the absent men. But the peers were impatient, and appealed to the king for no other business to proceed, be put forward or be heard until the treason case in hand had been finally put to rest. The king granted this request.

Finally, on 11 February, when no evidence could be alleged on behalf of the absent men, John Devereux, the court steward, representing the king, pronounced that the archbishop of York, the duke of Ireland, the earl of Suffolk and Robert Tresilian should be brought to Tyburn, there to be hanged forthwith on the gallows, and that all their goods should be confiscated, so that their heirs might not be able to enjoy them.

The Scots attempted to take advantage of the distraction caused by the political upheavals in the south, though without complete success, as Walsingham shows.

This year the Scots, who do not know how to be at peace, thinking that the English would put up no resistance, got ready to invade the north of England as soon as the current truce expired. They entered England with a large army, before the English could assemble any forces to withstand them. Since they encountered no opposition, the invaders marched onwards, bringing slaughter and rapine, taking many prisoners and burning everything in their path, except where the landholders paid to be spared.

With a great display of arrogance they approached Newcastle upon Tyne, and camped at Otterburn. Henry Percy the younger, Hotspur, was then in Newcastle with his brother Ralph. Both were knights, both eager for military glory, both hostile to the Scots, but Henry the more so, and it was he whom the Scots most feared, because of his great valour.

Henry himself was enraged that the Scots were rampaging about unchecked, and so, because they had challenged him to fight, he promised that he would join battle with them within three days, although his forces were far below theirs in numbers. True to his word, he fell upon them unexpectedly in their camp, and inflicted many casualties.

Otterburn

IN 1384, after nearly 30 years of uneasy truce, war broke out once again between Scotland and England. The Scots were more buoyant than at any time since their victory at Bannockburn in 1314. Taking advantage of Edward II and Edward III's domestic and continental commitments, they had gained territory on the borders while nominally keeping the truce; and, on Richard II's accession, had stopped paying the instalments of David II's ransom, half of which was still outstanding 13 years after David's death.

It was not until 1384 that the English could devote full military attention to their northern neighbours. Early in that year, John of Gaunt returned to Edinburgh, which he had last visited in 1381. But this time he came with an army; and he held the city to ransom.

The Scots had been encouraged to reopen hostilities by the promise, in August 1383, of French support. However, when they invaded the English borders a year later, there was no significant aid from the French. This materialized in May 1385 when the admiral of France, Jean de Vienne, arrived in Scotland with an army, and money – in the nick of time: in July, Richard II and John of Gaunt marched north in a grim expedition to chasten the Scots – and blood the young king.

The invading force was immense, and set several border abbeys ablaze, as well as inflicting fire damage on Edinburgh. But after two weeks the Scots' scorched earth policy had starved out the English invaders, who turned for home. The Scots and their French allies pursued them across the borders, but when a promised French attack on the south of England failed to take place, the expedition returned to the north.

The French presence in Scotland was more alluring in prospect than in practice. The French knights had expected to win conventional kudos in action against Richard II, and be treated as superior military beings. Instead, they watched while the Scots avoided pitched battles and ruthlessly burned crops. The success of these tactics only heightened the ignominy. Friction turned to fisticuffs. When the French left, they were billed for the damage they had caused; and Jean de Vienne had to remain behind in captivity as a surety for due payment.

The 'auld alliance' survived, but the fury of the English attack in 1385 – and the demonstration of the alliance's failings – had dented Scottish confidence. For two years, French attempts to invade England did not tempt the Scots to break the ensuing truces by joining them.

In summer 1388, however, when the last of the truces was coming to its end, and the English administration was in disarray, the Scots mounted a two-pronged attack against Ireland and northern England.

Above Otterburn today. Hotspur earned the admiration of the Scots here; but his prowess, celebrated by Shakespeare, was later turned against the crown.

On 5 August, at Otterburn in Redesdale, the defending English army, under the earl of Northumberland's eldest son, Henry Hotspur, set upon and was defeated by the smaller, diversionary Scots force led by the expedition's commander, James, earl of Douglas. Hotspur was captured (and later ransomed for an astronomical sum); Douglas's corpse was found by his victorious troops the following morning. The battle of Otterburn is commemorated in one of the most famous and evocative of border ballads: 'Chevy Chase', a celebration of the Scots victory, and of the chivalric ideal.

Richard's wish for revenge against the Scots was checked by his even stronger desire for peace with the French, who insisted that Scotland be included in the truce they made with the English in June 1389. Richard subsequently made occasional threatening overtures against Scotland, but his military involvement in Ireland made him anxious for peace in the north. The Scots felt secure enough to deny England a peace treaty while the terms were unacceptable to them. Seen from Scotland, Richard's reign ended as it had begun, with a series of truces, unenthusiastically observed by both sides.

The leader of the Scottish forces, James, earl of Douglas, another ambitious young man, realized that the occasion for which he had prayed a thousand times was now at hand, namely that Henry Percy was in his camp. Eagerly Douglas rode to oppose Hotspur.

It was a magnificent sight, to see two such fine young men join battle and strive for glory. Although neither was lacking in courage, victory fell to Henry Percy, at whose hands this, the greatest of the Scots, perished. The earl of Dunbar then came on the scene, with a large force of Scots. They killed many Englishmen and took Henry Percy and his brother prisoners, but only after Henry and the small band of men who had followed him into the field had slaughtered many of the leading Scots.

While the English magnates were still making preparations to oppose the Scots, the invaders, shamed and humiliated by the treatment which they had received in the battle of Otterburn, fled from English soil, taking their captives with them for they dared not await the arrival of the lords. Thus, the bravery of Henry Percy alone had served to free England both from the fear and the presence of the Scots.

1389

That year, King Richard II, influenced by certain tale-bearers, summoned the magnates and many of the leading men of the realm. He then strode into the council chamber where the assembled lords were awaiting his arrival and, taking a seat, he enquired of them how old he was. They replied that he had now completed his twentieth year.

'That being so,' said Richard, 'I am of full age to take control of my house and household, not to mention my kingdom. It seems to me to be unfair that someone of my station should be in a more restricted situation than the humblest of my subjects. After all, any heir within my realm, whose father is dead, is permitted to deal freely with his own estates when he has reached his twentieth year. Why should I be denied a right which is granted to anyone of lower rank?'

King Harry Percy

IN the latter years of Richard II's reign the great Percy family ruled the northernmost English counties virtually unchallenged. In time of war, they were under constant threat of Scots invasion, and even in periods of nominal peace, cross-border raids and local feuds ensured little tranquillity. To defend and control this turbulent frontier, the government relied on wardens of the Marches, who, although paid from the national treasury, were effectively independent warlords commanding subsidized private armies. Although they were chosen by the king, his choice was limited to the heads of leading border families. The most powerful – and certainly the most ambitious – of these were the Percys.

Percy influence in the north dated from the decades after the Norman conquest, when William de Percy accumulated 86 properties in Yorkshire. These were a solid base for 14th-century Percy expansion into Cumberland and Northumberland, where the family's estates included the castles of Alnwick, Warkworth, and Prudhoe with control of Berwick on Tweed. Henry, Lord Percy (1341–1408) was created earl of Northumberland at Richard II's coronation in 1377.

Northumberland's son Sir Harry Percy (1364–1403) materially assisted this rise. He started his military career at the age of 14 in skirmishes against the Scots, and soon won the nickname of 'Hotspur' from his enemies, either because of his fiery temper or, more probably, the speed of his riding. His most famous exploit was at Otterburn in Redesdale in August 1388, when he launched a surprise dusk attack on a Scots raiding force led by his rival, Lord Douglas. Although Douglas was killed in all-night fighting by moonlight, Hotspur was captured and the Scots claimed the victory. The battle nevertheless enhanced Hotspur's heroic reputation locally and nationally.

His fame and Northumberland's power made the Percys leading contenders for the wardenships of the Marches. Previously, the government had distributed one of the two wardenships – of the East and of the West March – to each of the border families in turn. From 1391 to 1396 the Percys held both simultaneously – until Richard II challenged their dominance by granting the West March to a courtier. Soon afterwards he raised their chief rival, Ralph Neville, to the earldom of Westmorland.

The Percys never forgave the king and were the first English noblemen to join Henry Bolingbroke; and it was Northumberland who captured Richard II by means of a false promise and handed him over to Henry. The Percys benefited richly from their kingmaking, for when Bolingbroke became Henry IV, he granted them control of the Isle of Man and North Wales, as well as over the borders.

After their great victory over the Scots at Homildon Hill in 1402, their next goal could only be the crown.

In July 1403 the Percys rose against Henry IV, ostensibly to crown Richard's 'rightful heir', the earl of March, who was the nephew of Hotspur's wife. However, their real intent was declared at the battle of Shrewsbury, when Hotspur's soldiers cheered for 'King Harry Percy'. But Hotspur was killed in the battle, and to prove that the great northern hero was dead, the king had his body salted and quartered; a quarter was displayed at Newcastle, and his head at York. Five years later, his father suffered the same fate.

Opposite *A statue of Henry Percy, earl of Northumberland, on the exterior of Beverley Minster in Yorkshire, the Percy heartland.*

Below *Henry Percy swears fidelity to Richard II on the Host in Conway Castle chapel. Despite this oath it was Northumberland who betrayed Richard into Bolingbroke's hands, a legacy of the king's clumsy attempt to play the Percys off against their rivals the Nevilles.*

Astounded, the barons replied that certainly none of the king's rights ought to be taken from him, and that he should rule his realm, as was due to him by law.

Richard declared: 'Listen to me! You all know that for a long time I have been subject to the control of guardians, and have not been allowed to do even the smallest thing without their consent. Well, now I am dismissing them from my council, and, like an heir attaining full age, I shall appoint instead those whom I choose, and I will conduct my own business myself. And my first command is that the chancellor shall hand the Great Seal over to me.'

When the chancellor, Thomas Arundel, archbishop of York, had handed over the Great Seal, the king clasped it to his chest, then rose swiftly to his feet and left the chamber. Within a few minutes, however, he came back and sat down, then handed the Great Seal to William of Wykeham, bishop of Winchester, whom he appointed chancellor despite widespread disapproval.

In early November, John of Gaunt, duke of Lancaster, returned to England after an absence of three years in Spain and Aquitaine, otherwise called Gascony. Having endured difficulties in 1386, in his early days in Spain, he had later enjoyed the greatest good fortune, not because of the strength of his men, nor the numbers of his warriors, but by manifest divine favour.

This year, to celebrate the dedication feast of St Mary's church in Cambridge, the Host was carried round the parish on the shoulders of two priests in a shrine which, far from being heavy, was so light that even a seven year old child could have borne it on his own without any difficulty. The procession, led by the two priests with the shrine, wound its way through the town until it reached the house of the Augustinian friars, which adjoins the market-place.

There, all of a sudden, the shrine, which had been resting evenly on the shoulders of the two men, reared up and strove, as if endowed with invisible power, to leap away from them. It then

William of Wykeham

WILLIAM of Wykeham was one of the most successful social climbers of medieval England. A Hampshire man, he came from an obscure family, but through the patronage of William Edington, bishop of Winchester, entered the service of Edward III in about 1349.

By 1356 he was clerk of the works at three royal castles, including Windsor; and in 1359, as their keeper and surveyor, his responsibilities were greatly enlarged. The basis of Wykeham's success in royal service was his efficiency in organizing the king's considerable building programme, especially the new royal apartments at Windsor Castle, which (much altered) still survive. By 1360 he had become Edward III's right-hand man, a position that was formalized in 1367 when he was appointed chancellor.

Like most 'civil servants', Wykeham was in holy orders, which meant he could not marry. However, it also meant that, in addition to his wages, he could augment his income with ecclesiastical benefices, and in 1367 Wykeham succeeded Edington as bishop of Winchester. The richest bishopric in England, its holder was among the wealthiest men in the kingdom, and Wykeham enjoyed its income until his death in 1404.

From 1369, he planned the foundation of New College, Oxford. At its heart it was to be a religious institution, providing prayers for Wykeham's soul, while its secondary purpose was to raise the quality of parish clergy by supporting students of theology.

New College, which came formally into being in 1379, was remarkable on three counts: its size – it had 70 scholars, twice the number at any other college; the provision, during Wykeham's lifetime, of specially designed buildings, many of which, including the chapel, dining-hall and archive store, still serve their original purpose; and the foundation of a 'feeder school', Winchester College, to provide boys suitably qualified for study at Oxford.

Boys, all of whom already had some skill in Latin grammar, were admitted to Winchester at between eight and twelve years old, and stayed until their eighteenth birthday or until they had qualified for university. The 70 pupils received free schooling, and Wykeham specified the groups from which these scholars were to be chosen: his relatives had priority, followed by the sons of tenants of the properties of his two colleges.

Wykeham's third project was rebuilding the nave of Winchester Cathedral. Started in 1394, the work was well advanced at his death, and today's nave is largely his achievement.

Above *New College* seen by contemporaries, with visitors strolling outside admiring the magnificent new structure and fine architecture.

Below *New College* today, quiet and peaceful.

became so heavy that the priests could scarcely support its weight, but neither were they able to remove the edges of the shrine from their shoulders or set it down. Thus they suffered and toiled, sweating and gasping for breath, and entreating the lay people to assist them.

Many laymen came up to lend a hand, but, amazing as it may seem, they could feel no weight at all. The priests were affected by these paroxysms for the whole time it took them to pass the house of the friars; and as soon as the procession had moved on from there, the shrine settled quietly again on the bearers' shoulders. Then an idiot, a truly wretched specimen of humanity, began to leap clumsily, or, as it were, to dance, in front of the Host: immediately a terrible punishment overtook him, for in the middle of his merriment he fell to the ground and died within a short time.

A variety of explanations were offered for these miraculous events. I shall not attempt to judge between the interpretations, for I prefer to leave such evaluation to others and not to make any rash judgements upon things of which I have no first-hand knowledge. I shall, however, venture to add one thing more: very shortly after this episode, Cambridge suffered a great and fearful plague. Perfectly healthy men, when stricken by this disease, went suddenly mad and died senseless, without the last rites.

About the same time, a swarm of gnats, so thick that it blotted out the daylight, attacked the royal manor of Sheen. The insects then began a vicious fight among themselves, at the end of which two thirds of the swarm lay dead on the ground, while the remaining third flew off victorious, their destination unknown. Brooms were needed to sweep up the heaps of dead gnats, which would have filled several bushel measures. I leave it to others to decide the meaning of this episode.

At about this time, in the priory of the Augustinian canons at Bridlington, which is in the diocese of York, so many undoubted miracles occurred at the tomb of John, a former prior of the house, that the whole of England marvelled. It was said of John that when alive he had walked

Heavenly holidays

MIRACLES – God's intervention in human affairs, directly or through his saints – were accepted as a matter of course in medieval England. They were likely to occur at any of hundreds of shrines, by far the most popular of which was the tomb of St Thomas Becket in Canterbury Cathedral. Pilgrims visited these shrines for a variety of reasons. Some came to do penance, loading themselves with chains or crawling round the church or cathedral on their hands and knees. Others made the journey to obtain the indulgences that most major shrines offered. These could also be obtained by proxy, and wealthy penitents sometimes bequeathed money to hire professional pilgrims for this purpose.

Many pilgrims treated the journey as a holiday. They could return with their souvenirs: pilgrim badges purchased at the shrine, and perhaps a handkerchief pressed (for a small fee) against it, and so endowed with miraculous power. The sick or crippled went on pilgrimage in search of a miraculous cure.

A shrine's popularity was related to the number of miraculous healings, and the stained glass windows round the site of St Thomas's tomb at Canterbury depict the saint curing ailments ranging from nightmares, piles and swollen feet to 'worms in the stomach' and blindness, and even reviving those on the point of death – or beyond it. The patient might be measured, and a candle of exactly equivalent length presented to the shrine in supplication, or as a thank-offering, where it would burn near wax or silver models of limbs and organs left by ex-sufferers.

Some saints specialized in particular illnesses, often linked to their martyrdom. St Pancras was invoked against headaches; St Apollonia, whose teeth were knocked out, against toothache; St Elmo, whose intestines were pulled out on a windlass, against stomach ailments; and St Vitus, for whom angels danced in prison, against epilepsy, fits and chorea (or 'St Vitus's dance').

Holy places also had particular properties. The spring of the virgin martyr St Winefred, at Holywell in North Wales, was believed to promote fertility, while at North Marston in Buckinghamshire the shrine of Master John Schorne, who conjured the Devil into (or out of) a boot, alleviated gout. He was one of a number of unofficial, uncanonized 'saints' whose cults sprang up spontaneously.

Most well-known shrines centred on a saint's body, but there were exceptions. At Hayles in Gloucestershire there was said to be a phial of Christ's own blood, while Walsingham in Norfolk displayed a replica of the Virgin Mary's 'Holy House', an ampoule of her milk and a wonder-working image of the Virgin.

Images of saints (and of the Virgin) were popular objects of veneration. At Worcester, a statue of Mary attracted more offerings than the once-renowned tomb of the Anglo-Saxon St Wulfstan. Images were sometimes endowed with distinctive personalities. 'Of all Our Ladies', Sir Thomas More heard a pilgrim remark, 'I love best Our Lady of Walsingham.' 'And I', replied his neighbour, 'Our Lady of Ipswich.' Other relics included the ear of

Malchus, hacked off by St Peter in Gethsemane and treasured by a West Country monastery, and 'a piece of the clay from which Adam was made', displayed with 'part of Christ's manger' at Canterbury.

Only a tiny Lollard minority rejected images, relics and shrines; most people had faith in their miraculous powers. Throughout the 14th and 15th centuries, the desire to go on pilgrimages was undiminished.

Opposite *St John of Bridlington.*

Below *St Thomas Becket's miraculous cures.*

Far below *St Nicholas calms the waters.*

on water, had raised the dead and had, by his prayers, filled the barns belonging to his house with miraculous harvests, so that crops which had been thought scarcely adequate to supply the household for one month, actually lasted for a whole year. His humility and his kindness to those who suffered were sure signs of his sanctity.

1391

On Christmas Day, a dolphin came leaping up the River Thames from the sea, as far as London Bridge. It may have been a portent of the storms which arose within the week. The citizens saw the beast and pursued it; with some difficulty, they captured it, then brought it into London, where its sheer size provided an interesting spectacle for the people, since it was easily ten feet long.

Dolphins are sea creatures who follow human voices, enjoy the sound of pipes, and gather together in flocks if they hear music. When they take mighty leaps through the waves, they foretell storms. The sea contains no swifter or more agile beasts. Frequently, dolphins jump right over ships' sails.

After copulation, the females wander away, to give birth to their whelps after a ten-month period of gestation; the young are born in the summer. They suckle their offspring, and carry their young in their mouths. They take care of the weak.

Tests on tails which have been cut off show that dolphins live for thirty years. They have mouths like other beasts, but set in their bellies; alone among marine creatures, they have tongues which move. Their dorsal fins are pointed, and bristle when the dolphins are angry, but retract when the beasts become calm again. They cannot breathe in water, but are said to take the air which they need from above the waves.

The sound of their voices is similar to human groans. They have a special name to which they will answer, for they are more accurately called 'Simones'. When the wind is in the north, they are more receptive to human voices, but when the wind is in the south, their hearing is dulled.

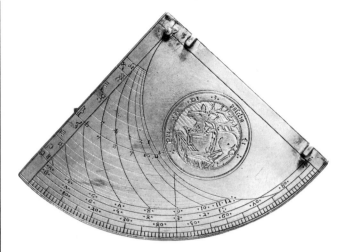

The natural world

MEDIEVAL natural philosophy attempted to describe the world 'as it must be rather than as the illusion of experience might make it appear'. It assumed that general principles ruled creation, and that creation was tied to spiritual forces which could be apprehended.

The *Travels of Sir John Mandeville* (*c.* 1375), an anonymous travelogue rich in geographical and scientific information, rapidly achieved a wide popularity. Full of marvels, it seems an odd mixture of fancy and fact. But 'Mandeville' claimed to report only what he himself had seen. As evidence that 'the earth and the sea be of round form and shape', he quotes sightings he made on the same star in Brabant and in Bohemia, as well as sailors' accounts that the night sky varies in different parts of the earth.

The dolphin in the Thames lent credibility to the fabulous stories told by seamen from the whale fisheries off the Bay of Biscay. A favourite one of these related how a boat beached on an island which, when the sailors made a fire to cook their food, turned out to be a whale. Other similar tales were found in bestiaries. Popular, and often brightly illustrated, these were scrapbook-like lists of animals with descriptions of the allegorical, symbolic or spiritual significance of each. The lion sleeps with his eyes open, in imitation of Christ who slept in 'death' in the tomb while as God he remained awake. The unicorn symbolizes the one God, and chastity.

More intellectually, animals were seen as imperfect reflections of ideal forms, and followers of this aspect of animal study aimed to deduce the nature of physiology from abstract principles. The 13th-century German scholar and philosopher Albertus Magnus was the greatest exponent of this scholastic biology. He was also a renowned botanist. Meticulously accurate in his descriptions of plants and flowers, Albertus studied plant physiology, pondered on the influence of heat and light on plant growth, and recommended afforestation as a remedy for soil erosion.

More practical aspects of botany were represented

above all in the medical 'herbals': lists of plants and flowers that were seen as 'simples', or elements, in complex medications. Many herbals were anonymous; all were derived from the *De Materia Medica* by the first-century Greek, Dioscorides. The writings of his followers, like the 12th-century German nun Hildegard of Bingen, provide a wealth of herbal lore and medicinal recipes, in which the symbolic and religious significance of the ingredients is critical.

Thirteenth-century encyclopaedias like Bartolomaeus Anglicus's *Concerning the Properties of Things*, which dealt with the sky, the earth and water, and the creatures in them, summed up contemporary scientific knowledge.

Alchemy, probably the largest branch of medieval science, was dedicated to the discovery of the 'philosopher's stone' which would transmute base metals into gold. Although it failed to achieve this aim, the search yielded by-products such as alcohol and inorganic acids, and developed basic laboratory techniques.

The 14th century was seminal in European mathematics and physics. Men like Thomas Bradwardine, archbishop of Canterbury, and the philosopher William of Ockham are seen as precursors of the age of Galileo. Richard Wallingford pioneered European trigonometry, while his astronomical timepiece at St Albans, built in the 1330s, was one of the mechanical marvels of the age.

Opposite *Horary quadrant, made in gilded brass in 1399, and bearing the king's badge.*

Below *Artist's sketches of wildlife.*

1392

This year, King Charles VI of France was stricken with madness, and fell into a frenzy, reportedly in the middle of preparing an unjustified attack on the duke of Brittany. He remained in that condition throughout the summer, but the winter brought some amelioration, and he appeared to have returned to his senses, although he never recovered completely, for he suffered fits of madness which recurred every year at the same season.

During the Christmas festivities, Charles VI was performing a dance in his hall with four knights of his household. He was costumed as a wild man of the woods, in a tightly fitting robe, daubed with resin and pitch to make the coarse threads of flax which were attached to it stick better.

But for the grace of God, however, he would have been burned to a cinder through the trickery of his brother Louis, duke of Orleans, who since the onset of the king's illness had begun to nourish ambitions towards the throne. For as King Charles led his companions in the dance a man, who had been recruited for this purpose, lowered a torch and set light to the flaxen threads on the outer layers of the king's garments. As the flame burned through the robe itself, which was tight-fitting and closely stitched around his body, it found the pitch and resin, and burned right to his skin.

Seeing the king of France in such peril, one of the ladies rushed forward and dragged him out of the dance. By her action the king himself was saved, but there was no way to save his four companions, who expired in a heap of burned skin and flesh.

1393

This year the King's Bench and the Chancery were moved from London to York, either (it was said) out of hatred for the Londoners, or as a mark of favour to the men of York, because the chancellor, Thomas Arundel, who was also archbishop of York, desired that his city should prosper. The innovation did not last long, however, for these institutions were brought back to London just as easily as they had been taken to York.

1394

Queen Anne died in June and was buried at Westminster. Famous as her funeral was for the vast expenditure which was lavished upon it, the occasion was infamous to an even greater degree, because at the very beginning of the service the king desecrated the holy place by attacking, wounding and spilling the blood of Richard fitzAlan, earl of Arundel.

In September, King Richard sailed for Ireland, accompanied by the duke of Gloucester and the earls of March, Nottingham and Rutland. The Irish were terrified by this huge force, and did not dare to risk an open battle; instead, they subjected the king's army to numerous ambushes. In the end, however, the English overcame them, and many of the Irish chieftains were compelled to submit to Richard, who kept several of them with him, lest they should stir up any more trouble. He remained in Ireland until after Easter 1395.

1395

Then Thomas Arundel, archbishop of York, and Robert Braybrooke, bishop of London, came from England with other representatives sent by the clergy, to beg King Richard to return home as soon as possible. They wished him to give support to the Catholic faith and to the Church, which was suffering badly at the hands of the Lollards and their supporters. These men devoted themselves to working out how they might grab all ecclesiastical property and, what was worse, do away with the whole structure of Church law. Having heard the deputation's report, the king was inspired by the Holy Spirit, and he returned to England as soon as he could, thinking it more important to help the endangered faith than to fight for temporal kingdoms.

In this same year that barbarian, Beyazit I, sultan of the Ottoman Turks, with three hundred and fifty thousand pagan warriors, fought a battle at Nicopolis against the prior of the Knights Hospitaller and a Christian army. Through the power of God, he was vanquished and one hundred thousand of his men were slain.

The death of Queen Anne

ANNE of Bohemia took seriously her role as Richard II's consort. At each crisis in his reign – the Peasants Revolt, the trial of Wycliffe, the executions after the Merciless Parliament, and the king's quarrel with London in 1392 – she advocated moderation and reconciliation. Her influence may well have been behind Richard's lenient attitude between 1389 and 1394, and if she had produced an heir and become a potential queen mother, Anne might also have had considerable power in the king's council.

One of Richard and Anne's favourite residences was at Sheen in Surrey. Edward III had spent a great deal of money transforming this royal manor house into a palace, and the work continued after his death. The great house looked out over the Thames towards a small island called La Neyt, where Richard built a set of private apartments including a chapel and a bathroom decorated with glazed tiles. It was at La Neyt that Queen Anne died in June 1394, at the tragically young age of 27.

The king was heartbroken. A major state funeral was held at Westminster, and when the earl of Arundel arrived late for the occasion, the king lashed out at him in a dramatic display of anger and grief. In April 1395 he sent orders to his clerk of the works that the entire manor of Sheen should be razed to the ground. Even the site itself was too painful to behold, and Richard never went there again. The most tangible sign of his mourning is the joint tomb he commissioned for Anne and himself in Westminster Abbey. The effigies of the king and queen are now damaged, but originally they clasped hands in an eternal expression of love.

Above Anne on her deathbed, surrounded by her grieving attendants.

Below Costly and elaborate effigy of the queen in Westminster Abbey.

The queen's death was a turning-point in Richard's reign. After 1394 there was no one close to the king to share his troubles. In 1396 he decided to accept Isabella of France – not yet eight years old – as his new queen.

Deprived of Anne and isolated from his friends, Richard became increasingly irascible and unpredictable. It is uncertain whether his tyrannical behaviour during the late 1390s was the result of schizophrenia or of a long-held desire for vengeance against his enemies. But it is clear that Anne's death removed the last psychological and political prop of Richard II's foundering regime.

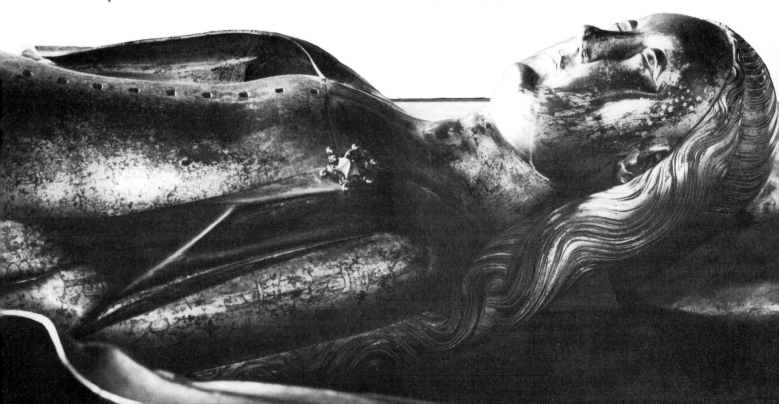

Since fortune did not favour him on the battlefield, he decided to try his luck in a naval campaign. But He who rules the sea and the land frustrated the sultan's designs, and drove him to flight in great confusion. Then the city of Constantinople, which had been besieged by Beyazit's enormous army, was freed by the intervention of the emperor of Constantinople, who arrived with a small Christian force and slaughtered five hundred thousand pagans in a miraculous fashion.

In 1395 Froissart returned to England after many years' absence. In his chronicle he describes his audience with King Richard II.

I, Sir John Froissart, then treasurer and canon of Chimay in the county of Hainault and the diocese of Liège, longed to go and see the realm of England. I had been present at Abbeville in 1394 and knew that a four-year truce by land and sea had been made between the kingdoms of France and England, their allies and dependencies [which would make this journey possible].

In preparation, I had had all my writings on matters of love and morality collected together and written out fair and illuminated. This made a very handsome volume, beautifully decorated, bound in velvet and adorned with silver-gilt studs, which I could offer as a gift to the king.

I obtained horses and other necessities and crossed from Calais, reaching Dover on 12 July.

I could not find anyone at Dover whom I had known in the days when I used to go to England. All the houses were full of new people and the little boys and girls had turned into grown men and women who did not recognize me in the least, nor I them.

I heard that the king of England was expected to arrive at Canterbury on pilgrimage on Thursday, that he was back from his nine-month campaign in Ireland, and that he liked visiting the church of St Thomas for the sake of the saint's holy and famous body, and because his father was buried there. And so I thought I would wait there for the king, which I did.

Richard II arrived next day in great power and might and bringing a large retinue of noble men and women. I mingled with these people but I did not know a soul: everything seemed new to me, for things had changed a great deal in England over the past twenty-eight years.

Then I thought I would approach Lord Thomas Percy, high seneschal of England, who was present; and so I spoke to him and found him courteous and friendly, very easy to talk to, and he offered to present me and my letters to King Richard. He advised me not to draw attention to my arrival for the time being, but to join the king's entourage; he would see, however, that I was well lodged. He chanced to put me into a house where he had already lodged a very pleasant English knight belonging to the royal household. This noble knight, Sir William de Lisle by name, saw that I was a foreigner and assumed that I came from France (they think all French-speakers are French, wherever they come from). He began to talk to me, and I responded to him, for all English noblemen are extremely courteous, friendly and approachable.

On the Friday morning, Sir William de Lisle and I set out on horseback together and rode to Leeds Castle [in Kent], where the king and all his company were gathered. I found Edmund, duke of York, there, and so I spoke to him and gave him the letters from the count of Hainault, his cousin, and from the count of Ostrevant. The duke remembered me very well and welcomed me warmly, saying, 'Keep close to us and our people, Sir John, do not leave us, and we will show you every kindness and consideration. We are bound to do so, for the sake of times past and of our lady mother, whose own man you were. We remember it very well.'

I thanked him for these words. Thus with help from him, and from Thomas Percy and William de Lisle, I was brought forward in King Richard's chamber and was presented to him in the name of his uncle the duke of York.

The king received me kindly and pleasantly and accepted all the letters I offered him. He opened

The Canterbury Tales

THE work of Geoffrey Chaucer's old age, *The Canterbury Tales* was unfinished when he died in 1400. His works as a whole reflect not only the court society in which he moved, but also the major French and Italian literary currents of continental Europe, and his eclectic reading of pagan and Christian authors.

Chaucer's wife, Philippa Roet, was sister to Katherine Swynford, John of Gaunt's mistress and ultimately third wife, giving Chaucer an established connection with the house of Lancaster.

Throughout his writing, Chaucer created a series of narrators with voices distinct from his own. *The Canterbury Tales* is related by a pilgrim who recounts all the stories he heard on the pilgrimage. He is the least competent of the story-tellers, but his account introduces the voices of his fellow pilgrims. Chaucer uses these characters to release him from responsibility for what is said, but never allows them to impair how a tale is told.

Although the sequence of the *Tales* is incomplete, the book's nature is made clear in the General Prologue, which presents a series of portraits drawn from contemporary society, from the Knight to the Cook, from the Parson to the less virtuous Friar, Summoner and Pardoner. There are also women: a Prioress, two nuns and, of course, the Wife of Bath. The array of pilgrims is so comprehensive that the prologue may be read as a satirical portrait of the estates of 14th-century English society. However, individual details prevent the portraits from being bland archetypes: the Reeve has a horse called Scott, the Friar's name is Hubert, the Pardoner sings falsetto and the Wife of Bath is gap-toothed.

On one level, the *Tales* can be seen simply as dramatic fiction; individual animosities develop between Miller and Reeve, Friar and Summoner, and pilgrims tell stories appropriate to their place in the scheme. But *The Canterbury Tales* is also the culmination of Chaucer's experiment in literary genres. The Miller's bawdy story of two men in pursuit of one woman is set against the Knight's Tale, a refined romance concerned with that same eternal triangle, and each exposes the limitations of the other. The *Tales'* enduring vitality comes from the way it is structured as a web of dramatic and literary oppositions, as well as from its variety.

Although the order of the *Tales* is not positively established from surviving manuscripts, the first and last stories were clearly in place. The Knight, the most noble of the pilgrims, is first; last comes the Parson who refuses to tell a tale but preaches a sermon instead. When he has finished, the 'makere' of the book, presumably Chaucer, takes his leave. In doing so, he retracts all his translations and compositions concerning 'worldly vanities', commending only his philosophical and religious writings, with his soul, to Jesus Christ.

Right *Portrait of Geoffrey Chaucer as remembered by Thomas Hoccleve.*

Below *A magnificent chest of elm wood (c. 1410), the front carved with scenes from the Pardoner's Tale. A riotous youth takes three bottles and is stabbed to death by his two companions (centre); they themselves are killed by drinking the poisoned wine.*

them and read them over at length, and when he had read them he told me that I was welcome; having belonged, he said, to the household of his grandfather, King Edward III, I still belonged to the household of the king of England.

Next Sunday, when most of these counsellors had gone back to London or elsewhere to their own homes, the duke of York and others mentioned my business to the king, and the king asked to see the book I had brought him.

I showed it him there in his chamber, for I had it all ready, laid on his bed. He opened it and looked inside and was very pleased with it – and so he should have been, for it was written out, flourished and illuminated, and was bound in crimson velvet fastened with ten silver-gilt studs, golden roses in the centre, and two large clasps gilded and richly worked and set with golden rosettes.

Then the king asked me what the book was about, and I said, 'Love.' He was delighted with this reply and looked into several parts of the book, and read it, for he spoke and read French very well. Then he handed it to one of his knights, a Sir Richard Credon, to be put into his private room, and he gave me a kinder and kinder welcome, indeed a wonderfully cordial reception.

In 1396, Richard II concluded a treaty of alliance with France. There was to be a 28-year truce and, as Walsingham relates, a marriage between the English king and Charles VI's young daughter, Isabella of France.

1396

On Saturday 28 October, the kings of England and France met at Guisnes to discuss certain articles of their treaty, after which they swore on the Holy Gospels to observe what had been agreed. Then King Richard invited King Charles to dine with him on the following day.

On the Monday, the king of France came to the king of England's pavilion. Isabella, the daughter of the king of France, she who is now the queen of England, was then conducted to the

The image of monarchy

RICHARD II was as strongly attached to Westminster Abbey and Palace as his ineffectual forebear, Henry III. Both kings shared an instinctive conviction that any apparent inadequacy as ruler could be outweighed by displays of regal magnificence and largesse, as if the setting could somehow impart majesty to the monarch; and both lavished money and energy at Westminster.

The abbey, rebuilt by Henry III, housed a magnificent series of Plantagenet tombs, but Richard was clearly determined to outdo his predecessors. A remarkably full contract details the opulent sculpture, painting and gilding that decorated the tomb he was to share with his first wife, Anne of Bohemia.

The grandest and most famous of Richard's commissions was the rebuilding of Westminster Hall. The 11th-century original, built for William Rufus, had been the largest hall in Europe, and few had surpassed it in the intervening three centuries. The new building was the same size as the Romanesque one and reused much of the original masonry; Henry Yevele was responsible for the gable walls, with their vast windows which provided the only source of external light. The *tour de force*, both technically and aesthetically, was the roof. The early wooden one, like the roofs of other vast halls, had been supported by twin arcades of columns. At Westminster, Hugh Herland, the royal carpenter, boldly dispensed with the supportive arcades and covered the vast span of the hall with the present braced hammerbeam roof – the largest medieval timber roof in Europe.

The egotist and the connoisseur in Richard were expressed in his interest in commissioning portraits of himself. His stall in the abbey, richly decorated, had an enormous painting of him hung on its back. First mentioned in the abbey sacrist's roll in 1395, it was probably painted by Gilbert Prince of London, who was the royal painter until 1397, when he was succeeded by Thomas Litlyngton. The painting is remarkable in that it has survived at all – and also as an early example of an individualized and recognizable portrait, catching to perfection the king's slightly fatuous, fading blond good looks, and his weak chin ill-concealed by a thin beard. It is also a magnificent icon of royalty; full-length and massive, with rich use of stamped gold.

Richard also appears in the Wilton Diptych, this time in profile. Once again he is instantly recognizable in his pale weakness, as his favourite saints present him to the Virgin and Child and a choir of angels. Like the full-length portrait, the Wilton Diptych (so called from the house where it was preserved) is of the very highest quality. It is not known whether it was painted at

Westminster, and it does not appear to be by the same hand as the full-size portrait, though the enormous difference in scale makes direct comparison difficult – the diptych is quite small and was clearly intended as a portable devotional image for the king to take with him on his travels.

It is made up of two hinged wooden panels with painted backs that can be folded shut to look like a book and to protect the two precious paintings inside. The Wilton Diptych has been dated convincingly to between 1394 and 1396, a time when the image of monarchy it portrayed was crumbling fast.

Left Jean Froissart, *the chronicler, offering one of his books to Richard at Eltham Palace.*

Below Contract for Anne of Bohemia's tomb. *The finest craftsmen were commissioned to carve marble bases and to make the effigies in gilded copper and latten.*

Overleaf The Wilton Diptych, *a portable image made for the king in the mid 1390s. Richard's coronation is commemorated, with eleven angels for his eleven years.*

pavilion, and King Charles presented her to our king, who took her by the hand and kissed her, thanking her father for so noble and welcome a gift. Richard went on to declare that he was receiving her according to the conditions agreed between the kings, so that through the relationship thus established both monarchs could live in peace and tranquillity, and could secure a proper state of harmony between their two kingdoms for ever, and that no more Christian blood would be shed, as was all too likely to happen if this alliance were not made here and now.

The new queen was entrusted to the care of the duchesses of Lancaster and Gloucester and the countesses of Huntingdon and Stafford, and of other noblewomen who were there. They conducted her to Calais, accompanied by a large escort of men and horses, and twelve carriages full of noblewomen and ladies-in-waiting.

This business accomplished, the kings went to their banquet in King Richard's pavilion. King Charles sat on the right-hand side of the hall, and was served in royal fashion, according to the custom of his own country, that is to say, he ate helpings of all the dishes of the first course at once from a single large dish, and likewise the second course. The king of England was served in the manner of his land.

After the feast, the kings kissed each other, then mounted their horses. The king of England set the king of France on his way, and finally they shook hands and parted company. King Charles rode to Ardres, while King Richard proceeded to Calais, where he married Isabella, the daughter of the king of France, a little girl of seven or eight years.

This meeting of the two kings was a great occasion, marked by heavy expenditure on gifts. Quite apart from the presents which he gave to King Charles and to the other French magnates, which cost in excess of ten thousand marks, King Richard spent, so it was said, more than thirty thousand marks. Soon afterwards, he returned safely to England with his new wife, but he lost his pavilion and most of his household furnishings as a result of a storm.

The little queen

ISABELLA of Valois was only seven years old when she became queen of England in 1396, two years after the death of Richard's first wife, Anne of Bohemia. Her father, Charles VI of France, was eager for a match that would end hostilities with England, and Richard had been toying with the idea of a Spanish marriage, which did not suit French policy in southern Europe. Charles suggested three adult brides, none of whom was a king's daughter, and then offered his six year old, eldest daughter Isabella, with a large dowry. Like Charles, Richard favoured a peaceful end to the expensive, and latterly unsuccessful, war, and he accepted the French king's offer.

The match was not popular in England, because of both her age and her nationality. There was, in fact, only a 20-year age difference between Richard and Isabella and

the king grew attached to the child, who plainly adored him – when the news of his death reached her, she was ill for two weeks.

The French court of Isabella's childhood was highly cultured, extravagant, pleasure-seeking and full of pomp. Richard is said to have spent £200,000 on maintaining the English monarchy's prestige when he went to France to fetch her; Isabella brought with her £50,000, the first instalment of her dowry. Because of her youth the little queen was accompanied by a French 'gouvernante', Lady de Coucy, and other French servants; later the king dismissed Lady de Coucy because of her extravagance and Isabella's English education was carried on under the watchful eye of the widowed countess of Hereford.

When Richard died, Isabella – then ten years old – and her household were moved to Wallingford in Berkshire while Henry IV tried to extricate himself from the embarrassing position in which her presence in England

Above *Richard greets the young Isabella.*

placed him. She should by rights have returned immediately to France, but this would have meant giving back her dowry and jewels. For Henry, the obvious and most satisfactory solution would have been to marry her to his heir, the future Henry V. The French, however, were opposed to an alliance with the man they believed had usurped Richard's throne, and Isabella, steadfast in her loyalty to her husband's memory, flatly refused to countenance the match. There was a prolonged dispute over her dowry, and the little queen endured two lonely years of widowhood before she was allowed home to France – at a cost to Henry of £4000.

In 1406 Isabella married her cousin Charles, the future poet duke of Orleans, who was four years her junior. She died in 1409 at the birth of her first child, a daughter. She was just 19.

1397

A parliament was held in London in January, at which the duke of Lancaster obtained the legitimization of his children by his former mistress, now his wife, Katherine Swynford. The eldest Beaufort – this being the surname which Lancaster had chosen for his children by Katherine – was created earl of Somerset.

Unfounded rumours began to spread, that King Richard II had been elected Holy Roman Emperor. Richard was so puffed up by this that from that time onwards he began to behave even more loftily than usual, to impoverish the common people and to borrow large sums of money from every available source. He carried this to such extremes that throughout the realm no prelate, no city, nor any individual known to be wealthy could avoid loaning money to the king.

That year, the kingdom seemed to be on the verge of enjoying a period of great stability, partly because of the royal marriage and the riches accumulated in aid of that, but also on account of the long truce with France, and the presence of so many noblemen, more numerous and higher in rank than any other realm could produce.

But the king's scheming behaviour soon threw all this into confusion when, without warning, he had his uncle, the duke of Gloucester, arrested at Pleshey in Essex and taken to Calais, where he was thrown into prison. Richard also invited the earl of Warwick to a banquet, and on that very day had him arrested and imprisoned likewise, after pretending to be well disposed to the earl and even having promised to be a gracious lord and true friend to him in the future.

Furthermore, Richard used deceitful promises to win over the earl of Arundel, who was powerful enough to have saved himself and freed his friends Gloucester and Warwick; when the earl submitted peacefully, the king despatched him to imprisonment on the Isle of Wight. Fearful lest the common people should be in uproar about the detention of these noblemen, the king put out a proclamation across the kingdom that these men

A taste for extravagance

THE greatness of late 14th-century English vernacular poetry and prose was largely due to the enlightened patronage of the court, inspired by Richard's preferences. By the age of 13 he was buying fine manuscript copies of popular romances like *Sir Gawain*, *Sir Perceval* and the *Roman de la Rose*, and throughout his life he kept illuminated books in his private chamber.

His court cookery book, *The Forme of Cury*, is one of a number that have survived. It emphasizes exotic ingredients and expensive spices imported from the Far East, but nevertheless shows that Richard's diet was sophisticated rather than gluttonous. Typical main dishes are shelled oysters or minced pheasant cooked in wine, ginger and other spices. The prologue to the book describes the king as 'the best provider of viands' in all christendom.

The luxury arts flourished under the patronage of Richard, who delighted especially in combinations of costly materials. The inventory of the king's treasure, compiled in 1399, includes an ivory mirror in a gold frame set with enamelled and jewelled roses, with a queen in enamel on its back; drinking glasses of painted and enamelled glass; silver ewers with engraved inscriptions in French and English; and jewelled chaplets for the king's head and girdles for his waist.

Above all, there are individual gems: rubies, diamonds and sapphires. As early as 1380, Richard owned three brooches representing his personal badge of the white hart, each of which was set with rubies, as well as two collars incorporating the French royal device of the broomscod. One of these was ornamented with four rubies, three sapphires and 27 pearls.

The king's love of fine clothes is legendary, and he was often accused of leading his subjects into extravagant habits. One of his gowns is said to have been worth more than £1,000, an astronomical sum in the Middle Ages. Another was made of white satin embroidered with leeches, water and rocks and ornamented with 15 silver-gilt whelks, 15 silver-gilt mussels and the same number of white-silver cockles; the doublet was embroidered with golden orange trees bearing 600 silver-gilt oranges. Stephen Vyne, Richard's embroiderer, was recommended by the duke of Berry. A patron of the arts, and son of the French king, the duke had the most fashionable court in Europe.

Richard introduced, but failed to popularize, linen handkerchiefs; their use is described in his wardrobe accounts. He also set great store by hot baths and personal latrines. A new bath house was added to his palace at Eltham in the mid 1380s; also a spicery and saucery to deal with the complexities of the new court cookery.

Two large bronze taps were installed to bring hot and cold water into his bath at La Neyt, the private lodging he had built on the Thames near Sheen, for which 2,000 hand-painted tiles were also commissioned.

Confident of his beauty, the king remained clean-shaven until well into his twenties. This was far longer than was customary, but it suited the adolescent, rather epicene qualities admired in men. When he did begin to wear facial hair he had it elaborately barbered into two small tufts on either side of his chin. These were worn with merely a wisp of a moustache, again suggesting the boy rather than the man.

Opposite *Richard II's badge of the White Hart, his personal emblem, set here in enamelled silver.*

Below *Splendour surrounds Richard even as he yields the crown to Bolingbroke.*

had not been arrested on account of past misdeeds, but for new crimes against the king, which would be explained fully in the next parliament. Events proved this proclamation to have been wholly untrue.

On 17 September, the parliament met in London. All the lords came in arms, accompanied by their retainers, such was their fear of the king.

The principal speakers at this parliament were three knights, all avaricious, ambitious and arrogant: John Bushey, William Bagot and Henry Green. These men clamoured insistently for the revocation and annulment of the charters of pardon.

Charters of pardon had earlier been granted by King Richard, to safeguard the lords appellant and the other parliamentary commissioners who had brought about the deaths of his supporters in the Merciless Parliament.

On receiving this request, the prelates had no difficulty in adjudging these charters to be revocable, without stopping to consider that such a repeal was damaging to the king's reputation, for mercy is the foundation of a royal throne, and anything which diminishes the king's mercy undermines the throne. The temporal lords, seeing the prelates' lack of moral courage, assented in their turn to the annulment of the charters, prompted more by fear of the king than by reasoned judgement. The clergy were browbeaten into agreeing to appoint a lay proctor, so that although they could not participate in processes involving judgements of blood, their lay proctor could do so on their behalf, if the need arose.

Revenge could now be taken in parliament against the king's enemies.

On 21 September, judgement was given against Richard fitzAlan, earl of Arundel, whose claims and demands for pardon, both under the terms of the charters and as granted to him personally by the king, were unavailing. He was condemned to drawing, hanging, disembowelling, burning of his entrails, decapitation and quartering.

The king, of his grace, reduced this sentence to one of beheading only, which Arundel suffered soon afterwards. The earl's countenance never faltered, not when he was awaiting judgement, nor when he received his terrible sentence, nor when he was taken from the place of his trial to the place of his execution, nor when he knelt and stretched out his neck for the sword. He grew no more pale than he would have done on receiving an invitation to a feast. He was led to the scaffold surrounded by a savage crowd of Cheshire men, armed with axes, bows and arrows.

After Arundel's death, the king was tormented by nightmares. As soon as he fell asleep, he seemed to see the earl's ghost dancing before his eyes and threatening him in a terrifying manner, as if he were saying, in the words of Ovid:

'I come, a shade, bearing your deeds in mind,
To shake my bones before your very eyes.'

Since King Richard II did not think it safe to allow his uncle, Thomas of Woodstock, duke of Gloucester, who was very popular, to stand trial in public, he ordered the earl marshal, Thomas Mowbray, to put the duke to death secretly. The marshal sent some men who carried out this evil plan by smothering Gloucester with feather-filled cushions and mattresses thrown over his face. So died this fine man, the son of one king [Edward III] and the uncle of another, who had been the chief hope and consolation of the entire kingdom.

After this, King Richard II cunningly prorogued the parliament until after Christmas, and ordered it to reassemble at Shrewsbury, on the Welsh border.

1398

When the parliament reconvened at Shrewsbury, the king persuaded all the estates of the realm to agree to an arrangement whereby the power of parliament should be delegated to a group of seven or eight men, whose task would be, after the end of the session, to determine petitions which had been laid before the parliament, but had not been dealt with fully.

The royal household

ALTHOUGH the Merciless Parliament of 1388 was unique in the savagery of the reprisals it took against Richard II's servants, it was neither the first nor the last parliament to attempt to curb the size and cost of his household. In an age when the government of England lay in the hands of the monarch, and was influenced above all by his character and preoccupations, the household was an ideal instrument for exercising his authority. The officials who ministered to the domestic needs of the king and his family could easily assume prominent roles in regional and central administration, by-passing the great departments of state if necessary, and consolidating the crown's power at the expense of vested local or baronial interests.

In building up the chamber – an inner ring of officials – of his household, Richard deliberately sought to free himself from the constraints imposed by parliament and by the royal council, dominated by the aristocracy. The number of chamber knights rose from three in 1376 to 17 in 1388; most were given important military and administrative positions throughout the country, and were also entrusted with diplomatic missions and other sensitive business. More yeomen and esquires were also appointed, whose activities made it necessary to employ a larger secretariat with independent powers of action.

Any royal writ or directive had to be authenticated by a seal; and Richard began to use his own personal signet. This meant he could act without having to consult either the chancellor or the keeper of the privy seal, although he was also able to instruct the chancellor's staff to sanction grants and payments. The signet gave the king far greater control over the distribution of patronage, and he exploited this to reward his closest friends and advisers at court. His indiscriminate generosity to a narrow clique of favourites antagonized the nobility, who saw their traditional position as the principal recipients of royal bounty seriously threatened.

The sheer volume of paperwork generated by the expansion of the chamber led to the creation of a signet office in the 1380s, staffed largely by clerks from the king's chapel. Most were former students of King's Hall, Cambridge, which had been founded by Edward II to provide better-educated and more professional administrators. The hall became a virtual 'seminary for civil servants', although its emphasis on the study of civil (or Roman) law aroused the suspicions of the common lawyers trained at the Inns of Court. They believed that while their discipline equipped them to uphold the liberty of the subject, civil law lent itself to the defence of tyrannical or despotic practices. Many lawyers sat in the

Above Westminster Hall, where the courts of King's Bench and Common Pleas met. Rebuilt under Richard II in the 1390s, it formed an administrative centre for his regime as well as an expression of royal power and magnificence.

house of commons, and this debate assumed an immediate significance when the reform of the royal household was discussed in 1388. Although they never came to trial, four clerks of the signet were detained in prison during the time that the Merciless Parliament was in session.

Another grudge against the king's clerks – all of whom were in holy orders – was their blatant pluralism: aided and abetted by their royal master, they acquired lucrative benefices and fat livings, which they invariably neglected for their official duties. The commons was still complaining, in 1397, about the 'multitude of bishops' who found preferment at court while abandoning their dioceses. But throughout Richard's reign, the lower house was mainly concerned about expense – and was at one with the lords in demanding draconian cuts in the number of household personnel.

Under colour of this grant, the men so deputed went on later to deal with other business generally handled in full parliament. Such proceedings, undertaken moreover at the king's wish, detracted from the authority of parliament and offered an evil example, damaging to the whole kingdom. To provide some specious justification and authority for his course of action, the king had changes and erasures made in the rolls of parliament, to alter the original terms of the grant.

At about this time, the duke of Hereford, Henry Bolingbroke, earl of Derby, laid an accusation against the duke of Norfolk, Thomas Mowbray, concerning certain words spoken with intent to discredit the king. The two were ordered to fight a judicial duel at Coventry. When they had entered the lists, both displaying rancour and pride in equal measure, the king took the matter into his own hands and proclaimed that the duke of Hereford had discharged his debt honourably.

But almost immediately afterwards, on no legal grounds whatsoever, the king imposed upon Bolingbroke ten years' exile, a decision which was contrary to justice, the rights of knighthood and the customs of this kingdom. At the same time, Richard condemned the duke of Norfolk to perpetual exile, decreeing implacably that no one should make any request or offer any plea to him for relaxation of the sentences on the two dukes, on pain of heavy penalties.

At this time, according to the Eulogium, the king 'ordered a throne to be set up in his chamber on which he would sit after dinner until evening, showing himself. He would talk to no one but would look at people, and whoever he looked at, whatever his rank, he had to genuflect.'

1399

John of Gaunt, duke of Lancaster, died on 3 February. His body was buried in St Paul's church, in London.

Soon afterwards, the king sentenced Lancaster's son, Henry Bolingbroke, duke of Hereford, to exile for life, instead of banishment for ten years.

This same year, King Richard demanded large sums of money from seventeen counties of the realm, putting their inhabitants in fear of their lives, by accusing them of having stood against him with the duke of Gloucester and the earls of Arundel and Warwick, for which reason he was prepared to proceed against them, as public enemies. He took new pledges of security from them, strengthened by sworn oaths. Then he sent some of the bishops and other highly respected men to these counties, to persuade the leading ecclesiastics and lay lords, as well as all the middle-ranking men there, to submit to the king and to send sealed letters acknowledging themselves to be traitors.

On the pretext of this 'admission', the clergy, the lay lords and the common people of these counties were coerced into granting insupportably large sums of money to the king, to win back his goodwill.

Despite his perilous situation at home, Richard II now resolved to return to Ireland, where Art McMurrough, formerly a supporter of the English crown, had declared himself king and had risen in revolt.

On 18 May, King Richard, leaving his kingdom in a state of great disturbance, set sail for Ireland, accompanied by men from his principality of Chester and by several magnates, including the dukes of Aumale and Exeter. He took the sons of the dukes of Gloucester and Hereford with him, somewhat in the manner of hostages, because he was so afraid of their families. He took along also numerous bishops and the abbot of Westminster. The abbot had been one of the committee of eight whom Richard had set up once before, in 1398; now he was to be at hand, to confirm on behalf of the clergy anything which was decided whenever the king wished to hold 'parliaments'.

When on the point of setting out for Ireland, King Richard removed from the royal treasury, without the consent of the estates of his realm, many valuables, relics and jewels, comprising much of the wealth of the crown, handed down from ancient times.

Richard II and Ireland

RICHARD II claimed lordship over all Ireland, but in practice his power was confined to the south-eastern province of Leinster and a few colonial outposts in Ulster. To the south and the west, in Munster and Connaught, he had virtually no authority. Even around Dublin, in the area later known as the Pale, English rule was often disrupted by tribal chieftains who lived in the Wicklow Mountains. By Richard II's time one of them, Art McMurrough, was calling himself king of Leinster.

The king's authority could be maintained only with the acquiescence of the nobility, successors of the men who had been given lands in Ireland after its conquest by Henry II in the 1170s. In the late 14th century many were absentee landlords; the most important was the earl of March, who claimed vast tracts of land in Ulster and Connaught. However, the resident Anglo-Irish aristocrats, the earls of Desmond, Kildare and Ormond, were more significant. They recognized the Plantagenets as their rightful lords, but regarded themselves as Irish.

Since the 1360s, the crown had made various attempts to stop the gradual erosion of its authority in Ireland, appointing powerful lieutenants from among the royal family or the resident nobility. In 1380 Richard's government gave this office to Edmund Mortimer, earl of March, husband of the king's cousin, but he died unexpectedly in the following year.

For a while, Richard looked upon Ireland as merely another reward for his friend Robert de Vere, and virtually handed over the sovereignty of the island to his favourite when he created him marquis of Dublin and duke of Ireland. This did nothing to improve the English colony's position, and after de Vere's fall in 1388, it became apparent that the king would have to visit and restore order to Ireland. In 1392 Art McMurrough attacked the English-held towns of Leinster, and the Westminster government began to plan a military expedition.

Richard eventually landed at Waterford in October 1394, accompanied by the duke of Gloucester, the earls of March and Nottingham, and the largest military force yet to land on the shores of Ireland. Overwhelmed, the Irish chieftains gathered before the king at Dublin to make their peace. Richard knighted the Gaelic leaders, believing that this would best ensure their loyalty. In 1395 his funds dried up, and he was forced to return to England.

Richard went on another expedition to Ireland in 1399; but within a month of his arrival news reached Dublin of Henry Bolingbroke's attempted invasion of England and the king departed hurriedly for Milford Haven.

After reaching Ireland, he seemed at first to be prospering, and to be stronger than his enemies. This brought little joy to the chieftains, who received successively worse reports of him, and who feared that he would subject them to harsher oppression than hitherto.

Henry Bolingbroke, formerly duke of Hereford, was now by right heir to his father's dukedom of Lancaster. He had been aggrieved by his initial banishment, but was even more incensed at being exiled for life and disinherited, and he came to the conclusion that such actions were an injustice to all who owed the king allegiance. Seizing the opportunity offered by Richard's absence, Henry decided to return from Paris to England, to seek his inheritance.

Accompanied by his long-standing adherents, Thomas Arundel, the erstwhile archbishop of Canterbury, and his nephew, the heir of the earl of Arundel, the new duke of Lancaster set sail with a retinue of moderate size, containing no more than fifteen lances (to use the popular expression), although he could have come in far greater strength: so great was his trust in the justice of his cause and the support of the people.

He did not wish to invade straight away; instead, he appeared to his countrymen now in one place, now in another, to see if the coastal districts were on the alert to resist him.

The king's uncle, Edmund, duke of York, had been appointed regent during Richard's absence in Ireland. When he learned that the duke of Lancaster was already at sea, and on the point of invading England, he summoned Edmund Stafford, the lord chancellor and bishop of Exeter, the treasurer, William Scrope, earl of Wiltshire, and the knights of the king's council, John Bushey, William Bagot, Henry Green and John Russell, to seek their advice on how to deal with this emergency. They suggested that he should retreat from London to St Albans, where he could assemble armed forces to resist the duke's advance.

Events showed the stupidity of this counsel. For men came from all over the land to declare that

they were not willing to harm the duke, whom they knew to have been badly treated. The worthless counsellors, Bushey, Bagot, Green, and Scrope the treasurer, realizing that the people of the realm would support Lancaster, abandoned the regent and the chancellor and fled to Bristol Castle.

The duke of Lancaster landed, without opposition, at the site where the old town of Ravenspur once lay, on 4 July. He was met by Henry Percy, earl of Northumberland, and his son, Henry Percy the younger, and Ralph Neville, earl of Westmorland, with a great many other lords who feared the king's tyranny. Within a short time, the army had grown to a force of sixty thousand men, whose unanimous wish was to begin by hunting down the king's evil counsellors. They marched swiftly to Bristol and besieged the castle, where they were prepared to meet with resistance.

The outcome was, however, that William Scrope, the treasurer, John Bushey and Henry Green were taken prisoner and beheaded summarily the following day, by popular demand. Of this group, only William Bagot escaped. He had not gone to Bristol with his associates, but had first of all fled to Chester and then sailed to Ireland.

King Richard II was still in Ireland when news reached him that the duke had landed in England. Within a short time he arranged for the sons of the dukes of Gloucester and Lancaster to be incarcerated in the castle at Trim in Ireland, under strong guard. Then, accompanied by the dukes of Aumale, Exeter and Surrey, and the bishops of London, Lincoln and Carlisle, he rushed to sail for England, aiming to engage in battle before the duke's forces could grow any larger.

When the king had reached England, however, and had learned of the size of the duke's forces, he lost heart for the fight, believing that the people assembled to oppose him would rather die than yield, as much out of hatred for him as out of fear.

He dismissed his household, giving them orders, through the steward, Thomas Percy, that they should hold themselves ready to return in better times. Richard himself, looking for somewhere to hide, travelled hither and thither for many days, always pursued by the duke's forces. Eventually he reached Conway Castle, and, having no hope of further flight, he requested a meeting with Thomas Arundel, whom he had ousted from the archbishopric of Canterbury, and with the earl of Northumberland. He told them that he was willing io abdicate, if granted honourable means of support and if a guarantee of safety were given to eight persons, whom he wished to specify by name.

When these terms had been accepted and settled, the king went on to Flint Castle, where he had a brief meeting with the duke of Lancaster. They then rode together to Chester Castle on the same night, with the duke's enormous army.

It was on 20 August that Richard surrendered to Lancaster, forty-seven days after the duke had landed in England. The royal treasury, together with the king's horses, equipment and household goods, fell into the duke's hands, but the king's household ministers, the magnates, lords and men of lower rank were despoiled by the Welsh and the Northumbrians. The king himself was taken to London, to be confined in the Tower until parliament assembled.

The story of Richard's deposition is told by an anonymous chronicler, probably a Burgundian. His dramatic and largely fictional account shows great sympathy for the fallen king.

On the morning of 2 September, very early, Richard heard mass at Westminster, as he had requested, after which he was taken to the Tower of London by the young duke of Gloucester and earl of Arundel. As he rode through London on a pony on the way to the prison, they kept well away from him so that he could be clearly seen by everybody; and a small boy behind him pointed to him and said, 'Look. It's King Richard who has done so much good for the kingdom of England.'

It is true that some people felt sorry for him, but there were others who were glad about his downfall and swore loudly at him, saying, 'Now we have got our revenge on this wicked bastard who has made such a bad job of ruling us.'

The next day, Henry Bolingbroke, duke of Lancaster, went to the Tower, along with the dukes of York and Aumale. When he got there he ordered Aumale to bring King Richard to him.

The duke went as he was told, but when the king had heard his message he refused to go with the duke and said that if Henry wanted to speak to him he must come in person and see him; otherwise he would not speak to him.

The duke went back and told Henry this; then Henry and all the other lords went to see Richard. None of them, however, showed any respect for King Richard, with the exception of Lancaster who took off his cap, greeted him respectfully and said, 'My lord, here is our cousin the duke of Aumale and his father, your uncle, and they wish to speak to you.'

The king's answer to this was, 'Cousin, they are not worthy to speak to me.'

'But please be good enough to hear them, my lord,' replied the duke.

'In the name of God, York, you are a villain,' said the king. 'What could you have to say to me? And you, Aumale, you are a traitor and unworthy of my time. And what is more, you do not deserve the title "duke" — nor "count" nor "knight" for that matter. I pray to God and John the Baptist that the hour when you and your evil father were born be cursed. It was because of you and your lies that my uncle Gloucester was put to death. It makes me sad to feel that I was ever so fond of such a traitor; there is no doubt in my mind that you will be the ruin of England.'

Aumale replied that the king was lying and he threw his hat at Richard's feet; the king immediately kicked it away and said, 'Traitor. I am the king and your master and so I shall remain; I will become even greater than ever I was, in spite of all my enemies. You are not worthy to talk to me.'

At this, Lancaster told Aumale to say nothing or else he would order the constable and the marshal to restrain him until he was quiet.

The king then asked Lancaster, 'Why do you keep such a close guard on me? I would like to know if you acknowledge me as your lord and king, and also what you intend to do with me.'

Lancaster replied, 'It is true that you are my king and lord, but it has been ordered by the council of the realm that you remain in prison until the day parliament assembles.'

Again the king swore and ordered that his wife, Isabella of France, be brought to him so that they could talk. The duke of Lancaster, however, informed him that the council had forbidden that too.

The king was so furious that he stormed away down the hall and was speechless with rage. When he finally got his voice back, these were his words:

"O God in Heaven, O Virgin Mary, O St John the Baptist and all the saints of Heaven, how can you allow all the great wrongs and treason that these people have committed and still wish to commit against me, my dear wife and lady, daughter of my dear and beloved lord and father, the noble king of France, who has no idea of the terrible state we are in, or of the danger that we now face?

"Now I see clearly that you villains are all traitors to God, my lady and myself; I am willing to prove this by taking on any four of the best of you, like the loyal knight that I am, for I have never forfeited my knighthood.

"My grandfather, King Edward, gave me the crown before he died, God bless his soul, and afterwards this was confirmed by the consent of all the nobles of the whole country. You too have recognized me as king for the last twenty-two years; how dare you treat me so badly? I think that you are lying and cheating me, your lord. This I will prove by fighting any four of you, and this is my pledge."

With these words, Richard threw down his hat, and Lancaster fell to his knees, begging him to say no more until the meeting of parliament, when

The Perpendicular style

THE essence of the Perpendicular style can be seen in Gloucester Cathedral, constructed in about 1350. Severe, angular tracery panels with predominantly vertical lines stretch across both window and wall, and the shafts that link columns and vaulting are nothing but tracery lines which extend down to cover their supporting pillars, like brittle icing on a fruit cake.

At Gloucester, the Perpendicular covered and re-fashioned the massive Norman choir, and the same is true of the nave of Winchester Cathedral, redesigned by William Wynford between 1394 and c. 1410. Canterbury's nave, however, was totally rebuilt rather than decorated, between 1379 and 1405. The man in charge was Henry Yevele, who had recently completed the nave of Westminster Abbey. Often described as the chief royal architect of the time, he is possibly the best-documented of English medieval architects. However, his very versatility – he signed contracts for bridges as well as churches – suggests that he was as much a contractor as an architect.

Neither Winchester nor Canterbury Cathedral use the fan vault, often considered synonymous with Perpendicular architecture. This type of vault is made from a series of linking half-cones adorned with severe tracery grids, like those lining the walls, which expand around the cones to form the distinctive fan shape. They were used for the first time in the second half of the 14th century in the cloister at Gloucester Cathedral, but it was the end of the 15th century before architects were prepared to build fan vaults over the broad spaces of a full-sized church.

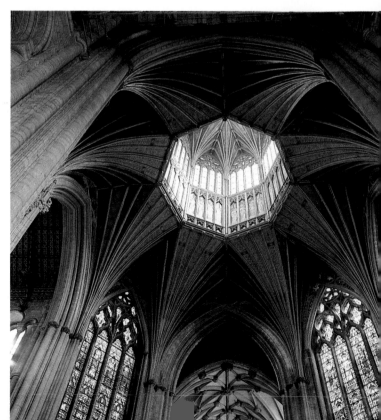

Top left *Nave of Canterbury Cathedral, in true Perpendicular style: first of its kind in south-east England.*

Above *Gloucester Cathedral: the cloister's fan vaults, the earliest known, were probably patterned from French rose windows.*

Right *By contrast, Ely Cathedral's octagonal crossing tower shows the florid extravagance of the Decorated style.*

Perpendicular was especially appropriate for comparatively small buildings, and many chantry chapels, self-contained units within larger churches, were constructed in this style. Its severity and lack of expensive detail meant that tracery grids could easily be applied to the flat walls, windows and towers of a parish church. Where the Decorated style had seemed overcrowded, Perpendicular provided a sense of elegant scale.

everyone could have his say. 'At least, sirs, in the name of God, let me be brought to trial, so that I may give an account of my conduct and answer all the accusations levelled against me.' Then Lancaster said, 'My lord, do not be afraid; nothing unreasonable will be done to you,' and took his leave of the king. Not one of the lords present had the courage to say a word.

After this meeting, parliament began on 30 September, and when Henry of Lancaster went in, he found, already seated, all the prelates of the country, bishops, abbots and others. Lancaster's four sons and two archbishops preceded him into the meeting, and his two brothers and the dukes of Surrey, Aumale and Exeter followed him, arm in arm, and all wearing his livery.

After the duke of Lancaster's entrance, Sir Thomas Percy, with a white rod in his hand, sat down opposite him and shouted, 'Long live Henry of Lancaster, king of England,' at which all the lords, prelates and people of London and England exclaimed, 'Yes, yes; we want Henry to be king. Nobody else.'

A few days later, when the duke of Lancaster was sitting on the throne, which had, of course, been Richard's usual seat, he sent one of the dukes to tell Sir Baldwin Pigot, a knight, to summon the lords of the council and the commons.

At this point, the bishop of Carlisle, a Benedictine priest, rose and spoke in favour of King Richard, and the duke of Lancaster ordered him to be seized and taken to the prison at St Albans.

When this had been done, the duke asked that King Richard's sentence be read out, and the recorder of London started to do so:

'My lords, it is ordered by the clergy, the lords and the commons of England that John of Bordeaux, also known as Richard of England, be sentenced to imprisonment in some royal castle; that he be given the best bread and meat that money can buy; and that if anyone should attempt to rescue him by force, he will be the first to die.'

This was the unfair sentence which parliament passed on King Richard II.

The death of a tyrant

KING Richard II was in Ireland when Henry Boling-broke invaded England in the summer of 1399.
Taking ship from Waterford, the king landed in Wales and tried to drum up military support in the principality and in Cheshire. Bolingbroke advanced on Chester and a deputation was sent to the king, at Conway Castle. Two of its members, the earl of Northumberland and the archbishop of Canterbury, suggested to the king that he should restore the Lancastrian inheritance to Bolingbroke, and surrender certain of his councillors for trial in parliament. Both swore on the Host that he would then be left free to rule and Richard agreed to the terms in good faith. But when he left Conway, Northumberland was lying in wait for him, and the king suddenly found himself a prisoner in Flint Castle. Bolingbroke had become the effective ruler of England.

Summonses were issued in Richard's name, calling a parliament to meet at Westminster at the end of September, and the king was taken south and lodged in the Tower pending this assembly. It was by no means clear what would happen next. Many of the nobility were opposed to Henry Bolingbroke's taking over as king, and a committee of experts rejected his claims to the throne as John of Gaunt's son and by right of conquest.

Bolingbroke became increasingly impatient of constitutional arguments, and took matters into his own hands: when parliament assembled he stepped forward and claimed the empty throne. The lords and lawyers were ambivalent, but Henry had made sure there was a large body of Londoners at the doors of Westminster Hall ready to acclaim him. It was necessary only to justify the revolution by discrediting Richard's regime. A list of crimes was patched together and proclaimed before parliament. The king was accused of breaking his coronation oath by ruling wilfully and with no regard for the rights of his subjects, and even of saying that the laws of the land were his alone to make and break. In the light of such damning evidence, Richard was declared a tyrant who had forfeited his right to rule.

He was told of his deposition on 1 October. Four weeks later he was taken from the Tower, disguised as a forester, and led to Pontefract Castle in Yorkshire. By February 1400, King Richard II was dead. Starvation is the most likely cause, though it is not clear whether this was self-inflicted or imposed on him by his jailer, Sir Thomas Swynford. His body was taken to London and buried alongside Queen Anne in the royal mausoleum at Westminster Abbey.

Henry IV was evidently anxious to quell the rumours that Richard had escaped imprisonment and death and

Above Richard II put into the Tower by Henry Bolingbroke. Later chroniclers claimed that Henry's sinful crime of usurpation was visited on his grandson Henry VI.

was about to reclaim the throne. However, these stories continued for some years, and were often a cause for concern to the new Lancastrian regime. Ironically, Richard proved more popular in death than he had ever been in life.

Richard II remains an enigma. He was at once intelligent and cultured, psychopathic and brutish. The patron of literature and art and the inventor of the handkerchief was also capable of acts of great cruelty and boorishness. It is probably best to think of him as a lonely and rather unhappy man, whose promising early career collapsed into a dangerous despotism.

89

HENRICVS ·IIII·

Part II

Henry IV
1399–1413

The advent of Henry IV ended the succession of the direct line of Plantagenet kings and replaced them with a cadet branch – the house of Lancaster. The deposed Richard II proved an immediate focus of opposition to the usurper, and although Richard disappeared, presumed murdered, in 1400, for the next five years Henry faced one rebellion after another. The Welsh and the Scots added to his problems, and the king became increasingly tired and ill; in his last years much power was wielded by his son the future Henry V. Thomas Walsingham again provides the main narrative for the first Lancastrian reign – and finds himself mildly pro-Lancastrian in sympathy. More extreme in their views are John Capgrave, who provides a eulogy of Henry IV, and the anonymous chronicler who relates Richard II's death with vivid intensity. Walsingham introduces his account of Henry's reign with optimistic comments about the new regime.

(Opposite: Henry IV)

Henry Bolingbroke was crowned King Henry IV at Westminster by Thomas, archbishop of Canterbury, on 13 October, a year to the day after he had been sent into exile. This was thought to be a miracle sent by God.

As an omen of the yet more abundant favour God was expected to show him, Henry was anointed with the divine ointment which the Blessed Virgin Mary, mother of God, had given to St Thomas Becket, the martyred archbishop of Canterbury, while he was in exile, prophesying that the kings of England who were anointed with this ointment would defend the Church and be merciful.

While parliament was in session, the king, with the agreement of all the estates of the realm, created his first-born son Henry, prince of Wales, duke of Cornwall and earl of Chester. Later in the same parliament he made him duke of Aquitaine and chief heir to the English throne.

In this parliament it was ordained that the statutes and Acts of the parliament held at Westminster on 14 September 1377, and later moved to Shrewsbury, were to be henceforth invalidated, revoked, and made null and void in all their details. By these statutes many honourable houses and other subjects of the king, together

Henry IV's struggle for the throne

In 1399 Henry IV seized the crown from Richard II by force, and had to struggle for nearly a decade to hold it for the house of Lancaster. France and Scotland were both hostile: in 1400 the new king mounted an expedition to Scotland but made few gains. Having crushed a major internal threat from Richard II's supporters in the same year, he was faced almost

Edinburgh
Leith
Haddington

Roxburgh
Jedburgh
Nisbet on Teviot
Redesdale
Coquetdale

Homildon Hill
Bamburgh
Dunstanburgh

Tweed
Tyne
Newcastle

Carlisle
Durham

Tees
Darlington

Pickering
Thirsk
Scarborough
Ripon

Knaresborough
York
Lancaster

Bramham Moor
Leeds
Pontefract
Ravenspur

Liverpool
Doncaster
Tickhill

Rhuddlan
Beaumaris
Conway
Flint
Chester
Trent
Bolingbroke

Caernarvon

Nottingham
Derby
Harlech
Tutbury
Castle Donington
Burton-on-Trent
Shrewsbury
Lichfield
Leicester

Aberystwyth
Rockingham
Higham Ferrers

Severn
Kenilworth

Leominster
Builth
Cardigan
Hereford
Brecon
Ross
Gloucester
Carmarthen
Haverfordwest
Monmouth
Thames
Wallingford
Tower of London
Milford Haven
Kidwelly
Windsor
London
Queenborough

Avon
Bristol
Dover

Pevensey

Launceston
Portland

Plymouth
Dartmouth
Restmorel
Falmouth

immediately with a major uprising in Wales under the leadership of Owen Glendower. For the next eight years, this occupied much of Henry's time and energy, and in its later stages furnished his young son, the future Henry V, with a valuable training in warfare.

Henry Percy, earl of Northumberland, and his son Hotspur, had in the meantime increased their domination of the north by defeating the Scots at Homildon Hill in 1402. Discontented by their treatment by the king, they made common cause with Glendower in 1403, and although the king crushed Hotspur and his

army at Shrewsbury later that year, the father remained a threat until his defeat at Bramham Moor in 1408.

In 1405, another rebellion had broken out in the north of England, backed by no less a personage than the archbishop of York, Geoffrey Scrope. Henry's execution of this prelate earned him great unpopularity, but by the end of 1408 he had brought the Welsh and the Percies to heel and held the young son and heir of the Scots king as his prisoner. The long struggle had, however, left him exhausted: for the last years of the reign real power was exercised by the future Henry V.

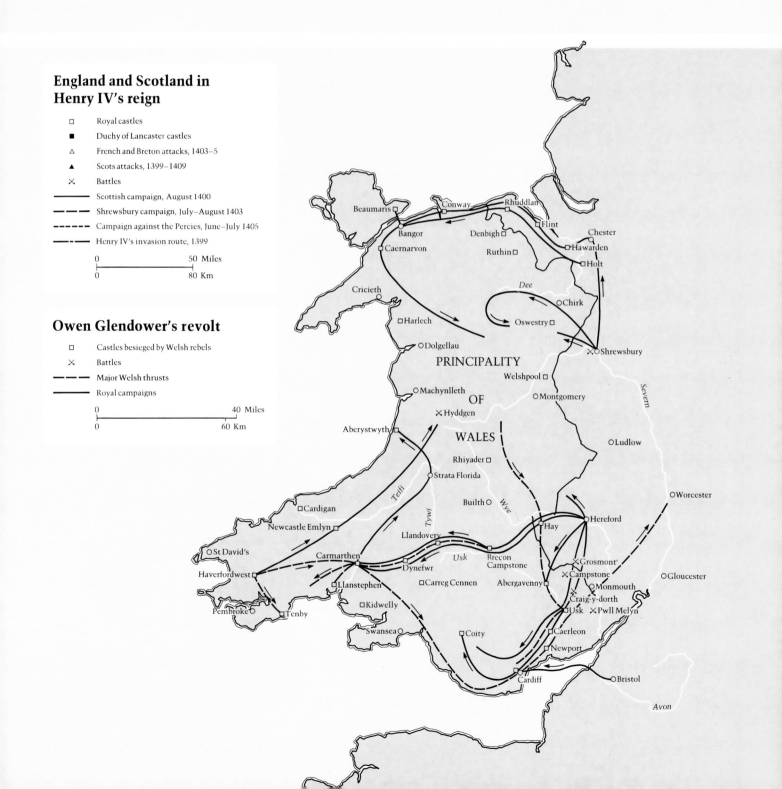

England and Scotland in Henry IV's reign

☐ Royal castles

■ Duchy of Lancaster castles

△ French and Breton attacks, 1403–5

▲ Scots attacks, 1399–1409

✕ Battles

——— Scottish campaign, August 1400

– – – Shrewsbury campaign, July–August 1403

- - - Campaign against the Percies, June–July 1405

–·–· Henry IV's invasion route, 1399

0   50 Miles

0   80 Km

Owen Glendower's revolt

☐ Castles besieged by Welsh rebels

✕ Battles

– – – Major Welsh thrusts

——— Royal campaigns

0   40 Miles

0   60 Km

with their heirs, had been disinherited. It was also ordained that the parliament held at Westminster in 1388 [the 'Merciless Parliament'] should be considered completely valid, for the honour and good of the whole kingdom.

John Capgrave gives a eulogistic account of the new king's prudence and wisdom.

Thus raised to the throne, King Henry IV followed the paths of justice, greatly honoured the servants of God and, drinking from the fountain of Scripture, did not go away thirsty. In my time I knew highly educated men who enjoyed his company and said that he had a very able mind and an excellent memory, so much so that he spent a lot of the day in solving and unravelling problems. For he was mindful of the great vow of Solomon in which he chose not wealth or honours but the succouring wisdom of God and, as the poet says,

'At his father's wish when he took up the crown
And God allowed him to choose whatever he liked;
Not victory nor length of years,
Nor treasure did he seek, but with humble mind requested
A wise heart to be given him, to defend his realm.'

Although this was said of Solomon, it came true with King Henry.

As Walsingham relates, Henry IV soon had to face a dangerous plot to depose him.

1400

In this year the earls of Kent, Salisbury and Huntingdon, thinking nothing of the benefits conferred on them by the king, went against the wishes of the common people of the kingdom and many of the nobles and gathered together a band of wicked men. By means of meetings and assemblies held at various places, they arranged to attack King Henry suddenly at Windsor Castle under the guise of a birthday game, and cruelly to kill him and his children; they would then seek out King Richard and restore him to the throne.

The first Lancastrian king

WHEN he became king in 1399, Henry Bolingbroke, duke of Lancaster, was about 33 years of age – a few months older than his cousin Richard II, with whom he had little in common. Unlike Richard, Henry of Lancaster had travelled widely, to tournaments near Calais, to a crusade against the pagan Slavs in East Prussia, and on a pilgrimage to the Holy Land by way of Venice. Recently he had been exiled in Paris.

He had won admiration throughout Europe for his 'singular virtues', including faithfulness to his wife, Mary de Bohun. Renowned as a fighting man and a jouster, Henry was also educated, literate and musical. Of stocky build, he cut an elegant and dashing figure, who was extravagant in his tastes and lavish in his generosity.

However, he had had no training for kingship. His invasion of England was made deceptively easy by Richard's unpopularity and his own skill as a military leader, but the crown was more easily won than held.

Although many lords and other landholders were opposed to Richard, few were wholeheartedly for Henry, who had to learn to confront critical parliaments and open rebellion at home as well as enemies abroad. His only real supporters were the tenants of his Lancastrian estates, many of whom had also been his comrades in arms, and the few people who found reconciliation with Richard impossible. Henry's two main allies on his path to the throne were Thomas Arundel, whom he restored to the archbishopric of Canterbury, and Henry, earl of Northumberland, head of the Percy family. Arundel remained his lifelong councillor, but the Percys, unenthusiastic for Henry even in 1399, supported him only so long as it suited their ambitions.

When the parliament which had deposed Richard met again as the first parliament of the new reign, it took away the titles conferred in 1397: the nephew and half-brother of Richard lost their dukedoms of Surrey and Exeter and reverted to being earls of Kent and Huntingdon, while Henry's half-brother was reduced from marquis of Dorset to earl of Somerset. One bishop, Carlisle, who had supported Richard in parliament, was deprived of his see.

Otherwise the revolution claimed few victims. Archbishop Arundel needed no government office to confirm his political standing. The earls of Northumberland, Westmorland and Somerset were appointed respectively constable, marshal and chamberlain of England. John Scarle, a senior Chancery clerk, became chancellor, John Norbury, an ever-loyal squire of Henry, was made treasurer and posts in the royal household were filled by Lancastrians. The judges and all the officers of Chancery and Exchequer were confirmed in their posts.

On 12 October at the Tower of London Henry knighted some 50 young noblemen; including his own four sons, and the next morning after their vigil they rode with him to Westminster, where he was crowned with all the traditional ceremony. At the banquet that followed, the king's champion rode into the hall offering to defend him against all comers. Henry replied that he would, if necessary, defend himself, and this he soon had to do.

Only three months later, on Twelfth Night 1400, when the royal household was at Windsor, it was revealed that the recently demoted lords and other supporters of Richard were plotting to capture the king and his sons. Henry, at his best in a crisis, rode to London gathering an army as he went. The rising, quickly suppressed, was only the start of his troubles. Both Scots and French were ready to take advantage of any English weakness.

Henry decided to settle the Scots first and invaded Scotland in the autumn of 1400. He reached as far as Edinburgh, but the Scots withdrew before him and he was unable to bring them to battle. Shortage of money and provisions forced him to return to England, where he was presented with another problem: the Welsh under Owen Glendower had risen in revolt.

The French continued to observe the truce made with Richard II, but urged the return of his young widow, Isabella, who remained in Henry's hands.

To add to Henry's difficulties, parliament made him no grant beyond the usual customs duties, and the king and his council, fearful of the unpopularity that would result from taxation, did not dare to ask for funds. Shortage of money was an enduring problem throughout the reign.

Above A Yorkist genealogy: Henry IV, with the sword, cuts off Richard II's line, while a prophet above foretells the punishment of his descendants.

Below Bolingbroke's coronation.

Through these terrible crimes they would regain the ducal titles and the possessions of which they had been deprived.

Fortunately, the king learned in advance of the treason they had planned; he left Windsor and hurried to London. These men, that is the earl of Kent and the earl of Salisbury, thinking that the king knew nothing of their secret conspiracy, went to accomplish their plan at twilight on 4 January. They arrived at the castle with an armed party of about forty men; but when they learned that the king had escaped, they were thrown into confusion and began to look for a way out. They rode fast towards Sonning, an estate near Reading where Richard II's queen, Isabella of France, was staying at that time.

The earl of Kent entered, with the earl of Salisbury, showing none of his despondency to the queen's household. When she came to meet them, he lifted his right hand to his face and crossed himself. 'God bless you,' he said. 'What has happened that Henry of Lancaster should have run away from me, when he used to be so proud of his strength and his fighting skill?' And then he added, 'Lords and friends, you must know that Henry of Lancaster has fled from me to the Tower of London, with his children and friends. And it is my intention to go to Richard, who was, is, and will be our true king of England, and who has escaped from prison and now lies at Pontefract with one hundred thousand soldiers to defend him.'

When he had sworn to this, the earl of Kent tore off the king's tokens, that is, the collars from the necks of certain men he saw there wearing these tokens, to express his contempt, and said that such tokens should not be worn in future. Then he tore the symbols of the crescent off the arms of the squires, and threw them away.

Queen Isabella was overjoyed, although for empty reasons, and departed in the direction first of Wallingford and then Abingdon, appealing to people along all the way to take up arms and go to meet their king, Richard II. She and the earls arrived at Cirencester under cover of darkness. The people of the town were suspicious of all this

display and thought that the rumours were lies, so they cut off all the entrances and exits of the earls' lodgings. When, at midnight, they tried to slip away, the townspeople, armed with bows and arrows, would not allow them to pass.

The two earls realized that danger lay ahead of them and resorted to their weapons, thinking that it would be easy to overcome the townspeople. They fought here and there from midnight until midmorning the next day. Finally, exhausted, they surrendered their weapons to the common people, and on their knees begged to be spared from death, until they had spoken to King Henry. This would have been granted, had a priest from their household not set fire to several houses in the town, with the idea that, if the common people were busy extinguishing the fire, his masters would have a chance to escape. This was in vain: the common people left their houses in danger of being burnt, and were incited by even greater anger against these lords to avenge the loss caused by the fire.

They led them from the abbey, and at dusk that night beheaded them. It is said that the earl of Salisbury, who all his life had supported the Lollards, scorned images, despised canons and sneered at the sacraments, ended his life without taking the sacrament of confession.

The earl of Huntingdon, Lord John Holland, was not with the other lords at Windsor Castle, but was at London awaiting the outcome of the plot. When he learned that the machinations had failed, he tried to escape by boat, but winds blowing in the opposite direction forced him back. So he went on horseback to Essex, with a knight called John Schevel.

He tried to escape the country by sea, but every time he put to sea he was driven back by the force of the winds, until he despaired of Neptune's help and abandoned his plan. In the end he returned to dry land and went to the house of a friend. While he was sitting at dinner with the knight named above, he was captured by the commons of the locality and taken first to the town of Chelmsford and then to Pleshey, which was a safer place to hold him.

The people of the region flocked there, and at sunset on 15 January he was brought out and was beheaded in the very place where their lord, the duke of Gloucester, had once been arrested by King Richard. He first confessed in tears that he had sinned in many ways against God and his king, because he had known about the plot of the other lords, but had done nothing to protect his sovereign lord.

At that time Lord Thomas le Spencer, who was called earl of Gloucester, attempted to escape, but was captured suddenly and taken to Bristol, where he was beheaded according to the wishes of the people. Various other accomplices in the conspiracy were captured and put to death, some at Oxford, others at London.

Two clerics were condemned at London, John Maude and William Ferby, who ended their lives by being hanged, drawn and beheaded. Bernard Brocase and John Schevel, knights, and many others, suffered a similar fate.

The bishop of Carlisle was accused of conspiracy: he was condemned, but spared by the mercy of King Henry.

Richard, the former king of England, heard about this disaster and was distraught. He killed himself by voluntary starvation, it is said, ending his days at the castle of Pontefract, on 14 February. His body was displayed at the more populous places that lay on the road from the castle to London, wherever they stopped for the night. This was after the celebration of the Offices of the Dead.

After the last rites had been said at St Paul's cathedral in London, it was ordained that Richard's body should be carried at once to Langley, to be buried in the church of the Dominicans.

The bishop of Chester, the abbot of St Albans and the abbot of Waltham performed the last rites, in the absence of the nobles and the people. There was no one to ask them to a meal after they had completed this task.

The anonymous author of the Traison et Mort de Richard II *gives a quite different account of the deposed king's death.*

In January 1400, Henry IV, facing a rising in support of King Richard, ordered a knight, Sir Peter Exton, to go and put an end to the days of 'John of London', as Richard was known. Thereby Sir Peter would carry out the sentence of parliament.

As soon as he left the king, Exton rode off to the castle where Richard was imprisoned, and found him sitting at his table, waiting for his dinner. Sir Peter called King Richard's squire and forbade him, on King Henry's orders, to taste the king's meat again; he should let him eat alone, if Richard so wished, for this would be his last meal.

The squire returned to Richard's cell. The king was still at his table, but was unwilling to eat because he was alone and his squire would not perform his customary duties in front of him. 'What is the news?' asked the king. 'There is none,' replied the squire, 'except that Sir Peter Exton is here. What news he brings, I do not know.'

King Richard asked his squire to carve him some meat and taste it as usual. The squire fell to his knees at King Richard's table, and begged the king to pardon him as he had been forbidden to do so by orders from King Henry. At this Richard was furious and, seizing one of the table knives, he hit the squire on the head with it yelling, 'A curse on Henry of Lancaster and on you!'

As he shouted these words, in rushed Sir Peter Exton and seven men, every one of them armed with an axe. When Richard saw them, he threw back the table, jumped in amongst the armed men, and snatched an axe from one of his would-be murderers. He now set about defending himself with great courage and strength, killing four of the eight, but Sir Peter had leapt on to the king's dining-chair and waited, axe in hand, until Richard came near.

It was astonishing how long Richard managed to hold out against all the armed men: but he did so like a true and loyal knight until at last, while defending himself, he stepped back towards the chair where Sir Peter was waiting. Sir Peter brought his axe down with such force that Richard staggered backwards shouting, 'Lord have mercy on me', and fell dead to the ground, where Exton hit him again on the head.

So died King Richard, and without confession, for which we should pity him, and anybody who says otherwise does not know what he is talking about.

When the king was dead, the knight who had killed him knelt beside his body and began to lament. 'What have we done? We have murdered the man who has been our king for twenty-two years. Henceforth, wherever I go, I shall be reminded of this deed which has cost me my honour.'

The next day, King Richard's body was taken to Pontefract, where it was given a pauper's burial. God have mercy upon his soul!

Richard's death did not quell the opposition to his successor. Walsingham describes Henry's troubles with the Scots and the Welsh, troubles that were to persist for most of his reign.

King Henry IV gathered an army and then set out for Scotland. But the Scots withdrew and did not come to fight; so the king left after laying waste to the countryside.

Meanwhile the Welsh seized the opportunity given by the king's absence to rebel, under the leadership of Owen Glendower. He had originally been an apprentice at Westminster, then a squire to the present king. A dispute broke out between him and Lord Reginald Grey of Ruthin, over lands which he claimed belonged to him by inheritance. When he saw that his reasons and claims were being ignored, he marched first against Lord Grey, destroying his lands by fire, and putting many of his family to the sword, an act of great cruelty and inhumanity.

King Henry entered Wales with an army. The Welsh, who were occupying Snowdonia under

Dress and adornment

SOME of the most fantastic fashions ever devised were worn during Henry IV's reign. Gowns trailed extravagantly and wide, hanging sleeves were *de rigueur* for both sexes – in 1399 the author of *Richard the Redeless* complained that they swept the ground. He also wrote of clothing 'cut all to pieces', a reference to the fanciful leaf shapes that were cut into the hems and sleeve edges of gowns; clothes had an almost ragged appearance at odds with the rich fabrics used in their making. In 1402 parliament puritanically petitioned the king to introduce legislation to control the width of fashionable sleeves and prohibit anyone below the rank of knight banneret from wearing them. Amounts of gold and silver fringing were also restricted.

The tailoring that underlay these flowing fashions had advanced considerably by 1400 when curved seams and buttoned closures were introduced. Sleeves could now be set neatly into armholes and clothes fitted closely to the curves of the body. Cloth was bought from a draper and taken to a tailor for making up. Garments were made from standard pattern blocks or ones specially made for individual customers and retained by the tailor.

Enormous quantities of cloth were used to make the voluminous gowns and for the hoods which men twisted into fantastic shapes – more than a yard of broadcloth for the tippet or tail section alone.

Women's head-dresses were equally extravagant. Their hair was rolled over their ears and enclosed in padded, jewelled nets; a veil was suspended above, extended at either side of the head by whalebone or dried plant stalks.

The decorative trimmings that embellished fashionable clothing included embroidery, jewels, belts and purses. Early 15th-century dress was an auditory as well as a visual experience: any movement was accompanied by the clinking sound of bezants (coin-like metal discs) sewn on to clothes and horse trappings, and the tinkling of hundreds of tiny gold and silver bells worn on belts and girdles. Wide, loose sleeves encouraged women to wear bracelets. Designs for brooches included stags, eagles, pelicans, huntsmen and pairs of lovers.

Badges and heraldic devices were increasingly popular. In 1407 King Henry IV paid a huge sum to Christopher Tyldesley, a London goldsmith, for a gold collar adorned with the motto SOVEIGNEZ (remember me) in enamelled letters and a quantity of rich jewels; from it hung a triangular pendant set with a great ruby and four large pearls. Another collar, of SS pounced with the motto SOVERAIN and adorned with an equally costly pendant, was made by the same goldsmith on a later occasion. By the time Henry V acceded to the throne in 1413, the Lancastrian collar of SS was established as royal livery. The pendant worn with it might be a family badge or indicate some political affiliation. Henry IV's customary pendant was an enamelled white swan, the device of the de Bohun family into which he married.

Opposite top *A jeweller's shop.*

Right *John, duke of Burgundy, loved jewels.*

Below *The Dunstable swan, an enamelled gold version of Henry IV's swan badge.*

Glendower, promptly abandoned their plan of revenge. The king set fire to the area, and several people died, whom fate presented to his soldiers' swords. He returned with his plunder of baggage animals and other livestock.

At the same time, the emperor of Constantinople came to England to ask for a subsidy to help fight the Turks. The king with his escort of nobles received him at Blackheath on 21 December, in a manner fit for such a hero. He took him to London, and entertained him there splendidly for many days, paying all the costs of hospitality and showering him with gifts.

1401

A parliament was held in London from 6 January. A statute [De heretico comburendo] was passed concerning the Lollards: wherever they were caught spreading their vicious teachings, they should be apprehended and handed over to the diocesan bishop. If they continued to defend their beliefs obstinately, they should be handed over to secular jurisdiction. This law was brought to bear against a false priest, who was burned at Smithfield in front of a large crowd.

Now that conditions in the kingdom had been made stable, and all necessary preparations had been made for her departure, Isabella, once queen of England, was sent back to France, her native land. She was not yet twelve years old.

At the same time, Glendower invaded England with his Welshmen, inflicting heavy damage.

1402

At that time, by great misfortune, certain Franciscan friars contemplated treason, but were caught before they could act. One of them, when asked what he would do if King Richard were alive and present, replied consistently that he would fight anyone to the death on his behalf. So verdict was passed against him, and he was hanged and drawn in the habit of his order. His fellow friars could not bear the disgrace and were granted permission to administer the last rites over his body.

That year the king sent his daughter Blanche in great state, with a large retinue, to Cologne. Prince Rupert, the emperor's son, came to meet her with an escort, and although he was still young, married the maiden, according to the custom of the region.

At that time the Scots, made restless by their usual arrogance, invaded England. They thought that all the northern lords had been kept in Wales by royal command. But Henry Percy, earl of Northumberland, with Henry his son, known as 'Hotspur', and the earl of Dunbar, who had lately left the Scots and sworn fealty to the king of England, suddenly cut off the retreat of the Scots with armed men and archers.

Their opponents, after burning and plundering in England, were trying to return to their own country, but they were forced by Percy to stop and choose a place of battle. They selected a hill near the town of Wooler called Homildon Hill, where they assembled with their men-at-arms and archers. When our men saw this they left the road and climbed the hill facing the Scots. Without delay our archers, drawn up in the valley, shot arrows at the Scottish formation to provoke them to come down. In reply the Scottish archers directed all their fire at our archers; but they then felt the weight of our arrows, which fell like a storm of rain, and so they fled.

The earl of Douglas, the Scots' leader, saw the flight. Not wanting to seem to desert the battlefield, he seized a lance, rode down the hill with a troop of his horse, and charged the archers. But he trusted too much in his equipment and in that of his men, who had been improving their armour for three years. For our archers, although they retreated, were still shooting, and with such vigour, determination and effect that they pierced the armour, perforated the helmets, pitted the swords, split the lances and penetrated all the Scots' equipment with ease.

Despite his elaborate armour, the earl of Douglas received five deep wounds. The rest of the Scots, who had not come down the hill, turned tail and fled from the arrows. But flight did not avail

Owen Glendower,
a prince of Wales

OWEN Glendower was descended in the direct line
from the princes of Powys in North Wales. He had
studied at the Inns of Court, which served as a university
for the richer members of society, but, like all his class, he
was also proficient in arms: he is said to have served in
Richard II's army. The occasion of his rebellion against
Henry was a dispute with Lord Grey of Ruthin, an
English marcher lord and a close ally of the king. Unable
to defeat Grey by process of law, Glendower decided to
take advantage of Welsh resentment at the occupation of
part of their country by these lords, whose ancestors had
won their lands by the sword.

Glendower was proclaimed prince of Wales in 1400
and on 18 September he and his followers burned the
town of Ruthin, the centre of his enemy's lordship, and
other English settlements. But within a week a force
raised from Shropshire and neighbouring counties by
Hugh Burnell, a loyal Lancastrian squire, overwhelmed
his small army.

The king, on his way south from Scotland, received
news of the rising at Northampton and immediately
marched towards Wales. However, by the time he
reached Shrewsbury on 26 September the revolt seemed
over and he was able to lead his army around North
Wales in a show of strength. Henry IV returned to
Westminster, leaving his son Henry, prince of Wales, in
nominal charge in North Wales with the earl of Northumberland's son, Henry Hotspur, as his chief councillor
and the real commander.

Glendower and his surviving companions went into
hiding, too wary to meet the king's army in battle, and
waged a guerrilla war against the English. On Good
Friday 1401 Conway Castle was captured by a party of
Welsh rebels while the garrison was hearing mass. In the
summer Henry IV returned to Worcester with his army,
determined to end the rebellion. Again, he failed to bring
Glendower to battle.

Another member of the Percy family, the earl of
Northumberland's brother Thomas, earl of Worcester,
was now given the command in South Wales, where
Glendower was also active. In 1402, however, the rebels
captured Lord Grey and Edmund Mortimer, the young
earl of March, who by the strict rules of primogeniture
was the true heir of Richard II. For the third time the king
set out on a punitive expedition against the Welsh, and
again withdrew without meeting Glendower in battle,
defeated by the stormy weather as well as the Welsh
leader's tactics.

Above *Owen's revolt heralded by a comet.*

In the mean time, the earl of Northumberland and his
son Hotspur defeated an invading Scottish army at
Homildon Hill in Northumberland. Although this relieved the king on one front, their victory gave him little
satisfaction, as it contrasted with his own lack of success.

Henry soon arranged for Grey to ransom himself, but
showed no eagerness to see Mortimer freed. The latter's
sister was Hotspur's wife; the Percys, who had been
negotiating with Glendower supposedly on the king's
behalf, and who were complaining that they had not been
paid for their services, now had a further grievance. In
1403 their discontent came to a head.

Hotspur proclaimed his revolt, and marched on
Shrewsbury. But the king arrived first, and defeated
Hotspur on 21 July, before Northumberland could join
him from the north or Glendower from Wales. Hotspur
died in the battle and Worcester was executed.

The king's victory ensured the eventual downfall of
Glendower as well as of the Percys. The prince of Wales,
Henry, now 16, slowly reconquered the country and
finally drove the Welsh leader into hiding. Glendower
was never captured and the obscurity of his end made
him a national hero. The legend grew until he came to be
claimed as the father of modern Welsh nationalism.

them, for our archers followed them, so that the Scots were forced to give themselves up for fear of the deadly arrows. The earl of Douglas was captured, as were many of those who fled, but many were drowned in the River Tweed because they did not know the fording places. It was said that the waters devoured five hundred men. In this battle no lord or knight dealt a blow to the enemy; but God gave a miraculous victory to the English archers alone, and the magnates and men-at-arms remained idle spectators of the battle.

Henry IV had meanwhile contracted a marriage alliance which promised well for English influence in France.

1403

In January the new queen, Joan, came to England, from small Brittany to great Britain, from a duchy to a kingdom, from a fierce people to a peaceful one, and, it was hoped, bringing with her good fortune. She had been married before to a nobleman, John de Montfort, duke of Brittany, to whom she bore six children. She bore none to King Henry, whom she was now marrying.

On 26 January she was crowned in splendour at Westminster in London.

At the same time Sir Henry Percy the younger, known as Hotspur, to whom fortune had always until then been kind, and in whom the hopes of all the people lay, suddenly revealed himself as an enemy of the king. Against everyone else's wishes, he drew to his side Sir Thomas Percy, earl of Worcester, his uncle. The earl of Worcester suddenly left the house of the king's eldest son, whom the king had entrusted to his special care, and went to his nephew, to add strength and a spirit of rebellion to his cause.

In order to excuse their conspiracy, the Percys wrote round to the provinces, saying that the cause they had taken up was not incompatible with the allegiance and loyalty they had given to the king, and that they had gathered an army for no other reason than to save their own lives, and for the better government of the country.

The rebellion gained strength from unbridled boldness and contempt for the king's clemency. Sir Henry Percy made haste towards Shrewsbury, hoping for help from Owen Glendower and Edmund Mortimer, together with men of Chester and Wales. But the king, when he became aware that this young man was hardened in wickedness, decreed that he must be opposed with all haste, together with his uncle, Sir Thomas Percy, before they could collect a larger army.

These men and their fellow-conspirators then had it declared throughout their territory that King Richard was still alive and was with them; in his name or cause they had declared war on King Henry. This announcement, although it was false, made a great impression on many minds.

When he heard of these announcements, King Henry, who was bold and strong in fighting, wisely gathered all the men he could, and went unexpectedly to Shrewsbury where the rebels were making havoc. Henry Percy suddenly saw the royal standard just as he was about to attack the town.

On 21 July King Henry IV and Henry Percy prepared their forces for battle about two miles outside Shrewsbury.

While the soldiers on both sides were awaiting the signal for war, the abbot of Shrewsbury and the clerk of the Privy Seal acted as messengers for the king, to offer Henry Percy peace and a pardon if he abandoned his attempt. Percy was softened by their means of persuasion, and sent his uncle, Sir Thomas Percy, back with them to the king, to explain the reasons for rebellion.

It is said that the king listened to every reason and lowered himself more than is appropriate for a royal person, but that Sir Thomas Percy, when he returned to his nephew, gave him an answer which was the opposite of what the king had said, thus exacerbating the young man's spirit, and inciting him to war, even though it was now against his wishes.

Therefore the archers of Henry Percy began the fight and launched their missiles. Men on the

Joan of Brittany

HENRY IV had been a widower for five years when he came to the throne in 1399. His wife, Mary de Bohun, had borne him four sons and two daughters who were still alive, and the succession seemed secure. But Henry needed a queen to grace his court and share the loneliness of a king's life. His second wife was Joan, daughter of Charles of Navarre, widow of Duke John IV of Brittany, and regent for her young son, the new duke.

There are several reasons for supposing Henry personally chose her as queen. There were close family ties between the English and Breton ruling families; Henry had visited Brittany before becoming king and was in constant correspondence with the duchy from the beginning of his reign. Negotiations were carried out in secret, and the marriage took the people by surprise.

The new queen brought no dowry from her father, but a large sum of money had been bequeathed her by her late husband, and she also had the income from her Breton dower lands. Despite this Henry gave her a dower much larger than that customary for queens of England.

Joan secured the tacit agreement of the king of France and her maternal uncle, Philip the Bold, duke of Burgundy, to her remarriage, but had to surrender her regency to Philip and leave her four young sons in Brittany. Henry therefore lost any hope of controlling the duchy in her name, or even of acquiring it as a firm ally.

The couple were married by proxy in 1402, and in person at Winchester on 7 April 1403. Joan brought with her a large train of Breton attendants, whom she retained even after protests in parliament. The marriage was never popular, but Henry was a generous and faithful husband and Joan a good wife to him.

For much of Henry V's reign, the new king was unmarried, and Joan continued to preside over her stepson's court as she had done over his father's. Henry treated her with the honour and respect he might have accorded his mother, which was indeed the name he gave her; grants were made, not to 'the queen', but to 'the king's mother, the queen'. When he concluded a truce with Brittany in 1417 he said he had done so in response to her appeals. Nevertheless, in September 1419, when Henry V was in France, Joan was arrested on the orders of her second stepson, John, duke of Bedford.

The reason given in parliament for this extraordinary action was that her confessor, John Randolph, accused her of attempting 'the death and destruction of our lord the king'. The council had to take seriously this accusation of witchcraft made against her, but it is unlikely that many at court really believed it; Joan had nothing to gain by Henry's death. Her real 'crime' was that her English dower absorbed too many of the crown's resources in wartime.

Joan was never formally charged and, after an initial imprisonment at Pevensey, lived in style and comfort in her own castle of Leeds, in Kent. Henry V ordered her release on his deathbed three years later, but not before the crown had availed itself of the income from her dower lands for those years, when it was most needed for war with France. For the rest of her life Joan lived in affluent retirement. She died in 1437 and was buried at Canterbury with Henry IV.

Top left *Effigy of Joan of Brittany on the tomb shared with her husband in Canterbury Cathedral.*

Below *Joan's coronation as queen following her marriage to Henry IV.*

king's side fell as fast as leaves fall in autumn after the hoar-frost. Nor did the king's archers fail to do their work, but sent a shower of sharp points against their adversaries ... Henry Percy and his ally, the spirited earl of Douglas, urged their men against the king's person alone, and concentrated their arms on him, in spite of the rain of arrows and the dense bodies of horsemen. When the earl of Dunbar had guessed their designs, he withdrew the king from his position at the front. This deed saved the king's life, for the royal standard-bearer was felled by the fury of the enemy, and his banner thrown down, and those who stood round him were killed. Prince Henry, the king's first-born son, who was experiencing his first battle, was wounded by an arrow in the face.

Meanwhile Henry Percy, while he led his men in the fight, rashly penetrating the enemy hosts, was unexpectedly cut down, by whose hand it is not known. When this was known, the rebels fled. But the earl of Douglas was captured, for the second time this year; fighting against the English he always found ill fortune. For in the first battle his head was pierced and he lost an eye, and in the second he was wounded and fell into a second captivity. Also captured was the earl of Worcester, Sir Thomas Percy, the originator of all the evil and the cause of the present misfortune.

1404

The lord of Castella, a Breton, landed at Dartmouth with a crowd of Frenchmen and Bretons, lured on by the Fates, and thinking that fortune would help them, as it had the previous year at Plymouth. But everything turned out against all their hopes, for their leader was killed by those people he most despised, that is, the peasants, as were the men who landed after him. Caught unawares they were captured or slain. The women earned much credit for this deed, for they beat the enemy down with violent blows from their slings.

So it came about that the enemy were killed or captured by women or peasants. Many men were killed because, although they offered large sums for their own ransom, they did not know a common language. These uncouth people interpreted them differently and thought they were making threats, when in fact they were earnestly begging for their lives. The king rewarded the captors and gave them purses stuffed with gold. He kept the prisoners in his power, to be handed over to harsher judgement later.

All through the summer, Owen Glendower and his Welshmen looted, burned and destroyed the area around his lands. He captured and killed many Englishmen, took many castles and razed them to the ground through treachery, ambush or open warfare, and kept some for himself as protection. John Trevor, bishop of St Asaph, when he saw that the Welsh cause was prospering, became a traitor and went over to Owen's side.

1405

At this time the bishop of Winchester, William of Wykeham, died, a very old man. Through his industry and generosity the English clergy had daily grown and increased. In Winchester he had established a college to teach young scholars, and at Oxford he founded a college for students of the finer branches of learning. A hundred scholars were educated in these institutions from funds he provided.

Another leading ecclesiastic, Richard le Scrope, archbishop of York, now joined Thomas Mowbray, the earl marshal, and Henry Percy, the earl of Northumberland, in a new revolt against the king.

Secure in the support of Northumberland and Bardolf, Scrope and Mowbray called out the citizens of York and many others; by way of encouragement they had manifestos in English nailed to the doors of the churches and monasteries in the city. A great number of knights, squires, townsmen and rustics joined the archbishop, who was highly regarded for his age, holiness, learning and amiability.

The earl of Westmorland, who was nearby, heard rumours of all this, and gathering his men, hurried to suppress the archbishop's force before it grew too big; but in vain, as he found the archbishop's army already much bigger than his own.

Spreading the word

ALTHOUGH reading matter of any kind was scarce in 15th-century England, the literate minority was growing. By the early 1400s it included most of the nobility and gentry, the swelling business community, and even a few artisans. At Lollard meetings, one group member was usually able to read their unauthorized English Bible and heretical tracts – a 15th-century *samizdat* literature.

The written word was not, however, the sole means of communication. The parish pulpit and manor court were local forums for announcing official news and legislation. The Church controlled a vivid range of visual media: stained glass, murals and brightly painted statues taught doctrine and morality. Street theatre – mystery and miracle plays performed on garish pageant carts, often with the brightly painted statuary of the church façade as backdrop – was a vivid way to instruct as well as to entertain.

State ceremonial could be used for propaganda purposes, as is shown by Henry IV's coronation, on Monday 13 October 1399. The king-making had taken place two weeks before in Westminster Hall, when an assembly of lords and bishops acclaimed the reading of the absent Richard's 'voluntary' abdication before an empty throne and accepted Henry's assertion of his right to the crown. This carefully managed public relations exercise, aimed at the influential in Church and state, was followed by the coronation at which the realm's most important body of commoners, the Londoners, could signal their assent.

Top right *An official proclamation.*

Below *A scribe's poster showing his work.*

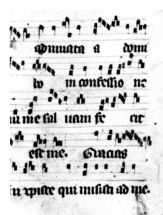

Chroniclers from the leading churches and religious houses recorded the official version which was broadcast as fully as possible. When Henry faced an uprising in January 1400 it was not because there had been a failure in communications – people simply did not believe in his claim to the throne.

English was by now the language of society as well as of the populace, and the chief medium for the growing literature of political squibs and verses. Many were written by clerks in, or on the fringes of, government service, and were commissioned by the regime – or rich patrons opposed to it. Numerous copies of some of them have survived, indicating a wide readership. Others were set to music and performed in the halls of the nobility and in market-squares or guildhalls.

Public pronouncements, too, could be made on bills posted on church doors and other public places. When Archbishop Scrope of York joined the 1405 rebellion against Henry IV, he ordered the rebels' grievances be 'written in English . . . and set upon the gates of the city, and sent to curates of the towns about, for to be preached openly'. (Scrope was executed; but a folk carol told the story of his 'martyrdom' and his tomb in York Minster attracted a popular cult, suppressed by Henry.)

Although bills were also used in private feuds – as an early member of the Paston family found when a Walter Azlak posted 'menaces', or threats 'of death and dismembering' on rhymed bills, in English, set up around the city – they were generally political. *Mum and the Sothsegger* was written to warn Henry IV of widespread grievances expressed in popular songs, verses and bills. The written word was beginning to make its mark.

Westmorland therefore tricked Scrope into a parley and persuaded him to lay down his arms.

Scrope and Westmorland shook hands on their agreement and a knight was sent from the archbishop's side to tell the people to lay down their arms and go home. Seeing the lords drinking together, and tired of their unaccustomed soldier-hood, most of them did so; thus one side increased while the other diminished. The archbishop did not realize that he had been deceived until he was arrested by Westmorland's men. An amnesty was proclaimed for all, but not observed, for later, when the king came to York, both the archbishop and the earl marshal were beheaded.

Henry IV aroused widespread opposition for executing an archbishop. To many of his subjects, the mysterious illness which overtook him soon afterwards, rumoured to be leprosy, seemed a judgement from God for his misdeeds.

The king next set out against the earl of Northumberland, Henry Percy, and arrived at Berwick. The earl fled from his sight in fear to Scotland, taking Sir Thomas Bardolf with him. Sir David Fleming, a Scot, took them into his protection. When the king learned of the earl's flight, he ordered the men in the castle to surrender it to him. When they persistently refused, he attacked it with a huge cannon, whose first shot knocked down part of one tower and terrified those inside so much that they chose to fall on their swords rather than await a second firing. The castle was thus handed over to the king, and of its defenders some were beheaded, others sent to prison. Once this castle had been handed over, the castle of Alnwick and other castles belonging to the earl came easily into the king's hands.

The king was overjoyed by this success, and returned without delay to Wales. There, on the contrary, nothing went well for him; everything happened as if bad fortune had struck him. Because of this nothing useful was achieved, and he headed back, losing carriages, carts and wagons, apparently about five hundred in all, together with a vast treasure and his crowns, because of violent and unexpected rainstorms.

He arrived at Worcester and summoned Thomas Arundel, archbishop of Canterbury, and various other bishops, revealing to them the bad fortune that had overtaken him and asking for their help. The archbishop replied that he would negotiate with the clergy on his behalf.

1406

A parliament was held [the 'Long Parliament'] which was prolonged uselessly for nearly a year. After a long delay over whether to give the king help, the parliamentary knights at last gave way and granted him the tax he was asking for, to the loss of the people. Because of this delay the soldiers' expenses were almost equal to the subsidy demanded.

A new tax was granted to the king by the clergy, to be levied on chantry priests and mendicant friars, and other religious men who celebrated anniversary masses. Half a mark was to be raised from each of them to lessen the burden of taxation on the clergy, who had always paid for them.

At the same time the earl of Northumberland and Sir Thomas Bardolf fled to Wales on the advice of David Fleming, who told them that the Scots were conspiring to hand them over to the king in exchange for certain prisoners. Because of this treachery, David was killed by the Scots, who were roused into civil war so violent that, once it had lost strength, they were forced to seek a year-long truce.

Northumberland and Bardolf then fled to France, to return to Scotland to foment rebellion in the next year.

Once the truce had been established on land, the Scots sent James I, their king's son and heir, abroad, so that he might grow up and be educated in French manners and the French tongue. But some sailors from Cley in Norfolk took him prisoner by chance, together with a bishop and the earl of Orkney, to whose care he had been entrusted by his father. They took him to England and delivered him to King Henry, who said jokingly: 'If the Scots were truly grateful they would

Public wars, private armies

BY the beginning of the 15th century English armies were generally recruited by contract: private arrangements between the king and his suppliers. These captains were usually nobles and gentlemen who undertook to provide an agreed number of soldiers for a fixed period of service in return for wages. A captain might rely entirely on his own retinue of followers, or arrange subcontracts with others; either way, English armies of the later 14th and the 15th centuries were raised by private enterprise. Kings thus condoned the existence of private armies, and relied on their chief subjects to provide soldiers.

There were many advantages, the most striking of which was that England did not have to pay for a standing army. Instead collections of noble retinues took the burdens of mustering, equipment, training and discipline off the hands of the government. It was a perfectly adequate way to raise armies, provided direction from the top was firm and unified.

Command was held by the king, his brothers and uncles, and noblemen and men of knightly rank, and there were two main types of soldier. Men-at-arms – a general term for knights, esquires and gentlemen – were, at best, encased from head to toe in expensive plate armour. Although trained to use lances on horseback, they fought on foot: the central episode of a battle was the confrontation between opposing men-at-arms, who bludgeoned each other with weapons like maces, flails and poleaxes. Early in the 15th century the proportion of men-at-arms to archers, the second type of soldier, was normally one to three, during the century it rose to one to seven or more.

Archers were useful in battle, siege and garrison duty and were cheap to recruit, even when mounted to keep up with the men-at-arms. All free-born Englishmen between 16 and 60 were required to keep, and practise with, the long English bow; even if the law was disobeyed (which was not unusual) a large pool of archers was available. They were good value for money and versatile; and their success prevented the science of the crossbowman and handgunner from flourishing in England.

The importance of artillery in battle and siege, however, was appreciated and there was an artillery train in every major army. Prince Henry used one in his campaigns against Glendower in Wales, and later as king, in his reduction of Normandy in 1417–19.

It is difficult to give an accurate estimate of the size of 15th-century armies. Town and castle garrisons were formed of surprisingly small numbers. A handful of men-at-arms and archers – a token presence – would suffice for even a city like Paris when it was under English rule. The largest single army raised for service abroad was to be

Above *An illustration from Froissart of the sort of scene that was all too common in the 14th and 15th centuries. Soldiers on campaign looted from indiscipline, greed and, often, from need, when pay or food ran short.*

taken to France by Edward IV in 1475. At 11,451 soldiers it surpassed by 2,000 the force Henry V raised for service in France in 1415. It was normally possible to raise rather more men for wars at home, and during civil wars lords called out their tenants for short periods. The relatively small numbers of fighting men were swollen by the host of people needed to service an army on the march.

English governments made remarkable efforts to feed armies at home and abroad, but it was inevitable that troops in foreign territory – and sometimes in England – should loot for sustenance. Occasionally there was a dearth of supplies of all kinds; in 1415, for example, the English army which ultimately won at Agincourt was hungry and bedraggled.

The reasons why men served in armies were complex. Nobles were members of a military aristocracy whose rank required them to fight; it was also their duty to serve the crown. As with lesser men, payment was an important incentive, although wages were frequently far in arrears. Abroad, soldiers were expected to enrich themselves through plunder. A town that refused to surrender would probably be sacked when taken and anywhere on the route of a march was fair game.

have sent this young man to me to be educated, for I too know French.' The young man and the earl of Orkney were sent to the Tower of London. The bishop had escaped by running away.

The French then went with speed to support Owen Glendower, with thirty-eight ships; but eight of these were captured, complete with weapons, while the rest escaped in terror to Wales. Shortly afterwards fifteen ships, carrying wine and wax, were captured by English merchants charged with patrolling the sea.

That summer the king and queen escorted the king's daughter, Philippa, born to him by his first wife, to the town of Lynn, to sail to Denmark to be married to the king. She was accompanied by noblemen, among whom were the archbishop of Bath and Lord Richard, brother of the duke of York. On their return after completing their mission, they had little or no good to report of the country.

Around 4 July, the English ships sailing to Bordeaux ventured into a part of the sea hitherto unknown to the English. They proceeded without particular caution and suddenly sank into a whirlpool, said to have been in the sea off Spain, and were swallowed up in front of their companions' eyes. The sea there is said to be full of whirlpools, and engulfs ships in hidden currents. The ships that remained were warned by the fate of the first to sail away. They arrived safely in Bordeaux, but in diminished numbers.

Towards Christmas the king demanded an immediate payment of a subsidy. Eventually he was granted a fifteenth part of the common people's money.

1407

In 1407 the siege of Bourg and Blaye in Gascony by the duke of Orleans was lifted. He had come with fifty thousand men to capture these towns. By the grace of God, who humbles the proud, for eight weeks no day dawned without falls of rain, snow or hail, mixed with winds and thunder, which drove both men and animals to their deaths.

It is reported that six thousand men died as a result of this misfortune. When he arrived, the duke, who was ostentatious beyond his fortune, had a gold cloth carried over his head by four knights; returning without victory, he merely rejoiced that the sky had cleared of rain.

At that time documents circulated in many parts of London which claimed that King Richard II was still alive and would return soon in glory and splendour to recover his kingdom. But shortly afterwards the lying fool who had committed such a rash act was captured and punished. This tempered the joy he had aroused in many people by his lies.

That summer a great plague, arising from corruption in the air, began to infect people's bodies. It was the worst plague that had been seen in the country for many years. It killed nearly thirty thousand of both sexes in London; in the countryside it hit the poor with even greater loss of life. Many houses, once packed with happy families, were completely emptied.

At that time Louis, duke of Orleans, was taking his pleasure in France with whores, harlots, incest and adultery, when he was killed by a knight with whose wife he was committing adultery. John, duke of Burgundy, was proscribed and treated badly because he presumed to defend the knight for his deed.

1408

This year excessive snowfall made the winter very harsh. It lasted through December, January, February and March. Many birds of the thrush or blackbird family died of cold or hunger.

At that time Henry Percy returned to England and proclaimed that whoever desired liberty should take up arms and follow him. Many men did so, thinking their wishes would be fulfilled. The sheriff of Yorkshire, with the knights from his region, met them near Bramham Moor. A great battle took place, and the sheriff killed the earl, Henry Percy, whose head he cut off. These events took place on 19 February.

Dick Whittington and his cat

DICK Whittington and his cat have been part of English folklore since at least 1605, when the story first appeared in print. Whittington was indeed three times lord mayor of London, but, although the theme of a cat helping its owner is found in many European folk traditions, it is unclear just how it came to be associated with him. Certainly, sculpture on the old Newgate, which Whittington rebuilt in an early example of prison reform, showed a man with a cat at his feet; and a medieval carving of a boy and a cat was found at Gloucester, in what was said to be the Whittington family home.

An anonymous commentator on early 15th-century England uses Whittington to illustrate his thesis that the merchants, rather than the nobility, created the country's wealth. 'In worship now I think on that son of merchantry Richard Whitingdon – lodestar and chosen flower that has brought England much in honour.'

The word 'worship' summed up the ethos of the rising merchant class. Where a noble or knight had his code of honour, the guildsman boasted his 'worth'-ship (or worthiness) and the honorific title 'his worship the mayor' was jealously competed for. When a wife addressed her husband as 'right worshipful' or a son wrote to his 'right reverend and worshipful mother', they were not using empty formulae.

The son of a west country, probably Gloucestershire, gentleman, Whittington came to London in about 1371. There were strong trade links between Bristol and the capital and Sir Ivo Fitzwaryn, the London mercer to whom Dick became apprenticed, may have been a friend of the Whittington family. Like the other London companies, the Mercers (chartered in 1393) dealt in a wide range of merchandise. However, they specialized in high-quality textile goods: the Merchant Adventurers, based in Flanders, was their 'overseas branch'. Richard married Sir Ivo's daughter Alice, became an alderman, and, in 1397, was elected mayor for the first time and master of the Mercers Company.

Now among London's élite, Whittington was able to buy royal friendship by advancing immense loans. When

Top left *Two of Whittington's spoons, bearing his arms, from a set made c. 1410.*

Above *The Whittington Stone, on the spot where he supposedly heard the Bow Bells.*

Richard II fell, Whittington was called to the council of Henry IV in December 1399. Debts from the old reign were repaid, and Whittington advanced the new king the considerable sum of £666 – the equivalent of five months' wages for a force of 300 professional archers. He features on the council rolls and as financier to Henry.

Whittington began his second term as mayor of London, in 1406–7 by successfully capturing an impostor who posed as King Richard II, thereby putting an end to the false rumour that the king was still alive. This term coincided with his headship of the Calais Staple – an important association of wool traders; and some years later he lent heavily to Henry V. He was knighted by Henry V, a real distinction of 'worth-ship'.

He was elected to his third term as mayor in October 1419. On his death in 1423, Whittington left rich endowments to Christ's Hospital and to found Whittington College (suppressed in 1548).

On 8 September more rain fell than ever before, even in the living memory of very old men.

On 1 November the cardinal of Bordeaux came to England. He was a powerful man in both words and actions, and had been sent by the college of cardinals to inform King Henry IV of the bad faith of Pope Gregory XII, as he had previously informed the king of France, Charles VI, and his subjects.

He wanted these two kings, thought to be exceptional throughout the whole world, to apply their judgement to induce Gregory to observe the oath that he had pledged, so that by the authority of these two kings a magnificent union might be brought about within the Church.

The king of France willingly agreed to this task. He sent ambassadors to Gregory, who, however, proved stubborn and uncooperative. So the king of France, on the advice of the doctors of the universities of Paris, Bologna, Orléans, Toulouse and Montpellier, decided to recognize neither claimant.

The king of England, when he had heard the cardinal's proposal, ordered all kindness to be shown to him, offering him generous resources for as long as he wished to stay in England.

1410

In 1410, as arranged, the cardinals of both colleges, that is, of Gregory XII and Benedict XIII, met at Pisa to create a new unity in the Church.

Prelates and highly respected churchmen from all the Latin-speaking world were chosen to assist the cardinals in this cause, and they all met here, bringing together a huge number of mitres in one place. Calling on the grace of the Holy Spirit, they agreed unanimously on one person and chose him to be the head of the whole Church, the two others having abdicated.

They named the new pope Alexander V, while Gregory and Benedict, who had decided to slip away from the council, muttered insolently against the decision.

The magnificent Medici

HEADED by Giovanni, the great Cosimo, his son Piero and his grandson Lorenzo *Il Magnifico*, the Medici excelled as politicians, patrons of the arts, and – under Giovanni and Cosimo – as bankers. The success of their financial operations throughout Europe provided them with such enormous wealth that they became rulers of Florence and commissioned the great works of art for which they are still celebrated.

Long established in Florence, they claimed descent from the giant-killing knight Averardo: the seven *palle* or red balls in their heraldic arms symbolized the dents the ogre's mace made on his shield. Rivals preferred to believe that the *palle* represented pills, and that the family originated as low-born doctors.

The Medici fortune was founded by the banker Giovanni de' Medici (1360–1429), who cultivated Baldassare Cosa, a Neapolitan ex-pirate, and probably lent him the money to buy himself the office of cardinal. When, on Alexander V's death in 1410, Cosa was elected Pope John XXIII by the Council of Pisa, he returned the favour by appointing the Medici papal bankers. The Medici often had to bail the pope out of financial difficulties – on one occasion they accepted his jewelled mitre in pawn – and paid his ransom when he was imprisoned for heresy, poisoning his predecessor, and for the mass seduction of Bolognese women.

However, the papal account conferred tremendous prestige on the Medici and at times produced over half their banking profits. As bankers to the pope, they could threaten defaulting debtors with excommunication.

The connection was equally advantageous to the pontiffs: the bank was one of the few with enough capital to meet the loans they needed, and its widespread branches – from Italy to London, Cologne, Geneva, Bruges and Lübeck – enabled papal funds to be moved swiftly around Europe.

The Medici were also convenient ecclesiastical office-brokers. Candidates for bishoprics paid their fees into the nearest branch of the bank, whose manager issued a papal licence to proceed. Moreover, popes like other clients could order a variety of commodities through the bankers' thriving wholesale trade: silk, spices, holy relics.

The Medici enterprise reached its zenith under Giovanni's son Cosimo (1389–1464). Ugly, witty and modest, and a tireless worker, who declared that even if he could obtain money by magic he would still prefer to be a banker, he was said to be the richest man in the world. As the close friend of three successive popes, his political and financial influence was tremendous: when he was exiled from Florence in 1433, no other banker would lend his enemies 'so much as a pistachio nut'. Cosimo was recalled, and for the rest of his life was ruler of the city in all but name.

Raised in the new spirit of classical humanism, he was an avid book collector – the Medici library included over 10,000 Greek and Latin manuscripts – and the generous patron of artists like Fra Filippo Lippi, 'Fra Angelico', and Donatello. Above all, he poured money into splendid buildings – churches and monasteries like the friary of San Marco.

His munificence provoked envy. 'Who would not build magnificently, if he could do so with other people's money?' demanded one critic; another, remarking his habit of adorning the buildings with the Medici *palle*, declared, 'He has emblazoned even the monks' privies with his balls.' When Cosimo died in 1464 the city mourned him as *Pater Patriae* – 'Father of his Nation'.

His son Piero (1416–69) was also a generous patron – notably of Uccello and Botticelli – but an indifferent banker. His grandson Lorenzo the Magnificent (1449–92) was worse, despite his princely qualities as diplomat, athlete, zestful poet and patron of Michelangelo. As a result of his neglect, branch after branch of the bank collapsed, and he lost the papal account when he quarrelled with Sixtus IV. In 1478 the pope condoned a plot by rival bankers to assassinate Lorenzo in Florence Cathedral. When it narrowly failed, he registered his pique by repudiating all papal debts to the family and confiscating their Roman assets.

The bank failed soon afterwards, and though Medici rule in Florence continued intermittently for another two and a half centuries, they never recovered their influence. They had lost the source of their power.

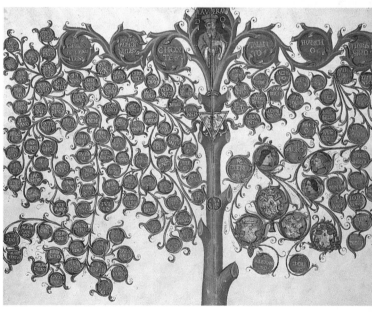

Top *Cosimo I 'il Vecchio', greatest of the Medici bankers and patrons.*

Above *A Medici family tree: their pride matched any noble dynasty's.*

Opposite *The Medici 'palle', here adorning the Old Sacristy of San Lorenzo in Florence.*

In the statute De heretico comburendo *(1401), parliament had enacted that anyone found preaching heresy should be arrested by the Church; if he refused to recant, he was to be publicly burned by the king's officers.*

Parliament was held at London during Lent.

A certain layman, a smith by trade, obstinately defended the heresy that there is no body of Christ as handled in the Church's Sacrament, but that it is an inanimate thing, lower than a toad or a spider, which are both live animals. He refused to abandon this belief, so he was handed over to secular jurisdiction.

The man was condemned and imprisoned at Smithfield, and Prince Henry, the king's eldest son, who was in London at the time, went to see him, and urged and advised him to come to his senses. But lost in his own mists he ignored this great prince's advice, and chose rather to be burned than to pay reverence to a living sacrament. So he was kept in prison and afflicted with consuming flames, which made him moan pitifully from the middle of the fire.

The prince was moved by his terrible shouting, and ordered the timber to be taken off the fire, to remove the heat from him. He offered the man comfort, although he was nearly dead, promising that even now he could live, and receive a pardon and three pennies from the royal exchequer for every day of his life, if he would only come to his senses and recant. But the wretched man, rekindling his breath, spat on this generous offer, doubtless because he was possessed by an evil spirit. So Prince Henry ordered him to be put back on the flames and to receive no more mercy. This trouble-maker died for his own sins, pitifully burned in the fire.

In this parliament the knights, or, to put it more truthfully, the satellites of Pilate, swayed by evil intentions and caring nothing for the good of the kingdom, made one crime their aim: to despoil the English Church. The king sought in the presence of parliament to obtain a tithe from the clergy for as many years as he might live, without his having

Heresy at stake

THE statute *De heretico comburendo* was petitioned of Henry IV by the English clergy and members of the house of commons, and was passed in parliament in 1401. It stated that 'divers false and perverse persons of a certain new sect' were preaching and teaching, in public and in private, new, heretical doctrines on the sacraments and authority of the Church. Furthermore, 'they hold and exercise schools, they make and write books, they do wickedly instruct and inform people, and . . . stir them to sedition and insurrection and make great strife and division among the people'.

The 'sect' in question was the Lollards, supposed followers of the teachings of John Wycliffe, an Oxford academic, whose theological tracts against transubstantiation and encouraging non-payment of tithes in particular, were condemned as unorthodox in 1382. Elements, sometimes distorted, of this intellectual heresy were accepted by members of the knightly and lower classes. The evangelism of Wycliffe's followers, the tracts they distributed and the newly translated vernacular Bible which allowed people to gain the Word direct rather than through the clergy, fundamentally undermined the Church's role. Many people believed that unlicensed preaching bred unorthodox opinions – which were difficult to control and could lead to rebellion.

It fell to the ecclesiastical courts to investigate suspected heretics. From 1382 sheriffs were authorized by bishops to arrest unlicensed preachers and bring them before the courts, but efforts like these failed to stem the tide of heresy. More secular support was needed and the statute of 1401 was the state's response.

Upon royal authority, it forbade preaching openly or secretly without episcopal licence, and teaching of, and instruction in, any heresy; and writing and dissemination of any heretical book. All suspect literature was to be delivered to the bishop for examination within 40 days of the statute's proclamation. Clandestine meetings and teaching sessions were forbidden. The bishops were empowered to arrest and imprison anyone suspected of defying the statute, until charges were answered or the heresy abjured.

Penalties were imprisonment or a royal fine according to the gravity of the offence. Obdurate or relapsed heretics were handed over to the local sheriff or mayor, who 'caused them to be burnt before the people in a conspicuous place, that such punishment may strike fear into the minds of others'.

This power to burn heretics brought England into line with continental practice. The ecclesiastical court could sentence but could not take mortal life or shed blood. The civil authorities were responsible for carrying out the sentence. They paid the executioner and provided the stakes, wood or straw.

Although Lollardy was the statute's main target, its dangers were probably exaggerated in an atmosphere of political instability and crisis. In 1399 the Lancastrian Henry IV had usurped the throne of Richard II, who had died in mysterious circumstances; and preachers were spreading propaganda suggesting Richard was still alive. Rebellion was on the horizon and the statute of 1401 was intended to deter, and inspire fear in, anyone spreading perverse political or religious teachings.

Above *A heretic returns to the fold.*

Left *More stubborn offenders burn.*

Ultimately, the Church's duty was to make heretics realize, and abjure, their error, not to burn them indiscriminately. Between 1401 and 1414 only two people were burned at Smithfield in London: William Sawtry and John Badby, a tailor from Evesham. Badby's screams in the flames were mistaken for repentance; half-dead, he was taken from the fire and promised life, liberty and threepence a day pension to abjure. However, he declined, was retied to the stake and met his fate.

Heretics were actively hunted down by secular and ecclesiastical authorities in 1414 after the Lollard leader John Oldcastle's rebellion, which linked dissent with political subversion; one supporter, the heretical baker Richard Gurmyn, was burned in 1415, and Oldcastle himself in 1420.

As late as 1494 the octogenarian Joan Boughton, an 'old cankered heretic', was burned for ranting that Wycliffe was a saint. However, between 1414 and 1522 there were over 400 abjurations of heresy, opposed to 27 burnings. The statute provided the ultimate penalty, but the stake consumed comparatively few victims.

to call a parliament, as well as a fifteenth part from the laity; but he was not granted it.

Parliament was extended from 20 January until almost the beginning of May. King Henry was eventually granted a fifteenth share from the laity, but not without great grumbling from the common people.

1411

War broke out between the dukes of Burgundy and Orleans. The latter, Charles, was the son of that duke of Orleans who had recently been killed in the dispute with John of Burgundy. The duke of Orleans had the support of the kings of Navarre and Aragon and the dukes of Berry and Brittany, together with Gascony and Aquitaine.

The duke of Burgundy, supported by Charles VI, king of France, and many others, saw the opposite party gathering such strength and numbers that he lost faith in his forces. So he sent ambassadors to England to seek the king's help against the duke of Orleans. He made Henry IV many offers, including his daughter's hand in marriage to Henry, prince of Wales, together with a huge sum of gold.

Prince Henry, who had since 1410 exercised a controlling influence in the king's council, agreed to support the duke of Burgundy.

The earl of Arundel and Sir John Oldcastle of Cobham were sent across to France with a band of armed men and archers in huge numbers. They were welcomed with great joy by John, duke of Burgundy, and escorted with full honour. But when they had waited in Paris for a long time, and already butcher's meat was being sold for more than its usual price, the English soldiers decided to venture out and, if fortune favoured them, to plunder the enemy's victuals for themselves.

Charles, duke of Orleans, and his household were staying in a neighbouring castle which was near the town of Saint-Cloud; a large part of his army was stationed midway between the two sides. The English soldiers sent out to forage decided to enter Saint-Cloud, but found the bridge across the

River Seine had been broken by their opponents. The enemy had spread over it some planks, which were narrow, but long enough to enable the townspeople to come out of the gates. They could then fend off the English or, according to what sort of encounter it was, retreat from the enemy if necessary.

A battle took place in which the French were put to flight. In their terror they slipped on the narrow planks and were drowned in the river. One thousand and three hundred were reported dead; the others fled into the town and told the weeping duke of the disaster. He saved his own life only by fleeing from a different part of the town. The English then looted Saint-Cloud, took many prisoners and returned with them to Paris.

In 1412 King Henry IV regained control over the council from his son and, increasingly concerned that the Burgundians would not uphold his rights in Gascony, switched his support to the Orleanist party, now also known as the Armagnacs.

1412

About 15 August, King Henry IV, by a decree of his council, made provision for aid to be sent to the duke of Orleans's party. He sent his second son, Thomas, duke of Clarence, with Edward, duke of York, and Thomas, earl of Dorset, and a large number of valiant men, to assist the duke of Orleans against the duke of Burgundy.

The men who had crossed the sea to give support to the other faction – the Burgundians – had not yet returned. Such a sudden change of policy caused astonishment to many people, for within a short space of time the English had supported both opposing sides.

The nobles then set out to support the Orleanists and landed in Normandy. But since the duke of Orleans did not come to meet them at the time they had agreed upon, they set fire to his towns, looted the villages and captured many boroughs. Eventually, although much later, the dukes of Clarence and Orleans met to negotiate; they came to an agreement that our men would cease from

Burgundians and Orleanists

AT the start of his reign, Charles VI of France had much in common with Richard II of England: he was a boy (12 years old) when he became king in 1380, and crowned almost at once; and like Richard he was dominated by his uncles: three dukes on his father's side and one on his mother's. Charles declared himself of age at Reims, in 1388, and dismissed his uncles, but within a few years madness overtook him. For the rest of his life lunacy alternated with sanity. In the early years Philip the Bold, duke of Burgundy, ruled when Charles was mad, while in his lucid intervals the young king favoured his brother, Louis, duke of Orleans, who took command. Each raided the royal revenues to maintain his estates.

Although England's possessions – Calais and the ever-shrinking duchy of Aquitaine around Bordeaux – were under constant threat, Henry IV, threatened by the Scots and by rebellion at home, was at first in no position to wage war on France. Fortunately for him, the French court was divided between Burgundy and Orleans, and Richard II's child widow, Isabella of France, was almost a hostage in England.

Although the duke of Orleans had been friendly when Henry was in exile in Paris in 1398–9, the Netherlands dominions of the duke of Burgundy, which depended for their prosperity on peace and trade with England, made him a more likely ally. Isabella was eventually restored to France where she was married to Charles, son of the duke of Orleans, and an uneasy truce was maintained, even though French help was sent to Glendower.

Philip of Burgundy died in 1404 and three years later his son, John the Fearless, had Louis of Orleans murdered in the streets of Paris. Isabella died and Charles, now duke of Orleans, married the count of Armagnac's daughter; the count took over the lead of the Orleanist party, now known as the Armagnacs. Several attempts at reconciling the two houses failed and by 1411 France was in a state of civil war. The Burgundians, driven out of Paris by the Armagnacs, sought English aid, in return for which they offered to hand over four Flemish towns and marry the duke's daughter to the prince of Wales.

Henry IV was not prepared to commit himself fully. Assisted by only a small English force, the duke of Burgundy forced his way back into Paris; he was accepted only with reluctance by the populace. The king of England, preparing an expedition to France, primarily to defend Calais, sent envoys to the Burgundians, but already the other side was competing for his favour.

The leaders of the Orleanist party sent two embassies to England, offering to help Henry to recover the entire duchy of Aquitaine in full sovereignty in return for his aid. While money was being raised for the expedition against the Burgundians, King Henry decided he was too ill to go himself. The prince of Wales was out of favour, and the king's second son, Thomas – created duke of Clarence – was chosen to command the expedition – but in support of Orleans rather than Burgundy.

The English army landed in the Cotentin in August 1412 and captured a number of small towns. However, the Burgundians and Orleanists made a temporary truce, and Clarence was paid to march his army to Aquitaine. By the time he reached Bordeaux, Henry IV was dead.

Above Charles VI with John the Fearless (far left) and the duke of Orleans (in black).

Below The 'bal des ardents' of 1392; Charles VI, dancing in wild man guise, almost died when Louis of Orleans set fire to the dancers' costumes accidentally (or not). The duchess of Berry wrapped the king in her skirts, saving him.

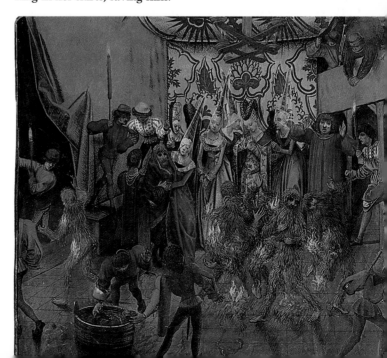

their unfriendly progress through the land, and put a stop to their looting. This was granted, and the English dukes withdrew to Aquitaine, to winter there. The duke of Orleans returned to his estates.

Meanwhile in England, King Henry IV was increasingly disabled, with consequences that one contemporary describes.

Prince Henry, the king's eldest son, and almost all the other lords of England, agreed to ask the king to lay down the crown of England and allow his eldest son to be crowned, because he was so horribly disfigured with leprosy. But when this was put to him by various lords in council, King Henry refused to give way and immediately set out on horseback over much of England, notwithstanding his leprosy.

Robert Fabyan, an alderman and sheriff of London who wrote in Henry VII's reign, gives a colourful account of the last months of Henry IV.

A great council was held at Whitefriars in London on 20 November, at which it was decided amongst other things that certain galleys of war should be made ready for the king's great journey that he intended to make, to visit Our Lord's Holy Sepulchre. Whereupon all haste and speed were made; but after the feast of Christmas, while he was making his prayers at St Edward's shrine to take his leave and speed him upon his journey, Henry IV became so sick that such as were about him feared that he would have died right there. For his comfort they bore him into the abbot's house and lodged him in a chamber, and there upon a pallet laid him before the fire, where he lay a certain time in great agony.

1413

At length, when he had come to himself, not knowing where he was, he asked of such as were about him what place that was. They said to him that it belonged to the abbot of Westminster. As he felt himself so sick, he asked if that chamber had any special name: they answered that it was named Jerusalem. Then said the king, 'Praise be to the father of Heaven, for now I know that I shall die in this chamber, according to the prophecy made about me before, that I should die in Jerusalem.'

And so he made himself ready, and died shortly after, on 20 March, when he had reigned 13 years, 5 months and 21 days, leaving after him four sons and two daughters.

When King Henry was dead, he was conveyed by water to Faversham, and from thence by land to Canterbury, and there interred by the shrine of St Thomas.

The triumphant king

IN May 1410 Henry IV named his councillors in parliament at the request of the commons. For the first time since 1399, the archbishop of Canterbury was omitted. The new list was headed by Henry, prince of Wales, freed by his own successes from the fighting in Wales. Sir Thomas Beaufort became chancellor, and other members included the bishops of Winchester (Henry Beaufort), Durham and Bath, and the earls of Arundel and Westmorland. The two Beauforts, the king's half-brothers, were the prince's closest advisers. The third brother, John, earl of Somerset, had recently died and been replaced in the important post of captain of Calais by Prince Henry.

For some time the king had been suffering from a debilitating and disfiguring disease, and he now withdrew from London to the Midlands. The prince of Wales, with the council, was in charge of government for nearly 18 months, until in November 1411 shortage of money forced the council to summon another parliament.

The king was at Windsor when the parliament was due to meet and wrote to say that he was too ill to reach Westminster in time. This was probably the moment when Bishop Beaufort suggested that Henry IV should be persuaded to abdicate in favour of his son. Certainly, the king realized that he needed to make a great effort to keep his crown and suddenly seemed to recover his former energy. In parliament on 30 November he thanked the prince and other councillors for their services, effectively dismissing them from office. Archbishop Arundel was restored to the chancellorship and the archbishop of York and the bishop of London replaced the Beauforts on the council.

The king's new attitude to parliament was even more surprising. Previously he had submitted to lectures by successive speakers. On this occasion the speaker was Thomas Chaucer, son of the poet Geoffrey Chaucer, elected to the chair for the third time, and, as a cousin of the Beauforts, a follower of the prince. When Chaucer made the usual speaker's protest Henry said that he wanted no novelty in this parliament, but wished to preserve his liberty and prerogatives as fully as his predecessors.

Although mortally ill, Henry was at last triumphant. The Scots had not dared to attack since their boy king James had fallen into English hands in 1406; the Welsh rebels were defeated and the French divided between the dukes of Burgundy and Orleans with both sides seeking English help. Rebellion had ended at home and the continuous carping of his parliaments was stilled. Finally, in the last year of his reign, the prince of Wales sought reconciliation with him.

Henry died on 21 March 1413, aged about 47. The fact that he was still king almost 14 years after landing at Ravenspur, and that after an unquiet reign he was able to leave an undisputed succession to his son, is evidence of his ability and character.

Below *Henry IV's effigy in Canterbury Cathedral.*

Part III

Henry V 1413–1422

Contemporaries saw Henry V's reign as a time of triumph. The English king not only regained many of his lost possessions in France, but also re-established his claim to the French throne. Pious, and a gifted leader who was admired for his military prowess, Henry V united his people behind him in pursuit of glory, his untimely death coming before the financial and political consequences of his ambitions had fully emerged. Unusually for an English king, his heroic exploits attracted several biographers. Tito Livio, an Italian humanist, wrote his florid but valuable version of the king's life in 1437. This work, which begins here with a description of Henry, has been interwoven with Walsingham's well-informed chronicle, which ends with the reign. In addition, there are extracts from an English writer lambasting French duplicity, from a Parisian source, and from a Scottish chronicler who gives a malicious explanation for Henry's death.

(Opposite: Henry V)

As his life was drawing to a close, the old king Henry IV gave due thanks and supplications to God and blessed Prince Henry his son, in the presence of a priest who held communion. Then, as the old king lay dying, the prince, now designated his father's successor, summoned a monk of exemplary purity to whom he confessed his past sins, and from that time his way of life and habits were completely changed. After the death of his father, his life was free from every taint of lustfulness.

Let me describe the prince: he was taller than most men, his face fair and set on a longish neck, his body graceful, his limbs slender but marvellously strong. Indeed, he was miraculously fleet of foot, faster than any dog or arrow. Often he would run with two of his companions in pursuit of the swiftest of does — he himself would always be the one to catch the creature. He had a great liking for music and found enjoyment in hunting, military pursuits and the other pleasures that are customarily allowed to young knights.

In the year 1413, on 4 April, the prince who was at that time twenty-six years old was crowned and anointed as King Henry V, with all the pomp and ceremony that was customary.

Henry V and France

Henry V is most widely remembered for his successes in France. Profiting from the divisions between the Burgundian and Orleanist parties, he mounted three major campaigns and brought large areas of France under English control. The battle of Agincourt came at an early stage in this process, in 1415, and its

importance was as much psychological as military. By the time of Henry's death in 1422 England was the dominant power in France, and her kings looked set to inherit both thrones. Henry V and the house of Lancaster had surpassed even his Plantagenet forbear, Henry II.

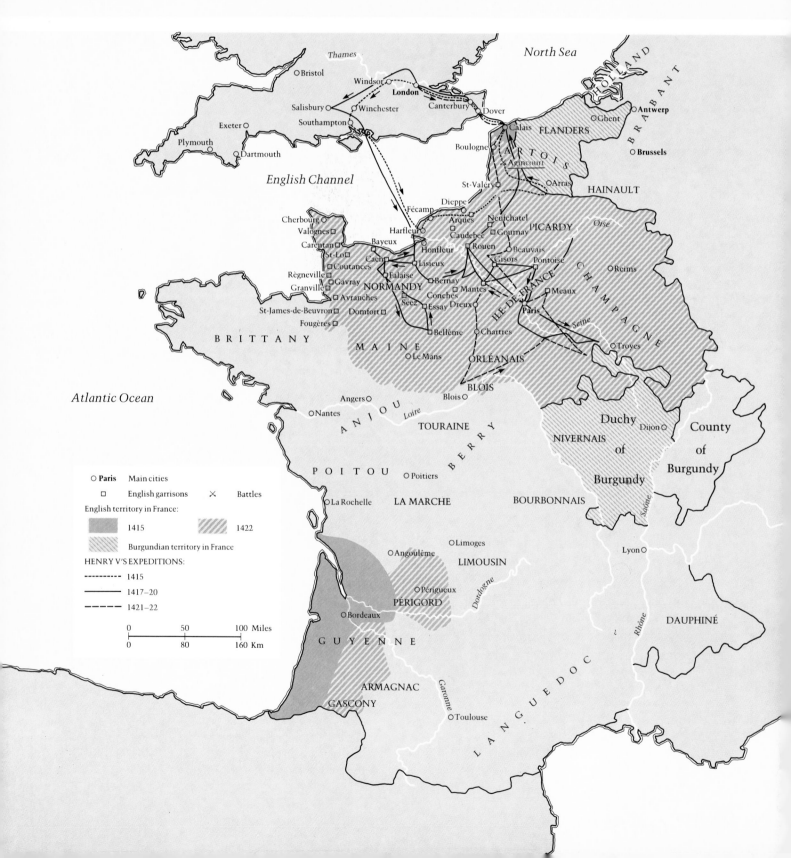

Legend:

○ Paris — Main cities
□ — English garrisons   × — Battles

English territory in France:
— 1415
— 1422
— Burgundian territory in France

HENRY V'S EXPEDITIONS:
- - - - - 1415
———— 1417–20
- - - - 1421–22

0   50   100 Miles
0   80   160 Km

The Holy Roman Empire

In the early 15th century the Holy Roman Empire was far stronger in idea than in reality. It formed a conglomeration of relatively independent states, many controlled by the Church. In the north, the Teutonic knights were continuing their struggle against the heathen Slavs and the Hanseatic league was building up a trading hegemony in the Baltic and the North Sea. In

the south, Venice and Genoa were carving out Mediterranean empires of their own. Holy Roman Emperors were nevertheless men of note, both as kings and princes in their own right, and because of the traditional prestige of their office. It was a major coup for Henry V when in 1416 he won the alliance of the Emperor Sigismund.

After Henry had received the eucharist from the priest, in remembrance of the passion of Our Lord at Eastertide, all the noblemen of the realm swore an oath of loyalty to him. He then gave instructions that, once more important matters had been taken care of, a royal palace should be built at Sheen. He also had two religious houses built on the River Thames, one for the Carthusian Order, to which he gave the name of Bethlehem, and the other, which is known as Syon, for the nuns of St Brigit. He sought and obtained indulgences for both these religious houses from the pope and endowed them with many privileges and a great income.

He then appointed men whom he considered to be honest and fair to be judges throughout his kingdom and selected other necessary officials for posts in all his lands.

Then, when affairs had been properly settled in Ireland, Scotland and Wales, Henry decided to win back the kingdom of France which belonged to him by birthright. First, however, he sought advice in all the schools and universities from men learned in divine and human law whether he might justly and without fear of wrongdoing seek to regain the crown of France by force of arms. Without exception they all agreed he might pursue this plan. The king then sent an embassy to France with instructions to present his claim to a council of the French and, if by any chance the French should refuse him justice, to announce to them that King Henry would come with an army to claim his rights.

The French, understandably, refused. The best-known though fanciful story of this diplomatic encounter is told by John Strecche.

1414

King Henry, conspicuous for the nobility of his character, in the second year of his reign sent to France certain ambassadors in state, fittingly caparisoned: a bishop, two learned doctors, and two knights. They met with the king of France and his council to request that a marriage be solemnly celebrated between Henry, king of England, and

Chosen by God

ONE writer describes Henry V as tall, clean-shaven and tight-lipped, sinewy and agile, more clerical than military in appearance. Determined to impress his subjects as a great king, he insisted on respect for his dignity, and any who insulted or underrated him did so at their peril, as the story of his angry reaction to the dauphin's mocking present of tennis balls was clearly designed to show.

The principal functions of a king were to defend the realm from its enemies and rule his people with justice, and in both Henry V fulfilled the ideal. He relished war, fighting in the thick of the battle at Agincourt and engaging in single combat in a mine beneath the walls of Melun. Like every good commander, he cared for his men and won their confidence; but he was also a stern disciplinarian, who executed on the spot any who disobeyed his commands. He was ready to take risks, and only superb generalship at Agincourt saved the expedition from disaster. However, the conquest of Normandy two years later was achieved by careful military and diplomatic planning, which always put him one move ahead of his adversaries. He studied the art of war and used artillery on a scale hitherto unknown, reducing strongly fortified castles and towns by bombardment and fierce assault.

Henry's ambitions were boundless, and infused with a sense of his destiny. He believed that he, and the English nation, had been chosen by God to humble the pride of the French, and that France and England should be joined together under his rule, bringing the Hundred Years War to an end and uniting christendom in a crusade to the Holy Land.

Opposite below *Henry on his throne, the embodiment of majesty and justice, as his subjects saw him.*

Left *Henry, whilst still prince, receiving a book on the principles of kingship from its author, Thomas Hoccleve. We do not know if this book caused the reformation of Henry's behaviour that Shakespeare described.*

He had no doubts about the rights of his cause – and presented himself to his subjects as the embodiment of justice. Shortly after becoming king Henry V accompanied the Chief Justice to the Midlands to investigate oppression. Throughout his reign, even while he was on campaign in France, humble petitioners brought their complaints to him and received royal writs ordering redress for them – and the shadow of his presence ensured peace and order in England. Stories circulated of how he suppressed feuds between nobles by threatening summarily to hang offenders.

At his accession Henry faced several challenges. The first, in the winter of 1413–14, was a rising of the Lollards under Sir John Oldcastle. A secret Lollard, even while serving under Henry in Wales and later in the king's household, Oldcastle plotted to have the king assassinated and, when he was detected, followed this with open revolt. It was easily suppressed, but the following year, as the king and nobility assembled at Southampton to sail to France, another assassination plot was revealed, implicating some greater nobles. They were mainly old enemies of the house of Lancaster who had never forgiven Henry IV's deposition of Richard II. All were summarily executed.

The failure of both plots strengthened the king's position, for it was seen as evidence of God's protection. At the same time Henry took positive steps to win the nobility's loyalty by fair treatment and bold leadership, while his severe and disciplined piety reinvigorated orthodox religion.

Henry V also breathed new life into royal government. He brought order into the crown's finances by planning his income and expenditure and refusing to live on credit, and scrutinized officials rigorously, punishing corruption and insisting on the crown's rights and dues. As a result, he won the confidence and support of the house of commons whose generous grants of taxes after the victory at Agincourt enabled him to plan the conquest of Normandy in 1417.

The king took the initiative and set the pace in all these spheres, advised and supported by the greater nobility and bishops. In addition to his brothers he could rely on his half-uncles, Thomas Beaufort, duke of Exeter, who defended Harfleur against the French in 1416, and Henry Beaufort, bishop of Winchester, chancellor until 1417, who lent the king large sums for his campaigns. By 1417, with nobility, Church and nation united behind him, Henry V was already becoming a legend.

the noble lady Catherine, daughter of the king of France; but they had only a brief discussion without reaching any conclusion consistent with the honour or convenience of our king, so they returned home. For these Frenchmen, puffed up with pride and lacking in foresight, hurling mocking words at the ambassadors of the king of England, foolishly said to them that as Henry was only a young man, they would send to him little tennis balls to play with and soft cushions to rest on until he should have grown to a man's strength.

When the king heard these words he was greatly moved and troubled in spirit; but he addressed these short, wise, and honest words to those standing round him: 'If God wills, and if my life shall be prolonged with health, in a few months I shall play with such balls in the Frenchmen's courtyards that they will lose the game eventually, and for their game win nothing but grief. And if they shall sleep too long on their cushions in their chambers, I will wake them from their slumbers at dawn by beating on their doors.'

Tito Livio treats of more serious matters.

In the mean time, the heroic King Henry V was concentrating all his resources on preparations for war. His first battle, however, was with heretics and others who were straying from the true doctrines of the Church. For there were at that time in England two knights, Sir John Oldcastle, whom the king himself, before his coronation, had dismissed from his retinue and sent away on account of his heretical views, and Sir John Acton, who was the leader of a sect devoted to a wicked superstition. These men, together with a vast band of followers of similar persuasion, made war against the priests, the Church, the king and the entire kingdom.

The king was at Eltham for the feast of Epiphany when he first heard news of this dreadful crime. He was told that the rebels had already gathered in a field not far from Westminster. The good king, making no public mention of this matter, at once made his way quietly to his palace at Westminster. He summoned thither a large number of men-at-arms who made an assault on the heretics and overcame them almost without a struggle.

An Englishman's castle

DURING the late 14th and the 15th centuries in England, well-to-do homes became less and less castellated and castles more and more like homes.

The great hall, with attendant kitchens and offices, the main living space in a castle, was usually placed along one of the walls of the inner court. When John of Gaunt acquired the effectively and thoroughly fortified castle of Kenilworth in Warwickshire in 1390, his principal addition to the late 12th- and early 13th-century building was a new great hall. Raised over an undercroft, and reached by a grand external flight of stairs, it was rivalled in span and splendour only by Richard II's hall in Westminster Palace.

Unlike Kenilworth, Bodiam Castle in Sussex, constructed in the late 14th century for Sir Edward Dallingrigge, keeper of the Tower of London, occupied a new site, and was built to a single coherent design. It reveals more clearly than most buildings the ideal residence of a major courtier of Richard II's reign. Sir Edward acquired a licence to crenellate in 1385, and Bodiam is in many ways

The charming manor house of Ightham Mote, also in Kent, is almost entirely unfortified except for its picturesque moat. The 14th-century hall was surrounded over the following two centuries by additional wings so that the building closed in on itself around a courtyard.

Crosby Hall is a rare and splendid example of a late medieval town house, which was removed from its original site in the city of London and reconstructed, lock, stock and barrel, in Chelsea. Originally built by Sir John Crosby, a wealthy city merchant, between 1466 and 1475, it stands above a brick vaulted undercroft, and has a gilded timber roof with elaborate pendant bosses, and a richly mullioned and stone-vaulted oriel window.

The finest of all merchants' private houses is in Bourges in France and was built for Jacques Coeur, banker to the French crown, and the dominant force in Mediterranean trade. It is irregularly set around a courtyard and its most striking feature is its sculpture. Internal fireplaces are designed like castles, with courtly ladies and armed lords peeping between the crenellations; or like merchants' houses, with the merchant and his wife playing chess at an open window. Above the gatehouse, realistic, life-size figures of Jacques and his wife lean out of *trompe-l'oeil* windows in perpetual stony welcome.

Above The south front of Penshurst Place, Kent, showing a decidedly domestic profile despite the crenellations.

Right The entrance to the chapel staircase in the French royal banker Jacques Coeur's house in Bourges, with carved figures over the doorway.

everything a castle should be. Based on early 13th-century French castles, it is fundamentally a rectangular enclosure with towers over the gatehouses and at the corners; living accommodation is built up against the enclosing walls. Attackers approaching from the seaward side would plunge through a decorative and undefendable gatetower into the lord's hall. Bodiam Castle was surrounded by a wide moat, and its castellated perfection would have come into its own as a setting for water-borne pageants or mock sea-battles.

Penshurst Place in Kent, by contrast, was originally built by Sir John Pulteney, lord mayor of London, in the 1340s, as a grand manor house with surrounding fortified walls, which were strengthened in the 1430s, when Penshurst belonged to the duke of Bedford.

The rebels were seized and put to death. The king's men crucified their captives, except for the leaders who were kept in chains for many days and afflicted with the torture they deserved. Thus the first great victory of the prince was gained for Christ and God's Church against evil heretics.

Meanwhile, as Walsingham relates, attempts were afoot to heal another danger to the Church – the papal schism.

At Michaelmas, Henry Chichele, the new archbishop of Canterbury, held a great council in London to discuss banning the privilege of exemptions bought from the Roman popes, which they had enjoyed until then. At this council men were chosen to represent the English clergy at a general council to be held at Constance, a town in Germany.

Thanks to the laudable efforts of Sigismund, the king of the Romans and Hungary, a most Christian man, who, when he was elected emperor of Germany, refused the crown until he knew without doubt who was to be preferred as pope, almost all the wisest bishops and prelates of the whole of christendom, and countless other clergymen, gathered there, including some very venerable prelates from England who were of powerful intellect and famed for their godliness.

When these men, together with the colleges of cardinals once belonging to Gregory and Pedro de Luna, and other prelates and doctors distinguished by their godliness, met at Constance, Gregory renounced the papacy, on condition that Pedro de Luna and Baldassare Cossa, who had respectively assumed the titles of Pope Benedict XIII in Avignon and Pope John XXIII in Rome, did the same. But John would not co-operate for some time, until he was advised and persuaded by the emperor, and in due course he agreed to renounce his claims, like the others. After this, indescribable joy broke out among all present, for they thought that at last there was an end to the discord.

Tito Livio describes how the king's preparations for war with France were marred by the discovery of a plot against him.

The end of the great schism

THE driving power behind the Council of Constance was Sigismund, king of Hungary and emperor designate of the Holy Roman Empire, who persuaded John XXIII, Alexander V's successor, to convoke the second general council since the start of the great schism. It met in the free city of Constance in November 1414, lasted until 1418, and was attended by cardinals, bishops, learned doctors and many other clerics, all of whom came as members of delegations from Italy, Germany, France, England and, later, Spain.

The council first proceeded against heresy, condemning the ideas of John Wycliffe, and sentencing two Bohemian thinkers, John Hus and Jerome of Prague, to death by burning. Of dubious legality, these killings roused heretical opinion in Bohemia and provoked civil war.

Next, the council enacted a series of decrees, the first of which – *Haec sancta* (its opening words) – was passed because the pope had absconded. John XXIII left Constance in the belief that the council had no legality without him, and would come to an end. *Haec sancta*, however, declared that the council 'holds power directly from Christ; and that everyone of whatever estate or dignity he be, even if papal, is obliged to obey it in those things which belong to the faith'. This was passed on 6 April 1415.

On 9 October 1417 another decree, *Frequens*, laid down the intervals at which future councils were to be held. The following month the schism was formally healed when the council deposed all existing popes and elected Martin V. He eventually commanded the obedience of all christendom except Scotland and the county of Armagnac. Church reform remained on the agenda but was set aside for the moment.

Above *John XXIII rewards a supporter.*

Left *Pope Martin V, who supplanted him.*

Sigismund and the English delegation had wanted to tackle reform before the papal election, but were thwarted by the hostility of the French and Italians in particular. Sigismund lost a valuable ally with the death of Robert Hallum, bishop of Salisbury and president of the English delegation, on 4 September 1417, and many delegates were anxious to bring the protracted business to a close.

The new pope, Martin V, was a conservative Roman aristocrat, and although he complied with *Frequens* by summoning the councils of Pavia (1423) and Basle (1431), he was no reformer. His chief preoccupations were augmenting papal revenues and reconstructing the papal state in central Italy. His re-establishment of the papacy as a power on the Italian political scene was a remarkable achievement, but he can be criticized for the methods he used – diplomacy, cunning, nepotism – and also because he made the papacy into just another Italian princedom.

With Martin V's election a great experiment in church government came to an end. During the Council of Constance the medieval Church had been more demo-cratic than at any other time in its history, and if *Frequens* had been observed faithfully it would have become a constitutional monarchy. Instead it reverted to the ab-solutist government which had existed before 1378.

1415

During an inspection of the army, a great conspiracy was discovered, led by three men. One of these was a kinsman of the king, an earl; the second was Henry Grey, who held an important position among the king's councillors; the third was Thomas Scrope, a knight who, until this time, had ever been an ornament of chivalry. When they had been arrested and confessed their crimes, they were punished according to the just custom of the kingdom.

In the third year of the king's reign, on 14 June, the king and all his army set off on their campaign against the French. They embarked on a thousand ships and, on the third night, they landed at Clef du Caus in Normandy.

Having taken Harfleur, the English marched towards Calais. The French army barred their way, and both sides drew up in battle formation at Agincourt.

On 25 October, at dawn, the most Christian of kings, Henry V, led forth his army in battle array, after his priests had duly said prayers and supplications and sung matins and masses. He gave instructions that many horses and a large quantity of equipment should be left in the charge of a small garrison, in the hamlet where he and his men had spent the night, and led forth only arms and men. The king trusted to divine guidance, God and justice, and behold, fortune offered him a safe position and a field protected in the rear by the hamlet where the army had passed the night and to the sides by thorny hedges. These shielded the king's army from the enemy's ambush or attack.

Henry himself was clad in fair and shining armour and wore a helmet topped by a golden crown. His surcoat was decorated with precious stones, which formed the coats of arms of the kingdoms of England and France, and he rode on a white horse. His men rode upon most noble steeds with golden harnesses, the richest reins and saddle-cloths embroidered with the arms of both England and France, following the king's example.

The Royal Navy

HENRY V was the first English monarch to recognize the need for a permanent royal navy always ready for action; previous kings had relied on their subjects to provide ships and men when a fleet was required.

When Henry became king in 1413 he inherited half a dozen vessels from his father, and immediately began to add to them by purchase, construction and capture. When he embarked on the conquest of Normandy in 1417 there were about 30 king's ships. Chief among them were four great vessels which had been constructed to overcome the carracks hired from Genoa by France. The titanic *Grace Dieu* with a displacement of 1,400 tons was a symbol of the king's determination but never seaworthy; but the *Jesus, Holigost* and *Trinity Royal*, with displacements of 1,000, 740 and 540 tons, were more useful. No less than seven of Henry's vessels were carracks of some 500 tons each, captured from the Genoese in 1416–17. Several balingers were also constructed. These small, easily manoeuvrable galleys could operate in river mouths and even far upstream as well as on the open sea.

Even with a fleet like this Henry could not win control of the Channel – medieval ships could remain at sea for only a few weeks before returning to port for repairs and more provisions. Sea battles were rare and ships could not hold set positions for long. However, the very possession of a fleet and the organization to maintain it where others had none, was a substantial advantage. By mounting constant patrols Henry was able to deter French raids on English merchant shipping and coasts and, when he invaded France in 1415 and 1417, the fleet enabled him to secure his lines of communication with Normandy. It was necessary to requisition merchant vessels to carry the men in these invasion armies, but for the day-to-day business of keeping the seas the king's ships were more than adequate. In 1416 they defeated the Franco-Genoese flotilla blockading Harfleur, and repeated the feat in the following year.

The French naval threat in the Channel ended when the northern coastline came under the control of Henry and Philip of Burgundy, and, above all, when the great French naval base at Rouen was captured in 1419. Very soon, however, the English fleet lay idle and rotting, its job done; funds were already stretched, and it made sense to dismantle the fleet. The process started before Henry's death in 1422, and was completed soon after. When the situation worsened, after 1435, as French seapower built up, the government, with no money to rebuild the fleet, depended once again on the resources of its subjects.

It was about half a century before an English king once again began raising a royal fleet. By 1480 Edward IV had

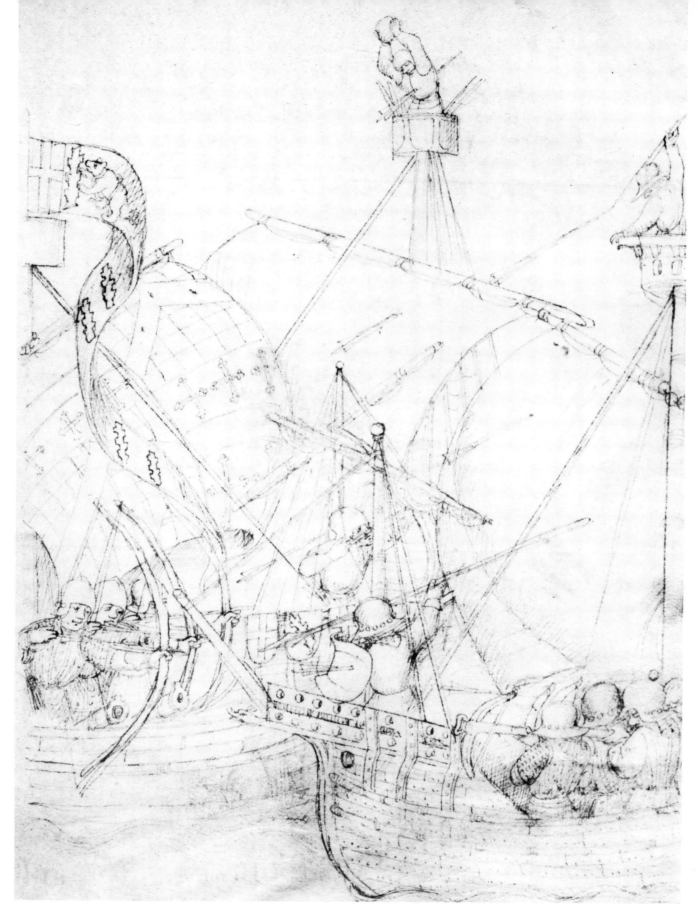

gradually increased the number of his ships to seven, and re-created the organization to maintain them. Their chief task, as before, was to mount regular patrols and to protect merchant shipping, like wool convoys and the North Sea fishing fleet. They were also used in military action, as in the 1475 French campaign. The number of

Above *A contemporary sea fight.*

vessels increased to 15 as a result of the war with Scotland in 1481, and these were used with success by Richard III during his brief reign. However, they could not prevent his rival Henry Tudor from landing in Wales in 1485.

Thus equipped for war, the invincible king addressed his men to raise their spirits for the impending battle.

'Be brave in heart and fight with all your might. God and the justice of our cause will be our protection and will ensure that all, or at least a great part, of those proud enemies whom you see before you now will be delivered into our hands and be at our mercy.'

The French, however, put such faith in their own numbers, in their mighty horses and in their fair and splendid arms that several of the great princes left behind their knights, their new recruits and their retinues and several left their banners and standards and swept into battle like men certain of victory.

Among these was the duke of Brabant who, although his standard had not yet been brought to him, gave orders that a banner be removed from a trumpet and attached to a lance to serve as a standard, as soon as the battle line was ready.

The French line of battle was drawn up with all possible soldierly order and was vastly superior in numbers to the English. For the French warriors were more than thirty deep, one behind the other. Indeed the battlefield was not wide enough to accommodate such a body of men. The English, on the other hand, were drawn up only four deep at the most.

The French army also boasted a thousand knights armed with lances, on each wing, who had instructions to break up the English battle line by a sudden assault. In addition, they had a great many guns which could send forth a thick hail of stones, great, little and middling, at the English warriors.

The king called a council of his advisers to discuss what plan might be best — for a large portion of the all too brief day was now past. It was their opinion that the English should advance, since delay would bring many dangers in a hostile country where they were protected by no treaty, particularly when their supplies were running so low, and the dangers would increase the longer

Agincourt

A T the battle of Agincourt an exhausted, hungry and heavily outnumbered English army utterly routed a fresh, well-provisioned French force perhaps ten times its size and inflicted such heavy losses that a shocked Parisian writer exclaimed, 'Never since Christ was born has anyone done so much damage to France.'

The campaign which led to this encounter began on 14 August 1415, when Henry V landed near Harfleur, at the mouth of the Seine estuary. His intention was to capture the port as a base for operations against Paris, but when the town capitulated six weeks later, his army was in a pitiful state. Dysentery – the dreaded 'bloody flux', brought on by marshy, insanitary conditions and aggravated by a diet of unripe fruit and dubious shellfish – had killed or incapacitated a third of his force, so there was no longer any question of striking inland. The only practical course was to garrison Harfleur and return home.

But Henry decided to march through French territory to the nearest English-held town – Calais, over 150 miles north by the shortest route. The English army soon ran into difficulties. Forced to make a long detour to cross the Somme, its spirits were already at a low ebb when, on 24 October, it sighted an immense French host ('like a countless swarm of locusts') blocking its road to Calais.

Two totally contrasting armies encamped that night – Henry's men in silence, the French noisily dicing for the noble prisoners they expected to take. The latter numbered some 50,000 or 60,000, while the English mustered some 5,000 to 6,000, five-sixths of whom were bowmen. The rest were armoured men-at-arms. Only about a fifth of the French force were archers; their main strength was in armoured men, including a large number of nobles and knights.

Early in the morning of 25 October 1415, the two armies faced each other across muddy fields, shut in on either side by the woods round the villages of Agincourt and Tramecourt. The English formed a single dismounted line; three small groups of armoured men were interspersed with wedges of archers, each wedge protected against cavalry by a hedgehog of sharpened stakes. There were so many French, however, that the enclosing woods forced them into three divisions, one behind the other. Most of the great nobles crowded into the leading ranks, anxious for a share in the glory. Like the English, the French were on foot, but with squadrons of armoured cavalry on each flank, ready to ride down the archers.

The French remained stationary for nearly three hours – 'God knows why, not I,' remarked an English eyewitness – and Henry eventually advanced first, halting within bowshot to shower the enemy with arrows. This

provoked a disastrous French cavalry charge: horsemen who had not been shot down or impaled on stakes galloped off in panic and disordered the front rank of their foot soldiers as they trudged through the mud to attack Henry's line. In an attempt to avoid the wedges of archers, this vanguard crowded into three jostling columns. The sheer weight of their first impact drove the English men-at-arms back 'a spear's length', but the French impetus was soon halted, and Henry's archers began to pour arrows into their flanks. Too tightly packed together to wield their weapons, the French stumbled over their own fallen casualties and blocked their own progress with man-high heaps of the living and dead. The English archers then ran in, stabbing and clubbing at the struggling mass.

The English took many high-ranking prisoners at this stage, including the dukes of Orleans and Bourbon and the marshal of France. However, when a new French assault threatened, Henry ordered his men to slay prisoners of lesser rank, lest they turn on their captors. Reluctant to lose so many ransoms, the English were slow to obey, and the king ordered a band of archers to do the grisly work. The half-hearted new attack by the French now materialized, but was swiftly turned into a wholesale flight: to their astonishment, the English had won the battle of Agincourt.

Among the French dead were three French dukes, the constable of France, nine counts, 90 lords and some 5,000 knights and gentlemen. English losses were incomparably lighter – the overweight Edward, duke of York (suffocated inside his armour), one earl, six or seven knights, and perhaps 500 others.

Tactically the battle achieved nothing, for Henry had to begin his attack on France anew in 1417. Morally and strategically, however, its effect was overwhelming. Agincourt wiped out half a generation of French nobility, afflicted the survivors with the shame and demoralization of total defeat – and paved the way for Henry's subsequent triumphs in France.

they remained there. The French, however, since they were in their own country and faced with no other enemies besides the English army, would gain strength and reinforcements from any delay.

Three French knights approached the king who asked them to inform their leaders that the English wished to engage them in battle immediately. The knights replied that the French would join battle at their own pleasure, not when the English decided.

King Henry listened to the French noblemen and said to them: 'Return hence to your camp then. But take care lest we arrive there before you.' Then turning to his men, he cried: 'Let the standards advance!' As soon as his troops were drawn up into their proper battle array, the king roused his men to fight, deciding to attack the enemy at once.

Then the whole of the English army fell on their knees and took up crumbs of soil into their mouths. They left behind all that they had carried on their belts and, with a great shout, they flew towards the enemy in a furious assault, each man carrying nothing but his arms and a sharp stake.

They met with the French army at twenty paces from the town of Agincourt; a great chorus of trumpets urged the hearts of all to battle and they came to grips with the enemy.

Then the battle blazed: man fell upon man. Neither side would give an inch but after three hours of fighting in the same spot every man either slew his opponent or was slain by him. No one thought of spoils, only of victory. No captives were taken and many met their deaths. In short, countless French warriors found they had been led – by fate and by their own pride – not to battle but to slaughter. However, when many of the French had gone to their deaths and an English victory seemed assured, the English stopped killing their enemy and took them captive instead.

A great many princes, lords and noblemen and the noble King Henry himself did not cease from the labour of battle, nor did the king fail his men by seeking to avoid dangers to his own life but, like

Sweet English melody

WHEN Henry V landed at Harfleur in August 1415 he was accompanied by his household, among them the men and boys of the royal chapel. This was not because of his piety or because of his love of music. It was simply that great men travelled with large establishments.

The sick lists record the names of John Dammett, John Burrell and Nicholas Sturgeon, 'chaplains' – all of whom recovered from their illnesses and went on to successful careers. Dammett may have composed one of the motets for the Agincourt thanksgiving in London later that year, Burrell received a stipend from the abbey of Meaux as his share of the victory spoils. Works by all three feature in the 'Old Hall' music manuscript, which was compiled for the royal chapel in the 1410s and includes the two 'Roy Henry' pieces – attributed to the king himself.

The English had a reputation as musicians. On its way to the Council of Constance (1414–18), the delegation led by the bishops of Norwich and Lichfield delighted the congregation in Cologne Cathedral with singing, 'better than any heard these thirty years'. A chronicler at the council judged only one church service, out of the hundreds given during the sessions, as worth mentioning:

the English celebration of the feast of St Thomas of Canterbury in 1416. 'They began the celebration early in the morning with great ringing of bells, burning candles and with singing in the sweet English manner.' Also in 1416, the German embassy with Sigismund at Canterbury distributed farewell thank-you cards to 'Blessid Inglond, ful of melody'; while Italian music collections are full of English pieces.

The early 15th century was the only time in history that English musicians helped shape the direction of European music. Henry V's victory at Agincourt, celebrated in the 'Agincourt Carol', meant that a generation of English nobles and churchmen were regular visitors to northern France – and with them came their music.

In Europe the *'contenance Angloise'* was hailed as a new art. The leaders of the school were John Dunstable, a chaplain to John, duke of Bedford, the king's brother and regent in Normandy, and Leonel Power, who probably served Henry Beaufort, bishop of Winchester. Their contributions were in two fundamental areas. The 'sprightly consonance' of the English style produced a sweet, continuous euphony, quite unlike the stark chords and frequent dissonances of the contemporary continental style. Using the intervals of the common chord, it provided the basis for harmonic music from that time on. Its impact was long remembered: as late as 1581, the musician Vincenzo Galilei, father of Galileo, traced the music of his day back to Dunstable.

Power, it seems, added a new formal device to this bewitching sound. He gave a sense of unity to the separate movements of the mass by basing each on the same theme – for example, a fragment of plainsong. Simple in concept, the 'cyclic mass' opened rich possibilities; the development of simple themes became a basic technique in later music.

Many people would have been unaware of such technicalities but would be impressed by the sheer size of an English choir. Heard at events like the celebrations marking the treaty of Troyes, or Henry's wedding to Catherine of France, they brought a new dimension to choral singing. At a time when church choirs rarely exceeded 20 voices and the chapel of the dukes of Burgundy – Europe's most splendid – numbered 30, Henry's chapel royal employed 32 men and 16 boys.

English secular music was equally highly regarded – John Bedyngham's love-song *'O rosa bella'*, found in many continental manuscripts, was used by later Flemish composers as a mass theme. Not until the 20th century did English music again win such prestige.

Opposite Various 15th-century instruments, most of them for use in secular music.

Below 'Gloria' by 'Roy Henry', a vocal piece possibly written by Henry V himself and certainly emanating from the Chapel Royal.

an unvanquished lion, he fought against the enemy with great ardour, receiving many blows on his helmet and armour.

At last an English victory seemed won, for the French army was scattered, slain and prostrate, but suddenly another enemy force, no smaller in size than the first, appeared, ready to fight and thinking that the English would be exhausted after the long and dreadful battle. The English were greatly outnumbered even by their French prisoners and were much afraid lest they should have to fight again against their own captives as well as the new army, even though they had already killed so many rich and noble Frenchmen.

King Henry very wisely sent messengers to the new French army, saying that they must either join battle at once or else retreat, and warning them that if they waited or joined battle the French captives would all be put to the sword and that they themselves would quickly be taken captive by the English: no mercy would be shown.

The royal message was taken at once to the French and they, fearing the strength of the English and thinking that they and their men might come to harm, retreated, covered in shame. And Henry V gave many thanks to God for his great victory.

The outstanding success of the English army under the brilliant leadership of Henry V was celebrated in the Agincourt Carol, composed soon after the battle, and giving thanks to God for the King's great victory.

In this battle were slain among the French the most noble dukes of Alençon, of Bar and of Brabant, and many others to the number of about ten thousand. The captives included the dukes of Orleans and Bourbon. Of the English, the duke of York, the earl of Suffolk and about a hundred others were killed in the first encounter.

Since evening was now approaching, the most victorious king took the advice of his councillors and went with his army to that same hamlet where they had spent the previous night. There, they

Poet and feminist

IN the later Middle Ages poetry was not the esoteric literary form that it has since become, but was essential to educated and aristocratic living, providing material for competitions and a form for private journals and correspondence. Professional writers like Guillaume de Machaut and Eustache Deschamps were extraordinarily prolific – Deschamps wrote over 80,000 lines, including 1,017 ballades – and even a professional soldier such as Marshal Boucicault found time, in the midst of the Hundred Years War, to organize a poetic competition on the theme of fidelity and inconstancy in love; the collection which resulted is known as the *Cent Ballades*. Although much of this vast production was mere versification, certain poets produced original and distinctive work.

One of these was Christine de Pisan, who, in 1431, was nearing the end of a literary career that had brought her the admiration of fellow poets and the favour of princes. Born around 1364 in Venice of Italian parents, she was brought to France as a young girl, married at 15 to a rising royal secretary and tragically widowed at 25 with three children and very little money. Desperate, she was obliged, in her own words, to 'become a man' and earn her living by writing; originally she had written poetry simply to console herself in her sad loss. She needed the support of a wealthy patron, and found it at the lively court of the king's brother, Louis of Orleans, and, later, at the Burgundian court of Philip the Bold and John the Fearless.

Christine was known to her contemporaries for her scholarly allegorical works – *The Mutation of Fortune, The Long Road of Learning* – and tender lyrics (*One Hundred Ballades of a Lover and his Lady*). Today, however, she is remembered chiefly for her energetic, indefatigable championship of women. In her lyrics, she often develops the idea that women are obliged by society to pay too high a price for love outside marriage, while in her longer mythological and allegorical works she frequently takes men to task for slandering women. She was a polemicist prepared to attack anti-feminist attitudes, and two of her most significant allegorical works, the *Book of the City of Ladies* and the *Book of the Three Virtues*, concern women's importance in history and the ways in which women of every class could learn to contribute usefully to their society. Appropriately, her last work, *The Tale of Joan of Arc*, was a celebration of the career of someone whose exploits must have confirmed Christine in her belief that the spirit of the great women of the past could live again in her own day.

Charles of Orleans was the son of Christine's first patron. A princely and gifted poet, his early life was marked by the tragedy of his father's assassination and he

Above *Christine de Pisan presents a copy of her works to Isabella of Bavaria.*

Left *Charles of Orleans, captive, dreams of his native country in his work.*

spent 25 years as a prisoner in England after the battle of Agincourt in 1415. Like Christine, he possessed an individual talent that distinguishes him from the mass of his contemporaries. He had sworn allegiance to love while still very young and spent a large part of his time in England composing a series of ballades to his mistress; it is not known whether she was real or fictional. On learning of her death, he asked to be released from his obligation to love, and his later work became increasingly introspective. His use of allegory for psychological analysis is profoundly original: his poems are peopled by an enormous cast of characters (Amour, Aventure, Désir, Espoir, Confort, Tristesse . . .) who comfort or attack him according to their nature and his mood. Although apparently slight, Charles's poetry is distinguished by its polished, refined beauty, which ensures it a place in anthologies and the French school curriculum.

135

discovered that their baggage and the many horses and other things which they had left had been pillaged by the French during the battle. The king dined, served at table by the noblest of the French captives.

The Orleanists, also known as the Armagnac party, were greatly weakened by Agincourt, and their leader, the Dauphin Charles, was gradually to lose popular support in Paris, Picardy and Champagne. Matters were made worse when Sigismund, king of the Romans, decided to support the Lancastrian claims in France.

1416

Then the invincible and forever august King Sigismund of the Romans, hearing that the arms and majesty of France and England had lately been involved in armed dispute, sent messengers to both kingdoms announcing his intentions to mediate between them, and set forth for France where he was received with all due ceremony. He discussed how the French might enter into a peace with the English and persuaded them to send an embassy, headed by the archbishop of Reims. This accompanied him on his journey to England, together with his most noble retinue – including the illustrious duke of Berry and many other eminent princes, lords and gentlemen, together with about a thousand knights.

King Henry V provided three hundred large ships to convey the most noble King Sigismund and his retinue to England. Their voyage was calm and favoured by a following wind towards Dover, where they were welcomed by princes of royal blood and other prominent Englishmen.

When King Sigismund came into the outskirts of London, the most victorious King Henry came forth to meet him with all regal pomp, attended by his brothers, their highnesses the dukes of Clarence, Bedford and Gloucester, and other members of the royal family. The two kings greeted one another with the utmost gentility, each exemplary in his graciousness. They then progressed to the city where a vast crowd of people was gathered, eager to see the foreign king. Indeed, those most

Birth of the Renaissance in France

CHARLES V, king of France from 1364 to 1380, and his brothers Philip the Bold, duke of Burgundy, and John, duke of Berry, were remarkably generous patrons of the arts, famous for commissioning only the best artists and craftsmen.

Paris was still a lively artistic centre in the late 14th century, with established traditions, particularly in manuscript illumination, and Charles chose Jean Bondol, a gifted illuminator, as court painter. Bondol drew with all the grace of the Parisian tradition, but was also conversant with current trends; he included a lively, well-observed portrait of his patron in the *Bible Historiale* of 1371.

Although Paris after Charles's death in 1380 lost its artistic pre-eminence to John of Berry's capital of Bourges and to Philip the Bold's great dukedom of Burgundy, it remained an important centre for book production. The Boucicault master worked there early in the 15th century, painting the *Boucicault Hours* – from which he takes his name – for Marshal Boucicault, and the *Dialogues de Pierre Salmon*, which contains a fascinating early interior 'conversation piece' showing Charles VI talking in the informality of his bedchamber.

Jean Fouquet (1415–80) was also based in Paris. Court painter to Louis XI, he was an accomplished book illuminator, but had been to Italy as a boy and was also influenced by the great Flemish painters, van Eyck and van der Weyden; paintings such as the portrait of Etienne Chevalier, treasurer of Charles VII, and St Stephen (*c.* 1451) are 'Renaissance' in form and content.

The court of Burgundy was based at Dijon until 1419. Melchior Broederlam of Ypres was court painter, but the sculpture of Claus Sluter, especially Philip the Bold's tomb, and the famous Well of Moses in the charterhouse of Champmol, is probably the finest testimony to early Burgundian patronage.

When the court moved to Bruges, Philip's grandson, Philip the Good, employed Jan van Eyck as court painter. Van Eyck also worked for wealthy merchants, while his younger contemporary, Rogier van der Weyden, was unconnected with the court. The works of both men could hold their own against the most advanced paintings of Renaissance Italy.

Left *The Fall of the Rebel Angels, from the* Très Riches Heures.

Below *A more mundane subject; February from the* Très Riches Heures *calendar.*

Opposite *Jean Fouquet's portrait of his royal master Charles VII of France.*

Overleaf *Two examples of Jean Fouquet's brilliance and imagination; both from the Hours of Etienne Chevalier (c. 1445). On the left, the martyrdom of Ste Apolline; on the right, an adoration of the Magi.*

John, duke of Berry, the least active politically of the three brothers, was the most active and lavish patron. He collected anything that was collectable and lived more grandly in his many castles than any other contemporary European prince. Two superb books are testimony to his artistic discernment and magnificent life-style: the *Très Belles Heures du Duc de Berry*, commissioned from Jacquemart de Hesdin before 1402; and the *Très Riches Heures*, painted by the three de Limbourg brothers between 1413 and 1416. The latters' calendar paintings capture life at the most elegant court in Europe, and, while they show the duke feasting in state and riding out to hunt, they depict his peasants with equal conviction. This perfect courtly world was as evanescent as it appears in the paintings: in 1416, John and the de Limbourg brothers died in an outbreak of plague. Bourges's brief prominence as an artistic centre was over.

In Burgundy, Philip the Bold's descendants inherited his good taste and interest in patronage – and their artistic and political intervention extended over both Burgundy and Flanders, with important centres at Dijon, Bruges and Ghent. Flanders was probably the most heavily urbanized area in contemporary Europe, and artists working there could depend on the patronage of rich merchants, including foreigners from England or Italy, as well as on ducal support.

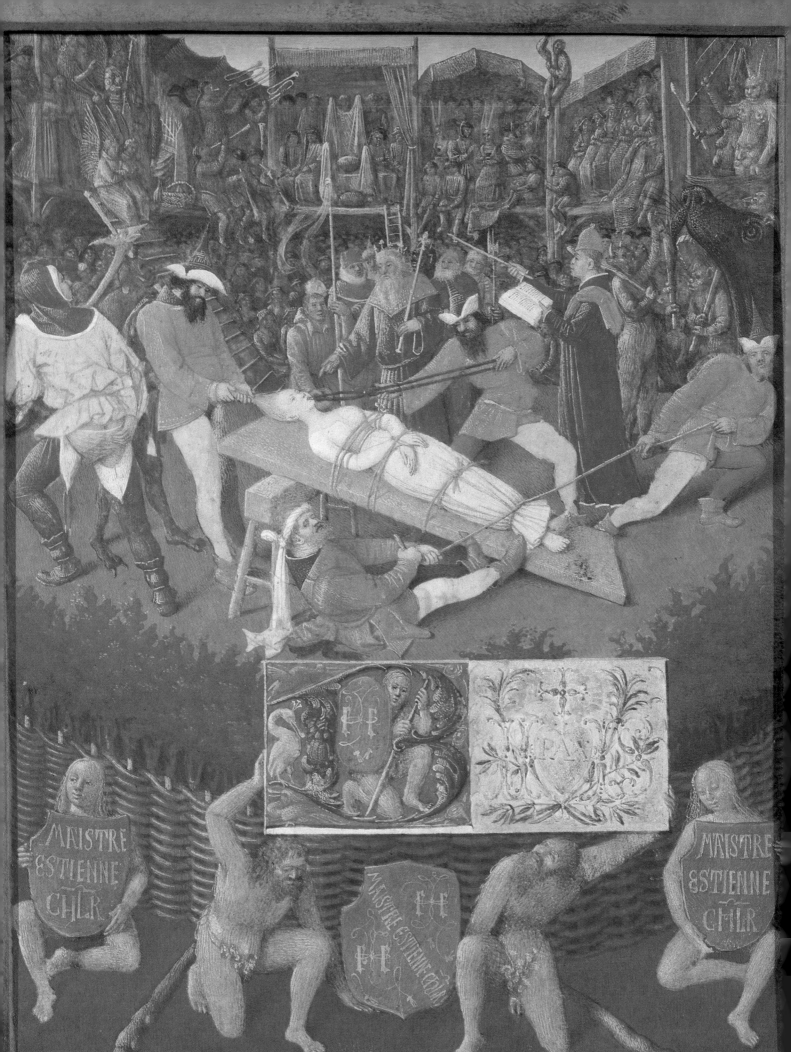

invincible kings and the other royal princes who attended them were scarcely able to make their way even through the broadest squares, so great was the throng of onlookers.

Finally they arrived at the palace of Westminster where all the king's treasures were displayed with royal magnificence and splendour in honour of the visit of the king of the Romans.

King Sigismund then began negotiations for a treaty. A council was arranged and King Henry, in order that the many and grave dangers of war and the damage that it brought should be avoided, proposed to the French ambassadors that, if they were to cede to him whatever had been in the possession of his great-grandfather, Edward, in 1360, together with those lands which he himself, enduring fearful dangers, had lately acquired, he would abandon the war. But the French refused to comply with any of his proposals and returned home to France, their resolve hardened.

Sigismund, king of the Romans, and Henry, king of England and France, during this time developed such mutual affection and regard that King Sigismund, at his own request, was admitted to the Order of the Knights of the Garter.

Walsingham, like Tito Livio, observes that despite the pomp and ceremony, Sigismund's visit did nothing to heal the breach between the French and English kingdoms.

All summer long it was thought that peace had been established between the two countries by means of the emperor's mediation. But the French refused to co-operate, and the peace negotiations were postponed, with the result that the French collected a fleet of cargo ships and galleys to harass the English. John, duke of Bedford, the king's brother, was sent against them with a powerful army. On 15 August he entered into battle with them, and captured three cargo ships, one hulk and four balingers. Three other cargo ships escaped; but one of these ran on to the sands and sank. Another large cargo ship went down off Southampton, and eight hundred men on board perished with her.

In order to display his heartfelt wish for peace, King Henry sailed in person to Calais, to remove from the French all grounds for recriminations: they had said that it was not their fault that they were not offering him an easy path to peace. When Henry met the emperor once more and learned that nothing could be got out of the French except the usual treachery and deceit, he poured scorn on their lies. However, he did make peace between the emperor and the duke of Burgundy, who had fallen out, after which the duke paid homage to the emperor.

Then the duke of Gloucester, the king's youngest brother, together with the king's vast household, escorted the emperor as far as Dordrecht, where he remunerated the English on an imperial scale, from the greatest to the humblest.

The scene changes once more to the Council of Constance, where the assembled cardinals are planning the election of a new pope.

1417

On the last day of October, the bishop of Winchester, Henry Beaufort, arrived at the council, intending to go on a pilgrimage to Jerusalem once the election of a pope had taken place. So great were his powers of eloquent persuasion that he stirred the cardinals into making peace and preparing themselves more speedily for the pope's election. They rapidly prepared the room for the conclave, and furnished it with beds for the cardinals and for the other electors who were to join them.

It was ordained by a decree of the council that six men should be chosen from every nation present, to enter the conclave with the cardinals.

From England came the bishop of London and the bishops of Bath, Norwich and Lichfield, the abbot of York and Thomas Polton, dean of York. Every nation wrote down the names of its representatives on a piece of paper and sealed it with wax, and these people entered the conclave on 8 November.

When they had gone inside, a layman brought in all the pieces of paper, sealed with wax, to the vice-chancellery in the conclave. With his arms bare to the elbow, he put all the pieces of paper on the table. Then a decree was made about the food that should be given to those in conclave: they should have bread and wine, one kind of pottage every day, and on one day a single kind of meat and on the other day one kind of fish.

Then the emperor, thirteen dukes and the important men of the city of Constance swore on the Bible that they would faithfully protect the conclave from outside disturbance, and that no food should be allowed in other than what was permitted. After this, the emperor in person searched the whole room, and locked the door after himself with two locks. At the entrance to the room a square opening had been made, one foot long and one foot wide, through which food could be passed for those who were shut inside, for however many days they were in conclave. The abbot of Bury St Edmunds and Prior John of Clerkenwell were appointed to taste the food of the English delegation. Then, when it had been passed to those inside, the opening was shut with three locks.

The assembled dignitaries began to confer about the business in hand. Some nominated the bishop of Winchester and some the bishop of London. Quite a few named the French cardinal. Nothing was decided on the first or the second day. On 11 November, however, which was St Martin's day, early in the morning the bishop of London arrived, and declared these words in front of the assembled cardinals: 'I, Richard, bishop of London, vote for Cardinal Oddo Colonna my lord.' As soon as they had heard this, everyone present suddenly, by the grace of God, agreed on the same person. So they stripped Cardinal Colonna of all his clothes and dressed him in new ones, set him on an altar and kissed his hands and feet. Then one of those who were shut inside the conclave quickly broke open the opening in the wall and shouted, 'We have a pope, Martin V.' [The new pope took his name from his election day.] Then everyone went out into the great church singing the *Te Deum*.

Two days later the pope was consecrated as bishop and celebrated his first mass, at which one hundred and forty mitred heads were present. The next Sunday, Pope Martin V led a solemn procession at dawn, which crossed from the south end of the church to the west end. There stood a priest holding some hemp and tow, and he burned these saying 'Behold, holy father, thus passes away the glory of the world.'

In July 1417, Henry V set off to France once more to consolidate his conquests: within seven months he had taken Caen, Bayeux and Falaise. At home, however, the Lollards were creating disturbances once again.

While Henry's armies were advancing in Normandy, the Lollards, led by Sir John Oldcastle, began to behave like madmen in England. Oldcastle appealed to the Scots with prayers and promises of money to invade England, which, in the king's absence, he promised, would be easy to subdue. Apparently he spoke to William Douglas, a Scot, at Pontefract, promising him a huge sum of money if he incited his people to rebellion and made a man who falsely called himself 'King Richard' among them come with them and behave as though he were king. The Scot, forced by 'holy hunger for gold', soon made his clansmen come, bellowing war-cries, to besiege the castle and town of Roxburgh. When he arrived he sent sappers to undermine the walls.

At that time it happened that the duke of Exeter and Lord Thomas Bedford arrived at Bridlington on pilgrimage. As soon as they heard news of this event, they went with haste to meet the enemy, gathering archers and armed men on the way. From the other direction, the regent of the kingdom, John, duke of Bedford, the king's brother, with some other English nobles, collected a huge army and reached the area. The Scots discovered this through their scouts, and, too afraid to stay there any longer, 'turned their cowardly backs in womanish flight'.

Their retreat was hardly surprising, since more than one hundred thousand men had apparently gathered to repel them. And in case anyone should suppose the army consisted of inexperienced peasants, who had come with no more than heroic words, the duke of Exeter, a very venerable man, swore openly that he knew the army contained forty thousand war-like men of exceptional skill and courage. They were equal to the most valiant in the whole kingdom, despite the fact that many were fighting with the king in Normandy.

At that time the leader of the Lollards, John Oldcastle, was seeking a hiding-place in various regions, and hid for many days near St Albans, on the abbot's land, in the house of a peasant, who had a suitable room. When news of this spread, some of the abbot's friends went there at night. They did not find him, but they captured several of his confederates and took them off to prison. The leader of the traitors himself heard of this and groaned violently, saying that his grand plan had lost its force now that his chief fellow-conspirators had been captured.

In this hiding-place were discovered books written in English, some of which had originally been decorated with images of the different saints. According to the custom of the false Lollard doctrine, however, these wicked men had rubbed out the heads of the images, and in the litanies they had erased the names of the saints, together with that of the Blessed Virgin. Writings full of blasphemy against the Virgin Mary were also found. These I have refrained from recording, because they were so horrific.

The abbot of St Albans sent a book defaced with such erasures to the king, along with other deluded writings which had been found there. King Henry then sent the book to the archbishop of Canterbury, so that it could be shown when he next preached to the people at St Paul's in London, and so that he might inform his hearers of the sort of madness that possessed the Lollards: they were men who would not allow even the names of the saints, let alone their images, to appear in their books.

At this time the vainglorious, inveterate practitioner of evil, leader of the Lollards, captain and chief of the traitors, John Oldcastle, once called

Sigismund the peace-maker

FROM 1410 to 1411 there were not only three claimants to the papacy but three would-be emperors of the Holy Roman Empire as well. The rival imperial candidates were Wenceslas, king of Bohemia, his brother Sigismund, king of Hungary, and their nephew Jobst. In 1411 Sigismund emerged as 'king of the Romans' – emperor elect.

In modern terms, the empire consisted of East and West Germany, Czechoslovakia, Switzerland and Austria; Belgium, Holland and Luxemburg; eastern departments of France such as Provence, Alsace-Lorraine and parts of Burgundy; and large tracts of northern Italy. Even England could be said to owe allegiance to Sigismund: in 1194, Richard I had formally acknowledged Sigismund's predecessor Henry VI as overlord.

The emperor's authority was, however, more theoretical than practical in most of his vast domains. England was a sovereign state, and the majority of the empire's lands were effectively independent. The French dukes of Burgundy, for example, controlled a growing body of territory in the imperial Low Countries, as well as the imperial county of Burgundy, which lay outside the borders of France. The Italian cities were among Europe's most important states and, in Germany proper, power

tione abbe. ad cari.
Ordo romanus ad bñdicendur
gem uel reginam. in imperatorem
imperatricem coronandos. 25
Dum rex in imperatore
tus uenit romã ad fus
impij coronã. Quando
descendit de monte g
et peruenit ad ponticellum consue
bro euangeliorum coram se posita
iuramentum prestare romanis
mondus rex futurus imperator i
me seruaturum romanis bonas c

was divided between a patchwork of great cities, church lands, princes, dukes and counts. Wars in Bohemia, and the increasing independence of the German princes, also hastened the decline of imperial authority; and Sigismund's activity in church affairs distracted him from the empire.

Hungary bordered on Islamic Turkey, and as king, Sigismund saw himself as the champion of christendom. Others believed that as titular head of the empire he was the last hope for ending the schism. To this end Sigismund proclaimed the Council of Constance in November 1414, and for four years the city was the focus of European diplomacy. In December 1415 the emperor arrived in Paris to win French allegiance from Pope John's rival, Benedict XIII, to encourage support for his policy of reform at Constance – an endeavour which was to meet with ultimate success.

Sigismund also saw himself as an international peace-maker and on the same visit to Paris tried to reconcile the differences between France and England. But three months after Agincourt, the French were not in a

Above Coronation order for a Holy Roman Emperor, *contemporary with* Sigismund. *The illuminated initial shows the moment of crowning.*

Opposite Sigismund enthroned after his *success against his rivals in the imperial* election. *Woodcut.*

conciliatory mood and so, in April 1416, Sigismund left for England, hoping – unrealistically – to persuade Henry V to modify his demands against the French. Henry V entertained him lavishly for several months, supplying him with large sums of money and lending him the palace of Westminster as his headquarters. He was enrolled as a knight of the Garter and attended magnificent public ceremonies.

By the end of his sojourn Sigismund had come to appreciate the English point of view, and on 15 August signed the treaty of Canterbury, an offensive/defensive alliance acknowledging Henry's claims to France.

143

lord of Cobham, was captured in England on the land of the lord of Powis. Those who captured him suffered danger and wounds, and Oldcastle himself was found hurt when caught.

At the same time all the different estates in the kingdom were assembled in parliament, discussing a subsidy to be raised for the king, who was suffering hardship in France. When the lords and commons heard that a public enemy had been captured, they all decided that parliament should not be dissolved until he had been questioned and heard in the same parliament. The lord of Powis, who had captured him by force, was summoned, and came to London with the wounded Oldcastle, and with a priest, who knew all his secrets.

Without delay Oldcastle was brought into the presence of the regent, the duke of Bedford, and all the representatives of parliament. An indictment was read to him concerning his treasonable offences, including his hostile insurrection against the king on the field of St Giles. He was asked how he wished to exonerate himself and to prove that he did not deserve to be condemned to death.

Straightaway, with the utmost arrogance and rudeness, Oldcastle replied that he recognized no one among them as a judge, since his lord, King Richard, was alive in the kingdom of Scotland. His reply was heard, and because there was no need for witnesses he was ordered to be taken away and hanged on the gallows and burned while hanging there. Many worthy people were present at the spectacle. It is said that he spoke his final words to Sir Thomas Erpingham, urging him to secure peace for his sect if he saw his resurrection on the third day. Oldcastle was so possessed by madness that he thought he would rise from the dead.

Tito Livio gives a vivid if idealized description of Henry V's long siege of Rouen, the key to Normandy.

1418

The most victorious King Henry V set out for Rouen with all possible speed as soon as he had full control over the Seine bridge, so that no other river or body of water should serve to obstruct his progress. The town of Rouen is situated as follows: it lies in open land at the foot of a hill and is surrounded by the stoutest of walls and the deepest of moats. Moreover, the meandering course of the River Seine is such that it practically surrounds the whole town of Rouen.

Besides this, the town itself is sizeable and, at that time, contained supplies for its townspeople, knights and a very large garrison. They lacked no sorts of artillery but were well provided with every variety. They had crossbows, large and even larger, able to inflict great harm, longbows, engines, catapults of many kinds stationed along the walls, over the gates and in the streets. They had also a great abundance of arrows, bolts and stones. In addition, they had set up a great many iron spikes outside the walls. They had attached spikes to wooden boards which lay concealed and hidden in the grass and under the straw, so that they would injure the feet of men and horses, in exactly the path by which the English would travel.

On 30 May, the most victorious king arrived at Rouen. Finally, after a long and bloody battle, the French were faring so badly that they were obliged to return, defeated, inside the walls. The king then set up his camp thus: he himself with his numerous band of noblemen in the flower of their youth, had the royal tent set up close to the town gate, which the common people call the gate of St Hilary.

The citizens, weighed down with the many cares that beset those who are under siege and mindful of the great and furious battles they had already experienced, feared lest they should now be oppressed by hunger and lack of sustenance. And so, by common consent, they compelled a great multitude of the poorer and less able-bodied people to leave the town, in order to alleviate the shortage of supplies. However, the king forced them to go back into the town, once they had been refreshed with a little food.

Every day the famine grew worse and Rouen would have been obliged to surrender had it not been for John the Fearless, duke of Burgundy, who now held Paris [and who had ousted control of

Rise and fall of the Lollards

HENRY V's biographer Thomas Elmham described how, in 1378, 'infortunate things and unprofitable harms began for to spring and (the more harm is) continued long afterwards'. One of these disasters was the great schism in the papacy. Another, in Elmham's eyes, was the birth of a man known as 'Lord Cobham, greatest and most beloved of the king's servants'; as 'the horn of Antichrist, arch-traitor to God and man'; and, long after his execution, as 'that blessed martyr of Christ, Sir John Oldcastle'.

Oldcastle was descended from a family of minor gentry with lands on the Herefordshire borders with Wales. He first made his mark as a soldier, serving with the future Henry V in the long wars against Owen Glendower, and soon became the young prince's trusted friend. Henry's influence helped him to rise in the world, especially after 1408, when he married a wealthy Kentish heiress and acquired the title of Lord Cobham.

However, the royal favourite was no friend to the Church. He sponsored a parliamentary demand for the confiscation of ecclesiastical lands, gave covert protection to Lollard preachers, and even encouraged the Hussite heretics in Bohemia. No charge could be proved against him until, in June 1413, a bundle of his Lollard manuscripts fell into his episcopal opponents' hands. Faced with this damning evidence, the newly crowned Henry V eventually agreed to his trial for heresy. Oldcastle was found guilty, but even then the king was reluctant to burn his old comrade, and insisted on a 40-day stay of execution in the hope that he would come to his senses. Instead, Sir John escaped from the Tower by night, and vanished into the London underworld.

Soon, messages were sent to Lollard congregations in the Midlands, the West Country and the south-east, telling them to meet outside the walls of London during the night of 9–10 January 1414. Oldcastle hoped that by then a band of conspirators disguised as festive mummers would have assassinated or kidnapped the king as he celebrated Twelfth Night on 6 January at Eltham Palace, leaving the Lollards free to sweep away the corrupt Church for ever. But on 5 January, the day before the mumming was to take place, some of the plotters lost their nerve and confessed to the authorities. The London conspirators were arrested in their hideout, and when the rebels from the provinces filtered into the midnight rendezvous, they were rounded up almost without resistance by the king and his waiting forces. Although a gathering of 25,000 Lollards had been

Above
Henry V informed of Oldcastle's plot.

predicted, scarcely 250 appeared – a ragbag 'army' of weavers, craftsmen and peasants, led by a handful of knights and gentlemen and perhaps two dozen priests. During the days that followed, at least 45 insurgents were hanged, of whom only seven were afterwards burned on the gallows for unrepentant heresy. Many rebels had joined the insurrection merely for the wages Oldcastle promised.

The 'Lollard knight' was nowhere to be found. He remained at large for nearly four years, during which there were constant rumours of Lollard conspiracies. Twice offered a pardon by Henry – who sought domestic harmony while he fought his French wars – and twice all but captured, Oldcastle was always one jump ahead of his pursuers: for some time he lived openly on his Herefordshire estates, protected by his neighbours' silence.

He was finally captured near Welshpool as he returned from a secret meeting with the son of his former enemy Glendower. Badly wounded in the struggle, he was carried to London where he was hanged for treason; his body was burned on the gallows for heresy.

Oldcastle's death ended the Lollards' last hope of triumphing through revolution. For over a century after his execution, he was vilified as a traitor to his king and his God, until, with the Protestant Reformation, he became 'the blessed martyr of Christ'. When Shakespeare (recalling the tradition that Oldcastle had once been the young Henry's boon companion) attached his name to the fat knight in *Henry IV*, he provoked an outcry – and the character was re-christened 'Falstaff'.

King Charles VI from the Orleanists]. He reassured them greatly with letters and messages, promising that not only he but all the princes and lords of France would come to their aid. Thus it was that the whole citizenry, to the loud sound of all the church bells, which had remained silent throughout the siege, went about the town giving thanks to Almighty God and making solemn supplications.

King Henry V, as soon as he learned the news, made an inspection of his camp and of the roads by which the enemy would approach. Soon, in accordance with his orders, vast and deep trenches were dug around the camp and the roads and alongside the open fields, and beside them were built earth mounds surmounted by fair and strong palisades, along which were many wooden towers. In these towers were stationed catapults, crossbows and longbows – so many that you could scarcely count them. Thus was King Henry's army protected against any unforeseen attack, if help should arrive for the besieged townspeople.

Then, lest the citizens themselves and their garrison should perchance burst forth while his men were engaged with the new French force, and so attack the English from the rear, he had other deep trenches dug and more ramparts and palisades constructed. Thus the most prudent of princes made the plight of the people of Rouen still more desperate and secured his own position against all possible attacks.

Daily the famine in the town grew worse. First the inhabitants shared out and consumed the flesh of their horses. Then they ate dogs, cats, mice, shrews and whatever else they thought edible in their famished state. Eventually, there was nothing left to eat at all. As a result of the famine, the city was invaded by the plague. People fell victim to it in their houses, in the streets, in churches and in the market-place. Sons expired before their parents and infants watched as their mothers died.

1419

Fearful in the face of these afflictions, the townspeople decided unanimously that they had no remaining hope but in the king of England's mercy. And so they sent a deputation of their most prominent citizens who were to go to the camp and ask the king's mercy, clothed in mourning and with cries of lamentation. On the king's instructions, the embassy was led into the camp and then into the presence of the king who was waiting for them attended by his retinue and noblemen.

Their pleas for the good king's mercy were successful, and they returned to the town where they summoned a meeting of the townspeople and garrison to tell them what the king had decided.

All were suffering dreadfully from disease and hunger, and readily, without exception, complied with the king's wishes. Soon afterwards the embassy, with the support of all the townspeople, returned to the camp to make an agreement with King Henry V.

Conditions – including the payment of a large indemnity – were agreed, and eighty of the city's leading men were handed over as hostages to the English.

The gates were then opened wide and the victorious king entered the town and fortress accompanied by a great crowd of dukes, nobles and other attendants. But first of all, lest some of his men should run off to pillage the town, the king appointed officers to watch over every quarter of the city, that damage and rapine might be prevented.

Henry V himself, moved to pity by the wretchedness of the townspeople, gave orders to his servants and retinue to fetch food for the crowd. A great quantity of victuals, brought at the most merciful wish of the king, came only just in time to revive the dying townspeople – and the most tender-hearted of princes had given instructions for the provision of food before anything else. But even fifteen days was not long enough to alleviate all the sufferings caused by the famine and the plague continued to take its toll on the citizens. Later, however, plenty and good health did return to the city. Indeed, the king appointed such worthy men as its prefects that Rouen was quickly restored to the flourishing state it had enjoyed in the past.

French Flamboyant

IN 1300, French architecture, which had until then dominated medieval Europe, was in decline, and the most interesting architectural experiments were taking place in England and Germany, hitherto on the artistic peripheries.

Paradoxically, the Hundred Years War breathed new life into the French architectural spirit. Many early medieval churches were destroyed or irreparably damaged by the fighting and the need to replace them stimulated architectural enterprise. Devastation was worst in areas that had been easily and consistently accessible to the English: the north-east of France, and Normandy. Rebuilding started in Normandy, probably the richest of these areas, followed, gradually, by the slightly less wealthy Somme valley and then eastern France.

The new Flamboyant style of architecture, which took shape towards the end of the 14th century, had a distinct regional quality; Paris did not play a major role in its emergence, as it had in previous manifestations of the Gothic spirit. Normandy was ideally placed to play the key role; an important aspect of the new style was its repertory of richly decorative tracery patterns derived from English Decorated and Perpendicular architecture, which first invaded the French architectural consciousness in Normandy – at the abbey of Saint-Ouen, Rouen.

Work started on this church in 1318, but it was mainly built during the long period of peace from 1380 to 1415; while the panelled severity of the English Perpendicular tradition is magnificently expressed in the unyielding granite of the choir of Mont-Saint-Michel, begun in 1446. The west front of Notre-Dame Cathedral at Rouen, rebuilt between 1370 and 1514 – the south-

west tower (1485–1507) on the proceeds of an ecclesiastical tax on eating butter – and Saint-Wulfram at Abbeville in the Somme valley, rebuilt in 1488, both in the Flamboyant style, incorporate complex combinations of flame-like forms, derived from English Decorated architecture.

Inspired by the 14th-century English obsession with polygonal plans – the east end of Wells and the porch of St Mary Redcliffe in Bristol are examples – French architects created the triangular porch of Saint-Maclou church in Rouen (*c.* 1436–1520) and the apse of the exquisite church of Caudebec-en-Caux (*c.* 1426), which Henry IV of France was to describe as 'the most beautiful chapel in the kingdom'.

Left *The interior of Rouen Cathedral, a masterpiece of the Flamboyant style.*

Below *A cathedral being built; from a contemporary French manuscript. The actual building is the Temple of Jerusalem, and no Gothic cathedral would have been gilded in this manner; but the architecture and techniques, including the crane at the top, are fifteenth-century.*

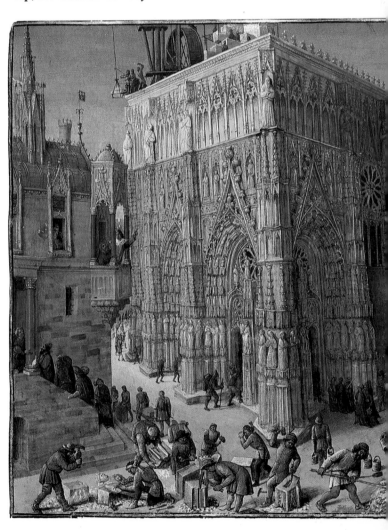

Henry V's victory at Rouen temporarily united the Orleanists and Burgundians against him. However, the Dauphin Charles had no wish to act as a puppet king in the hands of John, duke of Burgundy, and mistrust between the two factions remained deep. Walsingham laconically records the catastrophic error made by the dauphin's Orleanist entourage.

The duke of Burgundy was summoned to negotiate with the dauphin and his depraved companions [at Montereau] and was treacherously murdered by them. This was despite the fact that previously everyone had bound themselves by the same oath not to harm anyone of the other party who came to negotiate. The duke of Burgundy's son, Philip the Good, who was his heir, wanted to avenge his father's murder, and humbly sent a large number of representatives to the English king, pledging through them an oath to observe loyalty to him.

The murder discredited the dauphin and the Orleanists and rallied the wavering Parisians to the Burgundian cause. The Burgundians, anxious to avenge their duke, made a formal alliance with the English which gave Henry V an overwhelming influence in France. Negotiations for peace were now set in train, as Tito Livio relates.

1420

The most invincible king was giving thanks to God for his many victories when ambassadors came to him in Rouen from the so-called King Charles VI and from Philip, duke of Burgundy, with instructions to sue for peace. The king himself received them most graciously and sent the illustrious earl of Warwick, together with bishops, lawyers and a great many other advisers, to seek peace and forge a treaty. For he knew Warwick to be a man of most excellent worth, in peace and war, who had learnt much from Henry's own instruction.

And so these men went as ambassadors to the so-called King Charles VI and Philip, duke of Burgundy. Warwick made his way towards Burgundy, which was not far distant, and on the way he and the leader of his armed force took by storm

several fortresses which were in the hands of the Orleanists, supporters of the count of Armagnac. They then proceeded directly to Troyes where the most noble Charles VI, his wife and their virgin daughter, Princess Catherine, were staying. As soon as the ambassadors had rested and refreshed themselves, they began to discuss the peace.

After many days of shrewd negotiation on both sides, peace and concord were achieved between Henry and Charles. A marriage was arranged between the most pure virgin, Princess Catherine, and the most invincible King Henry. However, since many matters remained to be settled before the royal houses of the two kingdoms could be joined together and the proposed wedding take place, and since King Charles often suffered from grave ill health, it was agreed that Henry should come to Troyes, with a certain number of men as his armed escort, on a certain day so that negotiations could be completed. If he did not arrive in Troyes by that day, all the proposals hitherto agreed should be considered null.

When the above matters had been thus decided, the most noble earl of Warwick returned to the invincible king and, in a private meeting, showed him written documents and described in detail what had been agreed. King Henry rejoiced in many victories and constant good fortune both in peace and war of which he was not unmindful. Nevertheless, he gave instructions that his men were to be withdrawn from many towns and cities and were to join him at Pontoise where he would be waiting. These valiant soldiers quickly made their way thither, in obedience to the king's command. He then led them forth from the town into the open country. As was always his custom, King Henry ordered them into three lines of battle and two wings, before embarking on his journey to Troyes on 24 June.

They marched through the town called Saint-Denis, stopping for a while outside the walls of Paris, where the king held a parade of his valiant men, in full view of the townspeople. He then set off for the province called Brie and took an enemy fortress by storm. Some of the garrison he crucified, the rest he took with him as prisoners.

Heir to France

HENRY V had conquered Normandy by August 1419 and, with the capture of Pontoise, started to threaten Paris. The capital was held by the duke of Burgundy, John the Fearless, but was overshadowed by the rival Armagnac (Orleanist) forces to the south and west. The Burgundian–Armagnac feud had divided and weakened the French and Henry V had pursued negotiations with both sides, as each bid for his support. If he was to win the French crown he needed to ally with one or the other, while they would defeat him only if they put aside their quarrel and united in defence of France.

John the Fearless, who controlled Charles VI, now sought a meeting with the Armagnacs led by the dauphin, hoping to bring him too under his sway. But at their rendezvous at Montereau in September 1419 John was assassinated by the dauphin's men. John's son and successor as duke of Burgundy, Philip the Good, was left with no option but to ally with Henry V, and in May 1420 the treaty of Troyes was concluded between Henry V, Charles VI, and Philip.

The treaty provided for Henry V's marriage to Charles's daughter, Catherine, and his adoption by Charles VI as heir to the French throne. The dauphin was disinherited for his complicity in John's murder. Until Charles VI's death Henry was to rule France as his regent; thereafter the new Lancastrian-Valois dynasty would rule England and France as a 'dual monarchy': the two nations would have a common king, but each would retain its identity, governed by its own laws and nationals, and through its traditional institutions. Neither was to be subject to the other. The dauphinists could not accept this, and Henry pledged himself to continue the war against the dauphin until all France had submitted.

Normandy was a special case. It had been conquered piecemeal by the English and many Englishmen, from lords to humble soldiers and tradesmen, had been given lands there on which they settled as colonists. Henry V made a real effort to win the hearts of the native French, reviving their form of parliament (the estates of Normandy), appointing native officials at all but the highest levels, and giving the common people legal protection against the English garrisons. The economy began gradually to recover after the devastation of war, and measures were taken to restore law and order. None the less bands of brigands waged guerrilla warfare against the English from forest hideouts, threatening villages and travellers. When caught they were executed as traitors.

In Paris the English were more like an army of occupation than a legitimate government. They manned the Bastille and the royal castle at Vincennes but the administration was carried on by the duke of Burgundy's officials. The clergy and members of the university and parlement accepted the treaty of Troyes and retained their positions. Life in the capital began to return to normal.

In England the treaty, with its acknowledgement of English claims to the crown of France, was hailed as marking the end of the war. In France, however, it deepened the divisions between those who were prepared to receive Henry V as king and those who believed that only the dauphin could legitimately succeed Charles VI.

Above *Philip the Good, Henry V's ally.*

Below *Brigands menaced the English domains.*

He continued through the town of Provins and the town they call Nogent, on the River Seine. Gradually they drew near to the town of Troyes. As soon as he heard of the king's approach, Philip, duke of Burgundy, attended by a great many noblemen and knights, together with the leading men of Troyes, came forth to meet the victor king and received him with the great respect due to his majesty and also with great pleasure.

So the most victorious king, Henry V, entered the city with English and Frenchmen in attendance and went straight to the king of France, Charles VI, who was waiting for him in his palace. There he was received in the most gracious manner, with the most elegant words and gestures. For Charles, although he had been unwell for some time, had risen from his bed for this occasion. The most invincible king, accompanied by his great retinue, then made his way to his lodgings.

Troyes had been divided up into two parts. One half was for the lodging of the French. The other half was placed at the disposal of their English guests. And since the place assigned them was not great enough to accommodate all the English, a wall which separated the city from its suburbs was torn down so that every last man could be housed.

The king of England gave many prudent instructions regarding the health of his men, one of which is perhaps of little importance but since I found it recorded – and not without reason – I too consider it worthy to be told in my own history. The land around Troyes yields a great quantity of wine which is very potent and of a very dark colour. Now since the English were not accustomed to this most natural and common of refreshments, the most pious king, in consideration of their well-being, gave orders that not one of his men should dare to drink wine unless it was first diluted with water.

Let us now return to more important matters. Since, as has been said, King Charles often suffered from ill health so that he was unable to govern the state, his family or his own affairs, he had given power to Queen Isabella and to Philip of Burgundy, until he himself should be recovered. They,

together with his council, were to make peace and negotiate a treaty with King Henry on the following conditions. Henry was to swear in good faith to abide by the peace and observe all its provisions, on his own behalf and on that of his family, his heirs and successors. Charles VI himself, swearing a royal oath, promised on his own behalf and that of his family and heirs to ratify and confirm whatever his most noble wife Queen Isabella and Philip, duke of Burgundy, promised and decided during the peace negotiations.

The treaty of Troyes was Henry V's greatest triumph, for it made him the regent and legal heir to Charles VI of France. He was also to marry Charles's daughter Catherine, an event chronicled by Walsingham.

On 3 June, the day after Trinity Sunday, King Henry V of England married Lady Catherine, and appointed servants to her household, valiant English people. No French person remained in her entourage, except for three noblewomen and two maids, who were personal servants of their mistress.

The king of England, as regent and heir to France, turned to those [Orleanist] cities which had rebelled against him and the French crown, with a view to subduing them by force. He took the cities of Sens and Montereau, which surrendered to him immediately.

Then he went to the stronghold of Melun with his army and besieged it. At the siege were the kings of England, France and Scotland [who was Henry V's captive], the dukes of Burgundy, Bavaria, Clarence, Bedford and Exeter, the earls of March, Warwick, Huntingdon, Somerset and so on; and many other lords, barons, knights and squires, noble in birth and valiant in arms, whose names are not recorded.

The siege lasted fourteen weeks and four days. From 22 July to 1 November there was violent and almost daily conflict between besieged and besiegers, involving wounding, mutilation and the deaths of many of the besiegers; and it is said that more than seventeen hundred men died. The siege was worse than any the English had ever known.

Catherine of France

CATHERINE, daughter of Charles VI of France and Isabella of Bavaria, was the youngest sister of Isabella, Richard II's queen. She had first been proposed as a bride for the future Henry V during the peace negotiations of 1408, when the prince was 21 and she just eight. Nothing came of the suggestion and when Henry succeeded to the throne five years later he was still unwed. The idea of the match was revived soon after, but he did not win Catherine and the reversion of the kingdom of France until the treaty of Troyes in 1420.

Henry had met Catherine briefly in 1419 and had apparently been charmed by what he saw. Chroniclers on both sides of the Channel tell of his love at first sight, but the king's later behaviour suggests that his infatuation was short-lived. Catherine had only her beauty to recommend her, with neither the intelligence nor the personality to captivate for long a man of Henry V's qualities.

The couple were married at Troyes Cathedral in June 1420 and the following February Henry brought his queen to England. She made a state entry into London and was crowned by Archbishop Chichele. Before the king returned to France they were sure that Catherine was pregnant, and she remained behind in England to await the birth of their child. The future Henry VI was born at Windsor on 6 December 1421 and early in the New Year Catherine travelled back to France. She was staying with her parents at Senlis at the time of her husband's death and the king made no attempt to send for her. Few of his dying thoughts, so concerned with his son, seem to have been spared for his wife. Catherine accompanied his body back to England, a widow at 21.

During the first eight years of her son's reign, Catherine was accorded all the dignities of a queen dowager and never made the slightest attempt to use her position politically. With so young a widowed queen, the question of remarriage raised all kinds of problems. There was little point in Catherine returning to France, of which her son was now king. If she remarried in England, a new husband might have too strong an influence over his stepson – an unacceptable idea in the factional politics of Henry VI's minority. The suggestion that Catherine was contemplating marriage to her late husband's cousin, Edmund Beaufort, prompted parliament to pass a statute in 1428 prohibiting anyone from marrying a queen dowager without the express permission of the king – given only after he had reached the age of discretion. Catherine was not prepared to wait until her son grew up. Nor, as a contemporary put it, was she able 'to fully curb her carnal passions'. The result was a secret marriage in about 1429 to an obscure Welsh squire, Owen Tudor.

Above *The marriage of Catherine and Henry.*

Owen was possibly a member of the queen's household, but one of the oldest and strongest traditions surrounding the match is that Owen first came to Catherine's attention at a ball, when, distinctly the worse for drink, he fell into her lap. It was an unworthy match for a queen, but in choosing an insignificant commoner, she had hoped to avert the wrath of the council – the king's advisers. Although the marriage was not widely known in the country, the council was certainly aware of it and there has never been the slightest suspicion that the pair were not legally wedded. Catherine bore Owen four children: Edmund and Jasper, later raised to the earldoms of Richmond and Pembroke respectively by their stepbrother Henry VI, Owen, who became a monk, and a daughter who died young. Edmund was the father of the future Henry VII.

Some time before her death in 1437, the queen entered Bermondsey Abbey; in her will she refers to a 'grievous malady', from which she had long suffered. It is possible that this was a mental illness: her father, Charles VI, was subject to fits of madness, and her son, Henry VI, was similarly affected.

Eventually, the food supplies of the people being besieged became scarce and gave out. On 17 November, they surrendered to the mercy of the kings of France and England. More than four hundred valiant men from different camps were assigned as guardians, while the rest were allowed to depart, through the mercy of the king. For the kings of France and England the victory was as costly as it was glorious. They went to Paris and there celebrated Christmas and held a great parlement with much solemnity.

1421

When Christmas was over, and the official parlement had been dissolved, the king moved to Rouen. There he held another parlement in similar fashion with his Norman and English subjects. Once he considered that adequate provision had been made for the security and protection of the kingdom of France and the duchy of Normandy, he returned in haste to England.

Crossing through Picardy and Calais, he came on 1 February to Dover, and from there went to Canterbury, with his newly wedded bride and a small household. He had with him only the duke of Bedford, the earl of Warwick, and Sir John Cornwall, knight. He spent a few days at Canterbury, then went on to London, where he was received as he deserved by clergy and people, with pomp and celebrations of various kinds. On 3 March a mounted escort and a suitable procession went on ahead, and the queen was led to Westminster from the Tower of London. There, by the offices of the archbishop of Canterbury and other appropriate members of the clergy, she was solemnly crowned.

The coronation banquet for Henry's bride was of unsurpassed magnificence. A parliament was then held at London, when Henry V turned his attention to the state of the English Church, as Walsingham, himself a Benedictine, records.

Reforms were made, especially in the Order of the Benedictines, who were gathered there together in large numbers by royal edict. There were sixty abbots and priors, and three hundred or more

The food of kings

DIET in medieval England was generally monotonous, based largely on grains and vegetables. Boring at best, at its worst it was scarce and in bad years poor people starved. The food of the court was different and kings did not go hungry. Yet even their diet was at the mercy of the changing seasons and constrained by the difficulty of transporting and storing fresh produce – one reason why the court moved around the country was to consume food produced on royal estates. Royalty had also to obey the Church's laws about fast-days: meat and eggs were forbidden on Fridays and during Lent.

The upper-class diet was further restricted by misconceptions and snobbery. Raw fruit was believed to be harmful, and vegetables were regarded with suspicion. Bacon – a poor man's staple – was never eaten, and eggs and dairy products were served only in a luxurious form – French cheese, for example, or eggs cooked in cream – or with other ingredients in a recipe. There were many versions of frumenty (frumerty) made with whole wheat, and *de luxe* recipes included wine, spices and eggs.

Huge quantities of flesh and fish distinguished the aristocratic diet. Meat included domestic animals, poultry and game – mainly venison but also rabbit, which was a luxury, and wildfowl. Freshwater fish was sometimes 'wild' but was also extensively farmed; every substantial household had its fish pond. A variety of sea fish was available only in ports, including London; inland the choice was generally limited to smoked or salted herring, dried haddock or cod. Meat and fish were cooked with dried fruit like dates, figs, raisins, prunes – and with spices to pep up boring or tasteless ingredients. Many combinations of spices were devised. No distinction was made between sweet and savoury ingredients, which were often combined in the same dish, and concentrated, pungent tastes were popular.

The king and nobility drank wine every day, mainly imported from Bordeaux but also from Burgundy, Anjou, the Rhinelands, Castile and Italy. Sweet wines from the Levant were especially popular with the wealthy and powerful; Richard II ate oysters cooked in Greek wine, and a century later the duke of Clarence was said to have drowned in a butt of Malmsey.

Sugar was increasingly available during the 15th century. Used with spices as a condiment, it was also combined with almonds and moulded into sculptures called 'subtleties'. These made symbolic or political points and were presented at the end of each course at a banquet.

Food was not only necessary for nourishment, it was also a status symbol. Spices were used, not just for flavouring, but because they were expensive. This

The first course

Boar's meat with mustard	Eels in sauce
Frumenty with sea-bream	Pike
Pickled lampreys	Trout
Codling	Plaice
Fried merlin fish	Large crabs
Lombardy pork slices	Meat en croûte
Small pies	

A special confection

The second course

Galantine	Minced chicken
Bream	Conger eels
Sole	Mullet
Chub	Barbel
Roach	Fresh salmon
Halibut	Baked gurnard
Broiled rochet	Fried smelt
Lobsters	Damascus slices
Lamprey en croûte	Royal pork pie

A special confection in the shape
of a chef and a lady

The third course

Compôte of dates	Sauce of mixed herbs
Wild carp	Turbot
Tench	Perch
Gudgeons	Sturgeon, fresh and pickled
Whelks	Baked porpoise
Fried monkfish	Freshwater crayfish
Large shrimps	Baked eels and lampreys
White slices	Meat en croûte, decorated
	with four angels

A special confection in the shape of a tiger,
with St George leading it.

extravagance can be traced back to Richard II's court where pâtés and mousses, which took much labour to prepare, replaced the traditional roasts. Richard's chief cook wrote *The Forme of Cury*, the earliest English recipe book, in about 1390 at a time when there were constant complaints about the costs of the royal household. Recipe books of the 15th century testify to a continuation of this conspicuous consumption.

Three-course banquets were exceptional events, being reserved for coronations, weddings, great church feasts

Above *Catherine's coronation feast menu.*

and diplomatic occasions. However, even without these, aristocrats probably spent at least one-third of their disposable income on food for themselves and their retinues. They bought exotic ingredients, paid kitchen servants and fed multitudes of people, from those who dined on luxuries at high table, through the large numbers eating plain fare in the body of the hall, to the beggars who received the leftovers at the kitchen door.

153

Above *A man of rank's dinner with the serving-hatch visible in the far hall.*

Right *Gaston, count of Foix, at the picnic table during a hunt. Such meals combined two of the nobility's chief pleasures: hunting and eating in the grand manner. Jugs cool in the spring at left, while the dining hunters examine traces brought in by the beaters and decide which quarry to hunt.*

Below *A contemporary betrothal feast, held to honour the bride.*

monks, doctors and proctors. There had been reports to the king of treason by certain false monks. The abbots and their associates had been most lax. Monastic religion had lapsed from its original institutions and observances, and would have to be reformed by restoring them.

So the king took only four worthy men and humbly entered the chapter house at Westminster where they were gathered. He spoke to them about the former godliness of the order, about the piety of their predecessors and others in founding and endowing monasteries, and about modern negligence and lack of devotion. He then presented to them certain articles for their correction: and appealed to them to pray ceaselessly for himself, the kingdom and the Church. With energy and feeling he affirmed that if they did these things they would fear no enemy and that he would rely particularly on their prayers.

These articles and others were approved by the bishop of Exeter and others from the royal party, and diligently discussed by wise and valiant men of the congregation. The reforms were finally given formal agreement.

Meanwhile in Bohemia, Sigismund, who had in 1419 succeeded his brother Wenceslas as king, struggled against the Taborite heretics, the violent wing of the Hussite movement which had overrun Prague.

The most Christian and excellent King Sigismund of Hungary, Bohemia and the Romans, once elected Roman emperor, had made peace in the Church of God by means of his personal intervention. He had appointed a true pope and successor to Peter, Martin V, and then returned to his own kingdoms and dominions to fight the enemies of the faith, and to root out the Hussite heresy. This had flourished in Bohemia because of all the support that his elder brother, Wenceslas, had given it.

So Sigismund collected a huge host of armed men, and in 1420 laid siege to the town of Prague, where, above all other places, this heresy had originated, fixed its roots and grown to become a

rebel against him. It was so close a siege that when the citizens saw they could not resist such a great force, they submitted entirely to his power, agreeing to be his subjects and obey his counsel, orders and rule as long as he withdrew most of his army — which had devastated the whole of the country — and dealt amicably with them. They sent him food and gifts as a token of their promise and future loyalty, and received his messengers with respect.

Over-credulous and eager to avoid the shedding of Christian blood, Sigismund withdrew the strongest part of his armies and, accompanied only by his own retainers, awaited the hoped-for outcome. Deceitful and lying, the people of Prague saw that luck smiled on their designs and, making a sudden attack on his army, they caused great destruction before the emperor could come to the rescue. In the end he recovered his spirits, and charged three times, killing many and forcing the others back into the city.

With the remains of his army he withdrew to his lands, to return stronger and avenge this injury. He gathered a valiant force of princes, dukes, knights and other men-at-arms, and archers and siege engineers, together with the archbishops of Cologne, Mainz, Trier and others, and carried out his purpose. He did not cease pursuing the heretics until he had recalled them to the unity of the faith and the Church, or handed them over to be devoured by the sword or fire.

The dauphin and his Orleanist followers, whose support remained strong in most of central and southern France (except for Gascony), now began to fight back further north as well.

In this year [1421], during his absence in England, King Henry V's enemies captured Baugé, a fortified town which had formerly been restored to the king. Its English captain, Thomas, duke of Clarence, the king's brother, was slaughtered with all the others. Elated by the victory, the Orleanists became so foolhardy that it was feared that there would be rebellion and desertion by other cities which had been handed over to the English. The king was persistently urged by his loyal subjects to go quickly to that region with a large army.

That same year Queen Catherine of England bore her first son at Windsor Castle on 6 December. He was named Henry. John, duke of Bedford, his uncle, Henry Beaufort, bishop of Winchester, the king's uncle, and Jacqueline, duchess of Holland, who was staying in England at the time, acted as godparents. The English people were overjoyed and gave them gifts.

The future Lancastrian succession to both England and France was now secured.

Once everything concerning the kingdom of England and the war in Scotland [which had erupted once more] had been arranged in accordance with his wishes, King Henry V returned to France with an army of valiant soldiers and archers, one thousand or more in number, to avenge his brother's death to the best of his ability. But the dauphin refused to fight with him, although he had informed him otherwise through his messengers, and apparently had a greater army. He had sworn that if the opportunity presented itself he was willing to fight with the king of England; but at that time he was far away, devastating the countryside all around. It was claimed that the larger part of his army had deserted him and was unwilling to fight for him any longer.

The king pursued the dauphin in vain through lands which the dauphin himself had laid waste, causing great harm to his army. He laid siege to the town of Meaux, on the river, and the region of Brie, which was full of rebels. Because of the fighting and the lack of food, a great part of Henry's army was exhausted and fell sick, and most returned to England. Only a few of them came back again.

The local French peasantry was equally or worse afflicted by the depredations of war, as a contemporary citizen of Paris explains.

The king of England, who was besieging Meaux, sent his troops out pillaging over the whole district of Brie, and because of them and because of their opponents it was impossible to get any land ploughed or sown.

The labourers finally gave up in despair. They left their wives and children and said among themselves, 'What shall we do? It can all go to the devil, why should we care? We may as well do harm, not good, Saracens would be kinder to us than Christians. Come on, we'll do all the damage we can. Our rulers are to blame, traitors that they are! It's their fault we have got to leave our wives and children and go and hide in the forest like stray beasts. It's not one or two years since this dismal dance began, it's fourteen or fifteen. By now, nearly all France's nobility has died – by the sword, unshriven, by poison, by treason or by some foul unnatural cause.'

Complaints were made to the English commanders time and again but they only laughed and jeered. Then their men behaved worse than before.

Henry V himself was by now in difficulties, lacking both men and supplies. The unsympathetic, pro-French author of the Scotichronicon *relates a fanciful story about the king's final and fateful raid for provisions.*

1422

After a siege of three months, King Henry managed to take Meaux by storm – although many of his own men were lost in the battle. As his supplies were, by this time, running very low, he sent his men to scour the surrounding country for some food.

When they found nothing which could be eaten, the king sent them to raid the sanctuary of St Fergus or Feogrus (whose father had been king of Scotland) – though this is a sacred place which no one can attack with impunity.

The country people, trusting to the holiness of the place, had stored cattle and provisions there. These were seized and carried off by King Henry. At once, he was struck down with a cancerous sickness – that which the common people call 'St Fiacre's evil'. In consequence of this, he became sick in spirit also and gave orders that the captain of the captured city, the bastard of Vaurus, should be beheaded, his body then suspended by the armpits and his head impaled on a sharpened stake. So great indeed was the king's frenzy that he had more than three hundred of the townspeople put to death.

When, his sickness worsening, he questioned doctors as to its cause and origin, they answered that it was because he had desecrated the holy place of St Feogrus the Scot. When he heard this, the king frowned and said darkly: 'I go after Scots dead and alive and always I find them in my beard.' Then, as he lay on a litter, driven wild with pain, he gave instructions that he be carried to the Bois de Vincennes, near Paris. There he died with his entrails, genitals and lungs in a state of putrefaction. His body was conveyed back to England by his followers.

Walsingham's version of King Henry V's death is altogether more measured and sober, but he follows it with a panegyric of the king's character.

In the course of a lengthy illness, which he had contracted as a result of long and excessive labours, the king suffered from an acute fever, with violent dysentery, which so consumed his strength that the doctors dared not give him internal medicine and despaired of his life.

Seeing that his death was approaching, the king called together his dukes and others who were able to be present, to represent the kingdoms of England and France and the duchy of Normandy. He made wise arrangements, wrote his will and provided for his debts to be paid from his treasuries and numerous jewels.

After taking holy communion and the other sacraments that were the duty of a Christian, in true penitence, proper faith, certain hope, perfect charity and right remembrance, he gave up his soul to his creator on the last day of August, after he had reigned for nine years, five months and fourteen days.

King Henry V left no one like him among Christian kings or princes: his death, not only by his subjects in England and France, but in the whole of christendom, was deservedly mourned.

The Bohemian revolution

IN 1415, as the English authorities were attempting to stamp out the last embers of the Lollard movement, a more effective movement to reform the Church came to a head in Bohemia. From 1402, its figurehead had been John Hus, rector of the Bethlehem Chapel in Prague.

Originally an academic, he became a preacher of great influence and indefatigable energy: during his ten years at the chapel, he gave over 3,000 sermons, generally to packed congregations. A publicizer of beliefs already commonly held in Bohemia, rather than an innovator, Hus regarded himself as an orthodox reformer, the champion of the purified Church of 'the holy Bohemian nation, chosen by God'. As such, he had become a Czech national hero by 1414, when he was summoned to the Council of Constance. Hus went voluntarily to the assembly: he welcomed the opportunity to explain his reforms and was protected by a safe-conduct from the Bohemian-born Emperor Sigismund. However, the council was determined to try him for heresy. Thrown into prison, he was first accused of holding Wycliffite views, and later of attacking the papacy. When Sigismund withdrew his protection, Hus was faced with the choice between submission and death. In answer, he declared, 'I cannot abjure doctrines I never held, nor retract what I believe. I cannot lie to God.' On 6 July 1415 he was burned at the stake.

The Bohemian nation was appalled. A letter of protest against Hus's execution was sealed by most of the Czech nobility and the Church in Bohemia broke away from the papacy. To emphasize their rejection of corrupt ecclesiastical traditions, even moderate 'Hussites' insisted that laymen should receive wine as well as bread at mass – a 'privilege' previously reserved for the clergy. In many parts of Bohemia orthodoxy was swept away and worshippers gathered in fields or barns rather than churches. Alarmed by a projected papal 'crusade' against his country, Wenceslas IV – a friend of Hus – attempted to halt the religious revolution in 1419. A popular rising followed, during which the Catholic councillors of Prague were

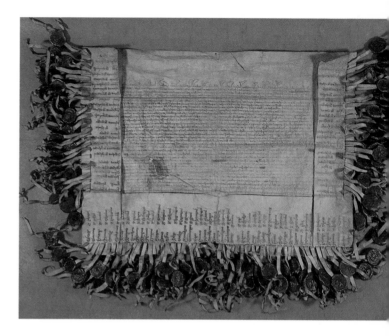

Above *Letter of protest from the Bohemian nobility objecting to the Council of Constance's treatment of Hus.*

Left *Hus is burned at the stake and, afterwards, his ashes are loaded into a cart.*

Opposite *Hus after his trial is dressed in the robes and devil hat of a heretic and led to the stake.*

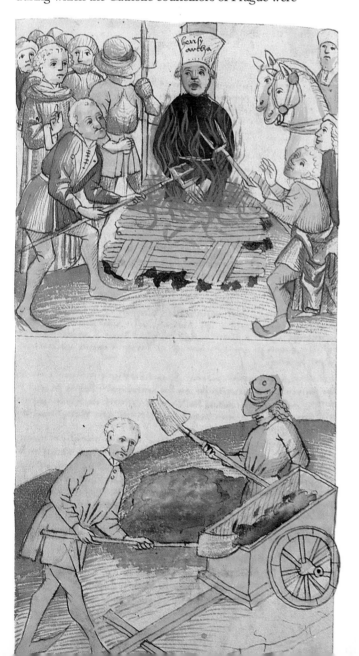

hurled from the town hall windows ('the first defenestration of Prague'). Wenceslas died of shock.

The heir to Bohemia was now Sigismund, who had betrayed Hus at Constance and who was resolved to enforce orthodoxy, if necessary by military means. In response to his persecution, thousands of Hussite peasants, convinced that the Last Judgement was near, assembled in great 'brotherhoods', sharing all their goods in common. The most important had its headquarters in a fortress, renamed 'Mount Tabor' after the scene of Christ's Transfiguration, where a one-eyed professional soldier, John Žižka, welded members of the brotherhood into a disciplined, dedicated revolutionary army, equipped with iron-spiked threshing flails and armoured 'war-wagons' bristling with cannon and handguns – a shattering 'secret weapon' against enemy cavalry.

Again and again, Žižka and his 'Taborite' forces routed Sigismund's armies and invading German 'crusaders' alike. After his death in 1424, when his followers took the name 'Orphans', the radical 'armies of the brotherhoods' continued to dominate central Europe until in 1434 they were defeated by an alliance of Bohemian nobles and moderate Hussites, and Sigismund was accepted as king. Yet the Hussite Church survived to the Reformation, the only medieval reform movement to successfully challenge the authority of Rome.

He was pious in soul, taciturn and discreet in his speech, far-seeing in counsel, prudent in judgement, modest in appearance, magnanimous in his actions, firm in business, persistent in pilgrimages and generous in alms; devoted to God and supportive and respectful of the prelates and ministers of the church; war-like, distinguished and fortunate, he had won victories in all his military engagements. He was generous in constructing buildings and founding monasteries, munificent in his gifts, and above all pursued and attacked enemies of the faith and the Church.

Thinking of his memorable deeds, people felt awe at his sudden and terrible removal, by the right hand of God above, and mourned inexpressibly.

When he learned of the death of his English son-in-law, King Charles of France, after celebrating solemn rites and masses in his chapel for Henry's soul, issued an edict summoning a large number of prelates and other lords, who had recently agreed on the peace between France and England, and had the same peace read out to them. By his oaths and theirs, the peace was reconfirmed over the body of the Lord and the holy gospel of God. Then the king wasted away through grief and desolation, and on 21 October, at dawn, he too departed this life.

All the French who had experienced the English king's just and prudent rule, after such a turbulent and dishonest tyranny, mourned for him with great lamentations. The people of Paris and Rouen, who honoured Henry's body in lawful funeral rites and gave him manifold offerings to the best of their powers, offered huge sums of gold to have his body buried in France, as a sign of their respect and as a unique way of consoling themselves.

But this could not be, for King Henry V had previously stipulated in his will that he was to be buried at Westminster, which was later done with full honours.

A legacy of war

AFTER his marriage and the signing of the treaty of Troyes in May 1420, Henry V returned to England with his queen early in 1421. He had been absent for three and a half years and during his brief visit he held a parliament and made a whirlwind tour, dispensing justice and raising money and men for a new campaign.

Back in France by June, he advanced south of Paris to the Loire, attempting to bring the dauphin to battle. By October he had settled down to besiege Meaux, the key to Champagne. Throughout a bitter winter he kept his men in place around the town, despite mounting losses from disease. Meaux finally capitulated in May 1422. It was the king's last triumph: he had contracted dysentery and by the end of August lay dying in the castle at Vincennes. His final commands were to confer the government of France on the elder of his two brothers, John, duke of Bedford, and to commit to the younger, Humphrey, duke of Gloucester, the guardianship of his son and heir, still less than a year old.

The government of England was speedily and effectively vested in a council of the most powerful lords and bishops under Gloucester as protector. In France, Henry's legacy was less secure. In the two years since the treaty of Troyes it had become increasingly clear that France was bitterly divided between the areas controlled by the Anglo-Burgundian alliance and those remaining loyal to the Valois Charles VII. Bedford faced a long military struggle to establish Lancastrian ascendancy, and relied on the support of Duke Philip of Burgundy, who controlled the areas east of Paris.

Henry's religious beliefs were deeply conventional and coloured by his conviction of his own destiny: he professed his intention 'to build anew the walls of Jerusalem' almost with his last breath. Nicknamed 'the priests' king', he involved himself actively in church affairs, choosing bishops, promoting new liturgies, reforming the Benedictine monks and suppressing heresy. He contributed to rebuilding the nave of Westminster Abbey, where he ordered his magnificent chantry tomb to be erected as close as possible to the shrine of Edward the Confessor.

Henry had restored the crown to its full dignity and authority after the calamities of the 14th century. He governed his subjects with justice and mercy and strove to extend his empire over France, the ancient enemy, to bring peace and security to both realms. Although all this was achieved in a remarkably short time, much remained to be done when he died and his death left the English in an untenable position in France. To England he bequeathed an unending war, which bred political divisions during the long minority of his son.

Below *Henry V's effigy in Westminster Abbey, his youth at death made plain. Dysentery cut short his brilliant career.*

Part IV

Henry VI
1422–1461

During the early years of Henry VI, who became king before his first birthday, the English effort in France was sustained. But the revival of the French, inspired by Joan of Arc; political strife at home; and the king's ineptitude compounded by bouts of madness: all had by 1452 lost the English most of their gains. Violence followed as the Lancastrian and Yorkist factions emerged to begin their struggles over the crown of England. The first phase of the 'Wars of the Roses' ended in 1461 with Henry VI's deposition. From 1440 the main narration is the chronicle attributed to John Benet, a rural clergyman with Yorkist sympathies; John Hardynge laments the evils of Henry VI's governance in florid style; wider perspectives are provided by the Flemish writer Jean de Waurin. Extracts from the Brut, an English chronicle, provide a stirring account of the first — and happier — years of Henry VI's reign.

(Opposite: Henry VI)

After the death of King Henry V his son Henry reigned; he was born at Windsor, and was known as King Henry VI.

Because he was under a year old, his father committed him to the guardianship of Henry Beaufort, bishop of Winchester, and Thomas Beaufort, duke of Exeter, his great-uncles.

The care of France and Normandy Henry V had entrusted to John, duke of Bedford, to be regent and ruler of both until young Henry, with the help of his council, should be able to govern them properly.

Humphrey, duke of Gloucester, he had appointed protector and defender of the realm of England, until the young king, with the help of the council of England, could rule the kingdom wisely, in his own and the country's best interests.

In the second year of King Henry VI's reign Sir John Mortimer [a distant claimant to the throne] escaped from prison in the Tower of London. He was recaptured, brought before the king's justices at Westminster, convicted of treason and sentenced to be drawn on a hurdle through the city to Tyburn and there hanged. This is how he died: may God have mercy on his soul!

The collapse of English power in France

In 1429 English power in France appeared strong an the young Henry VI seemed set for a glorious future king of both lands. However, the flagging cause of th French royal house was miraculously revived by Joan Arc, and during the 1430s Charles VII of Valois prof from the incapacity and peace-loving nature of the English king, the divisions at his court, and the incapacity of his captains of war. The English were swept out of France in the 1440s and in 1453 the longstanding and loyal colony in Gascony finally capitulated to the French. When Henry was depose 1461, England held only Calais and its march on the French mainland. Of crucial importance as a trading outpost and as a military bridgehead, Calais was to b retained – at great cost – until 1558. The Channel Islands were then the last outpost of the Plantagenet dominions.

France in 1429

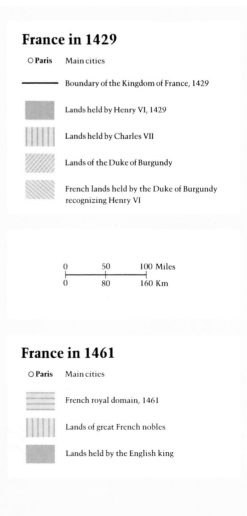

France in 1429

○ **Paris**   Main cities

——— Boundary of the Kingdom of France, 1429

Lands held by Henry VI, 1429

Lands held by Charles VII

Lands of the Duke of Burgundy

French lands held by the Duke of Burgundy recognizing Henry VI

| 0 | 50 | 100 Miles |
| 0 | 80 | 160 Km |

France in 1461

○ **Paris**   Main cities

French royal domain, 1461

Lands of great French nobles

Lands held by the English king

France in 1461

The rise of the Ottoman Turks

In Spain and in the Baltic, crusading forces were still gradually expanding the frontiers of Christendom in the 15th century, but in the Eastern Mediterranean it was Islam which was extending its power. The Byzantine Empire, fatally weakened by the Fourth Crusade in 1204, had subsequently suffered from sporadic western interference and internal divisions. During the 14th and 15th centuries the Ottoman Turks gradually built up

their power in Greece and Anatolia, surrounding and isolating Constantinople, the capital of the Eastern Empire. Promised help from the west failed to materialise and eventually, in 1453, the Emperor Constantine's great city fell to the Turks.

This was only the first phase of Turkish expansion: by 1566 Suleiman the Magnificent's power reached as far afield as the Persian Gulf, Hungary and Tripoli.

Territories of the Ottoman Empire in 1451

Conquests of Mohammed II 1451–81

0   200 Miles

0   300 Km

Henry's uncle, John, duke of Bedford, strove hard to uphold the gains of Henry V in France. The dauphin, now styling himself Charles VII of France – after the death of his father, Charles VI – and his Orleanist party began to recoup their strength and made an alliance with the Scots. Bedford and the English joined in a short-lived pact with Philip, duke of Burgundy. The Brut describes a major confrontation between the English and the Orleanists at Verneuil.

1424

On 17 August a battle was fought at Verneuil in Perche, between the duke of Bedford, regent of France, and the Armagnacs and Scots. The victory went to the English, thank God! Among the enemy slain were the earl of Buchan, the earl of Douglas, the earl of Moray, the counts of Tonnerre and Vendôme, and the viscount of Narbonne, who had in 1419 treacherously murdered Duke John of Burgundy while he was kneeling before the dauphin of France at Montereau. About ten thousand others were killed, but the heaviest vengeance was taken upon the proud Scots, for more than seventeen hundred of their high ranks drowned like dogs that day. Of them it may well be said: 'Bright was the crescent moon when they set forth; homewards they came at its baleful setting.'

Philip of Burgundy proved an untrustworthy ally to the English. In 1424 he made a truce with the dauphin and his party, which was to cause many problems.

In this year Humphrey, duke of Gloucester, the king's uncle, and his wife Jacqueline, the duchess of Holland, left England by sea for Hainault, to take over her inheritance of lands and possessions there. They received a respectful welcome as chief lord and lady of the region. Before long, however, the duke wished to return to England. He left his wife and all the money he had brought from England in a town called Mons, in Holland, whose citizens had sworn to be loyal to him, and to keep his lady safe until his return. But, in the event, they broke their word and handed her over to the duke of Burgundy, who sent her to the city of Ghent in Flanders, to be kept captive there. As God willed it, however, she soon escaped, dressed in men's clothes, going first to one of her possessions in Zeeland, then to another in Holland. Here, with the help of her friends, she held out against the duke of Burgundy and all his wicked schemes.

1425

In this year a serious quarrel arose between Humphrey, duke of Gloucester, and Henry Beaufort, bishop of Winchester, who harboured great feelings of hostility against the citizens of London. The quarrel began on the day the mayor of London was proclaimed, when the citizens came to Westminster; the mayor at that time was a draper called John Coventry. The following day the bishop of Winchester gathered a large band of men-at-arms and archers at Southwark.

The city authorities held the gate at London Bridge with a strong force of the same, so that no one could enter or leave, in an attempt to keep the peace between the two parties. Then, at eight o'clock in the morning, all the citizens of London took up their weapons, barricaded their houses and marched down to the banks of the Thames.

They hoped to cross the water and get hold of the bishop. But the archbishop of Canterbury, Henry Chichele, and others acted as go-betweens; in this way, praise God, it all ended peacefully.

Ten days later, John, duke of Bedford, with his wife, the duke of Burgundy's sister, sailed from France to England to find out if all was well with the king, and the state of the realm. As they approached London the mayor and aldermen, with many of the guildsmen, rode out to welcome the duke and duchess and escort them into the city, where they were to stay at the bishop of Durham's house. The bishop of Winchester rode through London with them, much to the annoyance of the citizens; but the duke's presence and possible displeasure prevented trouble.

In England, Gloucester and Beaufort were once more reconciled.

The last Lancastrian king

BORN at Windsor Castle on the feast of St Nicholas (6 December) 1421, Henry VI was barely nine months old when his father, Henry V, died at the château of Vincennes, near Paris, after dysentery contracted at the sieges of Melun and Meaux. Henry V never saw his only son, and his wife, the young, vivacious Catherine of Valois, went to France five months after the birth; when she next saw her baby he was king of England and, by the treaty of Troyes signed in 1420, heir to the kingdom of her elderly, insane father, Charles VI of France.

In 1422, the new king's accession raised two problems: how and by whom should Henry be brought up; and how should England and English France be ruled during his minority? Henry V's last will made arrangements for his son's upbringing, while, on his deathbed, he gave advice about future government. There were limits to what a dying king could do, but the outcome was generally acceptable. Respected soldiers and royal relatives cared for the king's welfare, nurses saw to his personal needs, and Catherine was at his side, holding his hand when he was brought to parliament in 1423. The question of govern-ment was more difficult. Two of Henry V's brothers were still living – John, duke of Bedford, competent and level-headed, and Humphrey, the cultured but volatile duke of Gloucester – as were two great-uncles, Thomas Beaufort, duke of Exeter (d. 1426), a loyal soldier, and Henry Beaufort, bishop of Winchester, an ambitious prelate whose cloth hardly concealed his ruthlessness. All four expected a place in the new regime.

The lords of England proposed a novel constitutional device for the realm's government: a protectorate. Although the special position of the royal uncles was recognized, none was given overriding power in England. Bedford became regent of English France, while, in England, Gloucester's commission was limited to protecting and defending the king and kingdom, in association with a council of leading men.

The king's closest relatives often argued, and this protectorate was a recipe for personal disputes, particularly between Bedford, Gloucester and Bishop Beaufort.

The protectorate nevertheless preserved public order until Henry was crowned king of England in 1429, before being taken across the Channel to his coronation as the king of France. This ceremony vested him with unique powers in his own right, and the protectorate therefore lapsed. Henry VI was just eight years old.

Above *The birth of Henry at Windsor. Nine months later he became king and inherited his great father's mantle.*

Below *The elaborate funerary effigy of Richard Beauchamp, earl of Warwick, who became the king's tutor in 1428. His son-in-law, Richard Neville the kingmaker, was instrumental in Henry's later downfall.*

1427

A little while after 13 January, King Henry VI's parliament was held at Leicester. At that parliament, Humphrey, duke of Gloucester, and Henry Beaufort, bishop of Winchester, were brought together and reconciled by the king, the duke of Bedford, and other lords who were present. On the same occasion the king created two new dukes: Richard, son of the earl of Cambridge, was made duke of York, and John Mowbray, earl marshal, duke of Norfolk. He also made many knights of the Order of the Bath.

In mid February, John, duke of Bedford, and his wife the duchess sailed to Calais. Henry Beaufort, bishop of Winchester, had sailed there a short while before, and on 25 March 1427 he was instituted as a cardinal in the church of St Mary in Calais, in the presence of the duke of Bedford, regent of France, and his duchess.

Before the mass, which the bishop was to celebrate, a kinsman of the pope brought in the cardinal's hat and very reverently placed it upon the high altar, where it remained throughout the service. When the bishop had said the mass and turned back to the congregation, a garment resembling a friar's cape, made of fine scarlet trimmed with fur, was put upon him. Thus arrayed he knelt before the high altar while the papal bulls were read out to him.

The first bull charged him with the dignity of the cardinalate, the second confirmed all the benefices, spiritual and temporal, held by him in England. After this the duke of Bedford, regent of France, went up to the high altar, took the cardinal's hat and set it upon the bishop of Winchester's head; then the duke bowed in obeisance to the bishop, and gave him precedence.

1428

This year, from the beginning of the month of April until 1 November, there was so much rain that not only the hay but all the grain crops as well were ruined; it rained more or less every day during that period.

On 1 September, Cardinal Henry Beaufort, bishop of Winchester, the king's great-uncle, came to London from the pope at Rome. All the priests and men of religion from in and around London went in procession to meet him outside the city, and on his arrival they showed him all the honour and reverence demanded by his status. The mayor and aldermen and many prominent guildsmen of London went out to Blackheath in Kent, welcomed him there with deference and respect, and accompanied him through the city and so to Charing Cross. There the mayor and citizens of London took their leave of him, and he rode on to Windsor Castle to meet the king.

On 8 November, between four and five o'clock in the evening, the duke of Norfolk with many gentlemen, knights, squires and yeomen, boarded a barge at St Mary Overy, intending to pass under London Bridge. But owing to bad steering the barge collided with the piles of the bridge, and overturned; most of the passengers were killed, but, as God willed, the duke himself and two or three other gentlemen, seeing the danger, leapt up on to the piles. They were rescued by ropes thrown down by people near the bridge, thank God!

In this year the earl of Salisbury set out with a great force of men-at-arms and archers. He was commissioned by the king and council of England to be the king's lieutenant in all the regions of France and Normandy, to destroy his enemies there and chastise rebels by a show of mighty power and strength. He left London with his men and equipment on 25 June. He and his troops made the sea-passage safely, thanks be to God for all his mercies! As soon as he landed in France he made vigorous attacks on the king's French enemies and slew many of them. He captured villages, towns and castles, forcing them to swear allegiance to the king of England. Then he laid siege to the town of Orléans. This siege lasted a long time, for Orléans was so strong, well-manned and provisioned that it could not be taken by any military device.

The earl became very angry at the lack of progress. Finally, as he was inspecting his dispositions with a view to attack, a wicked rascal inside

Royal training

IN his early years, while his uncles and great-uncles won prowess in the affairs of Church and state, Henry VI was put in the care of Dame Alice Botiller, expert in 'courtesy and nurture'. From 1428, he learned knightly accomplishments – 'good manners, letters, languages, as well as courtesy and nurture' – from the cultivated earl of Warwick, Richard Beauchamp.

Humphrey, duke of Gloucester, his uncle, was a forerunner of the English Renaissance and his servant, John Somerset, became Henry's doctor and 'master' in 1427, and helped him to acquire fluency in French as well as in English. Henry learned to recite the religious services by the age of six and his household continued to acquire books, including Bede's writings, religious tomes and *On the Rule of Princes*, which outlined the qualities expected of a king and the moral precepts he should follow. He also enjoyed reading chronicles, and was greatly interested in Alfred, whose canonization he was to urge on the pope in 1442. Like Alfred, Henry VI was to promote education and literacy among his subjects, not least at the universities: he founded King's College, Cambridge, which was closely linked with his college for poor youngsters at Eton, founded in 1441.

Henry spent most of his early years at Windsor or travelling between the royal residences and his mother's houses in south-east England. When he was 11, Warwick complained about sinister influences diverting him from his studies, and two years later the council warned about intrigues at court.

The king was 16 years old in November 1437 when he officially assumed his royal powers, and had begun to take a positive role in government a year before that. There is no sign that he was not physically and mentally up to the task of kingship. He was good-looking, intelligent and sharp – every inch a king. As a young man, he enjoyed hunting, gaming and spending money on fine hats and gowns. After his death, he was remembered as being tall, slim and well proportioned; when his tomb was opened in 1910 the bones were those of 'a fairly strong man' of about 50, Henry's age at death.

A strong character rather than formal education made a successful king in the Middle Ages. Emotionally, Henry was naïve even before his mental collapse in 1453. His piety and sense of Christian morality remained adolescent: his behaviour at the sight of naked bathers at Bath (1449) was prudish, and he was always uneasy in the presence of women. Despite the distinguished soldiers in his household, he developed no martial instincts, and was the first English monarch never to command an army against a foreign foe.

Easily influenced, he was surrounded by the political and personal bitterness engendered by his relatives; Bishop Beaufort was especially astute at exploiting his attitudes and weaknesses. Henry was shocked by the quarrel between the intemperate Pope Eugenius IV and the council of the Church at Basle over whether pontiff or council held supreme power; Henry supported the pope – as did Beaufort. He inclined towards peace with France – just like Beaufort – and was generous to the companions and servants of his youth. Pious and educated, he grew into a simple, pliable man who lacked subtlety and calculation.

Above *The young Henry VI carried by his mentor Richard Beauchamp.*

Below *Henry VI the grown king, his majesty more form than substance.*

the town fired a gun and the ball struck the earl a fatal blow. Much grief and sorrow was felt at his death for a long time; he had always been a man of great valour and courage, and a wise leader.

His body was shipped back to England and laid among his ancestors buried there in olden times. God have mercy on his soul! Amen.

It was at this point, when the dauphin's cause seemed lost, that Joan of Arc appeared. Waurin takes up the story.

While Orléans was under siege, a young girl came to see the dauphin of France, Charles VII, at Chinon, where he was then staying, saying that she was a maiden of about twenty years of age, called Joan. She was dressed in men's clothes, and she had been born in the area between Burgundy and Lorraine, in a town called Domrémy, quite near to Vaucouleurs.

Joan had spent a long time in an inn and was very capable when it came to horses, riding and leading them to drink, and she was also quite adept at other skills not normally performed by women.

She was sent before the dauphin of France by a knight called Sir Robert de Baudricourt, captain of Vaucouleurs. Sir Robert had given her horses and an escort of five or six men, and taught her what to say and do, and how to behave, since she claimed that she was inspired by divine providence and that she had been sent to Charles VII to restore him to the throne and regain possession for him of all his kingdom, from which she said he had been wrongfully driven out and exiled.

When she arrived at the court, Joan was in a pretty poor state, so she stayed for a couple of months in the dauphin's house. Several times she admonished him, as she had been instructed to do, with words designed to make him entrust to her troops, with which she would repel and drive away his enemies, exalt his name and increase his lands.

Joan said that all this had been revealed to her; but she did not at first inspire much confidence from the dauphin or his council.

At court, they thought she was a deluded lunatic, because she boasted of being able to accomplish tasks so difficult that the great princes thought them impossible, even if they combined all their forces in order to attempt them. Her words were mocked and ridiculed, for the princes thought that it was dangerous to believe blasphemy coming from the mouths of the people, and it is a great fault for a wise man to be deceived by believing too readily, in dangerous things.

However, when Joan had been at court for about two months, she was brought before Charles VII. She raised her standard on which she had painted a representation of Our Lord Jesus Christ: in fact all her sentences were punctuated with the name of God, and for this reason many people who saw her or heard her speak, like fools believed firmly that she was inspired by God, as she said. She was questioned several times by eminent clerics and other men of great authority in order to find out exactly what she intended to do, but she stuck to her ideas, saying that if the dauphin would believe her she would restore all his lands.

Now when she came to Charles, there were at court the duke of Alençon and several other great lords and captains with whom the king had been discussing the siege of Orléans. Soon after this, the maid went with Charles from Chinon to Poitiers, where he ordered that provisions, artillery and other necessary things should be taken to Orléans, in force, for her. She asked too if she could have a suit of armour to protect herself, and this was delivered to her.

Then with her standard raised she set off to Blois, where the troops were gathering, and from there to Orléans with the others, still in her suit of armour; during the journey, a number of men fell in behind her.

1429

The maid was extremely well received at Orléans, and some of the men expressed great joy at having her in their midst, so when the French troops who had delivered the supplies returned to the dauphin, the maid stayed there.

Chivalry and knighthood

Left *The jousts of St Ingilbert, in which three French knights opposed 36 foreign challengers over a week.*

Right *A shield with a knight and his lady.*

ALMOST every sovereign in 15th-century Europe had at his disposal at least one knightly order with which to reward his most loyal and deserving subjects. One of the first, and the most enduring, was the Order of the Garter founded by Edward III in 1348. This was followed by the king of France's Order of the Star in 1352 and, in the 15th century, by the duke of Burgundy's Order of the Golden Fleece (1430), modelled closely on the Garter, and by Louis XI's Order of St Michael (1469).

Clear distinctions were made between knightly orders with their limited membership, written statutes and regular meetings or chapters, and simple brotherhoods. Knights of the Bath, as created at Henry VI's parliament in 1427, fell into the latter category: their investiture, performed with extra ceremonial on special occasions, gave them precedence over ordinary knights bachelor. Special insignia – badges and collars – were common to both orders and brotherhoods. In addition to the Garter emblems, the kings of England had various personal devices which their retainers and others wore to signify allegiance, for example, the white hart of Richard II, the greyhound and white swan of Henry IV.

Knightly orders were founded for a variety of reasons – often diplomatic. Henry IV, anxious to secure his claim to the English throne, used the Garter to cement alliances: he created 51 foreign knights during his reign. Henry V admitted the Emperor Sigismund into the order as part of his campaign to secure him as an ally. The Order of the Golden Fleece was to unite the noble rulers of the duke of Burgundy's disparate collection of lands in loyalty to the duke rather than their own regions.

The Arthurian romances were a glamorous model for many orders, including the Garter, while the literary concept of courtly love inspired the votal orders: members vowed to perform a feat of arms in honour of a lady.

Originally societies of fighting men, the orders wore insignia first designed for battle or the tournament. By the 15th century, the ceremonial and practical aspects of these chivalric activities had diverged, and jousts and tournaments were linked only tenuously with real warfare. They taught war-like skills and how to handle weapons, but the tactics were theatrical rather than military.

171

Once she was asked to go out on a raid with the others by La Hire and other captains, but she replied that she would only go if the men-at-arms who had brought her were there too.

So they were recalled from Blois and other places to which they had by now withdrawn, and they returned to Orléans, where they were warmly received by the maid. She went out to welcome them, saying that she had observed and thought about the English and that if they would believe her she would make them all rich.

So, on that very same day, she set out on a lightning raid of one of the English strongholds, and she took it by force; this was only the first of many marvellous achievements for which she was responsible.

Joan of Arc so inspired the dauphinist troops that they began to turn the tide against the English forces. The Brut *glumly recounts the collapse of the siege of Orléans.*

A little before the following Whitsuntide, the siege of Orléans was raised by a dauphinist force under the duke of Alençon. All the magnates and captains besieging the town were dispersed – the earl of Suffolk and his brother, Lord Talbot and Lord Scales, with many of the English troops. They were all, every one of them, taken prisoner soon afterwards, which was a bad business.

In the same year, at midsummer, Cardinal Henry Beaufort, bishop of Winchester, went over to France on business for the king. Sir John Radcliffe, knight, with a great force of men-at-arms and archers, went over at the same time to give help and support to John, duke of Bedford, regent of France and Normandy, and the English troops remaining there by right of the king of England.

The dauphin and his armies, under the leadership of the maid of Orléans, were, however, inflicting considerable damage to English power in France: in July 1429 the dauphin was crowned king of France at Reims. The English soon followed suit by arranging for Henry VI's coronation.

Before Christmas on 6 November, which was a Sunday, King Henry VI was ceremoniously crowned king of England at Westminster by Henry Chichele, archbishop of Canterbury, and other bishops, with all possible ritual and honour.

On this occasion Cardinal Henry Beaufort, bishop of Winchester, and the prince of Portugal, with a fine retinue, came from overseas to attend the coronation and celebrations, in honour and respect for the king.

A French bishop and several knights and squires with their retinues had arrived earlier to stay in London to see the royal pomp and the king's crowning. The day before his coronation the king created thirty-six knights of the Order of the Bath at the Tower of London.

1430

On Friday 24 February, after the king's coronation at Westminster and the parliament held there at the same time, all the lords and commons of England in council recommended that the king should go over the sea to France to take possession of his inheritance, and assume the crown as rightful lord and king of that country.

The king, on the advice of his wise council, appointed his uncle Humphrey, duke of Gloucester, to be his lieutenant in England while he was overseas, to govern and protect the land against his enemies from all sides, and to see that justice and law be maintained in every way, for the well-being of his people and the safety of the realm.

The king came from Westminster to London with his lords and servants. He made an offering at St Paul's, then mounted his horse and rode through the city to bid farewell to the people of London. Then he rode to Canterbury, and remained there until after Easter, while the retinue to accompany him to France was being assembled and drawn up.

Then he arrived at Dover and, during the night, on 22 April, wind and weather being set fair and favourable, he boarded his ship there. When the tide was right they sailed, landing at Calais at seven o'clock on St George's day, 23 April, which was a Sunday. On landing the king went to Calais Castle, and stayed there until his retinue and equipment had made the sea-passage. Within three weeks from Easter they had all joined the king.

A little later, on the advice of his council, the king sent various magnates, knights and captains with their men-at-arms, archers and equipment to some of his towns, castles and garrisons in France and Normandy for the protection and reinforcement of his liege subjects and in maintenance of his claims and rights.

In the same year, on 15 May, an expedition was mounted in France near the town of Compiègne, in which eight hundred first-class troops, Orleanists and Scots, perished on the French side, while many of their higher ranks were taken prisoner.

In this battle the witch of France [Joan of Arc], known as 'la Pucelle', was also captured, dressed in full armour. Her followers, and all the French, were confident that her cunning sorcery would overcome the English army. But God was lord and master of our victory and her downfall, so she was taken and held captive by the king and his council for ever, at his will.

At that battle the English were under the command of John Montgomery and John Stewart, knights of the king's household, and their staff. John Montgomery had his arm cut off, and John Stewart was hit in the thigh by a bolt. But God granted them a return to health and the downfall of all their foes. Praise be to God!

Joan, who had been captured by the Burgundians, was sold to the English for £80,000. In May 1431 her trial began: a burgess of Paris wrote a detailed and lively description of the proceedings.

1431

On 30 May 1431, a sermon was preached in Rouen in front of my Lady Joan, called the Maid, who had been captured at Compiègne. She was standing on a raised platform so that everyone could see her, dressed in men's clothes.

There she was told what great and terrible harm she had caused in christendom and especially, as everyone knows, in the kingdom of France, and how she had attacked Paris with fire and sword on the day of Our Lady's holy birth; and other appalling sins she had committed and made others commit.

In Senlis and elsewhere she had led simple people into idolatry, causing them through her false hypocrisy to follow her as if she had been a holy virgin, telling them that the glorious archangel Michael and the saints Catherine and Margaret and many others appeared to her frequently and talked to her as a friend might talk to a friend – not by revelation, as God has at times spoken to those who love Him, but bodily, by mouth, like a friend.

She said that she was about seventeen years old, and felt no shame at the fact that she often used to go, in spite of father, mother, relations and friends, to a beautiful spring in Lorraine which she called Our Lord's and the fairies' good spring; local people always went there for help when they had fevers.

It was there, under a tall tree which gave shade to the spring, that St Margaret and St Catherine appeared to her. They told her she was to go to a particular captain, and so she did, asking no permission from either of her parents. This captain dressed her in men's clothes and armour, hung a sword at her side and gave her a squire and four men.

Then they set her on a good horse and she went to see the king of France [the dauphin]. She told him that God had ordered her to come to him, that she was going to make him the greatest lord in the world, that it was decreed that any who disobeyed her should be killed without mercy, that St Michael and other angels had given her a very rich crown for him and that there was a sword hidden in the earth for him too, but she would not give him that until the fighting was finished.

Joan rode with the king every day surrounded by men-at-arms, no woman with her at all.

She wore men's clothes and armour and carried a great cudgel in her hand. She used to hit her men hard with this if any of them did wrong, like a most cruel woman.

She said she was sure of paradise when her life was over.

She said too that she knew for certain that it was saints Michael, Catherine and Margaret who came and talked to her frequently, whenever she wished, that she had many times seen them wearing golden crowns on their heads, that everything she did was in obedience to God's command, and, besides this, that she knew much of what was to come.

She had often received the precious sacrament of the altar dressed like a man, armed, her hair cut short and round, wearing a scalloped hood, a tunic and scarlet hose tied with dozens of points.

Some great lords and ladies rebuked her for the scandal of this dress, and said she made a mock of Our Lord, receiving Him in such attire when she was a woman.

She replied at once that nothing could make her change it, she would rather die than give it up, no matter who forbade it, and that she could produce thunder and other marvels if she wanted to.

She said that someone had once attempted to molest her physically but that she had jumped from the top of a high tower and had come to no harm at all.

In various places she had had men and women killed, in battle and also in deliberate revenge, for she had anyone who did not obey her letters killed at once without mercy if she could. She said and maintained that she never did anything except at God's command, which she received frequently from Michael the archangel and from St Catherine and St Margaret, who caused her to do these things. They spoke to her not as Our Lord did to

Moses on Mount Sinai but personally and directly, telling her hidden things that were yet to come and ordering all she did, her dress and everything else.

Such and worse still were the false beliefs of my Lady Joan, and they were all demonstrated to her in front of the people, who were horrified at the dreadful errors against our faith which she had held and did still hold. However clearly her great wrong and wickedness were shown to her, she never hesitated or was ashamed but replied boldly to every charge like one wholly possessed by the enemy from hell.

This was quite clear, for the clerks of the university of Paris humbly entreated her to repent, to recant of her dreadful errors and to do penance; then it would all be forgiven her; otherwise she would be burned in front of the people and her soul would be damned to the depths of hell.

When she saw that they meant this, she asked for mercy. She recanted with her lips, she put on women's clothes – but as soon as she saw herself in that dress she returned to her former error and asked to have her men's clothing back.

Then, without a dissenting voice, she was condemned to death.

They bound her to a stake on the platform, which was made of plaster, and lit the fire under her. She died quickly and her clothes were burned away; then they raked back the fire and showed her naked body to all the people so that they could see the secret parts that a woman should have, and there were no doubts left in their minds. When they had stared long enough at her dead corpse tied there to the stake, the executioner got a big fire going again round her poor carcass and it was soon burned up, both flesh and bone reduced to ashes.

Many people there and elsewhere said that she had died a martyr for her own true lord. Others said this was not so and that the man who had supported her so long had done wrong. That is how people talked, but whatever good or ill she had done, she was burned that day.

La Pucelle

ONE of history's most enigmatic figures, Joan of Arc was 19 when she raised the siege of Orléans in May 1429 and changed the outcome of the war between France and England.

She believed she was inspired by God: from the age of 13, 'a poor maid, knowing nothing of writing and fighting', she had heard the voices of St Michael, St Catherine and St Margaret and seen visions, bathed in light, exhorting her to go to the aid of the dauphin, later Charles VII, and describing how her actions would influence events. Her future was mapped out, and the persistence of the voices made her mission urgent.

Small and sturdily built, with dark hair, she was totally fearless. Her conviction infused others with confidence and she was able to inspire even rough fighting men. She was strict and peremptory, and impatient, even rash, in action, disregarding strategy and the French commanders; the lord of Gamaches declared she was 'a girl who came from no one knows where and has been God knows what'. She loved the fray and turned the tide of the war. In uncouth, menacing language she dictated a letter to the duke of Bedford, commander of the English forces: 'Take yourself off to your own land ... I have been sent by the king of heaven to push you out of the whole of France.' Forceful rather than mystical and passive, she took remarkably little account of supernatural intervention. Even the 'miraculous' discovery of a sword at the church of St Catherine de Fierbois was of little significance to her; it had been excellent 'for giving good clouts and buffets'.

To the defeated and disillusioned English, Joan was 'a creature in the form of a woman. God knows what it is', while Bedford described her as 'a disciple and limb of the Fiend called the Pucelle that used enchantments and sorcery' and accused Charles of associating with 'a disorderly and disgraced woman wearing the dress of a man'.

The charges at Joan's trial for heresy and witchcraft centred on her perversion in wearing male attire – adopted as a practicality when six men escorted her to Chinon for her audience with the dauphin – and the nature and source of her voices and visions. Her courage and acumen in the face of questioning that attempted to prove that her inspiration was the work of the Devil were remarkable. She voiced her opinions and emphasized the importance of personal experience: 'It is for God to make revelations to whom He pleases.' There was humour, too. Did St Michael appear naked? 'Do you think God has not the wherewithal to clothe him?' Did he have hair? 'Why, should it be cut off?' Her direct communication with God seemed to preclude the Church's intercession. She faltered

Above **Joan of Arc in the armour which gave the English one pretext for her trial.**

and abjured only once, and promised to wear a dress, if communion were granted her, but her sentence would have been life imprisonment and few concessions. Defiantly, she resumed the male garb that had distinguished her. 'I have done nothing except by revelations, I have done nothing but by God's command.' She had believed and obeyed with a passionate and unquestioning intensity: 'I believed that it was an angel who spake with me and I had the will to believe it.'

Joan's constancy and defiance condemned her. In May 1431 she was burned as 'an heretic, idolatrer, apostate and relapsed; a liar, a pernicious miscreant; a blasphemer, cruel and dissolute'. Her death was in large measure a political act: in September of the same year a woman was burned for daring to pronounce Joan a saint.

In 1456, when the English had been defeated, the French Charles VII declared her trial an English attempt to defame him and sought – and gained – its annulment from the pope. Joan was rehabilitated by the Church, and Charles remarked, of a girl who changed the course of French history, that she had been 'a simple maid, a virgin, who at the instigation of God ... once fought on my side'.

The loss of Joan weakened French resistance and, as the Brut *shows, opened the way for Henry VI's coronation as king of France.*

King Henry travelled from Calais, through Normandy, to the city of Rouen, where he was received and welcomed as liege lord and king, with all possible ceremonial pomp and joyful respect. The citizens presented him with rich and royal gifts, and gave thanks to God for his arrival.

King Henry VI left Rouen for Paris on 2 December. He went first to Saint-Denis, where he received as fitting a reception as any king ever had in any city. At the place called La Chapelle, between Saint-Denis and Paris, the king and his lords were met by the provost and merchants of Paris, along with members of the three 'estates', a huge number of them, all dressed alike in fine robes of red satin and crimson cloth trimmed with marten fur, and blue hoods. The provost of Paris was wearing a gown of blue velvet, and the three masters of the Châtelet prison were also there, in blue with black hoods.

After these came nine great emperors, kings and queens. All, except the queens, were in armour, though the queens' horses, like the rest, had armoured trappings. The master of the chamber came next, and a great company of treasury clerks, all clad in violet robes trimmed with ermine, and scarlet hoods. The president and members of the parlement followed, in scarlet with fur-trimmed hoods and high round velvet caps. Such were the three 'estates' and the nine distinguished persons.

In front of the Saint-Denis gate, at the entrance to Paris, was a representation of the town's arms — gules, a chief azure, fleurs-de-lys or, on a field azure. There was also a real ship, with full rigging covered in silver leaf, and people in it.

As the king came up to the gate they hung over its side three blood-red hearts, larger than life-size. These opened at the king's approach, and out flew white doves and other birds. There were also banners, telling the king that the citizens welcomed him with all their hearts as their sovereign lord and king.

At the entry to the gate stood six men, bare-headed and dressed in blue, with chaplets of gold leaf. They held a canopy of cloth of gold, on six spearshafts. In the street was a fountain, with three mermaids swimming in the basin. It had three streams, one of spiced wine, one of red wine, and one of milk. There was as much spiced wine as they wanted for the English visitors, with waiters ready to serve them with cups and dishes. Three fauns sported atop the fountain, with others below, pretending to keep it flowing.

At the Châtelet there was a splendid arrangement of platforms hung with cloth of gold curtains blazoned with the king's arms of England and of France. Here, too, were banners all entreating justice of the king of England. Then a wild hart, caparisoned with the arms of Paris, was presented to the king.

King Henry rode on to the church of Notre-Dame to make his offering. All the streets from the Saint-Denis gate were hung with draperies and embroidered cloths, and most of the roadway was strewn with linen.

On Saturday 15 December, King Henry VI arrived at the Louvre, in Paris, in the afternoon, remaining there overnight. On Sunday he was ceremonially escorted from the palace to the church of Notre-Dame in Paris, and there he was crowned king of France by the cardinal bishop of Winchester, other English bishops, and the most eminent bishops of France. The coronation was carried out in a fitting manner, with all possible ritual and ceremony.

At the end of the service, when the king had been crowned, he went back to the palace and attended a banquet with most sumptuous food and wine. All comers, rich and poor, were bidden to the feast.

1432

After his coronation the king went back to Rouen, and thence to Calais, where the merchants of the staple and the citizens welcomed him with respect, honour and gifts.

From coronation to congress

IN July 1429, Charles VII (the dauphin), inspired by Joan of Arc, was crowned king of France. In response, the English mounted a propaganda campaign centred on the ten year old King Henry and his regal authority. His coronation at Westminster on 6 November 1429 was an essential prelude to his coronation as king of France and reflected his dual heritage as sovereign of both realms.

Henry's journey to France required greater planning. In April 1430 the royal household, more than 300 strong, crossed the Channel, at prodigious cost, with a large army. French kings – including Charles VII in 1429 – were traditionally crowned at Reims, but the military situation prevented Henry from reaching the city and his coronation as Henry II of France took place in Notre-Dame, Paris, on 16 December 1431. Cardinal Beaufort crowned the ten year old monarch, and the king and his entourage returned to Rouen with almost indecent haste, and to England in January 1432. Henry never again visited France.

Some Lancastrian advisers were worried about the future of English rule in France and the reliability of the Burgundian alliance which Henry V had considered essential; certainly, the duke of Bedford was exhausted and disillusioned. But they were not yet convinced of the need for peace, or whether anything more than a truce could be negotiated while the king was a minor.

Differences of opinion emerged about future strategy; Bedford wanted to defend Normandy, while Gloucester was committed to Calais, and Cardinal Beaufort inclined towards peace. Negotiations were leisurely and inconclusive, even at the grand Congress of Arras in the summer of 1435, when Beaufort was one of the mediators. English demands and concessions were unrealistic, and in September 1435, after the congress ended, the duke of Burgundy made an alliance with Charles VII. This delivered a mortal blow to English sovereignty in France and Henry VI burst into tears when he heard the news.

A turning-point had been reached in Anglo-French relations. At this juncture Henry himself began to take part in policy-making, supporting Cardinal Beaufort and the search for a lasting peace.

Top *The ten year old Henry VI crowned as Henry II of France, reaffirming English claims to the French crown. But Henry VI never visited France again and later favoured truce with the French.*

Right *The Royal Gold Cup of England and France, solid evidence of English exactions in France. Made in the 1380s for the duke of Berry, it was brought to England in 1434 and became part of the royal treasure.*

Within a fortnight he crossed the Channel and landed at Dover in Kent. The burgesses of the Cinque Ports were waiting to carry him ashore, and many people of Kent and Sussex, gentlemen and yeomen on horseback, dressed for the occasion, flocked to welcome him and accompany him to Canterbury. He stayed there for a day, and folk from all the surrounding countryside rode in to give their king a heartfelt welcome. They escorted him to his manor of Eltham, five miles outside London, where he stayed for five or six days before returning to the city.

On the ensuing Saturday the mayor and aldermen came again to the palace of Westminster, bringing a rich hamper of gold to present to the king. It contained a thousand pounds in gold, a welcome-home gift to mark his safe arrival.

Addressing him as 'your high and mighty grace' and 'beloved lord' they ushered him to his chamber.

Not long after Easter the king held his parliament at Westminster, lasting until 25 July. At the beginning of this parliament Henry Beaufort, the cardinal bishop of Winchester, returned from France and came to the king in London, to defend himself against allegations made about him by certain noblemen concerning some of his actions in France. He made such an excellent defence of himself to the king and his council that he was completely vindicated, and the opposing sides were reconciled.

1433

Shortly after Easter the archbishop of Canterbury, with other bishops and members of the clergy, and the duke of Gloucester accompanied by other noblemen, knights and squires, sailed to Calais to negotiate a treaty between the French and English. The duke of Bedford, the regent, went there from France, with many prominent Frenchmen, lay and ecclesiastical. The cardinal bishop of Winchester was also present.

The French, however, angered by Henry VI's coronation in Paris, were unwilling to negotiate.

John, duke of Bedford, with his newly wedded wife, the daughter of the count of St Pol, came over from France [to get funds for the defence of Normandy], arriving in London on midsummer eve, 23 June. The mayor and aldermen, with many distinguished citizens, escorted them with all respect and honour as far as Fleet Street, to the bishop of Salisbury's house.

1434

On 8 June, John, duke of Bedford, with his duchess, made the sea-voyage to Calais, returning to Normandy and France. They took with them a large force to maintain and strengthen the king's claims in those regions.

In this year also a great plague afflicted the men, women and children of London. Among the victims were distinguished aldermen and other prominent citizens. Many died, rich and poor alike. It was a time of deep sadness for everyone.

1435

This year Henry Beaufort, cardinal bishop of Winchester, and John Kemp, archbishop of York, with the earl of Huntingdon and other noblemen, knights, squires and clerics, went over to France, to the city of Reims, to try to negotiate a final peace between England and France. But the discussions soon broke up, on account of the overbearing pride and greed of the French. The English representatives stayed there from midsummer until the end of September; then they left and returned to England in safety, praise God!

In the winter of 1435 a bitingly hard frost began on 7 December, lasting until 22 February. It was a time of great affliction to everyone, for many died of the cold, and because of the shortage of wood and coal. The frost also killed tender plants like rosemary, sage, thyme, and many others.

Charles VII was anxious to maintain his links with the Scots. In 1436 his son, the Dauphin Louis, was married to Margaret, the daughter of James I of Scotland. The Scotichronicon describes the negotiations and Margaret's perilous journey to France.

Patronage and protectionism

THE towns and cities of 15th-century England were small by modern standards. London, by far the most populous city, had a mere 40,000 inhabitants, most of whom lived in overcrowded conditions within the confines of the square mile of today's City. Throughout the country major urban centres were cramped, noisy and dirty, and constantly at risk from fires – a risk increased by the illegal use of wood and thatch as building materials. Farm animals were kept in the cities and allowed to roam freely through the streets. As artisans, tradespeople and manufacturers lived cheek by jowl with ordinary householders, disagreeable industrial processes like lime-burning, tanning and metal-working were an ever-present nuisance. Even the patients of St Thomas's hospital in London could not escape the racket of local workshops, while pigs rooted around the precincts of Bedlam.

Municipal authorities were not ignorant of, or indifferent to, the connection between public hygiene and disease control. In London a great upsurge of civic pride led to the introduction of piped fresh water, improvements in sanitation and stringent regulations governing the sale and quality of foodstuffs. Throughout England wealthy town-dwellers endowed hospitals and almshouses which were used as schools, refuges for travellers, and homes for orphans and the elderly. Their chief purpose, however, was to care for the sick poor, who could not afford medical treatment. Patients benefited from careful nursing, plain food and clean surroundings – and were mercifully spared the attentions of doctors, whose services were invariably expensive and often fatal.

Some towns such as Coventry and York had already begun to decline as commercial centres but England's position as a focal point in European trade meant the great east and south coast ports flourished. Cloth remained the country's leading export and was exchanged for goods in the Mediterranean, the Baltic, France and even Iceland. Many programmes of urban development resulted from shrewd investment in overseas markets.

Rich and powerful merchants could salve their consciences as benefactors of the poor, but they were also resented because of their paternalistic and authoritarian behaviour. Power in English towns rested in a few hands. Only one quarter of the adult males in London played any part in civic affairs: government was dominated by a narrow clique of aldermen. Restrictions like these provoked popular protests, as in Norwich in 1433 and 1437, when the crown had to intervene to restore order.

Economic life was also hedged about by monopolistic practices. In larger towns each craft or commercial activity was organized within the confines of a guild, partly for protection against outside competition, but also to guarantee high standards of production and service. Regulations impinged on every aspect of members' lives, from their first entry as apprentices to their funerary rites and the support of their dependants; guilds also functioned as social clubs, welfare associations and religious fraternities. Eventually, their protectionism hindered the growth of a free market, and drove industry out into the countryside.

Above *A guild almshouse, the Hôtel-Dieu, survives in Beaune, France.*

Below *Dick Whittington on his deathbed endowing an almshouse.*

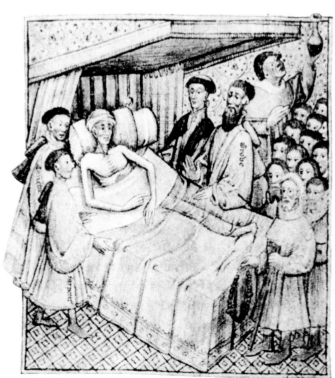

After the battle of Verneuil [1424], Sir John Stewart of Darnley, the constable of the Scots in France, count of Evreux, lord of Concressault and Aubigny, together with the archbishop of Reims and a splendid escort, had come with orders to renew the ancient pacts, alliances and friendships which had subsisted between the kings of France and of the Scots since the time of Charlemagne, and to request the hand in marriage of Lady Margaret, the king of Scotland's firstborn child, for the most noble Prince Louis, duke of Vienne and heir to the king of France.

1436

In 1436, her father sent her to France, accompanied by a splendid retinue, and, the following year, she was married.

The fleet which carried Margaret was under the command of John Cranach, bishop of Brechin, and Sir William Sinclair, earl of Orkney and admiral of the fleet. With them went many valiant knights and worthy men-at-arms.

With these were a hundred and forty chosen squires of gentle birth, most elegantly attired in matching apparel, and an escort of a thousand armed men, who were conveyed in three fair transports and six most excellent barges.

A Frenchman, Peter Chepye, was in command of one of these vessels. So swiftly did it glide across the water that it seemed borne on wings and those who saw its progress judged it could have left the rest of the flotilla far behind in under half a day. It was in this ship that the lady dauphiness travelled.

The English sent a hundred and eighty ships in an attempt to capture the dauphiness. But while they lay in wait for the Scots opposite the Pointe du Raz, all at once a fleet of Flemish merchantmen came towards them, carrying a cargo of wine from La Rochelle to Flanders. The Flemings made no attempt to resist and were captured by the English. But the English were to regret their prize for, without warning, on the following day, a Spanish fleet came to the rescue of the Flemings and their vessels and the English were left empty-handed.

While the English were busy with the Flemings, the fortunate dauphiness was able to evade them and landed at La Rochelle. She stayed quietly at the priory of Nieul, at two leagues' distance from La Rochelle, until the archbishop of Reims, with the bishops of Poitiers and Saintes and the worthy lords of Graville, Gaucourt and Pontoise, came to welcome her, and established her most worthily in a splendid lodging for a little more than two months, up until the wedding, which took place at Tours.

The marriage was performed with all pomp and ceremony by the archbishop of Reims. Once the wedding celebrations were over, the Scots were presented with many pleasing gifts and (apart from the few who were to remain with the dauphiness) returned safely home.

The Scottish king was unwilling to burden the whole kingdom with taxes in order to recoup the expenses of sending his daughter to France. Instead, he made courteous requests to the leading men of each estate and to the beneficed clergy. They were happy to comply and without compulsion made contributions in accordance with the size of their own fortunes.

Philip, duke of Burgundy, had abandoned the English and concluded a separate treaty with Charles VII at Arras in September 1435. As the negotiations neared their close, Bedford died, and the inhabitants of the Ile de France and surrounding regions rose against their English rulers. This enabled Charles VII to take back Paris in April 1436. The Brut describes how the English raised an emergency tax to fund their defence efforts.

In this year, King Henry VI held his parliament at Westminster. Here he was granted a tenth from the Church, and a fifteenth throughout the realm to finance his wars and maintain a defence against his enemies. In addition it was decided at this parliament that everyone, rich and poor, churchman or layman, should pay six pence for every poundsworth of lands, rents and freehold held in this realm of England; and this tax was to be carefully collected in order to meet the king's needs at this time.

Ritual costume

DRESS for ritual and ceremonial occasions is often frozen in time, a relic of styles that were once fashionable but, hallowed by tradition, have remained unchanged over the centuries. For example, the form, like the function, of most liturgical vestments was fixed long before the 15th century, and any changes that occurred then were relatively minor. *Opus Anglicanum*, the famous English medieval style of embroidery, was still widely admired and worked to an extraordinarily high technical standard. To accommodate the elaborate embroidery, the orphreys (decorated bands) grew wider on cope and chasuble and were generally more ornamental than previously. The chasuble itself changed shape. Originally cut in a circle, with a slit for the head, it became heavy and stiff with embroidery – and impossible for the priest to push back along his forearms. As a result the circle was curtailed at the sides into a fiddle shape.

Academic dress was closely linked to ecclesiastical costume. Masters and scholars at early universities were usually tonsured and wore sober, full-length gowns. Until the end of the 15th century the *cappa clausa* was regarded as the distinctive dress. A clerical, though non-liturgical, garment, it was similar to a loose cape with a hood and a slit in front for the arms. The hood derived from ordinary fashionable dress but in about 1450 had become a recognizable feature of academic and legal dress. It was provided with a vestigial liripipe, a remnant of the long tail used to pull the hood on and off or bind it in position.

The three grades of degree – scholar, bachelor and master or doctor – were differentiated by minor details of dress. At Oxford doctors of divinity, canon law, medicine and civil law wore a stalked beret – which was forbidden to masters of arts. Bachelors of all faculties were also denied any head-covering and were forbidden to wear fur or silk linings.

Judicial dress has changed little since the 15th century. Judges were appointed by the king and, as his legal representatives, wore grand, dignified robes – predominantly scarlet. Minor judges and secondary legal officers wore mustard-coloured gowns. All judicial dress consisted of the same components: a closed gown with narrow sleeves, a shoulder cape and, over all, a one-sided mantle called an *armelausa*. Cape and mantle might be lined with fur, and a coif and skull cap were worn on the head.

Civic dress, which started to evolve from the livery which had been worn by officials of 14th-century guilds, was often a parti-coloured robe with one plain and one striped half – another style which, once fashionable, had become 'fossilized' as part of ceremonial dress.

Left *Two judges in full dress.*

Below *Thomas Bekynton, bishop of Bath and Wells, wears robes and mitre.*

Richard, duke of York, with the earl of Suffolk and other noblemen, knights and squires, men-at-arms and archers, with all the supplies and equipment needed for war, went over to Normandy as the king of England's lieutenant, to rule those countries and guard them against the king's enemies, and for the protection of his subjects.

In the same year, about midsummer, the duke of Burgundy with all his forces from France, Flanders and other countries, besieged Calais and the garrisons stationed there. Then the Spanish fleet with other ships, huge vessels, strong and fully manned, came and laid siege to the town of Calais by water. But the earl of Devon brought his navy from the west coast, with other well-manned English ships, and when the Spaniards heard of his arrival they withdrew and made off without delay.

Then the count of Mortain and Lord Camoys led a band of their men out of Calais and broke the duke of Burgundy's siege. They penetrated to his main stronghold, killing most of the defenders. This happened before the duke of Gloucester landed in Calais with his fleet and army.

While all this was going on in Calais and Flanders that year, the king of Scotland led a huge force of troops and artillery to besiege first the town of Berwick, then Roxburgh Castle, inflicting grievous losses on his way. But the earls of Northumberland and Westmorland came with their followers and raised the sieges, so that he fled with his troops and made for Scotland.

1437

On 3 January good Queen Catherine, wife of Henry V and mother of Henry VI, died at Bermondsey Abbey, just outside Southwark, in Surrey. On 8 February she was brought to St Katherine's by the Tower of London, and from thence through London to St Paul's, escorted by noble lords and ladies, also the mayor, aldermen and guildsmen of London, with a company of canons, priests and friars. After this her body was taken to Westminster, where she was buried with royal honours in the Lady Chapel. God have mercy on her soul! Amen.

Attitudes to death

IN the 15th century England witnessed schism in church and state, and almost constant war. All was not as it should be, and, as tangible evidence of this, God wreaked vengeance, chiefly in the form of periodic visitations of the plague. Sensitivity to man's mortality increased correspondingly. Attitudes to death were largely determined by beliefs about the afterlife. Certain measures could be taken, especially by the wealthy, to ensure a swift passage through purgatory. Penance and charitable acts were important and they are a major feature in contemporary wills.

Funerals were elaborate, often with processions of paupers carrying candles, to whom alms were distributed from the deceased's estate. A chantry might be established for a priest to say masses for the deceased, his or her family, the monarch and any other patron. A fine chantry chapel or tomb showing the high rank of the person who had died was often constructed. This was a matter not of pride, but of station: the assertion and acceptance of the deceased's part in the correct order of rights and obligations under God.

The hierarchical view of death is dramatized in *The Dance of Death*. Originally French, the poem was brought to England by John Lydgate who translated it to accompany a series of paintings set in St Paul's graveyard

in London. Death, an animated skeleton, invites people of
all ranks to join his dance. Even a child, too young to
speak properly, is included; and only two of the dancers,
one a hermit and the other a Carthusian monk, gladly
welcome Death's blandishments.

After death, the individual soul depended on prayers to
help it on its journey to heaven, and eye-catching tombs
were designed to remind the living of this need. A
common epitaph began, 'Pray for the soul of . . .', and
accompanied an effigy of the deceased. A striking new
fashion in the 1420s showed the deceased as a cadaver or
skeleton; effective and instructive, it reminded bystanders
of the fate of all mortal flesh. Cadaver tombs sometimes
had two effigies, showing the deceased at the summit of
his earthly career with, underneath, a pathetic and

*Above Charles VI of France's funeral in
1422. His effigy lies on the bier. The chief
mourner (the duke of Bedford) and
members of the parlement of Paris wear
red robes because 'the king never dies'.*

Opposite The horrid reality of death.

emaciated cadaver. The first English example of this is the
tomb of Henry Chichele, archbishop of Canterbury, who
died in 1443, but whose tomb had been in place since
c. 1427 as a focus for his prayers and personal devotion.

Death was to be feared as the sinner's reckoning, but
also to be embraced as a release from this world:
separation of soul from body was, after all, a prelude to
their reunion at the Last Judgement.

On Monday 23 January, during the hard frost, the city gate at London Bridge collapsed and fell on to the frozen surface of the Thames. It dragged with it buildings from inside and outside, causing great damage to the city and the bridge. In this year, too, many limestone walls in houses, churches and cellars broke up in many places and crumbled into dust.

The king held his parliament at Westminster from 13 January until the following Easter. At the beginning of Lent news reached him and the rest of the country that James Stewart, king of Scotland, had been treacherously assassinated at St Johnstone by a Scottish squire.

Waurin gives a graphic account of James's death, and the horrible fate which overtook his murderers.

At this time an amazing act of cruelty was carried out in the kingdom of Scotland. The king of this country was staying at St Johnstone, in the middle of his kingdom, on the River Tay, where he was being lodged in a style befitting a young and trouble-free prince, in a Dominican friary, just outside the town. But on the first Wednesday in Lent some of his enemies spotted him and the leader of these evil men was his uncle, the earl of Athol, and he had thirty men with him including Robert Stewart and Sir Robert Graham.

One night they went to the bedroom in which they were sure the king was sleeping, to carry out their evil deed, but to their frustration found a guard, which was usual for such a distinguished prince, so they postponed their attempt. The next day, 21 February, however, on the stroke of midday, they went back and broke into the king's bedroom, and cruelly and viciously hacked James I to death, some of their thrusts going straight through his heart.

While the murder was going on, the queen, his wife, and sister of the earl of Somerset, tried to help and save him, but was badly wounded twice by the murderers, who, when they had done this, hastily left the scene of the crime to ensure their own safety.

News of this barbarous act spread first through the abbey and then to the town as the cries of the queen and then of other members of the family were heard. A large crowd gathered and went to their lord King James's bedroom, where they found his dead body lying, covered in wounds. They also saw the wounds of the queen, which prompted great pity in their hearts and made them cry in their sympathy for her.

On the following day James I was solemnly buried with royal honours in the Carthusian monastery at Perth.

After this, all the nobles and lords of Scotland met to decide on a course of action, and they unanimously decided, along with the queen, their mistress, that no effort should be spared in tracking down, bringing to trial and punishing these murderous traitors. This was immediately carried out and finally they were all captured and put to death with various tortures.

It must be made known that the earl of Athol, the king's uncle and leader of the murderous conspiracy, had his stomach slit open and his innards burnt before his own eyes, was quartered and his four limbs were placed outside the four largest towns in Scotland. Robert Stewart was hanged and quartered.

Robert Graham was put on a cart on which a gibbet had been built, and to which they tied one of his hands, the one with which he had murdered his lord the king, and he was led through the main streets of the town. Around him were three executioners, who pushed red-hot iron stakes between his thighs and buttocks and in other parts of his body, and then he was quartered.

All the other guilty members were horribly tortured and all of them had been brought to justice within forty days of the murder of the king.

The reason Athol had committed this horrendous crime on his nephew was that when, in 1424, the king had returned from England, where he had been a prisoner for a long time, he punished a number of noblemen, of his own family and

The Kingis Quair

JAMES I of Scotland was born in Dunfermline in 1394, the son of Robert III's old age. Robert ruled his kingdom in name alone, real power being exercised by his brother, the duke of Albany. James's early years were spent in St Andrews, under the tutelage of Bishop Wardlaw and in the company of Henry Percy, exiled son of Hotspur. Early in 1406, however, his father determined to send him to France for his education and safety, James's elder brother, David, having recently been murdered under mysterious circumstances. The journey went badly wrong. After being stranded throughout February on the inhospitable Bass Rock, James embarked on the *Maryenknyght* of Danzig, only to be seized off Flamborough Head and delivered up to Henry IV. For the next 18 years he was the enforced guest of the English monarch.

News of his son's capture all but killed Robert III, who died in April 1406. The duke of Albany continued to govern Scotland and appeals to him for assistance fell upon deaf ears. James remained in captivity and in 1420 accompanied Henry V on campaign in France, sometimes confronting Scottish troops supporting their French allies. He was dubbed knight and invested with the Order of the Garter, but his highest prize after the king's death and before his release in 1424 was the hand of Joan Beaufort, whom he married in Southwark and took home to Scotland as his queen.

James put his years of exile to good use and returned home a musician, poet and man of letters. His greatest accomplishment was the poem *The Kingis Quair*, started while he was a prisoner. Set as a dream-vision, it describes youth's liberation from fortune by philosophy and love. It reveals a broad, attentive reading of Chaucer and Lydgate and is a self-consciously literary blend of many popular themes. Yet *The Kingis Quair* is also an intensely personal spiritual autobiography, the story of the love of one man, a prisoner, love for a real woman:

> 'The bird, the beste, the fisch eke in the see,
> They lyve in fredome everich in his kynd;
> And I a man, and lakkith libertee . . .'

James I was crowned in Scone in 1424. As king he attempted to impose his version of the strongly centralized bureaucracy of Lancastrian England upon the culturally divided Scottish nation. His methods were not popular, particularly the heavy taxation he imposed in an effort to pay the £40,000 demanded by the English for his keep when he was a prisoner. He executed the duke of Albany's son and successor in 1425, along with his two sons, ending the threat from Albany's line. He was,

Above *James I, king of Scotland, with his English queen, Joan Beaufort, daughter of the earl of Somerset. His enforced absence from his native land was precipitated by the threat from his uncle the duke of Albany, who was suspected of ordering his brother David's death and who stood to succeed to the throne if James was also eliminated. His captivity in England served at least to protect him from his uncle's machinations and gave him the leisure to become one of the leading poets in the Chaucerian tradition.*

however, less successful in his attempts to control the unruly Highlanders.

James confiscated baronial lands both as a punishment and as a way to increase crown revenue, but the nobility were increasingly alienated by his vigorous approach to government. An alliance of Archibald, fifth earl of Douglas, Malise Graham, earl of Strathearn, Graham's uncle, Sir Robert Graham, and the Stewarts of Atholl, who revived their claim to the throne, took up arms and defeated the king at Roxburgh in 1436. On 27 February 1437 while James was entertaining the papal legate at the Dominican friary in Perth, he was murdered in a private chamber; unarmed, he had tried to escape through a sewer. His zealous administration was later to be recalled with regret during the near anarchy of James II's minority.

others, who had governed the country in his absence and who had not carried out their duty to pay his ransom or to rescue him from the English. Among these noblemen there were some who were close relatives of the earl of Athol, which is what prompted his intense hatred of the king. However, for a long time Athol had pretended to be one of James's most trusted and faithful servants, while harbouring this deep-seated loathing of him; and eventually he could hold it back no longer, as you have already heard.

The king of Scotland had a son of about twelve years old, also named James, who, with the agreement and authority of all three estates of Scotland, was confirmed as king of Scotland and was placed into the capable hands of a famous and courageous knight, Sir William Crichton, who had also been looking after him while his father was still alive. The right-hand side of this new king's face was red and the other half white.

Meanwhile England's population was, as the Brut *relates, severely afflicted by a dearth of foodstuffs.*

Throughout the whole of that year there was a great shortage of grain. A bushel of wheat cost twenty-two pence, rising at the end of the year to twenty-six pence; a bushel of rye cost sixteen pence, later eighteen pence, and of barley ten pence, later twelve pence. The bread sold to the common people was very poor stuff. A gallon of red wine was ten pence, while sweet wines like Rumney, Malmsey, Claret and Tyrian were sixteen pence. Meat and fish were very expensive for a long time, which was hard on the common people all over the country. In the north a bushel of wheat cost forty pence for most of the year.

Many persons, notable and common, died of the plague throughout the land, especially at York and in the north. God have mercy on their souls! Amen.

1439

On 22 April, between two and five o'clock in the morning, a severe storm of thunder, lightning, hail, wind and rain had occurred, giving rise to

Shopping centres

THERE were four possible places to shop during the Middle Ages: markets; fairs; shops (in towns); or at home, from travelling pedlars and chapmen or merchants. Of these transactions, the great majority occurred in markets and fairs.

Markets were numerous and took place frequently. They served restricted communities and traded in humble merchandise, especially food. They were usually founded or fostered by the local lord of the manor, to whom they were a source of prestige and profit: he charged rents to the stallholders, imposed tolls on merchandise, and, for a fee, provided weights and measures. It was prudent to obtain a royal charter granting the right to hold a market – and kings were happy to give them – normally for a fee, although the concession could be freely given to someone who had rendered outstanding service to the crown. By the early 14th century there were about 3,000 markets in England but from about 1340 to 1600 the number declined sharply – to about 1,000 – and trade became concentrated in fewer and more specialized centres.

Typical rural markets were held once a week and sold grain, cattle and poultry, dairy products especially cheese, bacon, wool and cloth. There might be up to three weekly in towns, where selling sometimes became very specialized; Ipswich had separate markets for timber (imported from Scandinavia), butter and wool, while Lincoln had separate ones for six different commodities.

Fairs were rarer than markets, lasted longer, and provided a wider range of goods. They were generally held once a year, often to coincide with the festival of the patron saint of the village church, or at some convenient time in the farming calendar – early summer, when livestock was ready for selling, or autumn, when crops were harvested – and lasted for three days. But there were wide variations. A substantial minority were twice-yearly and could last for as long as two weeks. Although some,

like the Nottingham Goose Fair and Yarmouth Herring Fair, specialized in particular products, most fairs offered a wide range of goods, many of which were imported: high-quality cloth from Italy and Flanders, wine from Gascony, wax and furs from Scandinavia, pottery from northern France, spices and seasonings from the east – cloves and pepper were often part of tenants' rents. A great fair was profitable for its lord, who was usually also lord of the local market: the abbot of Ramsey in Huntingdonshire said his fair at St Ives was as valuable as ten manors.

Plays on biblical and moral subjects were performed at some fairs, which also attracted travelling entertainers of all kinds, as well as confidence tricksters and quack doctors – who were so numerous that in 1421 Henry V issued an *Ordinance against Meddlers with Physic and Surgery* to try to curb their activities.

Disputes had to be settled quickly – the parties were generally not local residents but had travelled some distance to the fair. They were recognizable by their dusty feet (*piepoudre*) and, as a result, the tribunals were known as pie powder courts.

great terror. But Our Lord and his blessed mother Mary preserved and protected his creatures through it all, praised be their names! Amen.

On 23 November in the same year, between three and four o'clock in the afternoon, there befell a terrible storm of wind and rain, thunder and lightning, with dense smoky fog. The appalling noise was heard all over the land, causing great alarm. There was an earthquake, too, shaking the ground everywhere.

On the Monday after Trinity that year the earl of Huntingdon and other noblemen, knights and squires, with men-at-arms and archers, left London for the coast to take over the rule and protection of the city of Bordeaux and the regions of Gascony and Guyenne, in the interests of our liege lord the king and the welfare of the realm of England.

Later that year a truce was concluded with the French which gave the English a breathing-space both in Gascony and in northern France. Sporadic negotiations continued for three further years, but they achieved little beyond agreement on the ransom of Charles, duke of Orleans, who had been captured by the English at Agincourt. The story is taken up by the chronicler John Benet.

1440

At around Christmastide, the town of Harfleur was besieged by Lord Talbot and taken for the king of England.

Before Christmas, the duke of Orleans, who had been a prisoner in England for twenty-five years, was released from captivity, on condition that he help negotiate a peace treaty between the kingdoms of England and of France. He married the daughter of the duke of Cleves.

1441

On 23 June, Richard, duke of York, crossed the Channel to France; he was accompanied by five thousand soldiers.

War, peace and ransom

IN 1437, when Henry VI was 16 years old, and ruler in fact as well as name, the time seemed right to make peace with France. The king, repelled by the misery, waste and expense of the war, decided to use Charles, duke of Orleans, the highest-ranking prisoner captured at Agincourt, to advance the cause of peace, in the belief that he would influence his kinsman, King Charles VII.

Yet not even Henry contemplated surrendering hard-won territory, still less his title of king of France. His dilemma was heightened by the fierce clash between Cardinal Beaufort, his great-uncle and the apostle of peace, and the militant Humphrey, duke of Gloucester, his uncle and, unless and until Henry fathered a child, his heir presumptive; they flung insults at each other whenever France was discussed. The peace conference near Calais failed in the summer of 1439, but Orleans was nevertheless released.

Charles of Orleans was 21 when he was captured in 1415, and spent the next 25 years in England. He put his time to good use and wrote poetry, ballades and lyrics that earned him a high reputation as the last of French courtly poets; his writings reflect a deep longing for his native land. However, his political significance as a dove of peace was exaggerated. Gloucester denounced his release as unwise and a betrayal of the past; Henry saw it as a way towards a higher goal.

In 1440 a ransom was agreed with the French king: 40,000 nobles down and 80,000 marks in six months' time; if Orleans arranged peace, the ransom would be cancelled. As Orleans swore his oath to adhere to these terms in Westminster Abbey on 18 October 1440, Gloucester stalked out. Charles crossed the Channel early in November, was greeted by the duchess of Burgundy – but failed to gain even an interview with Charles VII.

This bold but ill-conceived initiative on the part of Henry was accompanied by the consolidation of Lancastrian rule in Gascony and in northern France, although it was soon clear that the English lacked the resources to defend both indefinitely. Confused and inept arrangements for command in France had followed the death in 1439 of the admired earl of Warwick, Henry's lieutenant there, and dynastic rivalry was taking root among the English nobility. Cardinal Beaufort's nephews, John, earl of Somerset, and Edmund, count of Mortain, received temporary commands (1439–40). Like the cardinal, they were descended from John of Gaunt. Richard, duke of York, was the king's cousin and England's premier duke after Gloucester; he had been lieutenant in France from 1436 to 1437 and resented losing his authority. The issue was all the more sensitive because Henry was still unmarried and both branches of his family — York and the Beauforts — could regard themselves as having a good claim to be his heirs.

York was reappointed lieutenant in July 1440 and was urged to treat with Charles VII. By 1442 Henry VI was studying marriage proposals from a southern French noble, the count of Armagnac, and commissioning portraits of his daughters; such an alliance might have protected Gascony but it outraged Charles VII. Then, in 1443, John Beaufort, newly created duke of Somerset, was given command of an expeditionary force which seemed to cut across York's authority as lieutenant. When Somerset landed in Normandy, he crossed the Breton frontier, attacked a Breton town and alienated the duke of Brittany, a valued English ally. He returned to England in disgrace and died in 1444 – possibly at his own hand. These contradictory policies and incompetence played into Charles VII's hands and defeated Henry VI's intentions.

Finally, a far-reaching step in the search for an honourable peace was conceived: Henry VI's marriage to a princess of the royal house of France. By the beginning of 1444, the name of Margaret of Anjou, niece of the French queen, was being mentioned.

Opposite *Charles of Orleans in the Tower where he wrote some of his best verse.*

Below *Charles's assent to his ransom terms.*

On 30 August, suddenly and with no apparent cause, there was a riot involving about sixty very well armed southerners in Oxford. In an outbreak of great violence, they broke a window of Master William Wytham, a doctor of civil law, who was at that time principal of the White Hall in Turl Street.

They made a great commotion, calling the members of the White Hall 'Scottish dogs' and shouting 'Fire! Fire! Fire!' Then, through a gate which had been opened by Wytham, they let fly two hundred arrows. But God was protecting the members of White Hall and scarcely any of them were wounded.

On the following day, despite the instructions issued by the chancellor, assisted by Thomas Bayley, then mayor of Oxford, some of the armed men just mentioned, from both parties, had an encounter at around two o'clock in the afternoon, in Queen Street, opposite the gate of the college which is commonly called Broadgates, in the parish of All Saints.

Again, the fight was ferocious so that many of the southerners were battered and knocked to the ground. Thirty of them hid in the college cellars and did not dare even to show their faces, fearing they might lose their lives.

About twenty-four of the northerners, full of triumphant glee, came upon men hurrying towards Carfax and also thirty Welshmen who were hastening to the defence of the college of Broad-gates. The northerners beat some of these, others they knocked to the ground, while the rest fled.

One of the latter was wounded in the neck by an arrow and died eight days later. However, thanks to the Lord's protection, not one of the northerners sustained an injury.

On the following day, in London, there was a great set-to between the men of the court and the townspeople, during which five of the court party received fatal arrow wounds.

At around this time, there were disputes in diverse parts of England.

Sports and pastimes

THE violence endemic in 15th-century English society often broke out in riots, as in Oxford and London in 1441. One way of canalizing and diverting it was in participatory sports, such as football. Already a national obsession, it was practised on village greens on all possible occasions. Its festival matches, violent mêlées traditionally held on Shrove Tuesday, might involve two or three villages in extreme cases and the goalposts could be several miles apart. So popular had it become that it was banned by Edward III, Richard II and Henry IV because it undermined the fighting capacity of England's archers.

Because archery was used in war as well as sport it was made compulsory to practise its skills; in the middle of the 15th century, for example, a statute compelled every man to own a longbow and ordered that butts be erected in every village for target practice.

Tennis, played with a hard ball in an enclosed space – often a dry castle moat – was an increasingly popular if dangerous sport favoured by both the English and French royal houses; and an early form of cricket was played in the villages as well as at court.

One of the most popular outdoor sports was hunting, enjoyed mainly by the king and great barons, and sometimes by the higher clergy. Game included the hare, hart, wolf, wild bear and fox and was shot with bows and

arrows or pursued with greyhounds, which were a favourite present for the ladies who often accompanied their lords.

Falconry was as popular as hunting. Hawks were valued gifts and were protected by royal edict; the penalty for stealing or destroying their eggs was imprisonment. The most common game was water-fowl: the birds were frightened to make them rise so that the hawk could seize them. Falconry was forbidden to the clergy by church canon, but some high-ranking clerics defied the law.

No special dress was worn for hunting or falconry although the hawk's caparison included special gloves that prevented the bird's talons from injuring the falconer. These are frequently listed in 14th- and 15th-century royal inventories, as are the hood or cap that covered the bird's head when it was not flying at game and the leather strap that held it to the falconer's wrist.

Shovel-board was a popular indoor diversion. Flat metal weights were pushed across a table to land as close

Above A boisterous game in progress in the streets of a medieval city.

Opposite Two knights enjoy the quieter pleasures of chess; its martial symbolism made it popular with men of war.

as possible to the opposite end, without falling off. Points depended on a player's proximity to horizontal lines on the table top.

Dice, chess, backgammon (called 'tables') and cards were regularly played and – with the exception of chess – regularly prohibited by law because they encouraged gambling. Chess, known in England before the Norman conquest, was popular in royal and aristocratic circles.

Children played many of these games, as well as skipping, leapfrog, marbles and blind man's buff.

On 7 July, many men and women were arrested, apparently for plotting the death of his most illustrious majesty, King Henry VI.

Eleanor Cobham, who was at that time duchess of Gloucester, sought sanctuary in Westminster Abbey. Later, of her own free will, she left the sanctuary of the abbey and was locked up as a prisoner in Chester Castle.

Many of her household, who were accomplices and accessories, were placed in the Tower of London. A priest, whose name was Roger Boling-broke, was hanged, drawn and quartered.

The king, who had taken over the reins of government in 1437, aged 15 years, was meanwhile proving himself a poor leader and politician. He was, however, noted for his great piety, as Capgrave tells us.

In 1441, the most pious King Henry founded two splendid colleges and devoted great care and expense to their buildings. He graced the laying of the foundation stones with his presence and with great devotion offered his foundations to Almighty God. The first is at Eton near Windsor, dedicated to the Blessed Virgin; the other, King's College at Cambridge, in honour of St Nicholas. Of the laying of the King's College foundation stone, a certain outstanding poet wrote:

> By thy light, O holy Nicholas,
> King Henry the Sixth founded this work.
> He who later placed the anointed stone at
>   Eton
> Erected this, all mindful of his clergy.
> It was one thousand four hundred years plus
>   one
> Since the Lord's passion.
> It was the nineteenth year of his reign, of
>   April
> The second day, when the king bent here his
>   knee.
> O Nicholas, confessor of God, denizen, like
>   the Virgin,
> Of heaven, grant the king the joys of the
>   highest place.

The duke and the witch

HUMPHREY, duke of Gloucester, was the fourth and youngest son of Henry IV and his first wife, Mary de Bohun. Born in 1391, he probably studied at Balliol College, Oxford – the Lancastrians were the best educated and most intellectual of English medieval princes – and was a great collector of books and patron of scholars from an early age. He gave money and books to the new university library at Oxford – later the Bodleian – and is honoured as its founder. Affable and energetic, he was also shallow and irresponsible.

When Henry V died, Gloucester made a bid to be regent on behalf of the infant Henry VI. He was given the title of protector but the council ensured that real power remained in its own hands. In 1422 Humphrey made a rash marriage to Jacqueline, the exiled countess of Hainault, Holland and Zeeland, whose previous marriage to John, duke of Brabant, had been annulled. Hainault was claimed by the duke of Burgundy, and when Gloucester invaded the territory on behalf of his wife in 1424, an alliance vital to English interests in France was threatened. Gloucester also quarrelled with his Beaufort uncle, Henry, bishop of Winchester, and their rivalry dominated domestic politics throughout Henry VI's minority and beyond.

Ultimately unsuccessful in the Netherlands, Gloucester gradually lost interest in Jacqueline's affairs, although he supplied her with money and men until their marriage was declared invalid in 1428. This coincided with the duke's own affair with Eleanor Cobham, one of her English ladies.

The daughter of Sir Reginald Cobham of Sterborough in Kent, Eleanor bore him two children out of wedlock before she persuaded him to marry her in 1431. It was an unpopular match: the new duchess was proud, determined and ambitious. When his elder brother Bedford died in 1435, Humphrey became heir presumptive to the throne; Eleanor was only one step away from being queen and, until Henry married Margaret of Anjou in 1445, she was England's first lady.

Like many well-born women, Eleanor was interested in necromancy – predicting the future by communicating with the dead. Not unnaturally, she wished to know if and when she would become queen – and, to this end, employed priests who practised necromancy and witchcraft in her household.

Gloucester was successful and popular in the 1430s when he was captain of Calais, but by 1440 his anti-French policies were superseded by Cardinal Beaufort's peace negotiations. Politically isolated, his influence with the king was waning. His opponents used Eleanor's

Above **Humphrey kneels before the Man of Sorrows.**

dangerous dabblings, which came close to heresy and treason, to discredit him. In the summer of 1441 three priests – Roger Bolingbroke, the duchess's personal clerk, John Hunne, her chaplain, and Thomas Southwell, canon of St Stephen's chapel, Westminster – were found guilty of conspiring to bring about the king's death by witchcraft.

Tried on the same charges, Eleanor admitted five of the 28 counts and was convicted of witchcraft and treason. The ecclesiastical authorities sentenced her to do public penance in the streets of London and pronounced her divorce from Duke Humphrey. The secular authorities condemned her to life imprisonment; her associates were executed. She was held at Chester, then Kenilworth and finally on the Isle of Man, where she died in *c.* 1457.

Would that, following the king's example, his subjects were inclined to adore the sign of the cross when his priests approach. I know many men leading a lusty life who have been encouraged by the king's most devoted example to greater fervour in the faith and a more sincere embrace of Our Lord's glorious sign.

May this greatly please the king, that his subjects should be reformed by his good example. For it is said, and experience proves it of him, that in no wise does he wish the Church or churchmen to be harmed; in this he is a true follower of Constantine the Great.

In 1442 the French launched an all-out attack on Gascony. The English, crippled by poor finances and political dissensions, were unable to sustain their defences either in the south or in Normandy. Then in 1444 another truce was arranged and Henry VI married a French princess, Margaret, daughter of René, duke of Anjou, and niece by marriage of Charles VII. She was to prove highly influential in English affairs. On her persuasion Henry VI handed over Le Mans and other fortresses in Maine to Charles VII in 1448, and the truce was extended once more.

In England, Margaret fomented further discord in an already highly charged political climate, as Waurin shrewdly observes in his analysis of English affairs in the 1440s.

The very noble duke of York, governor general of the duchy of Normandy and consequently of all the conquered territories, had been appointed to this post by Henry V.

York's duty was to guard and protect this country from the French, our enemies, and during his time in office, he governed admirably and had many honourable and notable successes over the French in different places and in various ways.

Everything he did was highly commendable, not only for himself, but also for the honour and furtherance of the crown of England, and for the exaltation of his master the king, whom he served with due reverence and loyalty, as all noble hearts should serve their sovereign lords.

The new universities

IN 1400 there were 45 universities in Europe: 100 years later the number had risen to 79. The new foundations included the first three in Scotland: St Andrews (1413), Glasgow (1451) and Aberdeen (1494). Universities were also established in areas of France under English rule – at Poitiers (1431), Caen (1432) and Bordeaux (1441).

The new movement affected England differently. Oxford and Cambridge, in existence since the 13th century, still had a monopoly on university education. But great advances were taking place within these centres of learning. They were organized by colleges – independent associations of scholars which originally provided accommodation, and were now also taking on much of the teaching. Between the mid 14th century and the Reformation, Oxford acquired six new colleges, and Cambridge nine. Across the country, new grammar schools sprang up to provide basic skills in literacy and numeracy; in London the Inns of Court gave a popular training in law and estate management.

The average student in late medieval Europe went to university in his mid teens and left after a few years with a smattering of education but no degree. Others spent four or five years studying the seven liberal arts – grammar, logic, rhetoric, arithmetic, geometry, astronomy and music – which equipped them for the oral examinations leading to the degrees of B. A. and M. A. A few high-fliers were allowed to go on to the more advanced subjects and win doctoral degrees in theology, canon law, civil law and medicine. Originally, different universities had developed different specialisms – Paris for theology, Bologna for law, and so on – and students had travelled widely in search of the greatest teachers and libraries. In the 15th century, however, wandering scholars were something of a rarity. Most Englishmen were content with the choices and the standards at Oxford and Cambridge.

The greatest educational foundations of the age were Henry VI's twin colleges at Eton and Cambridge. In 1440 the king decided to create a community of 25 scholars at Eton, within sight of his own palace of Windsor, and, in the same year, he set up a rector and 12 scholars in what would become King's College, Cambridge. These foundations were originally devoted more to the salvation of Henry's soul than to the advancement of knowledge. But in 1441 the king's attention was drawn to William of Wykeham's work at Winchester College and at New College, Oxford. Determined to outdo his predecessors, he considerably increased his endowments to Eton and King's so that each could maintain 70 scholars. By their sheer size and wealth, the colleges were set to become major centres of learning in England.

Henry VI laid the foundation stone of King's College chapel on 25 July 1446; and, for the rest of his reign, devoted time and money to the building programmes at Eton and Cambridge. The money ran out after Henry's deposition in 1461, and neither project was completed in his lifetime. At Eton the original plan had been to build a church as long as Lincoln Cathedral and almost as wide as York Minster; but the college authorities were forced to make drastic cuts, and only the choir was completed. Cambridge fared better. The original work at King's, by the master mason Reginald Ely, was well advanced by 1461, and both Edward IV and Henry VIII were pleased to contribute to its completion. The crowning glory was the great fan vault, erected under the supervision of John Wastell in the early years of the 16th century. Today, King's College chapel stands as the ultimate monument to the Perpendicular style of architecture, and Henry VI's most worthy achievement.

Above *Eton College, one of Henry VI's most famous foundations.*

Opposite *A bronze lectern effigy from King's College chapel of Henry VI, who laid the chapel's first stone in 1446.*

Below *The foundation charter of King's College, Cambridge, with Henry VI kneeling (at the right) during the opening of parliament. Behind him kneel the lords, and below them the commons. The scroll under the royal arms names him as founder.*

Nevertheless, in spite of all these qualities, envy, which never dies and is the enemy of all virtue and nobility, reared its head amongst the princes and barons of the kingdom of England, and was directed at the duke of York, who was gaining in honour and prosperity. What is more, he prospered far too much for the liking of those who did not devote themselves loyally to the benefit of the king and his country.

Above all, envy prompted the duke of Somerset, who despised the duke of York and who found a way to harm him. He was well liked by the queen of England, Margaret of Anjou, daughter of René, duke of Anjou, and the king of France's niece.

She worked on King Henry, her husband, on the advice and support of the duke of Somerset and other lords and barons of his following, such that the duke of York was recalled from France to England. There he was totally stripped of his authority to govern Normandy, which he had done well and for some time, and despite his having acted commendably throughout the whole English conquest of France.

In York's place, the duke of Somerset was appointed due to the solicitation and exhortation of the said queen and of some of the barons who, at that time, were in positions of power in the kingdom.

It must be pointed out that this change and others that took place in the kingdom were due to the simple-mindedness of the king, who was neither intelligent enough nor experienced enough to manage a kingdom such as England, which had been further enlarged by the conquest of Normandy and other areas of France.

This only goes to prove the proverb, 'Cursed be the land where the prince is a child or rules like one', for in the absence of a prudent prince, we have seen much trouble and several kingdoms and provinces ruined and destroyed, with subsequent suffering for the poor people. Certainly, this was nearly the case in the aforementioned kingdom, for in this instance, there was much dissension which almost put an end to all happiness.

Above *François Villon himself, from the 'Testament', composed in prison. A man with a criminal past, he was also an able and forthright poet.*

Opposite *The frontispiece from the first folio of the 'Testament', a work in which a bequest to a prostitute appears with profound personal reflections.*

The prince and the poet

IN the middle of the 15th century, a Milanese ambassador in France remarked that 'King René is the one who governs this entire realm.' It had not always been so; for much of the early part of his life, René, duke of Anjou and self-styled king of Sicily (the traditional title of the rulers of Naples), had had to struggle to ensure his own political survival. A dispute with Philip the Good of Burgundy over the succession to Lorraine led to a prolonged period of imprisonment, while his claim to the kingdom of Naples, to which he had succeeded on the death of Queen Joanna II in 1435, was successfully contested by Alfonso of Aragon.

Abandoning his dreams of conquest abroad, René returned to France in 1441, and began to consolidate his position. Charles VII had married his sister Mary, and spent much of his childhood at the Angevin court; this relationship proved to be of great importance to René, who was constantly with the king, as a member of the royal council, and as a companion in festivities and tournaments and on campaigns in Normandy and Lorraine. In May 1444 a two-year truce was signed with the English on condition that Henry VI marry a French princess; René's younger daughter Margaret was chosen.

During this happy period of his life René was able to develop his wide-ranging artistic talents. Although an artistic 'jack of all trades', he was master of at least one: he was unsurpassed as an illustrator of manuscripts. René was also known as a musician, and his development as a writer probably owed much to his friendship with Charles of Orleans, to whom he addressed five rondeaux (his first known writings) on the occasion of the 1444 truce in which both princes were involved.

René's court was renowned for its brilliance. A centre for writers, artists and musicians attracted by his generous patronage, it was also a place where the chivalrous tournament existed side by side with the pastoral idyll, and where life was softened by silks and porcelains from the east. To this court, early in 1457, came François de Montcorbier, Master of Arts, convicted murderer, thief and poet, otherwise known as François Villon.

Little is known of the life of the greatest French poet of the later Middle Ages. Born around 1431, he was a young child when his father died and he was adopted by Guillaume de Villon, chaplain of Saint-Benoît-le-Bétourné in Paris's Latin Quarter, where he later studied at the Sorbonne. He was convicted in 1455 of killing a priest, and in 1456 was involved in a robbery at the college of Navarre. As a result he left Paris in December 1456, after composing his *Lais* ('Legacies'), a light-hearted parody in which he bequeaths valuables such as his hair-

clippings and his old shoes to friends, relatives and officials. This was the start of five years of wandering. Villon did not spend long at René's court. Although it has been suggested that he found his true home among the Coquillards, bands of roving bandits who terrorized the countryside in the 1450s, this is unlikely; the Coquillards were rounded up in Burgundy between 1455 and 1457, and Villon was still travelling four years later. The occasional verses composed in Coquillard slang are probably the wishful thinking of a petty criminal or the verbal game of a poet.

In 1461, Villon was imprisoned by the bishop of Orléans at Meung-sur-Loire – and pardoned by Louis XI who had just succeeded to the throne. He composed his major work, the *Testament*, in the winter of 1461–2. It is an amplification of the earlier theme of the *Lais*, where he reflects on the iniquities of others, especially the bishop of Orléans, and on his fear of death and old age; he concludes with a second series of burlesque legacies.

Villon was condemned to death in 1462, but the sentence was commuted by the parlement to a ten-year period of banishment from Paris. Nothing is known of him after this date; possibly he did indeed meet his end on the gallows that had inspired some of his greatest poetry.

Sensieut vnst petit traittie dentre
lame denote z le aier lesql sappelle le
moztissiemt de vaine plaisance fait
z copose p irne toy de seale duc dariou
p luy made z ititule a tresreuered
pere en dieu larcheuesq de toure
lesql traittie fu fait en lan mil·iiij·
·lb· Et dusl comence le proesme·

Tresreuerend pere en dieu se
han par la duine strace ar

Left *René of Anjou writing in his study.*

Below *Amour takes René's heart; from his romance 'Le Coeur d'Amour Epris'.*

Above *From René's 'Livre des Tournois': before a tournament, ladies and judges inspect the contenders' helms, pointing out those guilty of unchivalrous conduct.*

At the time we are talking about, there were, in the kingdom of England, two parties contending for the government and administration of the king and his people. In one of these parties there was Humphrey, duke of Gloucester, King Henry's uncle, Richard, duke of York, and several other princes and notable barons; the other was an alliance between the dukes of Somerset and Suffolk, Lord Say, the bishop of Salisbury and several others not named here.

It must be noted here that the duke of Gloucester had previously acted as regent for the king, his nephew, and had governed extremely well, to the benefit of the king and all his people.

Now, however, William, duke of Suffolk, from the other party, was the principal adviser to the king, and was also well loved by the queen. It was through her and Edmund, duke of Somerset, and other men of his party that they managed to talk to the king in private, and point out to him that Normandy was costing him a lot to maintain, in wages to the soldiers he was keeping there under the duke of York and in other sundry daily expenses. So they recommended to him that the country of Normandy should be handed back to the French in order to avoid all these expenses.

This was how it happened that the duke of York, governor and regent of Normandy, was recalled, as I have already mentioned, and the duke of Gloucester removed from the privy council of the king, his nephew.

Shortly after his return from Normandy, something even worse happened to the duke of York which was provoked by the duke of Suffolk and other members of his party, for in 1449 he was expelled from the court and exiled to Ireland.

So the duke of Somerset and his supporters, being responsible for all these deeds and having increased their standing with the king, were over-joyed, and managed to influence the king to appoint Somerset governor of Normandy. Somerset carried out his duties so negligently that soon afterwards, due to his misconduct, the whole country was returned to the control of the king of France.

Margaret of Anjou

THE daughter of René, duke of Anjou, self-styled king of Sicily, Naples and Hungary, and a niece by marriage of Charles VII of France, Margaret was a fitting bride for Henry VI, even without a dowry. Although her father was rich only in titles and talents, the marriage in 1445 was a symbol of peace between England and France; the English initially gained only a two-year truce, but there was optimism that a permanent peace would follow. The war-impoverished English crown was therefore able to raise enough money in gifts for a splendid and expensive embassy led by the duke of Suffolk to be despatched to fetch the new queen. The cost of refurbishing royal palaces which had been effectively without a queen for 20 years was a further drain on the crown's resources.

Margaret had been brought up in Italy and was learned as well as beautiful. She was 16 at the time of her marriage. Henry was 23 and, as a papal envoy observed, he was more like a monk than a king and avoided the company of women. Nevertheless, the marriage seems to have been at least averagely happy; the couple chose to spend much of their time together. For eight years Margaret was childless, a major dereliction of queenly duty – and politically crucial, for Henry had no close heir presumptive. When she finally gave birth to Edward, prince of Wales, in 1453, her husband had lapsed into mental illness and was unable to recognize his infant son.

Margaret came from a family which for several generations had relied for political survival on the determination and resources of its womenfolk and she instinctively took up her husband's burden. But she had never learned that in England, unlike France, the crown was expected to be above faction. Margaret was politically

partisan and vindictive, and her lack of political judgement and moderation was one of the causes of the fall of the house of Lancaster.

When Edward, duke of York, seized the throne in 1461 and defeated the Lancastrians at Towton, the deposed king and queen escaped north into Scotland. Margaret ceded Berwick to the Scots in return for aid and went to France where, with the backing of Louis XI, she organized expeditions against Edward IV in the north of England, where her support lay. Henry was captured in 1465 and Margaret never saw him again. However, she did not cease her attempts to regain his throne.

Her greatest chance came in 1470 when Warwick the Kingmaker defected from Edward IV and fled to France. Although they were old and bitter enemies, they formed an alliance which led to Henry's restoration as king. Within seven months, however, before the queen and her son landed in England, Edward had defeated Warwick at Barnet. Henry was murdered in the Tower of London

following Margaret's defeat at Tewkesbury and the death of the prince of Wales. Edward IV put Margaret in the custody of her old friend Alice Chaucer, duchess of Suffolk, at Wallingford in Berkshire, and in 1475, after the treaty of Picquigny, her cousin Louis XI ransomed her for £10,000. To obtain her release she had to renounce her title and all her dower rights in England. It was an unjust demand on Edward IV's part, and Louis was not acting out of motives of chivalry. The French king wanted Margaret to surrender all claims on her parents' inheritances to the crown: in return he granted her a small pension on her father's death. Margaret retired to a small château near Saumur in Anjou, where she died in obscurity in 1482.

Benet gives a laconic account of the collapse of the English in Normandy.

1449

Around 15 August, about thirty fortified towns in Normandy were lost. When the king heard this news, he summoned a great council at Sheen which was attended by all the dukes, earls, barons, knights and squires in England. They all agreed to aid the king with the expenses of his wars. Around 8 September, the king received his half-yearly six thousand shillings and with this money paid off the first instalment of his loan from the nobles.

Much of this taxation depended on the profits of the wool trade, which still remained England's most important source of wealth.

During this time, Rouen was taken in an assault for the king of France, after it had been betrayed by its inhabitants. The earl of Shrewsbury and others were taken hostage, while the duke of Somerset fled to Caen. Besides this, the king of France took the town of Harfleur, the lands of Anjou and Maine, and all of Normandy around the River Seine.

1450

On 31 January, Thomas Cheyne, who was known as Bluebeard, was captured in Kent. He had summoned many men together so that they might rise up against those they called the traitors — that is to say, against the king, the evil duke of Suffolk, the bishop of Salisbury and Sir James Fenys, who had lately been made Lord Say. Thomas said that he was a servant of the king of the faeries. On 9 February, at Tyburn, Thomas Cheyne was drawn and hanged, and his entrails were torn out and burnt. He was then beheaded and quartered.

On 27 February, which was a Friday, between six and seven o'clock in the evening, an extraordinary lightning flash was seen which lit up the sky for three seconds. Just at that time, the storeroom, hall, kitchen and some chambers of King Henry VI's manor at Eltham were struck and burned down by that thunderbolt.

Pure new wool

ALTHOUGH the wool trade was in relative decline during Henry VI's reign, it was still England's main source of wealth, and few people recognized the downward trend. Other countries – Spain, for example – exported more fleeces, but none could match the quality of the finest Cotswold wool.

'Alle naciouns afferme up to the fulle
In al the world ther is no bettir wolle.'

The export trade to Flanders was funnelled through Calais so that the merchant staplers, whose company was based there, could control their monopoly and the government its single largest source of revenue. The duty and subsidy on wool amounted to £2 per sack of 364 pounds' weight for residents of Calais and considerably more for other merchants. There were two exceptions to the Staple monopoly: coarse-quality north country wools might be exported direct to the Low Countries from Berwick and Newcastle upon Tyne; and Italian dealers could buy the privilege to ship direct on Venetian, Genoese and, later, Florentine galleys.

Above *Lavenham, a typical wool village.*

In 1454, 51 graded quality ratings were listed in England. The finest wool came from the march of Shropshire and Leominster, closely followed by the Cotswolds. Areas of Lincolnshire and Gloucestershire, then Wiltshire, Yorkshire, and finally Suffolk and Sussex are other regions listed. Although not the best, 'Cotes' or 'Cotswold' were generic terms for all grades of quality wool: the region produced far and away the most.

Most Cotswold wool was exported but increasing amounts were bought by local cloth manufacturers. Those on the Stroudwater near Cotswold were typical; transport from England's premier wool area was cheap, there were large deposits of fuller's earth in the valley, a fast stream to power the waterwheels of the fulling mills and easy access to the great port of Bristol. Nearby Castle Combe, now 'the most beautiful village in England', was a noisy mill town where sweated labour lined the pockets of the landowner, Sir John Fastolf, who invested profits from the French wars in the new cloth industry. Wool was increasingly bought by specialist 'broggers' or woolmen who acted for the London staplers and Italian merchant princes: riding the wolds and downs, bargaining with large growers, haggling with small-time farmers, was tiring all-weather work. It might also expose foreigners to outbursts of xenophobia; in the 1450s a parliamentary petition complained of 'Italians who ride about for to buy wool in every part of the realm, gaining knowledge of the privities [secrets] of the same'.

Wool was exported as clippings, when it was sold by the sack, or as wool-fells (skins with the wool on them). Many grades were recognized, down to sweepings from the packing-room floor. 'Sarplers' of clipped wool or bundles of fells were taken by packhorse train to the port, weighed by the shipper's agent and possibly repacked. When the wool reached its destination its quality was inspected once again – at Calais the Staple's agents also checked to ensure it had been properly graded. Large sums of money were involved and fraud and smuggling were common. The government used duties as security for loans and paid its Calais garrison from them; it even regulated payments between merchants from different countries as a measure of bullion control. The 'wool' churches of Suffolk and the Cotswolds, with their superb angel roofs, window traceries and fine monumental brasses, testify to a trade which, for all its fluctuations and gradual decline, was the basis of England's wealth.

In the wake of the loss of Normandy, the duke of Suffolk was impeached by the angry house of commons. The king refused to take the advice of parliament and instead banished Suffolk from the kingdom for five years, to the fury of many of his subjects.

On 27 April the evil duke of Suffolk took three or four ships with two hundred men and set sail for Brittany. But on 30 April, at sea off Dover, he encountered some ships, among them the great vessel *Nicholas of the Tower*, together with many smaller vessels.

The evil duke was then arrested and brought to justice [by the vessel's occupants]. After two hearings, he was condemned to death.

On 2 May, at about ten o'clock, he was beheaded in a rowing boat. His truncated corpse was left on the sea-shore near Dover and lay for a month before it was buried in a church in Suffolk.

On 6 June, parliament was dissolved at Leicester, after the lords and commons had granted that whoever spent twenty pounds in a year should give the king ten shillings, and that for every pound spent above twenty, the king should have twelve pence.

Just as parliament was concluding its session, some men rose in rebellion in Kent.

This marked the beginning of Jack Cade's rebellion, a widespread popular reaction to Henry VI's misrule.

The Kentish rebels had chosen as their captain a most bold and subtle man, Jack Cade, who called himself 'John Mortimer'. He led five thousand men. On 11 June, which was a Thursday, the Kentish men came as far as Blackheath, by Deptford, and on the following Saturday, the king, with a great army of soldiers from different parts of England, made his way as far as the house of St John, by Clerkenwell, to overcome the Kentish captain.

The king sent the archbishop of York, who was a cardinal and at that time the chancellor of England, the archbishop of Canterbury and the duke of Buckingham to Cade, as his emissaries. These men were instructed to treat with the captain and to discover the reasons for the insurrection. And the captain told them of the many changes which he thought the king should make in his government of England.

When the king heard of Cade's opinions, he refused to make the changes he asked. The captain with all his followers stayed at Blackheath for eight days awaiting the king's pleasure, for he meant no harm to the king, nor to England itself, and he had no wish to hurt anyone, nor to take their property. And he made an announcement to this effect.

After a while, however, all the people decided that it would be best to rise up against their lords since the king was surrounded by traitors, namely, Lord Say, the treasurer, Lord Dudley, Thomas Daniel and many others.

The king then made haste to arrest Lord Say and have him put in the Tower of London. Besides this, the king made a proclamation to the effect that all traitors would be arrested, wheresoever they were found.

He next set up a commission whose members were instructed to bring to justice the extortioners, traitors and villains against whom Cade and the men of Kent had made their accusations. But Cade and the men of Kent were not thus appeased.

On that same day, 4 July, Cade came to London again and rode through the whole city brandishing his drawn sword. He extracted the sheriff of Kent, Crowmer, from Fleet Prison and took him first to the mound beside the Tower of London and thence to Mile End, where he beheaded him and another man. He had the two heads impaled on spears and carried to Cheapside.

Meanwhile, the justices were indicting about twenty men, among them Lord Say, for treason and extortion. Lord Say was released from the Tower for a short time and appeared before the justices, who asked him what answer he wished to make to the charges.

He replied: 'The king has made me a lord and a baron and, according to the laws and statutes, I may not be judged except by my peers.' When they heard this, the common people wished to have him killed at once, in front of the justices.

Then one of the junior officers said that they should allow him to have a confessor; and so he made his confession and was afterwards taken from the Guildhall and led by the junior officers and the men of Kent to the Standard in Cheapside, where he was beheaded forthwith.

Then Cade came, bearing the two heads impaled on spears, and impaled the head of Lord Say on a third spear, longer than the other two.

He despoiled the body of Lord Say and, having tied his feet to his own saddle, dragged him naked, with his arms outstretched, out of Newgate and thence through the Old Bailey, through Ludgate into Watling Street and thence through Candle-wick Street to the bridge. There Jack Cade circled a great stone, beating it with his sword. He put the three heads on a tower and dragged the headless corpse of Lord Say to St Thomas's hospital in Southwark.

When the people of London realized that Cade was breaking the promises he had made in his proclamation, they turned against him.

On the following night, at about ten o'clock, Lord Scales and Matthew Gooch, a squire, together with aldermen of London, came to blows with the men of Kent on London Bridge and this affray continued until eight o'clock on Monday, 6 July. Many on both sides were killed. Of the Londoners, Matthew Gooch, and an alderman, Sutton, who was a goldsmith, met their deaths, and forty other men besides. Of the men of Kent, about two hundred were killed.

It was then that the men of Kent felt obliged to accept the royal charter and general pardon, which they had previously refused. So the men of Kent went away into Kent, and the men of Essex into Essex. However, the newly created sheriff of Essex and many others went off in pursuit of Cade and, on 12 July, they came upon him beside the sea and killed him.

On the following day, they took his body to London and, on 15 July, he was quartered and beheaded and his quartered body, with the head tied to the chest, was drawn from Southwark to Newgate. Afterwards, his head was placed on London Bridge, although he had not appeared before a court of law and had been condemned not according to the law, but according to the king's wish.

Consequently, all the people of Kent, Essex and Wiltshire decided to rise up again in protest at the ill government of the kingdom of England.

When the king heard this news, he sent the archbishop of York, the duke of Buckingham and others to Rochester, in Kent, together with a newly appointed justice – the other justices did not dare to show their faces since they themselves were guilty of extortion. And at Rochester they sat in eyre with full powers, so that the men of Kent would be appeased and would not rebel.

On about 8 September, the duke of York landed in Wales, on his return from Ireland to England. Lord Dudley and the abbot of Gloucester, who had been accomplices of the wicked duke of Suffolk, now grew greatly afraid of the common people of England, and so they came to the duke of York at Ludlow Castle, seeking a safe refuge. On 29 September, which was a Sunday, the duke of York, with fifty thousand men, came to London, to the king at Westminster, where he received a most gracious welcome.

On 6 November, the king convened a parliament at Westminster, which was attended by all the dukes, earls and barons, each with a great retinue of armed men. The armed men, who had come with the nobles to parliament, learned on 30 November that neither the king nor the nobles had spoken of punishing the traitors whose actions were a scandal throughout England, in particular, the duke of Somerset, whose negligence was responsible for the loss of Normandy. So they cried out thrice in Westminster Hall, to all the lords, earls and barons, saying, 'Give us justice! Punish the traitors!', so that the king and the lords were much afraid.

On the following day, however, in the afternoon, about a thousand men suddenly rose up against the duke of Somerset, meaning to kill him. But the earl of Devonshire, on the duke of York's request, calmed them and prudently arrested their leader, who was taken in secret from the Friars' house on the Thames to the Tower of London, so as not to provoke the common people.

In the mean time, the common people were ransacking the house of the Friars. On the following day, however, the duke of York arrested one of them and took him to the king, who instructed the earl of Salisbury that he was to be beheaded at the Standard in Cheapside. These instructions were fulfilled.

On 3 December, which was a Thursday, the king, with all his dukes, earls, barons, knights and squires, accompanied by some well-armed soldiers, to the number of about ten thousand, marched through London.

1451

At around this time, the king of France began an assault on Gascony.

Waurin gives a fuller account of the collapse of the English in Gascony.

In May, the king of France, who was staying at that time in Tours, ordered the count of Dunois, his commander-in-chief, to go to Guyenne to bring the region under his control. With this purpose in mind, Dunois came to Tours at the beginning of May, and ordered several knights and squires to prepare themselves to go and conquer Guyenne.

On 2 June, the count of Dunois sent men to lay siege by land and sea to the castle at a place called Fronsac. This was the strongest in the whole

Jack Cade's rebellion

IN 1450 a major popular uprising occurred in the south of England. The participants, who included some gentlemen, yeomen and craftsmen as well as labourers, protested about Lancastrian government at home and abroad, echoing the views of parliament and certain nobles. Jack Cade, its mysterious leader, took the pseudonym of John Mortimer, presumably to link his cause directly with Richard, duke of York (a Mortimer through his mother), whose criticisms of Henry VI's regime and its conduct of the French war were well known.

The rebels denounced abuses in government, questioned the competence of the king's advisers, and complained about the self-seeking of his servants. By invoking the names of Richard, duke of York, and Humphrey, duke of Gloucester, as being of similar mind, the rebels appealed to the higher ranks of society and to London.

When the rebellion started in May, Henry VI, who was at Leicester, sent his nobles to investigate before following them to London on 13 June. He confronted the rebels at Blackheath and they, who had already declared respect for him, withdrew. Henry nevertheless refused concessions and allowed his men to go on the rampage in pursuit of his opponents. Many royal retainers deserted, and defeated soldiers from Normandy added an explosive element. Henry panicked. He agreed to the arrest of Lord Say, his most hated adviser, and deserted London for the Midlands on 25 June. When the rebels returned to Blackheath on 29 June their morale was high, though their numbers diminished, and their aims were clear. Their ranks now included mutinous retainers and disgruntled soldiers, as well as the original 'rustics'. The London masses were sympathetic and Cade forced an entry to the city on 3 July.

He tried to maintain discipline and act within the law, but there was looting and burning, and Lord Say and his brother-in-law, the sheriff of Kent, were executed. City opinion turned against Cade, and during the night of 5–6 July the people of London battled on London Bridge to keep the rebels out; hundreds were killed and the bridge partly burned. It marked the beginning of the end. Cade escaped – he was captured and mortally wounded some days later – and the rebels dispersed. Many people – onlookers, townspeople and monks, even loyalists, as well as rebels – accepted a general pardon to protect them-selves in the aftermath of rebellion.

Although Henry was initially conciliatory, repression followed later. New leaders appeared and disturbances continued throughout southern England after York's return from Ireland in September and when the duke of Somerset's defeated forces slunk back from Normandy. Henry tried to restore order in London and in 1451 toured the disaffected areas, garnering 'a harvest of heads' as he went.

This was the most serious crisis of his reign so far. The rebellion had practical aims coherently publicized; it was discriminating in its targets at home and abroad; and the king could not avoid responsibility. The rebels' complaints coincided with those of a wider public and included proposals to improve the personnel, policies and finances of the king's government. It was Henry VI's tragedy that in spurning the rebels he also spurned those who shared their grievances.

Opposite *The petition of Cade's rebels.*

Right *Retribution followed Cade's revolt, to punish the traitors and cow others.*

region of Guyenne and had always been guarded by English troops, because it is the royal seat and the key to Guyenne and Bordeaux, and so the English had to hold on tenaciously and defend it to the best of their ability, which in fact they did; for the French attacked in great force, but the English defended it courageously.

In spite of all this, though, after about fifteen days of siege, the English inside began to see the enormous strength in numbers of noblemen and warriors before them, and realized that they did not even represent half of the king of France's forces, as less than a quarter of them were even in this region.

They also saw the bombards, cannons and other pieces of artillery ranged against them, and the increasing proximity of the trenches and tunnels. Moreover they knew that in every siege begun by the French – there had already been several – the invading army had been too strong for all the forces that the English king then had in the duchy of Guyenne.

The English then spoke with the count of Dunois, and the agreement they reached was that if the English had not been relieved, or the French beaten by them, before 23 June, they would hand the town of Fronsac over to the king of France, as would the English in Bordeaux too; the latter would make arrangements with the local barons to hand over all places in Guyenne still under the control of the king of England. To ensure the security of the treaty and that all promises be loyally upheld, hostages were taken.

[Fronsac was handed over as promised] but the besieged in Bordeaux were confident of eventual help. They too had agreed with the French lords that if, by 23 June, sufficient reinforcements to defend themselves had not been sent by the king of England, then they should surrender everything without further delay.

When that day arrived, the French troops were drawn up and ready to fight their enemies, and, by whatever means they could, defeat, subjugate and submit them to the control of the French king, by fair means or foul, wherever they might be awaiting battle, from sunrise to sunset, on the agreed day.

It was, in fact, at sunset on that day that the beleaguered English, seeing that they had failed in their attempt to get help, had a herald cry out in anguish at the help which had never arrived. When they heard this public cry, the French lords left their troops and went to bed down for the night, as there was now nothing else to be done.

The next day, however, the chancellor of France returned with several other notable lords, to speak to the men in Bordeaux, and demanded of them everything which served their purpose, so that at the end of their meeting, they came to the decision that on the following Wednesday, they would be ready to hand over the keys to all castles, harbours, doors and gates of the city, and swear to be good and loyal subjects from that time onwards, and become natural subjects of the king of France according to the agreement and promises made between them; and that is exactly what happened.

Benet continues his dispassionate account of English politics.

1452

The king heard that the duke of York, the earl of Devonshire and Lord Cobham were marching towards London, with twenty thousand men, so he rode to Northampton and sent the bishop of Winchester, the count of Eu and Lord Stourton to the duke of York, to tell him not to rise up in arms.

The duke replied, commending himself to the king's good grace and saying that he had never rebelled against the king and would obey him always. He asserted that his uprising had been directed against those who betrayed the king and the kingdom of England and that he was not against the king and desired nothing but the good of England. He wished to tell the king of those who were encompassing the destruction of his two kingdoms, that is to say, of England and France. And these men were Edmund, duke of Somerset, who had been responsible for the shameful loss of

The fall of Gascony

AFTER 1429 when, inspired by Joan of Arc, Charles VII was crowned at the royal cathedral of Reims, no honourable Frenchman could doubt that he was true king of France; and that Henry of England's coronation at Notre-Dame in 1431 had been a charade – in the wrong cathedral, by the wrong bishop and without the sacred regalia.

But in Gascony, linked to the English crown by three centuries of tradition, allegiance to the *petit roy goddon* held firm – *goddon* was from the English oath 'goddam'. Local government, administered from Bordeaux by Gascon and English constables and seneschals, was staffed mainly by local Gascons. The economy depended on the English wine trade and a king-duke in distant London was seen as preferable to rule from Paris.

Although a French push against Gascony in the early 1440s faltered against determined local defences, negotiations in 1444 led to a truce between France and England, the marriage of Henry VI to Margaret of Anjou – and (in 1448) the English surrender of Maine, a territory vital to the southern defences of Normandy.

Brittany's allegiance was equally important and in March 1449, an English force, aiming to pressure its duke, sacked Fougères, the Breton fortress. Charles VII ordered his commander, John, count of Dunois, into Normandy at the head of three French and Breton armies. Local resistance groups were already active and the English garrisons surrendered piecemeal. Normandy was freed from English rule by mid 1450 and, in October of that year, a French force well supplied with modern guns and brilliantly commanded by Jean Bureau, took Bergerac in Gascony.

Lcur cmuoioit ges a plante.

Coment ceulp de Bordeaulp se rendirc

Above *The surrender of Bordeaux.*

Left *Castillon-sur-Dordogne besieged by Jean Bureau's forces in 1453.*

Charles prepared for a spring campaign against Bordeaux and, well aware of the 'singular affection' in which the Gascons held the English, issued stern orders to his army against looting and theft. In the spring of 1451 the French under Dunois advanced against the fortresses which guarded the Gironde estuary while a fleet blockaded it against English relief forces. Bordeaux, offered diplomatically generous terms by Charles VII, capitulated formally on Tuesday 29 June and Dunois took possession. Bayonne capitulated in August. However, the high-handed methods of French royal agents prompted a party of Gascon nobles to work for the restoration of English rule and London sent John Talbot, earl of Shrewsbury, to support them. By November 1452 he had recovered Bordeaux and its neighbouring territories.

In spring 1453 the French besieged Castillon where Bureau constructed a heavily defended artillery park. This enabled him to rout the English forces when they attempted to relieve the siege. Bureau next moved his artillery against Cadillac, Blanquefort and, in October, Bordeaux. The city's navy was harassing the besieging French forces and Charles called up a fleet from La Rochelle: an example of how throughout the Norman and Gascon campaigns the French made skilful use of their overwhelming numerical superiority. On Friday 19 October Bordeaux was rendered up to the French king. The generous terms of 1451 annulled, the rebellious city lost its privileges and was ordered to pay a fine of 100,000 gold crowns.

all Normandy, and John Kemp, the archbishop of York, who was a cardinal and the chancellor of England.

On 27 February, the king came to London, accompanied by a great army, and stayed as a guest at the lodgings of the bishop of Winchester. On 1 March, the king rode to Blackheath and thence to Welling, with twenty-four thousand armed men. The bishop of Winchester and others then negotiated for peace between the king and the duke. And on 2 March, the king allowed the duke to present a petition and thus they were reconciled at Blackheath, where the duke of York, the earl of Devonshire and Lord Cobham knelt before the king.

The duke of York put forward two articles against the duke of Somerset, accusing him of losing Normandy and Gascony, and later he pledged an oath before the king in St Paul's church in London, in front of the high altar, swearing that he had never rebelled against the king and would not rebel against him in the future.

After 29 September [in response to a petition from the Gascons for deliverance from the French], the earl of Shrewsbury put to sea, with a hundred ships, heading for Aquitaine. He sailed up the River Garonne where he overcame and captured thirty-three ships. On 21 October he took the town of Bordeaux by storm and went on to take thirty-two villages and castles in Aquitaine.

1453

After Easter, the king sent a thousand men to Gascony. They besieged the town of Fronsac and seized control of it. But around 10 August, John Talbot, the earl of Shrewsbury, and his son, Lord de Lisle, were killed at Castillon. At the end of September, the town of Bordeaux was again lost.

In the eastern Mediterranean the great city of Constantinople, capital of the fast-fading Byzantine Empire, had been under increasing threat from the Ottoman Turks for more than 50 years. In 1453 it finally fell to the Ottoman Sultan Mohammed II.

The fall of Constantinople

IN 1453 the English were preoccupied with events in France. The defeat of John Talbot, earl of Shrewsbury, at Castillon on 17 July meant the end of any hope of recovery from the military setbacks of the last 50 years and Bordeaux had finally become a French city on 19 October. Understandably, there was little interest in tidings from the east where Constantinople, the ancient capital of the Byzantine Empire, had fallen to the Ottoman Turks on 29 May after a brief two-month siege.

The resistance of the defenders of Constantinople is a stirring story: against hopeless odds, and knowing there could be no relief, they fought until overwhelmed. There were no more than 7,000 men (including volunteers from the west) to defend the four-mile length of the city's land walls; while, against them, Sultan Mohammed II amassed more than ten times their number, and an artillery train of 50 cannon including the largest piece in the world, especially cast for the siege. The city's great walls, constructed a millennium before, crumbled before the sultan's might.

Constantinople was sacked and its population massacred or enslaved. At the last minute several Venetian and Genoese vessels escaped laden with refugees, but the last emperor, Constantine XI, fought to the death. The great 6th-century church of St Sophia was reconsecrated by the Muslims as a mosque.

The wonder is that Constantinople lasted as long as it did. The Byzantine Empire had collapsed in the 14th century when it was attacked by Serbs and Bulgars in Europe and Venetians and Genoese from the sea. It was also riven by internal feuds and threatened in Asia Minor by the rise of the Ottoman Turks. In the 13th century they were merely a small outlying tribe which began to wage religious war against the eastern Christians: barely 100 years later their dominion had reached the Danube, and only Constantinople, Salonica and the Morea (southern Greece) remained in Greek hands.

The Byzantine Empire's greatest legacy was its Orthodox religion, which the Turks allowed to continue, but Christian rule in the eastern Mediterranean was now confined to a few isolated islands such as Rhodes, last bastion of the Knights of St John.

The fall of Constantinople was the last act in the story of a great empire, which had already ceased to play its historic role – preventing Muslim advance into Christian Europe – a century before it was destroyed.

Opposite The siege of Constantinople in progress. On the left, Turkish galleys are hauled overland to break into the harbour.

Meanwhile in England the king had fallen very sick. Henry's lack of response to his new-born son, Edward, is described in one of the Paston letters.

At the prince Edward's coming to Windsor, the duke of Buckingham took him in his arms and presented him to Henry VI, beseeching the king to bless him; but the king gave no answer.

Nevertheless the duke stayed with the prince by the king; and when he still had no answer, the queen came in and took the prince in her arms and presented him as the duke had done, begging the king to bless him. All their labour was in vain, however, for they departed without any answer or look from the king, saving only that once he looked on the prince and cast his eyes down, without any more sign of recognition.

Benet gives a terse account of the political arrangements consequent upon the madness of Henry VI.

1454

The king's council perceived that, if the king did not recover, England would soon be ruined under the government of the duke of Somerset. So the noblemen of the kingdom sent for the duke of York.

On 10 April, the earl of Salisbury was made chancellor and on 16 April, the duke of York was made protector of England for the duration of the king's illness, until such time as Prince Edward should come of age. Around 19 May, the duke of York rode to York, with a vast army of men, in an expedition against the duke of Exeter and the earl of Egremont, for those lords were rebelling in Yorkshire and breaking the king's peace. However, they fled when they heard of the approach of the duke of York.

On 23 July, which was a Wednesday, the duke of York arrested the duke of Exeter at Westminster, taking him first to his own house and later putting him in Pontefract Castle. The duke of York and the king's council deposed the duke of Somerset from all the offices he had held from the king.

The mad king

Henry VI matched up badly to the ideal of kingship. He failed to keep the peace amongst his nobles or to uphold law and order in the land. Worst of all, he was incapable of leading his men in war. It was only when France was lost and England about to descend into civil war that Henry was persuaded to take the field. The contrast with his father could not have been sharper. In every sphere where Henry V had excelled, Henry VI was grossly deficient.

The weak link in his genetic chain came not from the Plantagenets but from the Valois. His maternal grandfather, Charles VI of France, had been subject to fits of insanity which made him a danger to his servants and a liability to his realm. In August 1453 Henry VI fell into a trance-like condition which affected him periodically for the rest of his life. The symptoms were dramatic: complete amnesia, no sense of time or place, no physical co-ordination, and extreme inertia. Some modern doctors have diagnosed catatonic schizophrenia or depressive stupor. Contemporaries, less charitable, called it madness. In their desperation, the royal councillors commissioned doctors and surgeons to administer a bizarre combination of ointments, cordials, suppositories, head shaving and haemorrhoid removals. But all attempts failed, and the court had to accept the embarrassing reality that Henry VI had crossed the thin line between inanity and insanity.

For a while the council tried to act as though nothing had happened. But the longer the king's condition lasted, the more inevitable a formal regency became. There were three possible contenders for this job: Henry's wife Margaret, and his cousins Edmund Beaufort, duke of Somerset, and Richard, duke of York. Henry's henchman Somerset was discredited as a result of the reversals in France, and sent to the Tower. Margaret was a more formidable candidate: in October 1453 she was brought to bed of a baby boy, Prince Edward, and so had possession of the heir to the throne. But she, like Somerset, was unpopular and the third contender, Richard of York, was eventually created protector and defender of the realm in March 1454. He fulfilled this office with integrity and industry, remaining loyal to the Lancastrian regime which he served. But at Christmas 1454 the king regained his senses and the regency was no longer required. Somerset returned to court and York faced a future in the political wilderness unless he took up arms to preserve the place he had held in the king's council.

Ironically, it was thus not Henry's madness but the recovery of his sanity which made the Wars of the Roses inevitable.

Above *Henry VI probably inherited his
mental instability from his grandfather,
Charles VI of France, who attacked his
followers in a fit of madness in 1392.*

Below *A warrant from the king's council,
dating from 1454 and signed by Richard of
York as protector (in the centre), during
the king's incapacitation.*

On 31 December, by the grace of God, the king recovered his health, at Greenwich.

1455

On 6 February, the duke of Somerset was released from the Tower of London on bail. Very shortly afterwards the duke of York resigned his office to the king at Greenwich, after he had governed England most excellently for a whole year, miraculously calming rebels and villains, according to the laws and without unnecessary violence; and he resigned his office much honoured and much loved.

Then the king, in response to the intercession of the archbishop of Canterbury and the duke of Buckingham, pardoned all those who had entered into recognizances for the duke of Somerset. Once more, the duke of Somerset became head of the government under the king, although in the past he had almost ruined the whole of England with his misrule. On 7 March, the earl of Salisbury resigned the office of chancellor. Master Thomas Bourgchier, the archbishop of Canterbury, was made the king's chancellor and the earl of Wiltshire was made treasurer.

Soon after Easter, another dispute arose between the noble duke of York, on the one hand, and the evil duke of Somerset and the duke of Buckingham, on the other. For Somerset was plotting the destruction of the noble duke of York. He offered advice to the king, saying that the duke of York wished to depose the king and rule England himself – which was manifestly false.

Because of this, around the middle of May, the duke of York and with him the earls of Shrewsbury and Warwick, approached London, with seven thousand well-armed men. When the duke of Somerset heard this news, he suggested to the king that York had come to usurp the throne. For this reason, the king sided with the duke of Somerset.

The two factions – Lancastrians and Yorkists – now saw that conflict was inevitable and gathered their forces. The armies met at St Albans, where the first battle of the Wars of the Roses took place.

Mental diseases

MEDIEVAL medical texts distinguished five types of mental disease: phrenitis (acute inflammation of the brain), delirium (abnormal reactions accompanied by fever), mania (violent behaviour), melancholia (depression and lack of interest in people and events) and amentia (lack or loss of mental faculties). Other recognized mental illnesses included epilepsy and lycanthropy, which was characterized by wandering through cemeteries and woods at night imitating wolves and wild animals.

Mental disorders were generally attributed to an excess of black bile in the body, which caused an imbalance or flux of noxious humour to the brain, resulting in melancholia. However, physicians and laymen based their diagnoses on what they saw. Demonic possession was said to cause sudden falls in epilepsy and exorcism by a priest or a pilgrimage to a healing shrine was recommended. Moon-struck beings (*lunatics*) were treated with peony root worn around the neck, a potion of black hellebore, or a regimen of solicitude and comfort including music and soothing baths. Purgatives and blood-letting were said to remove corrupt humours; the most extreme form, trepanation, expelled a noxious humour from the cranium.

Although no moral distinction was made between the holy fool possessed of Christ, whose extremes of asceticism might result in wild appearance and behaviour, and the demon-possessed lunatic, tormented by the Devil, disturbed behaviour posed a social threat. Society's reactions depended on whether the person was non-violent or violent: ultimately a patient was confined if it was deemed to be for his or her good. Non-violent sufferers who caused no public disturbance were left at liberty, in the custody of their families; if the family was too poor – or non-existent – they could be left to roam the streets, objects of ridicule and abuse. Alternatively, they might be confined to a hospital like St Mary of Bethlehem in Bishopsgate, London, known as Bedlam; on one occasion six of 14 patients were 'out of their senses'. John of Arundel, physician to Henry VI, was its warden, and was succeeded by William Hobbes, surgeon to Edward IV.

Legally there were two groups of mentally ill under the king's prerogative: natural fools or idiots whose illness was congenital and permanent; and *non compos mentis* or lunatics whose condition was acquired after birth. The latter included people who suffered from psychiatric disorders but were capable of temporary or permanent recovery. The king had custody of any idiot, and of his lands and revenues, and provided for him until he died and his land reverted to his heir. Lunatics and their kin retained their lands under the king's protection to support themselves, and a lunatic 'come to right mind' resumed full control of his possessions.

By the late 15th century custodial rights over idiots, lunatics and their lands were granted to private individuals – at a price, in the case of idiots. King's Chancery issued the writs *de idiota inquirendo* and *non compos mentis*. Mental disability had to be established before a jury and was evaluated on common-sense criteria, like memory.

Henry VI inherited a genetic component from his Valois grandfather Charles VI, whose condition has been described as 'a manic state of raging madness in a violent, choleric, fast-living person'. In hot pursuit of would-be assassins of his constable in the forest of Le Mans in 1392, he was startled by a stranger who tried to warn him of an ambush. The clash of a dropped lance sent him into a demented rage and he is said to have killed four people before he could be restrained. He was prescribed isolation and medical purgatives – and religious offerings were made on his behalf. Henry's condition was non-violent: as a result of depressive stupor he lost control of his limbs and was unable to speak. Treatment included potions, head purges, laxatives, gargles, baths and blood-letting. Although he recovered, he had no memory of the 18-month period of his worst bout of illness. Probably a psychosis, it had momentous political consequences.

Left *The seal of the wardens of the hospital of St Mary of Bethlehem, alias Bedlam, in Bishopsgate. Founded in 1247, by the 15th century it was specializing in the treatment of lunatics.*

Below *Diana's arrows striking various victims. The very name 'lunacy' suggests one popular tradition regarding madness: the mad were moonstruck, victims of the baleful influence of the moon. This was a plausible explanation in a society where astrology was treated as a serious science.*

215

The earl of Warwick arrived at St Albans with two thousand armed men, and the duke of York with three thousand, and the earl of Salisbury with two thousand – and all these were well prepared for battle. The king then engaged in battle with his nobles. The fighting was furious. The duke of Somerset and the earl of Northumberland were killed, together with Lord Clifford and many others, to the number of about a hundred. The king was wounded in the neck, as was the duke of Buckingham, who was taken prisoner.

Thus all who were on the side of the duke of Somerset were killed, wounded or, at the very least, despoiled. The king, who was left on his own, fled into the house of a tanner, to hide. And to this house came the duke of York, the earl of Salisbury and the earl of Warwick, declaring themselves the king's humble servants. And when the king perceived this, he was greatly cheered. These noblemen, together with the king, went into St Alban's abbey, where they all spent the night.

The next day, which was Friday, the king came to London, attended by his nobles, and there he stayed as a guest of the bishop of London. And the earl of Warwick carried the king's sword to London. On the following Sunday, the feast of Pentecost, the king went in a procession to St Paul's church in London, where he wore his crown.

The growing disorder in English society, and the dangers this brought to the security of the realm, were pointed out by John Hardynge in a florid poetic address to the king.

In your realm there are no justices of the peace that dare take the responsibility to suppress the quarrellers. Such is the extent of the sickness that has taken hold that they will not recognize the rioting or the fighting so common now throughout your people.

This I dread most fearfully, that from these riots shall more mischief arise, and from the sores unhealed, a scab will form, so large that nothing may restrain its growth. Wherefore, good lord, if you will give me leave, I would say this to your excellency: withstand misrule and violence.

Withstand, good lord, the outbreak of fighting, and punish hard all the rioters that in each shire now gather together against your peace, and all their supporters, or else, truly, the fairest flowers will fall from your crown and noble monarchy, which God defends and keeps through his mercy. Whoever may beseech you on behalf of any troublemaker, whether he be a duke, an earl or any other estate, blame him as much as the other for the discord and fighting.

The law is like a Welshman's hose; it is the right shape for each man's leg. So supporters subvert it and twist it and its might is crushed under foot and the rioter's rule might completely take the place of your law.

Consider now, most gracious sovereign lord, how long your family have reigned, in wealth and high esteem, and continually upheld law and peace; and think that these qualities are the fairest of flowers of all in your monarchy and of the greatest importance, and will very soon surprise your foreign foes.

Benet pursues his relation of the political up-heavals in far more prosaic style.

1456

On 13 January, parliament met at Westminster. In this session, the duke of York and the house of commons devoted much trouble to the question of the resumption of grants for the king, which almost all of the lords were resisting. And the lords went to the king and accompanied him to Westminster in an attempt to persuade him to refuse the resumption. Then, in front of the king, the duke of York resigned his office and left parliament before the session was over.

Later, the king sent for the earl of Warwick and the duke of York. They came to him and were received most graciously by the king, though the queen loathed them both.

Before this, around 15 August, the king of Scotland invaded England, with one hundred thousand men, and burned twenty villages, but he

Richard Plantagenet
Duke of York
Died 1460.

Edward Plantagenet
Duke of York
e in 1461 Edward IV
King of England

Lancaster versus York

THE conflict which split the English aristocracy for more than three decades – from 1455 to 1487 – is generally known as the Wars of the Roses. Although it was not until the 18th century that this precise title was used, the idea that the red rose represented the Lancastrians and the white the Yorkists first appears in the Crowland Chronicle, completed by 1486, and it was given wider currency by Shakespeare. During these troubled years the white rose was the most popular of several Yorkist badges; and although Henry VI seems not to have used the red rose to represent his party, the propagandists of Henry VII adopted it as such in creating the red and white Tudor rose, symbolizing the union of the two houses.

The outbreak of open war between Lancastrians and Yorkists was the direct result of Henry VI's recovery from madness early in 1455. During his insanity, the nation had been ruled by a council of nobles under the protectorship of Henry's kinsman, Richard, duke of York, the greatest magnate in the realm and (some said) the rightful heir to the throne. But as soon as Henry came to his senses, the old 'court party' resumed its sway over monarch and government.

The real power behind this Lancastrian faction was the queen, 'a great and strong-laboured Frenchwoman', who hated York as a threat to the succession of the son she had at last borne Henry. Her principal ally was Edmund Beaufort, duke of Somerset, newly released from the prison to which his old enemy York had consigned him. Margaret had also recently gained the support of two influential northern noblemen, Lord Clifford and Henry Percy, earl of Northumberland. Their enmity was directed principally at York's strongest supporters, the earls of Salisbury and Warwick – both members of the powerful northern Neville family, with whom the Percys had been at loggerheads for generations.

When the Lancastrians regained power, York and his friends were excluded from their former government offices, and, expecting that worse would follow, they withdrew northwards and began mustering men. Their apprehensions were confirmed when Somerset called them to a 'great council' (packed with his supporters) at Leicester, where he presumably intended to enforce their submission. The Yorkists marched south in full force, to encounter the royal party at St Albans on 22 May 1455.

The Lancastrians barricaded the streets of the town, with the duke of York's forces (some 3,000 to the Lancastrians' 2,000) ranged in the fields outside. At first the two sides negotiated. The Yorkists protested their loyalty to the king, but insisted that Somerset and his henchmen must be handed over to them: the Lancastrians refused, and emphasized their possession of the puppet-monarch by hoisting his royal standard. York retorted by storming the barricades, while Warwick broke into St Albans through back lanes and gardens. Northumberland and Clifford fell in the street-fighting and Somerset may have been cut down by Warwick himself.

Victory went to the Yorkists, who also gained control over Henry – the duke became protector once more. The king had not put on armour, and was slightly wounded in the neck by an arrow. There was no question of deposing him: the king retained the loyalty of the whole nation, including most nobles, who as yet favoured neither the 'Red Rose', 'Lancastrian' party nor the 'White Rose' 'Yorkist' party but were simply anxious for a peaceful settlement.

The king also wanted peace and, even after the close of York's 'second protectorate' in February 1456, tried to remain on good terms with the duke. But Margaret, 'being a manly woman, used to rule and not be ruled', sought revenge, and set about creating a new Lancastrian party, centred on the kinsmen of Somerset and Northumberland and the remnants of the old court faction. She moved the seat of government from London (strongly Yorkist in sympathy) to the West Midland Lancastrian estates.

Meanwhile Henry ordered the duke of York and the Nevilles to found a chantry for the souls of those killed at St Albans, and to compensate their relatives. As a sign that old enmities were forgiven, the rival factions walked arm in arm – York with the queen, and Percys with Nevilles – through the streets of London on 24 March 1458. This 'loveday' charade pleased the well-meaning king, but achieved nothing else: the streets were filled with supporters of the 'reconciled' parties, heavily armed and glaring suspiciously at each other. Within less than two years Lancastrians and Yorkists were again at war; and so well did the king's supporters succeed that by the end of 1459 York and his major adherents were all in exile.

was routed by the duke of York. And the king, on the queen's advice, rode to Chester, rather than London, for the queen hated London.

On 4 December, there was an earthquake across the sea – beyond Rome, in the kingdom of Naples and in other lands and kingdoms. The earth sucked up villages and men, women and children – they say one hundred and twenty-five thousand – who never appeared again. And where the earth used to be, there is now nothing but filthy water.

1457

On 24 August, which was a Sunday, the French invaded England and almost destroyed the town of Sandwich, killing many English people. They ransacked the town completely and then played tennis there. However, as they were crossing the Channel, many Frenchmen perished.

After Michaelmas the king held a great council at Westminster, attended by all the lords, spiritual and temporal. In this council, Master Reginald Pecock, bishop of Chichester, was accused of heresy. He had written many books which explained the sacred scripture in the English tongue and he composed a new *paternoster* and a new *credo*, inserting in his *credo* the following words: 'He descended into hell, and on the third day he rose from the dead.' And grave heresy was found in his writings.

Because of this, the aforementioned Reginald, the heretic, submitted himself to the archbishop of Canterbury for punishment, renouncing his wicked views. On 4 December, in front of the cross in the cemetery of St Paul's in London, before the archbishop of Canterbury, the bishop of London and countless other men, he again renounced his false opinions and then, in front of the assembled gathering, four of his books were burned.

1459

After 24 June, the king held a great council at Coventry which was attended by the queen and the prince. However, the archbishop of Canterbury,

Art with knowledge

IN Renaissance Italy, and above all in the rich, bustling city of Florence, artists seem to have developed a new way of perceiving, and a new precision in portraying, the world around them. Painters started to represent people and things as solid objects in a precisely calculated spatial perspective. At its finest, in the works of Masaccio or of Piero della Francesca, who worked at Arezzo and Urbino, this sense of space and solidity gives a measured grandeur to early Renaissance painting. Occasionally, as with Paolo Uccello, the quest for calculable space reached such obsessive proportions that his paintings acquired a strange, nightmarish surreality. 'Oh, what a sweet thing is perspective,' he is supposed to have said, when his wife tried to persuade him to come to bed.

The Dominican friar, Fra Angelico, was more popular than either Masaccio or Uccello with the major Florentine patrons. He clothed his mastery of perspectival space in soft colours, silvery light and a gentle contemplative grace that was ideally suited to his most extended series of works – the decoration of the Medici-patronized convent of San Marco in Florence.

There was also a heightened consciousness of the heritage of classical Rome, and a determination to produce buildings (Alberti and Brunelleschi) and sculptures (Brunelleschi and Donatello) that imitated, even emulated, its great works. However, while Alberti and Brunelleschi were designing their consciously classical buildings in Florence, the largest and most impressive church under construction in Italy was Milan Cathedral, built between 1385 and 1485 and totally Gothic in conception and character. Local Italian architects could not cope with the immensity of the building – a staggered five-aisled church – and French experts were called in

during the early 1390s. A record of stormy chapter meetings, with arguments as to whether the building should be built to the square or to the triangle, has been preserved. Ironically, in an Italy where painters were beginning to understand the geometric basis of perspective, it was a French Gothic architect who in the midst of the Milan chapter meetings shouted in exasperation, '*Ars sine scientia nihil est*', 'Art without knowledge is nothing', a perfect motto for the early Renaissance, and the late Gothic world.

Opposite *Milan Cathedral.*

Above *One of the remarkable frescos of the Twelve Months from the cycle commissioned by Duke Borso d'Este for the Palazzo Schifanoia in Ferrara, showing the Triumph of Minerva and the Month of March.*

Right *A panel from Ghiberti's Paradise Gates on the Baptistery in Florence: a work central to the early Renaissance.*

the duke of York and other lords were absent. Because of this, on the advice of the queen, the aforementioned lords were indicted by the council at Coventry.

When they heard this news, the duke of York, the earl of Warwick and the earl of Salisbury decided to go to the king. The king met with many of them near Coventry, before riding on to Nottingham. On 21 September, which was a Friday, the earl of Warwick came to London with five hundred very well armed men. And the earl of Salisbury, advancing against the king on the following Sunday, was met near Newcastle under Lyme by eight thousand soldiers who had been sent against him by the queen. The earl of Salisbury entered into negotiations with them, asking that they might permit his passage. When they refused to allow this, the earl, with his three thousand men, engaged in battle with them and killed or captured, in all, two thousand of them. The rest fled.

Again, in a similar fashion, the duke of York, the earl of Warwick and the earl of Salisbury met with an army of twenty-five thousand soldiers near Worcester. The king came against them too, together with his lords and forty thousand soldiers.

The duke of York realized that the king was approaching, so he turned and withdrew to Worcester, for he had no wish to engage in battle with the king. When the king pursued him to Worcester, the duke moved on to Tewkesbury; and as the king was still following, the duke crossed the Severn and made for Ludlow. But when the king came too, they engaged in battle at Ludford Bridge. [This time the Yorkists were defeated.]

On 13 October the duke of York fled to Wales, and the earl of Salisbury, the earl of Warwick and the earl of March fled to Calais. The king ransacked all their property between Worcester and Ludlow, and then made the duke of Somerset captain of Calais.

The king then held a parliament at Coventry, which began on 20 November. In this parliament, the duke of York, his son Edward, earl of March,

the earl of Rutland, the earl of Warwick, the earl of Salisbury and many other knights and squires, were declared traitors throughout England.

York, in Ireland, and March, Warwick and Salisbury, in Calais, planned their return to the struggle against the Lancastrians. Among the minor families supporting the king at this stage were some of the Pastons of Norfolk and their connections.

1460

Around 24 June, the earls of March, Warwick and Salisbury and Lord Falconbridge landed in England from Calais. And, on 2 July, which was a Monday, they entered London with a vast band of armed men. They were accompanied by a legate from the papal court who carried papal bulls, stating that the pope had excommunicated three English peers, namely the earls of Wiltshire and Shrewsbury and Lord Beaumont, and he had also excommunicated all others who had opposed those peers who sided with the duke. The king was then at Northampton.

On 5 July, Lord Falconbridge left London with ten thousand men, and the earls of March and Warwick with a great many also. They were followed by the archbishop of Canterbury, the bishop of Ely and the bishop of Exeter who approached the king, accompanied by a large armed force. The earl of Salisbury and Lord Cobham waited in London for Lord Scales and Lord Molyns. They had remained at the Tower of London with the intention of attacking the city. And they inflicted great harm on London.

The king set up camp with twenty thousand armed men near Northampton, in a field which lay in between the village of Hardingston and a monastery known as de la Pré. The earls of March and Warwick and Lord Falconbridge came against them with forty thousand armed men.

On 10 July, which was a Thursday, they engaged in battle. The duke of Buckingham was killed and so were the earl of Shrewsbury and many others who were fighting for the king — altogether about five hundred in number.

The Pastons and their letters

THE Pastons of Norfolk are immortalized in their private letters and papers, written between 1422 and 1509. Preserved by the family until the male line became extinct in 1732, they passed into the hands of a succession of antiquarians who had them published. They were written, in English, to family, friends, servants and associates and are the most important document of 15th-century English social history. The letters show how, during the Lancastrian period, a family could rise to the landed gentry from relative obscurity as the Pastons meet, deal with and emulate famous contemporaries.

William Paston's education in law, and marriage to an heiress, was the family's first step towards social better-ment. Two of his five sons – John, the eldest, who became a lawyer, and William – went to Cambridge. A belief in the importance of education is one reason for the family's rise; in 1458 William's widow, Agnes, directed her son Clement's tutor: 'If he has not done well, and will not amend at all . . . truly belash him until he will amend.'

The first John Paston continued to increase the family's wealth and standing, particularly through his connection with Sir John Fastolf whose fortune had been made in the French wars. His frequent absences from home resulted in a large number of letters, mostly to his wife, who defended their properties when her husband was else-where. The elopement of their daughter Margery with their bailiff John Calle in 1469 caused much trouble: the bishop of Norwich directed the girl to remember 'how she was born, what kin and friends she had, and how she should have more if she were ruled and guided by them'; if she did not, what shame and loss she would suffer.

The niceties of rank are demonstrated by the family's attention to elaborate funerals and the concern about tombs shown in their wills. Failure to erect a tomb for John in Bromholme Priory where he was buried, after a costly funeral, was an enduring source of embarrassment.

Paston family affairs were interwoven with national affairs during the early years of the Wars of the Roses in East Anglia, which culminated in the Yorkist success at St Albans in Hertfordshire in 1461. William Paston's son-in-law, Robert Poynings, died in the battle fighting for the Lancastrians, and John was briefly imprisoned in the Fleet by Edward IV, the first Yorkist king, but his son John, William's grandson, joined the royal household. The letters illustrate how difficult it is to determine which families held to which side in the Wars of the Roses.

They were written at a time when East Anglia was a thriving literary centre. A turbulent region, it generated a series of anonymous political verses. It also produced the prolific John Lydgate, a monk of the abbey of Bury St Edmunds, who wrote for lay patrons, and Margery Kempe, wife of a burgess of King's Lynn, who employed an amanuensis to write down her memoirs. Parts of the letters are self-consciously literary: conventional ex-pressions between lovers, and snatches of verse.

Where a century earlier French had been the *lingua franca* of England's rulers, in the mid 15th century English was spoken at the Lancastrian court; and its growing use as the language of affairs helped to foster literacy. The Paston letters illustrate this development and show the richness and variety of the English vernacular.

Below *One of the Paston letters.*

Then the earl of March and the earl of Warwick waited with the king at Northampton. The bishop of Winchester, who was chancellor, and the bishop of Durham, who was clerk of the privy seal, fled; the earl of Wiltshire also made his escape together with many others who were enemies of the duke of York and the earl of March. On 16 July, which was a Wednesday, the king came to London, with a great many attendants, and stayed with the bishop of London.

On 2 August, the king set out on a pilgrimage to Canterbury.

Around 20 July, the king of Scotland with a great army laid siege to Roxburgh Castle and took control of it, but on 3 August, he was killed there. Then the Scots quarrelled among themselves as to who should be the guardian of their new king, who was only eight years of age. So they abandoned Roxburgh Castle and returned to Scotland.

Around 8 September, the duke of York returned from Ireland to England. Then on 7 October, which was a Tuesday, the king opened parliament at Westminster.

On 10 October, Richard, duke of York, came to Westminster to the king's palace where he stayed for three weeks, without speaking with the king or even setting eyes on him. He then claimed in parliament that the king's title should be 'King of England and France and Lord of Ireland'. This title met with the approval of parliament. So on 31 October the king and Richard were reconciled. On the next day, in St Paul's church in London, the king wore his crown and led a procession of dukes, earls and lords, as a symbol of concord.

Thus it was resolved in parliament by the king and all the lords and commons that King Henry should enjoy the thrones of England and France and the dominion of Ireland, for as long as he should live.

The duke of York was made heir apparent to the kingdoms of England and France and to the dominion of Ireland, and the duke received from the king, as an annual pension, ten thousand

Yorkist victories

BETWEEN July 1460 and March 1461 there were three violent changes in political fortunes in England and no less than five battles were fought on English soil. Executions of captured nobles added to the bloodshed, which reached a climax with the struggle at Towton, one of the bloodiest engagements in the wars.

The first of the battles was Northampton. In June 1460 the Yorkist earl of Warwick made a carefully planned comeback from Calais, taking control of London before marching on Henry VI's fortified camp at Northampton in July. A downpour put the Lancastrian artillery out of action, and the treachery of Lord Grey of Ruthin allowed the Yorkists into the entrenchment. The result was the capture of Henry, the death of four leading Lancastrian nobles and the reassertion of Yorkist control. However, when Duke Richard, head of the house of York, returned from Ireland in September and claimed the throne, neither parliament nor the judges would support his replacing Henry, the anointed king. The duke had to be satisfied with being named as Henry VI's heir and ruling the kingdom in his kinsman's name.

His position was by no means assured by Warwick's victory. In the north, Lancastrian support rallied under the duke of Somerset and the earls of Northumberland and Devon. To counter them Richard marched north in December with Warwick's father, the earl of Salisbury, and a force of some 6,000 men. The winter campaign ended in disaster for the Yorkists. At the end of December the army left the shelter of Sandal Castle in Yorkshire and was defeated outside Wakefield. Duke Richard fell in the battle. His severed head was decorated with a paper crown and displayed to the populace at York, along with the earl of Salisbury's.

Queen Margaret, the driving force behind the Lancastrian cause, joined the victors from Scotland and together they marched on London. In the Welsh Marches York's eldest son Edward defeated a Lancastrian army at Mortimer's Cross at the beginning of February: it was later said that the battle was accompanied by an omen which Edward took as his device – a golden 'sun in splendour'. But the Yorkist cause received a setback on 17 February when Warwick was brushed aside at St Albans. Only the advance guard of his army was heavily engaged on that day, but during the night the remaining soldiers melted away. In the confusion Henry was abandoned and allowed to rejoin his wife and supporters. The road to London lay open, but Margaret made a crucial blunder. She failed to occupy the city rapidly – hoping to calm its inhabitants' fear of her northern army – and gave Edward time to get there first and rally the flagging Yorkist cause. Margaret therefore retired to the north.

The Yorkists, who could no longer claim to be ruling in the name of Henry VI and the interests of the realm, were forced to proclaim Edward king. Their aim now was to depose Henry rather than simply purge the kingdom of evil counsellors, as before. Margaret was supported by the majority of English nobles who had taken up arms – about 20 lords compared to half that number who backed Edward – and many gentlemen. To deal with this Lancastrian threat, Edward carefully gathered an exceptionally large army as he moved north during March.

Battle was not long delayed. On 29 March the two armies, each numbering about 50,000 men, met at Towton on the road from Pontefract to York. The battle was long and hard, and fought in inclement weather. At last the Lancastrian army broke, suffering grievous casualties in the rout; the earl of Northumberland and four Lancastrian lords fell, and many gentlemen were taken and executed in the pursuit.

Towton was a major victory for Edward although the greatest prizes eluded him: Margaret fled to Scotland with her husband and son, where she was joined by the dukes of Somerset and Exeter and other Lancastrian nobles. In Northumberland and Wales important castles continued to hold out in the name of Henry VI, who was captured only in 1465.

But Edward's victory was decisive in that the major Lancastrian families were broken and resistance was confined to peripheral areas.

Opposite *Wakefield Bridge: Yorkist forces lost a battle here but later won the war.*

Below *Henry's capture after the battle of Northampton; corpses piled on his right. He regained his freedom nine months later.*

marks. All the lords, spiritual and temporal, swore allegiance to Richard, duke of York, and the duke of York swore allegiance to the king and the lords, saying that for his part he would abide by all the conventions and compacts agreed.

On 5 December, the duke of York, the earl of Salisbury and the earl of Rutland left London and went to Sandal Castle with twelve thousand men. The duke of Somerset came against them on 30 December [at the battle of Wakefield], together with about twenty thousand men. About a thousand were killed, including the duke of York himself.

1461

On 3 February, Edward, earl of March, fought in Wales at Mortimer's Cross with the earl of Wiltshire and the earl of Pembroke, and they fled. On 12 February, the king left London accompanied by the duke of Norfolk, and went to Barnet. That same day, the earl of Warwick left London to go to Ware with a great ordnance and met with the king at St Albans. Meanwhile, the duke of Somerset and the earl of Northumberland came from the north as far as St Albans, laying waste all the towns and villages that stood along their way.

The king went out against them, about a mile from the eastern quarter of St Albans, where the duke of Norfolk, the earl of Warwick and the earl of Arundel fled. They abandoned the king, who was then captured by the other lords.

The queen then came to meet the king in St Albans but the king had gone thence to Dunstable. While the queen was waiting in St Albans, her men ravaged the whole of Middlesex, as far as London.

She sent a chaplain and a squire to the mayor of London, requesting money, but they returned empty-handed.

On 26 February, the earl of March, Edward of York, came to London, accompanied by the earl of Warwick, together with twenty thousand knights and thirty thousand foot soldiers. A few days later he went through London in a procession, and in the afternoon he rode to Westminster, where he was chosen and made king of England and France and lord of Ireland. Edward of York was at that time nineteen years old.

Thus Henry VI was deposed from the throne of England and France because he had ruled like a tyrant, as had his father and grandfather before him.

Edward moved north again and joined battle with Margaret and a large Lancastrian army at Towton. As Waurin relates, Edward's victory made the Yorkist hold on the crown decisive.

There was great slaughter that day at their encounter at Towton and for a long time no one could see which side would gain the victory, so furious was the fighting. But at last the supporters of the king, queen and duke of Somerset were utterly defeated and the earl of March remained victorious.

King Henry himself and his wife Queen Margaret were overthrown and lost that crown which his grandfather Henry IV had violently usurped and taken from King Richard II, his first cousin, whom he caused to be wretchedly murdered, as was plainly told above.

Men say that ill-gotten goods cannot last.

The end of the Lancastrian line

HENRY VI is often regarded as a foolish and incompetent king who pitched England into the Wars of the Roses. Others believe him wilfully a failure. Such a verdict judges him in the light of the last eight years of his reign (1453–61), after his mental collapse; it ignores his uniquely difficult inheritance in England and France, and his long minority. Henry was interested in government, in peace with France, in rewarding his friends and servants, and in his subjects' educational and spiritual welfare. Eton College near Windsor and King's College, Cambridge, are his enduring monuments. But he was not shrewd, prudent or far-sighted, nor was he a good judge of character. Despite his long minority, he was the least experienced of kings, and the advisers he chose to help him proved unworthy. His peace policy was bold but too precipitate, and rewarding his supporters created jealousy and strife at court. After the final collapse of his French lands in 1453 he was a pathetic shadow of a king who all but abandoned his responsibilities. His qualities, admirable in a private person (and exaggerated by later writers), were not those of a successful monarch.

After Edward IV's accession in 1461, Henry spent four years as an exile in Scotland or a fugitive in northern England, until he was seized in Lancashire and taken, bound to his saddle, to the Tower of London where he was imprisoned for five years. He was restored to the throne in October 1470, after Warwick's invasion, when his subjects were exhorted, 'Return, O backsliding children, saith the Lord.' The king was deposed for the second time early in 1471 when Edward IV returned from exile, and was returned to the Tower where he died on the very night that the victorious Edward of York reached London (21 May). Henry was probably killed on Edward's orders, for political reasons: his son had died at Tewkesbury and the main Lancastrian line was now extinct.

The next morning, 22 May, Henry's body was displayed at St Paul's; on the way to the cathedral it bled on the pavement – proof, it was later said, of the dead monarch's sanctity. Henry was buried at Chertsey Abbey the following day. Within a year or two, he was being venerated and his tomb was a place of pilgrimage. His statue on York Minster's rood screen was removed to discourage venerators, but in 1481 the first of his many and varied miracles occurred. Richard III ordered that the body be reburied in a grand ceremony at St George's, Windsor, in 1484, apparently to exploit Henry's growing reputation for sanctity in a public act of reconciliation with a king whose death he had witnessed.

Henry VI's rehabilitation reached its highest point under Henry VII, who realized that his dead kinsman's reputation was an asset to the new, precarious Tudor dynasty; according to popular belief, the saintly king had foretold Henry VII's accession. Henry VII sought his canonization, commissioned a book of miracles to support his cause in Rome, and planned a second reburial for Henry in the new chapel at Westminster. For Tudor chroniclers, Henry VI had the stylized qualities of sainthood, valuable propaganda for the dynasty they supported; his real character had been lost along the way.

Below *The Tower, Henry VI's last home.*

Part V

Edward IV
1461–1483

Henry VI's reign left England in a state of lawlessness and confusion. A strong hand was needed to restore royal authority, and this Edward IV provided. Yet he fell into conflict with the earl of Warwick, 'the kingmaker', who by 1470 had gained sufficient support to bring Henry VI briefly back to power. Edward was forced to fight to regain the throne, but subsequently earned great respect both at home and abroad. Narrative sources for the early part of this important reign are relatively sparse; however, a useful outline with a mildly Lancastrian bias is given by John Warkworth, while the History of the Arrival in England of Edward IV provides an unequivocally Yorkist description of that king's recovery of the throne. Edward's later years are analysed by John Russell, bishop of Lincoln, in a highly informative continuation of the Crowland Abbey chronicle. There are also extracts from works by the Italian humanist Dominic Mancini, and by the Flemish Jean de Waurin who narrates events at the start of the reign.

(Opposite: Edward IV)

When Edward, duke of York, had won the day at Towton, he gave thanks to God for his glorious victory. Then many knights, earls and barons came into his presence, bowed to him and asked him what they ought now to do for the best, to which he replied that he would never rest until he had killed or captured King Henry and his wife, or driven them from the country, as he had promised and sworn to do. The princes and barons of his company said:

'My lord, then we must make for York, for we are told that Queen Margaret and some of her supporters have gone there for safety.'

But as soon as the queen heard this news, she and her people packed up everything they could carry and left York in great haste for Scotland.

When Edward, duke of York, heard that his enemies had fled, he was extremely sorry; none the less he went to York and entered the city. All its clergy came out to meet him and did reverence to him as their sovereign lord and prince, humbly begging him to forgive them if they had in any way offended him, although they did not think they had; and he freely forgave them. Edward stayed a full week in the city, and all the lords and princes with him, with much joy and celebration. He then

Henry VI versus Edward IV

Between September 1459 and March 1461 six major battles took place on English soil between the Lancastrian and Yorkist factions. The outcome was victory for Edward IV and the establishment of the house of York on the English throne. In September 1470, however, Edward was driven into exile by the earl of Warwick and Henry VI was returned to the throne. But in March 1471 Edward landed at Ravenspur and within a matter of weeks had swept aside the Lancastrians once more. Henry VI was killed and Yorkist authority now seemed unassailable.

England's overmighty subjects ▶

The 15th century saw the heyday of the 'overmighty subjects' – great nobles who had large estates and private armies and who wielded great authority and influence in the regions. The most powerful could make and unmake kings – as did the earl of Warwick; and to ensure his political survival Edward IV was compelled to come to terms with those who posed the greatest threat. This map gives a general indication of the areas dominated by these families during Edward's reign, but cannot reflect the fluctuations in their power and alterations in their spheres of influence.

Irish Sea

North Sea

Ouse
Humber
York
Towton ✕
Hull
Wakefield ✕

Chester ○
COUNTY PALATINE OF CHESTER

Lincoln ○
Newark ○

Harlech ○
Shrewsbury ○
Trent
Nottingham ○
Lynn ○
Caistor ○
Norwich ○
Yarmouth

Severn
Stamford ○
Leicester ✕

Ludlow ○
Coventry ○
Northampton ✕
Cambridge ○
Mortimer's Cross ✕
Warwick ○
Daventry ○
Worcester ○
Ipswich ○

Hereford ○
Banbury ○
Colchester ○

✕ Tewkesbury
Cheltenham
Burford ○
Dunstable ○

Carmarthen ○
Gloucester ○
Cirencester ○
Oxford ○
Barnet ○✕
St Albans ✕

Pembroke ○
Berkeley ○
Abingdon ○
London ○

Malmesbury ○
Thames
Windsor ○
Kingston ○

Bristol ○
Chipping Sudbury ○
Sandwich

Bath ○
Canterbury
Avon
Dover ○
Wells ○
Hythe ○

Taunton ○
Glastonbury ○
Salisbury ○
Winchester ○
Winchelsea ○
Romney ○
Yeovil ○
Shaftesbury ○
Hastings ○
Southampton ○
Poole ○
Portsmouth

Exeter ○

Plymouth ○

English   Channel

England's overmighty subjects

Royal Franchises in England and Wales
Royal estate
Lands held by Duke of Clarence
Other noble estates

0   50 Miles
0   80 Km

Henry IV versus Edward IV

········· Henry VI's advance, June–July 1460
—·—·— Lancastrian movements, Nov. 1460–Feb. 1461
— — — Yorkist advance, June–July 1460
— —— Duke of York's advance to the North, Dec. 1460
———— Edward IV's movements, Feb.–Mar. 1461
——— Edward IV's advance, 1471
— — — Queen Margaret's advance, 1471
- - - - - Lancastrian movements, 1471
✕   Battles

0   50 Miles
0   80 Km

left York with a noble escort of earls and barons, and they rode till they came to within two leagues of London where they found a number of archbishops, bishops and abbots, with many other churchmen, also the mayor of London and all the principal burgesses and merchants of the city, who did all the honour to the young duke of York that is proper to be done to a king.

He rode into London along the main thoroughfare of Cheapside as far as the great porch of St Paul's cathedral, where he dismounted and went up into the church.

Here the duke gave thanks to Our Lord, kissed the relics and made his offering, then came out and remounted his horse and with a great noise of trumpets and clarions he rode as far as the River Thames, where he found his barge prepared and hung with rich tapestries.

He went aboard, and all the princes and the others with him, barons, knights and squires, embarked on other barges provided for them, and so they all came ashore at Westminster.

The duke and his people entered the palace, which was nobly prepared and hung with splendid tapestries, and he was led to his own chamber where great honour was done to him.

Then some days later, when everything had been arranged for his coronation, Edward called the earl of Warwick and Lord Fauconberg to him and said:

'My lords, you have been friends and fathers to me and the source of all the good I have and hope to have; may God give me grace to be worthy of it.' They replied that he should have no doubt of that, and that they would always be his good and loyal subjects.

Despite the outward pomp of his coronation, Edward's position was far from secure. Henry VI and Queen Margaret, who had taken refuge in Scotland, were a focus for Lancastrian disaffection, and Edward's new kingdom was divided and disorderly. John Warkworth traces some of the measures he took to consolidate his power.

The first Yorkist king

EDWARD IV was born at Rouen on 28 April 1442, the first son of Richard, duke of York. Henry VI's lieutenant-general in France, Edward's father as a high-born nobleman was expected to take a major part in political and military life. Moreover, as a descendant of Edward III through both the male and female lines, he had a claim to the throne. In 1442 this did not matter. By 1459, when Lancastrian authority was tottering, it did and York took to arms. The Yorkists were so comprehensively defeated by the Lancastrians at Ludlow that they fled, the duke to Ireland and his foremost colleague, Richard Neville, earl of Warwick, to Calais. With their lands confiscated and given to government supporters – York had been England's richest landowner – the exiles' only option was a comeback: achieved in the summer of 1460.

In parliament an unsatisfactory compromise was stitched together: Richard, duke of York's claim was acknowledged, but the mad though by no means old Henry – he was younger than Richard – was to remain king for life; the duke and his heirs were to succeed him. This patchwork was not acceptable to Queen Margaret, who had her own son, the prince of Wales, Henry VI's heir, born in 1453. The armed conflict was renewed. York was killed at Wakefield in December 1460, but his son Edward won at Mortimer's Cross, and although the earl of Warwick lost at St Albans in February 1461, Edward was acclaimed as king with Warwick's support, at London, in March. At Towton later that month the Yorkists by a supreme effort overcame the Lancastrians: on Palm Sunday 1461 Edward, aged 18, declared himself king.

Edward was six feet three inches tall and of a big build, handsome, affable and accessible. Although he had no pretensions to scholarship or to more than conventional piety, he was not a philistine and took much of his library with him on his travels. His court circle included some notable patrons of learning, like George Neville, archbishop of York, but his own literary tastes were mainstream, and his extensive building schemes were mainly secular rather than religious in emphasis. Even St George's chapel at Windsor, which he reconstructed magnificently at great expense as a royal mausoleum, was intended as much to glorify the house of York as to 'serve Almighty God'.

Edward could be charming. In 1475 the Milanese ambassador described how his London neighbours – hard men of business – were elated to have talked to him and had given him the money he had asked for. But contemporaries were above all struck by his extravagance, laziness and love of luxury. His expenditure on items such as 'chambers of plesaunce' with rich hangings, on personal finery, exotic food and jewels was prodigious; on one occasion he reputedly offered as much as £3,000 for a huge ornament decorated with diamonds and rubies. He was also licentious and debauched; even Sir Thomas

More, in his otherwise flattering portrait of the king, wrote that 'he was of youth greatly given to fleshly wantonness'. His pursuit of pleasure often distracted him from the cares of state. De Commynes commented that his preoccupation with hunting, coupled with over-confidence, allowed the Lancastrians to recover power in 1470–1.

The crisis of 1470–1 did, however, bring out energy and determination in Edward. As a military commander he showed himself confident and decisive; as a ruler he began to seem more ruthless and determined. In his later years despotic tendencies and an increasing lack of political grasp underlay the charming façade. Behind the smiles there was a carelessness that was not attractive to everyone – the Paston family, for instance, when the king turned a blind eye to the injustices done to them by the dukes of Suffolk and Norfolk. A lightweight as a man and as a king, Edward never discarded his childish addiction to the superficial.

Opposite *The great seal of Edward IV.*

Below *Edward IV enthroned. The gartered figure (left) may be the young Richard III.*

In the first year of his reign, King Edward summoned a parliament, at which King Henry and all the others who had fled with him to Scotland from England were attainted; and because he found great comfort in time of need from his commoners, he ratified and confirmed the franchises bestowed upon all the cities and towns, and granted more liberties than they had had before to many new cities and towns, and had charters drawn up with the intention of creating more goodwill and popularity.

1462

Queen Margaret, Henry, duke of Exeter, Henry Beaufort, duke of Somerset, and other lords that had fled England had retained certain castles in Northumberland: Alnwick, Bamburgh, Dunstanburgh and Warkworth. These they had stocked up and filled with Englishmen, Frenchmen and Scotsmen, and by possessing them they controlled most of Northumberland.

King Edward and his council, realizing what harm might come from this, sent commissions to the south and to the west country. They raised large sums of money and besieged these castles in the month of December.

1463

Now Pierre de Brézé, a knight from France [who was grand seneschal of Normandy] and the best warrior of that time, was in Scotland to help Queen Margaret. When he found out that the castles were besieged he raised twenty thousand Scotsmen and marched upon Alnwick and the other castles.

On hearing of this, King Edward's men withdrew from their siege and were afraid; but the Scottish army supposed that this was a tactical move and so did not dare go near Alnwick Castle.

Yet if they had made one bold attack they might have taken and routed the besieging lords and commoners, for they had been troubled for so long by the cold and the rain that they had no courage for a fight.

When, however, those that were besieged in the castle saw that the army had withdrawn and that the Scots were afraid, they came out of the castle and left it undefended, so King Edward's troops went into the castle and took it.

After that, the castle of Bamburgh was handed over to King Edward in a treaty drawn up by Henry, duke of Somerset, who held it. King Edward granted Henry one thousand marks per year for it, which he was never paid; so after six months Henry left England and went to Scotland. King Edward now possessed the whole of England, except a castle in North Wales called Harlech, which Sir Richard Tunstall was in charge of, and which was later taken by Lord Herbert.

In this same year, there was heavy snow and severe frost, which allowed men to walk on the ice, and it was extremely cold.

There was also a meeting of parliament at Westminster which granted the king a revenue of a fifteenth part of men's possessions, and half as much again, which caused the people to complain bitterly.

1464

In that year, the earl of Warwick was sent into France to look for a wife for the king. The fair lady in question was the niece of the king of France, and the earl of Warwick managed to arrange this wedding. However, while the earl of Warwick was away in France, the king was married to Elizabeth Woodville, a widow, whose husband Sir John Grey had been slain in battle on King Henry's side, and whose father was Lord Rivers. The wedding took place in great secrecy, on the first day of May 1464.

The Italian Dominic Mancini, writing some 20 years later, gives a detailed and highly coloured explanation for Edward's marriage.

Edward IV, though he was then king of England, allowed himself to be ruled by his appetites in all things. In his choice of wife too he was governed by lust. For he married a woman of

Warfare and the people

THE Wars of the Roses straggled across a generation from 1455 to 1487, but, apart from establishing who was to be king, they had relatively little effect on the population as a whole. Unlike continental wars, which were protracted campaigns of sieges and scorched earth, the English conflict was simply politics in arms. Decisive battles were not sought in Europe, and locust-like armies were in the field for months; in the English conflicts, men went to war to fight for a political decision and, because they had to pay for their supplies, were on the march only for days or, at the most, weeks. Towns were neither besieged nor sacked – apart from Stamford in 1461 – and, with the exception of the old-fashioned castles of Northumbria and North Wales, the houses of the great, now built more for pleasure than war, were neither defended nor attacked. The Wars of the Roses consisted of sharp encounters in the fields and back gardens of small towns: St Albans (twice), Barnet, Northampton, Tewkesbury. In 1460–1 there were four battles in four months.

Except for 1459–61 and 1469–71 no general collapse of law and order was associated with these political

Above *Attacks on civilians were uncommon.*

Left *Most communities were undisturbed.*

conflicts. Ordinary people were affected by a wider social evil, and one which fostered the wars: the power of leading men to pervert justice for their own ends and to use their retainers to prosecute their own causes by murdering their opponents and destroying their possessions. Sir Thomas Malory, thrice a member of parliament, and a distinguished poet, was a noted lawbreaker. In 1449 he and his men attempted – unsuccessfully – to ambush and kill the duke of Buckingham; in 1450 he twice committed extortion and rape, and in 1451 terrorized the monks of Combe Abbey. His activities eventually landed him in gaol, where he wrote the *Morte d'Arthur*, one of the greatest books of the age.

Despite the violence and lawlessness endemic in society, the English nobility took little interest in continental advances in the art of warfare and built their houses more for comfort than security. All over England, parish churches were reconstructed and refurbished in the Perpendicular Gothic style, which reached its perfection during these decades. Although poetry was often tinged with morbidity and melancholia, literature as a whole showed no particular preoccupation with the horrors of civil war. These were, it seems, more an invention of Tudor propagandists anxious to promote the value of peace than a product of their own times.

low stock, called Elizabeth, against the wishes of the magnates. They would not stoop to show regal honour in accordance with her exalted rank to a woman of such humble origins, who was, moreover, a widow with two sons.

The king was moved to love her by reason of her beautiful person and elegant manner, but neither his gifts nor his threats could prevail against her jealously guarded virtue. When Edward held a dagger to her throat in an attempt to make her submit to his passion, she held still and showed no sign of fear, preferring rather to die than to live unchastely with the king. This incident only fanned the flames of Edward's desire. He judged her worthy to be queen whose virtue could withstand the approaches of even a royal lover.

The marriage caused the nobles to turn against Edward – later, indeed, he was even obliged to make war on them – while the members of Edward's own house were bitterly offended. His mother was furious and offered to submit to a public enquiry, asserting that Edward was not the child of her husband, the duke of York, but was conceived in adultery. For this reason, she claimed, he had no right to be king.

Edward had two brothers then living and they, for their part, were sorely displeased at Edward's marriage. The duke of Clarence, who was closest in age to Edward, showed his anger more openly. He criticized Elizabeth's humble origins bitterly and in public and asserted that the king ought to marry a virgin, not a widow, which was contrary to established custom.

The other brother, however, Richard, duke of Gloucester, was better able to dissemble his thoughts and was in any case, because of his youth, less influential. He said and did nothing that might have been used against him.

Warkworth traces the growing rift between Edward IV and the earl of Warwick.

When the earl of Warwick came home and heard of Edward's marriage, he was most displeased with the king, and the rift between them

Elizabeth Woodville

ELIZABETH was the daughter of Richard Woodville, later Earl Rivers, and Jacquetta of Luxembourg, widow of Henry V's brother, John, duke of Bedford. She was a maid of honour to Queen Margaret and in 1452 married Sir John Grey, son and heir of Lord Ferrers, by whom she had two sons. Her husband was killed at St Albans in 1461, fighting for the Lancastrians.

In 1464 Edward was the most eligible bachelor in Europe, with the reputation of a successful philanderer. A number of foreign royal brides had been proposed for him, but on 1 May 1464 he secretly married Elizabeth at Grafton Regis, the Woodville family home. No one knows when he first met and fell in love with her. A popular contemporary explanation of the marriage was that Elizabeth rejected his advances and declared that a wedding ring was the price of her favours. For a king of England to marry one of his own subjects – and one who was a widow five years his senior – was impolitic and Edward's council took the view 'that she was not his match, however good and however fair she might be and he must know well that she was no wife for a prince such as himself'.

Elizabeth was certainly fair, but although she may have been virtuous she was not good in any real sense of the word. She was greedy, ambitious, arrogant and unscrupulous and, for the first time since Eleanor of Provence's Savoyard relatives embarrassed Henry III two centuries earlier, the queen's family was closely involved in English politics. Not very affluent, and highly ambitious, the Woodvilles – five brothers and seven unmarried sisters – and the two sons of Elizabeth's first marriage, were mainly provided for by a series of highly advantageous marriages; Edward did not make them lavish grants of land or money. Once he had acknowledged his secret marriage, the king gave Elizabeth a magnificent coronation. Suitably dowered by Edward, although not as generously as the Lancastrian queens, she managed her finances carefully and lived within her means. She did her duty promptly and bore the king three sons and seven daughters; her first three children were girls and the future Edward V was not born until 1470 while his father was in exile and the queen in sanctuary. Nor did Elizabeth interfere in political matters.

Although Edward's infidelities were well known, Elizabeth had considerable influence over him, which she used to advance the interests of her relatives. On more than one occasion the easy-going king was manoeuvred into legally and morally dubious actions. His tampering with the laws of inheritance to provide endowments for the queen's Grey sons and his own younger son, Richard,

our moost goode and gracious. Queue Elisabeth Sister vnto this oure ffraternite: Of oure blissed ladi. And modir of merci. Sanct Mary vppon the

Above *Elizabeth Woodville in royal regalia.*

Below *The marriage of Edward and Elizabeth.*

was deeply resented by the landowning classes as well as the deprived legitimate heirs.

The Woodvilles' prominence at court, their greedy, grasping behaviour and their suspicion and antagonism towards possible rivals added to their unpopularity. But Edward's major error was to allow them to dominate the prince of Wales and his council. After his death fear of a Woodville-dominated minority made it possible for Richard III to usurp the throne and led to the deaths of Edward V and his brother Prince Richard, and the queen's brother, Anthony, Earl Rivers, and her son Richard Grey. But although Richard III had Elizabeth's marriage declared invalid and her children bastards, he gave her a generous pension.

Elizabeth, together with Lady Margaret Beaufort, now began to promote a marriage between her eldest daughter, Elizabeth of York, and Margaret's exiled son, Henry Tudor, earl of Richmond, whose successful invasion led to the restoration of Elizabeth's position as queen dowager. After a short period at court when her daughter became queen, Elizabeth retired to Bermondsey Abbey where she died in 1492 aged 55.

grew greater and greater from this moment on, for that and other reasons. The king removed the bishop of Exeter, Warwick's brother, from the post of chancellor and made the bishop of Bath chancellor of England.

After this, the earl of Warwick took on as many knights, squires and gentlemen as he could to swell his forces, and the king did all he could to reduce the earl's power. They were brought together several times, but they never again found pleasure in each other's company.

In May, the duke of Somerset and other leading Lancastrian nobles raised a large band of north country men to support King Henry's cause, and Lord Montague, at that time earl of Northumberland, attacked them with ten thousand men. The commoners fled, and the nobles were captured and later beheaded. [Henry, who was with the expedition, escaped and remained in hiding in the north of England.]

At that time Montague, the earl of Warwick's brother, whom the king had made earl of Northumberland, was a very powerful lord, and Edward, fearing that he might join forces with Warwick, encouraged the people to demand the rightful heir, the son of Henry Percy who had been slain at York field, as earl of Northumberland — which is what duly happened. Afterwards, however, the king made Lord Montague a marquis and made his son duke of Bedford. He then betrothed Bedford to his eldest daughter, putting him in line for the throne. So Montague received much flattery from the king, but no lordships, although Edward always promised him that he would give him land one day.

In the same year, 1464, Edward IV changed the coinage of England, which proved most profitable to him. He made an old noble a royal, the value of which was declared to be ten shillings; but the new coins contained some alloy, which reduced their value and made them weigh more; and he changed the design. He also made a groat worth threepence and an angel noble worth six shillings and eightpence, and with all these changes caused great harm to the common people.

Balancing the books

ENGLISH monarchs relied on two major sources of income to pay for the government and defence of the country and to support themselves and their dependants. It was understood that except in times of crisis the king would 'live off his own': the revenues from his estates would cover routine items of expenditure. However, because of the high cost of commitments like the garrison at Calais, parliament assigned certain customs dues to the king on a regular basis, sometimes even for life, to ease his financial burden. The house of commons had established firm control over the money supply by the middle of the 15th century and, because it was generally unwilling to sanction further taxation in peacetime, prudent rulers tried to avoid unnecessary appeals for money.

Edward IV needed a minimum annual income of £50,000 to cover his basic outgoings, and at first found it hard to make ends meet. When he mounted the throne, in 1461, he gained possession of all Henry VI's estates, together with his own extensive Yorkist inheritance and numerous properties confiscated from the Lancastrians. These netted about £30,000 a year, but he had to make so many rewards to his supporters that he himself reaped only part of the proceeds. Consequently, even though he received a grant of customs (worth an average of £25,000 a year) for life, in 1465, Edward still faced a worrying short-fall in revenues. To make good this deficit he borrowed from London merchants, trading conglomerates and foreign bankers. Whereas Henry VI's finances had been so chaotic that few people were prepared to advance him credit, Edward appeared a far sounder proposition; it says much for his business acumen that he was able to free himself from debt by repaying loans worth over £97,000 before he died.

Some of the methods he used to raise money involved a distinct element of coercion, if not intimidation: his request that all employees of the crown make donations to the royal coffers, his devaluation of the coinage and his practice of approaching wealthy subjects for 'benevolences' or gifts were all short-term expedients to tide him over temporary periods of financial embarrassment.

His attempts to improve the efficiency and profitability of the administrative system were of more lasting value. The crown estates had previously yielded unrealistically low rents, so Edward placed his property in the hands of farmers who paid their dues directly into the chamber of the newly reformed royal household rather than to the exchequer as before. The chamber became the principal department for the collection and disbursement of revenue, bypassing the exchequer with its outdated and cumbersome practices, and placing most aspects of

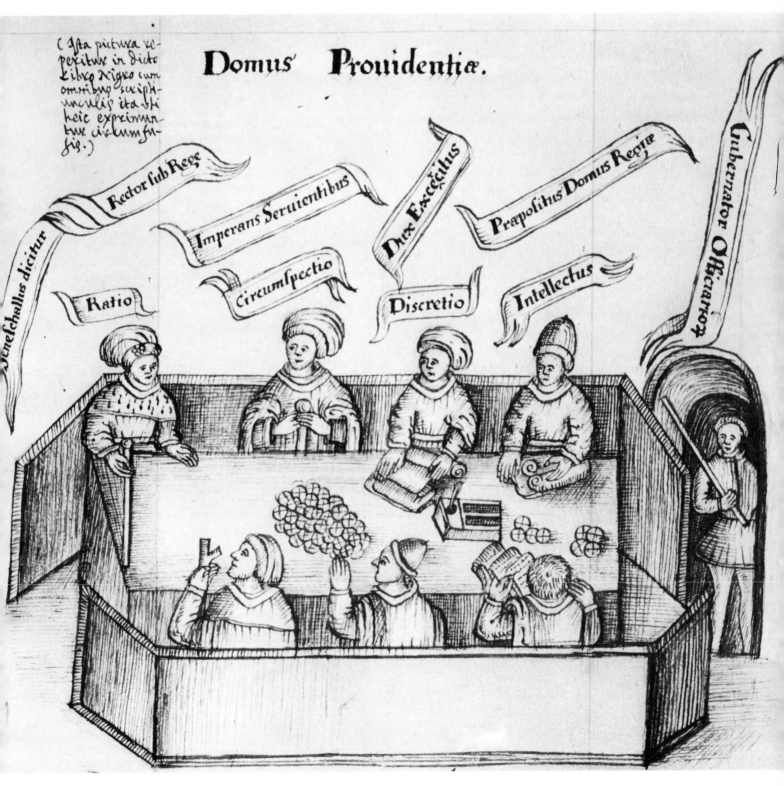

Domus Prouidentiæ.

Above Edward's royal household officials.

financial policy directly under the king's personal control. He further increased his income by tightening up procedures for collecting customs, and stamping out corruption by the officers concerned; at the same time unexploited feudal dues and rights were more thoroughly investigated for payments the crown might have overlooked. Although not all these innovations produced the desired results, Edward was one of the few medieval English kings to die solvent – a notable achievement,

especially as he was constrained by the need to provide for a horde of grasping relatives and courtiers. His continuous struggle to balance the books left him little freedom in the sphere of foreign policy: the financial equilibrium and independence he enjoyed could last only while England remained friendly with her continental neighbours, and to some extent at their mercy.

1465

In this year, King Henry was discovered in a wood called Cletherwood, near Bungerly Hippingstones in Lancashire. He was captured by Thomas Talbot, son and heir to Sir Edmund Talbot of Bashall, and John Talbot, his cousin from Coleby, and others, while he was dining at Waddington Hall, and taken to London on horseback, with his legs tied into the stirrups. There, he was brought to the Tower of London, where he was kept for a long time by two squires and two yeomen of the crown, and their men, and anybody was allowed to come and speak to him.

1466

Lord Hungerford was taken and beheaded for high treason at Salisbury. At different times and in different places throughout England, men were arrested for treason, some of whom were put to death and some escaped.

1468

A little before Michaelmas, a blazing star estimated at about four feet high appeared in the west in the evening, moving from the west towards the north, and it was visible for five or six weeks.

Meanwhile King Edward, as Waurin relates, had arranged an advantageous marriage for his sister Margaret.

On 29 June 1468, Margaret of York, sister of Edward IV, king of England, landed at the port of Sluys in Flanders. A marriage had been arranged between her and Charles, duke of Burgundy, in spite of all the efforts of Louis XI, king of France, to prevent it. He had done his utmost to make an alliance with the English in order to destroy the duke of Burgundy, so it was generally said, and he had succeeded in winning over the earl of Warwick to his side, and with him almost the whole commons of England.

It seemed very probable that if he had not married the king of England's sister, the duke of Burgundy would have had the kingdoms of France

Louis XI

T HE reign of Louis XI of France (1461–83) coincided exactly with that of Edward IV in England, and although Louis was the direct and undisputed heir to his throne, his problems were very similar to those of his English counterpart. The power struggles within the kingdom of France offer interesting parallels with the Wars of the Roses.

A man of immense energy and industry, Louis had rebelled against his father Charles VII, and as punishment had been sent into comfortable exile in the Dauphiné. As king, he was cruel and conniving, autocratic and ambitious. His greatest delight was in the intricacies of diplomacy: known as 'the universal spider', he believed that the best way to maintain his interests was by weaving elaborate webs of alliance and counter-alliance around his enemies. His confidant Philippe de Commynes described him as 'the cleverest man I have known at extricating himself from an adverse situation', a comment that nicely sums up the complicated politics of his reign.

Above *Louis XI meeting with Charles the
Bold, who subsequently died fighting
Louis' forces.*

Opposite *Louis enters Paris riding under a
canopy and sporting the royal fleurs-de-lys.*

Charles VII had already done much to rebuild the
Valois heritage, and Louis continued his father's work. He
encouraged trade and administrative reform, so that royal
revenues increased by 250 per cent in the course of his
reign. The biggest problem, however, came from the
nobility who ruled as independent princes in their own
regions: the dukes of Brittany, Orleans, Anjou, Bourbon,
Alençon and, most powerful of them all, Burgundy.

In 1464 the king faced a major alliance of discontented
nobles led by his brother Charles. The rebels called
themselves the League of the Public Weal and rampaged
over the kingdom; for several months the king's fate lay in
the balance. Louis survived, but at a price: Charles was
given the duchy of Normandy and the duke of Burgundy
regained territory on the borders of Flanders. There were
few direct threats to the crown after this, but it took the
rest of Louis' reign and all his prodigious determination to
re-establish royal influence in the duchies.

The focus of attention was Burgundy and its dukes,
Philip the Good and Charles the Bold. For some years,
Louis tried to counter their power by making an alliance
with England. But in 1474 Edward IV and Charles the
Bold came to terms in the treaty of London and agreed to
divide the kingdom of France. Louis was able to buy off
the English invasion that was threatened in 1475 as a
result of the treaty; and alliances were made with the Holy
Roman Emperor Frederick III, the duke of Lorraine, and
the Swiss confederation. With their help Charles the Bold
of Burgundy was defeated and killed at the battle of
Nancy in January 1477.

He had no son to succeed him as duke of Burgundy
and his only daughter, Mary, now became Europe's most
sought-after spinster. Louis immediately proposed a
marriage between the 19 year old Burgundian heiress and
his own seven year old son. However, when her future
father-in-law started annexing her lands Mary, understandably annoyed, married Maximilian, the emperor's
eldest son. The resulting military campaigns culminated
in the peace of Arras of 1482. Louis was given Picardy
and the duchy of Burgundy, which considerably increased
the size and security of the Valois lands.

When the king died in 1483 almost all the great nobles
had been subjugated or reconciled to the crown. Only
Brittany held out. Louis XI, by the twists and turns of his
diplomacy, rebuilt the authority of the Valois monarchy
within France and established it as a major force in
international politics. Like Edward IV in England, he set a
pattern for the great Renaissance monarchies to follow.

and of England as enemies both at the same time; and it was to obviate this great danger that the duke had deigned to conclude this marriage.

For this reason, therefore, Anthony Woodville, Lord Scales, brother of the queen of England, Elizabeth Woodville, arrived with the princess and other lords and ladies of that country, thirty of them altogether.

The duke of Burgundy sent his brother, the archbishop of Utrecht, with the count of Charny and others of his household to Sluys to meet them, and on the following day, Sunday, my lady Isabel of Portugal, dowager duchess of Burgundy, went to Sluys to welcome her daughter-in-law, took supper with her and then returned to Bruges. On Monday the duke went to see his lady, stayed until after dinner on Tuesday and then went back to Bruges. A week later the lady left Sluys and stayed at Damme, a short league from Bruges; and on Sunday morning the duke went to Damme with only a handful of people, married the lady Margaret of York and immediately returned.

As soon as the duke was back, all the lords and officers of his household went to Damme to meet their mistress and brought her to Bruges, where she made a splendid entry into the town in the following manner.

First came the embassy from Britain and then the members of the duke's council, all very richly dressed and adorned; next came, in order, all the domestic officers of the duke's household; next the duke's knights and chamberlains; then the princes and great lords very richly dressed; after them followed drums, minstrels, trumpets, clarions, heralds and kings-of-arms each according to his rank, in great number; then came the duke's four sergeants-at-arms carrying their maces.

Then came Margaret of York, seated in a litter very richly hung with cloth of gold over crimson velvet; surrounding the litter were twelve knights wearing the duke's order, some of the greatest men, all on foot, each with a hand to the litter, and in this manner they all went to the duke's palace. The lady was wearing a surcoat of blue

Caxton

SINCE 1456, the year of Gutenberg's 42-line Bible, presses had spread through Europe – to Cologne in 1464, Rome in 1467, Paris in 1470 and Florence in 1473.

In 1476 William Caxton set up his printing business in the precincts of Westminster Abbey. The site was well chosen. Church indulgences provided profitable work and the abbey was conveniently placed, near the palace of Westminster, to catch the interest of courtiers, and of parliament when in session. Caxton, in his 50s, had retired after a successful career as a mercer in Bruges.

Printing had come comparatively late to England, but Caxton's venture was highly original. Printing was usually introduced by German experts called in by a churchman or other wealthy patron, and the first book was a religious or scholarly Latin text. Caxton's press was a commercial enterprise, run by a native, and its first book, *Dictes and Sayings of the Philosophers*, was written by a layman, Anthony Woodville, Earl Rivers, in English.

Born in Kent, Caxton was apprenticed to a senior member of the Mercers, the city of London's leading company. His master died in 1441, leaving him some money, and in 1450 he was in Bruges, where the Mercers had what amounted to a continental branch. By 1453 he was prosperous enough to become a full mercer.

Early in the 1460s, Caxton was elected to the

Opposite *Caxton's trademark and initials.*

Above *The Squire, from Caxton's Chaucer.*

governorship of the English Merchant Adventurers in Bruges. He was a leading figure in the foreign community and an influential voice in English trade policies. Edward IV used him in commercial negotiations with Burgundy and when the king's sister, Margaret, married Duke Charles the Rash of Burgundy in 1468, Caxton led the English reception for her at Sluys.

A year later he started a translation of the fashionable *Recueilles d'histoires de Troyes*. Duchess Margaret was his patron and he soon had orders from 'diverse gentlemen' to supply 'as hastily as I might this said book', which he 'practised at great expense to ordain' in print.

Block printing had been known in China for centuries. But Gutenberg (a goldsmith by training) combined movable metal type, an ink that would 'take' on metal, and, above all, the printing press, adapted from the wine press. Caxton went to Cologne to learn the trade in 1471–2 and probably there met Wynkyn de Worde, his assistant for life. He returned to Bruges with a press, type, matrixes and arrangements for ink supplies.

The demand for books had risen so fast by the mid 15th century that booksellers were commissioning numerous copies of popular titles 'on spec'. In Florence, Vespasiano da Bisticci kept 50 scribes fully employed. In the north, Bruges was a major centre of the book trade. Caxton went into partnership with Colard de Mansion, dean of the city's booksellers' guild, and his *Recuyell of the Historyes of Troye*, the first book printed in English, appeared in Bruges in 1473.

The Game and Playe of the Chesse and four books in French followed before Caxton moved to London where he established himself as an editor and translator as well as a printer. His books included translations of Ovid and Christine de Pisan's *Order of Chivalry*, Gower's *Confessio Amantis* and Malory's *Morte d'Arthur*, both English classics, and the first definitive edition of Chaucer's *Canterbury Tales*. Caxton also pioneered the standardization of English at a time when it comprised many, often mutually incomprehensible, dialects; and laid down the criterion of good prose – 'short, quick and high sentences eschewing prolixity'. Few European literatures were so well served by their early printers.

cloth of gold and her dress was made of white cloth, with deep armholes like a *journade* without sleeves. Over this a mantle of crimson cloth of gold hung down behind her. Her hair, which was very beautiful, she wore loose, and on her head was a very rich crown.

The litter was followed by ten young noble-women mounted on fine white pacing horses, richly furnished and adorned. Then came three chariots very richly harnessed and covered with crimson cloth of gold, then three more covered with scarlet woollen cloth.

Next came the Bruges merchants of various nations, all richly dressed and decorated, that is to say, the Genoese, Florentines, Lombards, Spaniards, Germans and English.

At the lady's entry into Bruges several notable mysteries were performed in the streets through which she passed, which were a pleasure to behold. At the various crossroads, in particular, there were all kinds of wild beasts, some spouting forth a constant flow of wine, some of claret, others of hippocras or milk.

When the princess had reached the palace of her husband the duke, she was received by the duke's mother and by many other noble ladies old and young who were present almost without number. She was soon seated at dinner, which was noble and abundant with a variety of dishes and with rich dishes between the courses, which would take too long to describe, so for the sake of brevity I shall pass them over quickly. This much I can say to sum it up: that never in my life have I heard of any feast better provided in any respect; so the duke's noble generosity demanded, as all who knew him are well aware.

On 7, 8 and 9 May in the same year in Bruges, Charles, duke of Burgundy, re-established the feast of the Order of the Golden Fleece which his father, good Duke Philip, had founded in his own day, and made it exactly the same as it had been before. All the knights of the order, twenty-four in number, were summoned to the feast, and they all came in person or in proxy.

Textiles and tailoring

DURING the 15th century Italy was the European centre of silk production, and its economy benefited greatly from the design and manufacture of magnificent figured silk textiles, velvets and cloth of gold. Truly luxurious dress meant silk, and royal inventories, travellers' tales and household accounts show its vital importance for making official and ceremonial clothes.

The chief manufacturing regions for silk textiles were in northern Italy, in a band stretching from Genoa to Venice. Although they used only a simple drawloom, Italian weavers produced weaves ranging from plain smooth cloths such as damask, taffeta and shot silk to patterned textiles such as figured and brocaded velvets. Cloths of gold, the most expensive fabrics, combined an intricate pile weave with lavish gold or silver content in the yarn.

To exploit the techniques of velvet and brocading to the full, it was necessary to use bold designs and treat them as low reliefs by contrasting cut and uncut areas of pile; many of the finest 15th-century velvets are splendidly three-dimensional. Animal motifs, popular in 13th- and 14th-century silks, were used less and less frequently early in the 15th century and, by 1450, had been supplanted by floral motifs, especially the pomegranate.

In spite of their enormous popularity luxury textiles like these were the exception rather than the rule, and silk never took the place of linen and wool for everyday wear. English wool had few serious rivals for most of the Middle Ages, although it was the 15th century before finished cloth was exported. Previously raw wool had been supplied to foreign manufacturers; under Edward III the highest grade of woollen cloth in Europe had been dyed and finished in Florence from English wool which was woven in Flanders.

A number of different specializations were involved in the manufacture of clothing, and their activities were carefully controlled. Tailors were responsible for gowns, hoods and clothes in general but not for hose, which were produced exclusively by hose-makers. Embroidery was also a separate profession. Tailors were permitted only to make clothes to order, not for sale, and had to use new cloth, while the second-hand dealers were forbidden to sell cloth at all. The money paid to tailors was negligible compared to the price of cloth, and they had little influence on fashion.

Summer and winter clothes were distinguished mainly by weight of cloth; silk and linen were worn in warmer weather, wool, often lined with fur, in colder. As always, fur was a symbol of luxury and elegance. Marten, gris, vair and ermine were generally reserved for royal or court dress while beaver, otter, hare and fox were worn by the

lesser nobility and middle classes; lambskin, sheepskin and goat were for the common people.

Vair was the belly skin of the northern squirrel and the grey back and white belly, combined to create a shield pattern, was known as *menu vair* (little fur) or miniver. Thousands of bellies could be expended on lining just one

Above A street of drapers, with bolts of cloth and cut-out patterns on the stalls.

suit. Fur was bought through the Hanseatic League, with its Russian trading posts, or at Bruges, strategically placed between the northern producers and Mediterranean buyers.

243

1469

In this year, the earl of Warwick received a safe-conduct from the duke of Burgundy and went to Saint-Omer, where the duke and the lords of his court gave him a noble welcome. These lords went to meet him and accompanied him to his residence; then he went to the duke who at that time was staying in the abbey of Saint Bertin, and here the duke entertained him like a friend. Two days later he went to see his cousin the duchess at Aire and was received with every kindness, for never could anyone have imagined what his true purpose was.

When the welcome and the feasting were all done, Warwick took leave of the duke and the duchess and withdrew to Calais. The duke also left Saint-Omer and went to Ypres, as did his wife the duchess, neither of them giving a thought to the troubles now being caused to Edward, king of England, at the determined instigation of the earl of Warwick.

And I, the author of these chronicles, wishing to learn and to have accurate material to complete my work, asked leave of the duke of Burgundy to go to Calais, which he granted me, because he knew that the earl of Warwick had promised me that he would make me welcome and would give me help to find everything I might want. So I went to see the earl of Warwick, and he kept me nine days in all honour and kindness, but as for what I was wanting, he did little enough about that. However, he promised that if I went back to him after another two months, he would provide part of what I needed; and when I took leave of him he paid all my expenses and gave me an excellent palfrey.

I could see that the earl was engaged in important business; and this was the marriage then being negotiated between his daughter, Isabel Neville, and the duke of Clarence, King Edward's brother, which took place within the castle of Calais five or six days after I left. There were very few guests and the celebrations only lasted two days, for Clarence was married on a Tuesday and on the following Sunday he returned to England.

Warwick had by these nuptials cemented a valuable alliance in his plots against Edward IV. Warkworth describes how the earl's own and his confederates' schemes bore fruit in an armed uprising in the north.

Immediately after this, and by their arrangement, there was an insurrection in Yorkshire by many knights, squires and commoners, numbering twenty thousand men in all. Sir William Conyers was the captain of these men, and he called himself Robin of Redesdale. The king ordered Lord Herbert, earl of Pembroke, with forty-three thousand Welshmen, the best in Wales, and Humphrey Stafford, earl of Devon, with seven thousand archers from the west country, to go out and fight against them.

On their way to meet the men from the north, they had an argument about their encampment, and so the earl of Devon left the earl of Pembroke, along with all his men. Robin of Redesdale attacked the Welshmen on a plain beyond Banbury, and they fought bitterly; Pembroke was taken, along with his brother, and two thousand Welshmen were killed. So the Welshmen lost the battle on 26 July.

At the same time, Lord Rivers was captured, and one of his sons, in the Forest of Dean, and brought to Northampton, along with the earl of Pembroke and Sir Richard Herbert, his brother, and all four of them were beheaded there by order of the duke of Clarence and the earl of Warwick. Stafford, who was earl of Devon for only half a year, was captured by the commoners of Somerset at Bridgwater and immediately beheaded.

After this, the archbishop of York found out that King Edward was in a village near Northampton, and that all the men he had raised had fled from him. So, on the advice of the duke of Clarence and the earl of Warwick he went with a few horsemen, and captured King Edward. He kept him in Warwick Castle for a while, and then took him to the city of York, where the king, by making eloquent promises, escaped from the archbishop of York's hands, came to London and there did what he liked.

Warwick the kingmaker

THE Nevilles were the most powerful family in England in the 1460s; and Richard Neville, earl of Warwick, was their greatest member. The eldest son of the earl of Salisbury, and nephew by marriage to Richard, duke of York, Richard became Edward of York's principal supporter after both their fathers died at Wakefield. Warwick was at Edward's side when the young man made his formal claim to the throne in March 1461, and again when he made good that claim in the battle of Towton later that month. In the early years of his reign, Edward had few other friends among the established nobility; and although Warwick had not made him king, the goodwill of the Nevilles undoubtedly kept him in power.

Warwick's father had married the heiress to the earldom of Salisbury, and Richard claimed another heiress – to the earldom of Warwick – as his bride. By 1461, when he was 33, he had extensive lands and power in Yorkshire, the West Midlands, southern England and South Wales, and, with a net income of about £3,900 a year, was the wealthiest of the earls – the archetypal over-mighty subject.

Richard had no sons and, as the laws of inheritance dictated that the vast Neville estates would be split between his two daughters, he began to hunt for suitable sons-in-law in 1461 when Isabel was just ten and Anne a mere five. However, after Edward's marriage in 1464, all eligible bachelors were being snatched up for the sisters of Edward's new queen, Elizabeth Woodville. This created considerable friction between the Nevilles and the court, and was one of the main reasons why Warwick eventually defected from the Yorkist camp.

Foreign policy was the other cause of tension. Warwick favoured a treaty with Louis XI of France, but the king preferred an alliance with Burgundy. Warwick was put in charge of the Anglo-Burgundian talks, but used his influence to carry on an independent correspondence with the French king. By the late 1460s there were signs of open conflict between the king and Warwick.

The first opportunities for rebellion came in 1469, when major demonstrations broke out in Yorkshire and Lancashire under the leadership of Robin of Redesdale and Robin of Holderness. As Edward moved north to quell the disturbances, Warwick, who had been scheming for some time with Edward's younger brother George, duke of Clarence, seized his chance: on 11 July the 20 year old prince secretly married Isabel Neville. The following day Clarence and his new father-in-law issued a manifesto declaring that the king, by his reliance on the Woodvilles and his refusal to admit the advice of the great

Above *The kingmaker as a mourner on a tomb.*

Below *The bear badge of Richard Neville.*

nobility and princes of the blood, was bringing upon himself the fate of Edward II, Richard II and Henry VI. The battle lines were drawn.

For a short while it seemed that history was about to repeat itself, and that the Nevilles would help another Yorkist pretender, Clarence, to the throne. Warwick defeated the royalist earls at Edgecote and captured Edward and imprisoned him, first at Warwick and then at Middleham Castle in Yorkshire. However, widespread disorder broke out and, unable to gain control, Warwick was forced to release Edward. Rallying his supporters, the king marched on London and regained power in October. During the spring of 1470 a rising in Lincolnshire gave Warwick and Clarence brief hope, but it was soon crushed and Neville fled to France to plot with Margaret of Anjou. Richard Neville, the arch-Yorkist, was about to become kingmaker to the Lancastrians.

In the same year, a proclamation was read out at the King's Bench in Westminster, in the city of London and in the whole of England: a general pardon was to be granted to all manner of men for all manner of insurrections and crimes; and also a whole fifteenth part of every man's goods should be collected and paid on 11 November and on the following 25 March, which annoyed the people, for not long ago they had already paid a great tax of a similar amount.

In 1464, one of the brides proposed to Edward IV had been Isabella, half-sister of Henry IV of Castile, but he had instead married Elizabeth Woodville. Now, in 1469, Isabella's marriage to Ferdinand of Aragon allied two great kingdoms.

1470

In the tenth year of King Edward's reign, in the month of March, Lord Willoughby, Lord Wells his son, Thomas Delalond, a knight, and Sir Thomas Dimmock, the king's champion, drove out of Lincolnshire Sir Thomas Burgh, a knight of the king's house, pulled down his home, and took all the goods and cattle that they could find.

They then gathered all the commoners of the shire, some thirty thousand in all, and shouted 'King Henry!', denying King Edward's rights. This was thought to be the work of Clarence and Warwick, as had been the rising at Banbury Field of Robin of Redesdale.

When King Edward heard of this, he chose his captains and gathered a great crowd of men, sent a pardon to Lord Willoughby and an order that he should come to see him, which he did. When the king was sure of him, he led his army towards Lincolnshire, to the place where Lord Wells and all his men were gathered, and ordered Lord Willoughby to send a letter to his son and all his men, saying that they should surrender to the king, as their sovereign lord, or else he made a vow that Willoughby would lose his head.

The letter was dispatched, but they paid it no heed, so the king ordered that Lord Willoughby's head be cut off, despite his pardon.

The Catholic monarchs

THE kingdom of Spain, which was to become the dominant power in 16th-century Europe, was born out of the marriage of Ferdinand of Aragon and Isabella of Castile in 1469. This union of the heirs to two great kingdoms took place secretly at Valladolid – Ferdinand smuggled himself into the city disguised as a muleteer – and provoked a storm of reaction in Castile. When Henry IV of Castile died in 1474 Isabella had to fight her rival Joanna, reputedly Henry's illegitimate daughter, for the throne. In 1479 Joanna was finally defeated and retired into a nunnery, and Ferdinand acceded to the throne of Aragon. The Catholic monarchs – he cunning and parsimonious, she pious, industrious and regal – spent the next two decades building up royal authority and bringing order to their kingdoms. They did not attempt to unite them, retaining their separate institutions and customs.

Aragon, orientated towards Mediterranean trade and culture, had particularly close links with Sicily and Naples, which it had controlled earlier in the 15th century. Although the monarchy was weak, it had more authority than that of Castile, a kingdom bedevilled by succession disputes, over-mighty nobles and overstrained royal finances since the mid 14th century. Despite these domestic troubles its people continued to wage a long and slow crusade to sweep the Moors out of the Iberian peninsula, as they had done since the 11th century. This finally ended when Ferdinand and Isabella conquered Granada in 1492, the year in which some 200,000 Jews were expelled from Spain.

Control of religious orthodoxy was as important to the Catholic monarchs as extending political authority, and they had a useful weapon in the Inquisition. Set up by Pope Gregory XI in the 1230s to combat heresy in western Europe, the Inquisition soon acquired unprecedented powers to imprison on suspicion and to assume a person guilty until proved innocent. Torture of the accused was permitted; if it produced a confession he was condemned to imprisonment for life and his goods were confiscated; if he did not confess he was handed over to the lay powers and could be burned at the stake.

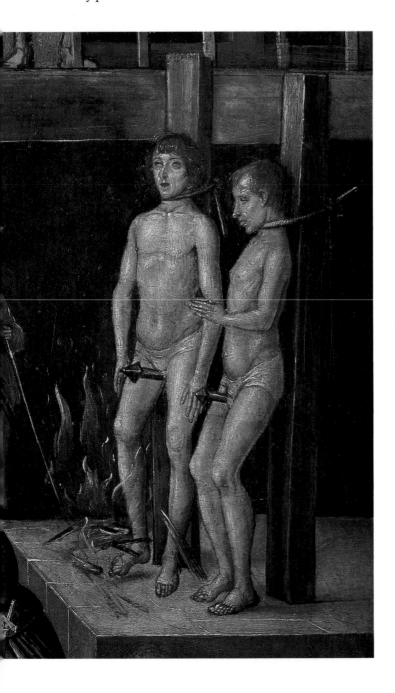

Above *Ferdinand and Isabella kneeling before the Virgin and Child. Behind Ferdinand is Torquemada, appointed inquisitor general of Aragon and Castile in 1483.*

Opposite *Isabella of Castile.*

Left *The fate reserved for stubborn heretics.*

No lay power had exercised control over the Inquisition until, in 1478, Pope Sixtus V issued a bull allowing Isabella to appoint inquisitors in Castile, to supervise their work and to receive the profits. In 1484 the system was extended to Aragon. In both kingdoms the Spanish Inquisition became an effective agent of political control and created a rigidly orthodox society. Contemporary observers admired its effectiveness, but its methods aroused intense opposition – which lasted until the Inquisition's final abolition in the 19th century.

After Isabella's death in 1504 Castile was ruled by her daughter Joanna the Mad, until incapacity drove her into the cloister and Ferdinand her father assumed control once more. Joanna had married Philip, archduke of Austria, son of the Emperor Maximilian I, and when Ferdinand died in 1516 Joanna's son, the young Emperor Charles V, added Spain to his Hapsburg dominions and brought it into the mainstream of European politics.

Edward then led his army against his enemies and used the full force of his artillery against them, supported by his infantry, and the commoners soon fled. There were, however, many men of Lincolnshire slain, and Wells, Delalond and Dimmock were captured and beheaded.

When the duke of Clarence and the earl of Warwick heard the battle was lost, and that their part in it had been discovered, they fled west to the coast, boarded ships there and went towards Southampton, where they were expecting one of Warwick's big ships, called *The Trinity*. However, Anthony, Lord Scales, the queen's brother, was sent there on the king's orders; he fought with the duke and earl and captured their ships with many men on them. So the duke and earl were forced to flee to the king of France, where they were received with honours.

King Edward then came to Southampton and commanded the earl of Worcester to sit in judgement of the men who had been captured in the ships; and so twenty gentlemen and yeomen were hanged, drawn and quartered, and then beheaded, after which they were hung up by their legs and a stake was sharpened at both ends; one end of this stake was pushed in between their buttocks, and their heads were stuck on the other. This angered the people of the land and forever afterwards the earl of Worcester was greatly hated by them, for the irregular and unlawful manner of execution he had inflicted upon his captives.

When the duke of Clarence and the earl of Warwick were in France, a blazing star appeared in the west, shaped like a flaming spearhead, which was seen by some of the king's household, and which frightened them deeply.

In the mean time, in France, the said lords were discussing what to do for the best. The only solution they could find was to write to Queen Margaret and arrange a marriage between Prince Edward, King Henry's son, and another of Warwick's daughters, Anne Neville. This was arranged and duly and honourably carried out in France. There, it was agreed by all that King Henry should take joyful possession of England again, and reign

Beyond the earth

MEDIEVAL astronomy derived from the 1st-century work of Ptolemy, whose *Almagest*, the culmination and summary of the ancient Greek tradition, presented the wonders of the heavens as an ordered whole, amenable to human reason governed by mathematics. When the first Latin translation appeared in the 1170s, Ptolemy and his Arab commentators opened new worlds to European thinkers. In the mid 13th century the Englishman John Sacrobosco produced treatises on arithmetical time reckoning and spherical geometry which remained popular and influential into the 17th century.

The sphere was the perfect form, expected in the divine creation, and no thinking medieval man supposed the world was flat. *The Travels of Sir John Mandeville* (1370s) described, 'for simple unlearned men', why 'a man may environ all the world and turn again to his country': the round world was set within a series of invisible celestial spheres, kept in motion by separate intelligences, which carried the moon, the planets and, beyond, the stars. Not until the 16th century was the sun, rather than the earth, proposed to be at the centre of the universe.

The universe was thought to be unique and finite, and subject to scientific principles. But even 'learned men' were unsettled by heavenly portents like comets, which were thought to be atmospheric 'exhalations' sent, like the star of Bethlehem, by God.

Astrology also reached Europe from Arabic sources, although the idea that the heavenly bodies have direct influence on human affairs is an ancient one. Many churchmen regarded it as a black art; others considered it 'the great science', linking natural philosophy with mathematics, and saw astronomy as a mere preparation for astrology. In the 13th century Roger Bacon described the rise of the world's religions in terms of astrological

Below *An astronomer with an astrolabe.*

planetary conjunctions. A specialized astrological mathematics developed with its own university chairs, the first of which was in Italy. From the late 13th century rulers began to employ court astrologers to cast horoscopes, advise on auspicious times for undertakings and foretell the future.

Although in the 14th century the French mathematician Nicholas Oresme used logic to demonstrate that these ideas were illusory, astrology's popularity did not decline; as today, the astrologers' public was larger than that of the scientists.

Of key importance in both astronomy and astrology, the astrolabe also reached Europe through Islam. A handheld brass disc engraved with a terrestrial sphere, it was fitted with a rotating star grid and a pointer or 'alidade' to fix a star's altitude above the horizon. Astrolabes could help to solve problems of spherical geometry, and check astronomical or astrological predictions, and were also used as teaching aids in astronomy. They became popular with educated laymen. Chaucer wrote a treatise on them for his son and the 15th-century Parisian instrument-maker Jean Fusoris stocked them along with portable sundials and other instruments. The astrolabe had joined the world of vogue gadgetry.

Above *God presides over the celestial spheres.*

Below *A treatise on lunar eclipses from 1476.*

Above *An astrolabe of the type used in astronomy, astrology and navigation.*

Opposite *The astrolabe in the margin of an astrological treatise.*

as well as he did before, and after him his son Prince Edward should rule, and be succeeded by any of his heirs rightfully begotten; and if it should happen that he should die without rightful heirs, then the kingdom of England and the lordship of Ireland should pass to George, duke of Clarence, and his heirs, for ever more.

It was also agreed that Henry, duke of Exeter, Edmund, duke of Somerset, and all the knights, squires and others who had been exiled and dishonoured in the cause of King Henry, should come back to England and retake possession of their property and its inhabitants. All these conditions were written, indented and sealed by Queen Margaret and the prince, her son, on one side, and the duke of Clarence and the earl of Warwick on the other. And moreover, to make it sure, they exchanged solemn and binding oaths, and all this was done on the king of France's advice.

In the same year, a little before Michaelmas, the duke of Clarence and the earl of Warwick landed in the west country and assembled a great number of men. Lord Montague had gathered six thousand men, at King Edward's command, to resist them. However, Montague hated the king and intended to capture him; so when he was within a mile of King Edward, he declared to his people that he would side with the earl of Warwick, his brother, and take King Edward if he could, and all those that stayed with him. Immediately, however, one of the men went from this gathering and told King Edward all about it, and told him to stay away, for he was not strong enough to take on Lord Montague.

Then King Edward made great haste to the town of King's Lynn, and there took ship on 29 September in the tenth year of his reign, along with Lord Hastings, the king's chamberlain, Lord Say and other knights and squires. The king sailed over the sea to Flanders, to his brother-in-law the duke of Burgundy, for help and support.

Edward's change of fortune was rapid and dramatic, but Philippe de Commynes blames it in part on his pursuit of pleasure.

King Edward escaped with two barges, and one of his own small boats, and some seven or eight hundred men with him, whose only clothes were their battle dress. They had nothing but what they were standing in, and they hardly even knew where they were going.

It was very strange for this poor king – it would not be improper to call him this – to run away like that and be persecuted by his own servants. More than any other prince of his time, he had, for twelve or thirteen years, indulged in his own pleasure, for he had thought of nothing but women, far more than is reasonable, and of hunting and of looking after himself well. When he went off on a hunt, he would take with him several tents for the ladies. In fact he had become very dear to them, but he did have a character as suited to this as any man I have ever seen; he was young and as handsome as any man who lived in his time; I hasten to add, at the time of this adversity, because he did become very fat later.

Warkworth describes the process of Henry VI's subsequent reinstatement as king.

At the beginning of October, the bishop of Winchester, with the compliance of Warwick and Clarence, went to the Tower of London where King Henry was imprisoned by King Edward's command, and took him from his keepers, who were neither feeding nor clothing him in a manner befitting a prince.

They released him, found him new clothes, paid him great reverence and took him to the palace of Westminster, where he was restored to the crown again. All his letters, writs and other records bore his regnal year in the following style: 'In the forty-ninth year of the reign of Henry VI, and the first of his readeption to royal power.' All his supporters, in fact most of the people, were full of joy at this. Yet when he had been removed from the throne by King Edward, most of the English people had hated him, all because of his deceitful lords, never because of his own faults. They were therefore very glad of a change. They had expected prosperity and peace from Edward IV, but it was not to be. One battle followed another, and there was

Edward IV's mistresses

ACCORDING to Sir Thomas More, Edward was wont to say that he had three concubines . . . one the merriest, another the wiliest, the third the holiest harlot in his realm. But the king was being modest: his mistresses numbered far more than three. Mancini describes him as 'licentious in the extreme . . . he pursued with no discrimination the married and the unmarried, the noble and the lowly; however, he took none by force'. But Edward's subjects did not take his activities amiss; his other kingly attributes more than compensated for his excessive enjoyment of all the sensual pleasures of life.

The names of only three of the king's mistresses are well known. Elizabeth Lucy was the daughter of Thomas Wayte, a member of the minor Hampshire gentry. The affair lasted several years, from about the time of Edward's accession to his marriage in 1464. Their son, Arthur, was brought up at his father's court; in 1472 the king's tailor was ordered to provide clothes for 'my lord the bastard'. At Edward's death he disappeared into the shadows, to emerge again in 1501 when the Tudor dynasty was firmly established and his half-sister, Elizabeth, was married to Henry VII. Arthur seems to have had a sister of the full blood, also called Elizabeth, but virtually nothing is known of her.

The story put about by Richard III – that Edward IV's marriage to Elizabeth Woodville was invalid and his children bastards, because the king had previously contracted to marry Lady Eleanor Butler – is unlikely to be true. But Eleanor, daughter of John Talbot, earl of Shrewsbury, had died in 1468 and could not contradict it. It will probably never be known whether or not she was Edward's mistress when he was very young.

The best documented of Edward's mistresses was Elizabeth (more commonly known as Jane) Shore. Her father was a wealthy London merchant named Lambert and she married the goldsmith William Shore. Sir Thomas More writes that when she became the king's

Above *Allegory: a lover embraces Amor.*

Below *Reality: a brass of Elizabeth Shore.*

'merry harlot', her husband put her aside; certainly she had her marriage annulled in 1476 on the grounds of her husband's impotency. The king took especial pleasure in Jane, 'for many he had, but her he loved'. More paints a charming picture of her: 'proper she was, and fair: nothing you would have changed, unless you would have wished her somewhat higher . . . yet men delighted not so much in her beauty as in her pleasant behaviour. For a proper wit had she and could both read well and write, merry in company, ready and quick of answer, neither mute nor full of babble.' The king's favour she 'never abused to any man's hurt, but to many a man's comfort and relief'.

Immediately after Edward's death she was taken into the protection of his closest friend, William, Lord Hastings, who had long wanted her. When in June 1483 Hastings was arrested by the protector, Richard of York, duke of Gloucester, Jane was accused of complicity in his treason and was also arrested and had all her goods seized. After Hastings's execution, Richard of Gloucester caused the bishop of London to make her do penance as a harlot, walking through the streets clad only in her kirtle with a lighted taper in her hand. She was released from prison when Thomas Lynom, Richard III's solicitor-general, fell victim to her charm and offered to marry her. She was still alive, though an old woman, when More was writing in 1518. Sir Thomas's work is sometimes dubious as history, but his portrait of Jane rings true. Clearly she had entranced him too.

More refrains from giving the names of Edward's wiliest and holiest concubines; he says they were somewhat greater personages and content to be nameless.

widespread disorder, and the common people lost much of their money and goods. Firstly, a tax of a fifteenth part of all their property was levied, and then another fifteenth to pay for the fighting. These and many other factors had reduced England to the direst poverty.

Many people thought, moreover, that King Edward was to blame for harming the reputation and the esteem of the merchants, for at that time, both in England and abroad, these were not as great as they had been before.

In the following February [1471], Henry, duke of Exeter, Edmund, duke of Somerset, Jasper Tudor, earl of Pembroke, King Henry's half-brother, and Henry Tudor, earl of Richmond, along with many other knights, squires, gentlemen and yeomen, came back to England and returned to their lordships and land, as all forfeitures passed in King Edward's time were annulled by parliament. Thus King Henry regained possession of both his crown and his dignity, and all his men of their inheritance.

Queen Elizabeth, King Edward IV's wife, had stocked up and fortified the Tower of London when she heard of her sovereign husband's flight, and now secretly left the Tower and took sanctuary at Westminster with all her children.

The queen herself was heavy with child at this time, and soon after her arrival in sanctuary she gave birth to a son [in November 1470], who was called Prince Edward of England. She was to remain there, in great trouble, until King Edward came back to her.

The Great Chronicle of London *gives a pro-Lancastrian view of the readeption of Henry VI.*

Thus was this holy and virtuous prince, King Henry VI, after long imprisonment and much insult, derision and scorn, patiently upheld by many of his subjects and regally restored to his rightful place, at which he did not proudly rejoice, but meekly thanked God and gave all his mind to serve and please Him and required little or nothing of the pomp and vanity of this world.

Over-mighty subjects

ONE of the greatest problems facing any medieval monarch, particularly one who owed his throne to the support of a powerful group of noblemen, was that of disciplining his 'over-mighty subjects'. In an age when the crown had neither a standing army nor a police force to rely upon in periods of national or international crisis, rulers were dependent upon the military prowess of the great lords and their armed retainers; at the same time, they were aware of the need to keep them in check, lest their private quarrels escalate into civil war.

Edward IV generally adopted a pragmatic and tolerant attitude to the nobility and tried to win them over into his service through promises of patronage and advancement. He was only partly successful. Some nobles refused to be seduced from their old loyalties to the house of Lancaster, while others – like his brother George, duke of Clarence, and the rapacious Neville clan – were so overweeningly ambitious that they turned traitor against him. As soon as he became king, Edward realized the urgent need to reward those who had fought for him and his father – and to build a wider and more permanent base of support among the aristocracy as a whole. He was remarkably

clement towards his former enemies: only 14 members of the peerage were attainted for treason, and most of the rest were rehabilitated immediately.

Edward relied upon an inner circle of about a dozen lords, some of whom he had himself ennobled, for help in government; he harnessed their ambition for high office by bolstering their authority in the regions where he employed them as his lieutenants. William, Lord Hastings, acquired unrivalled influence in the Midlands, and Sir William Herbert, earl of Pembroke, was unchallenged in South Wales. The Nevilles were dominant along the Scottish border, and Sir Humphrey Stafford, earl of Devon, in the south-west. This delicate balance of conflicting interests and personalities, hard enough to maintain at the best of times, was seriously upset by the king's marriage, in 1464, to Elizabeth Woodville, whose grasping relatives were avid for promotion. A spectacular series of seven marriages into the nobility established them on the political scene, as did the elevation of Elizabeth's father, Richard, Earl Rivers, and her brother, Anthony, Lord Scales, to the upper reaches of the nobility. The rest of the baronage regarded these developments with a mixture of resentment and dismay.

The failure, in 1471, of the Nevilles and their fellow-conspirators to restore Henry VI permanently to the throne and their defeat by the Yorkists at the battle of

Above *Warkworth Castle, a Percy family seat.*

Opposite *The Neville family at prayer.*

Barnet created a power vacuum in the north, and Edward altered his strategy there as a result, during the second half of his reign. However, when he restored the Percys, in the person of Henry, fourth earl of Northumberland, to their former authority on the East March and accorded almost vice-regal powers to his brother Richard, duke of Gloucester, he replaced the Nevilles with two 'over-mighty subjects' on an even grander and more impressive scale. He followed a similar policy in Lancashire and Cheshire, with the Stanleys, and in Wales, with the Woodvilles; in each case he consciously and deliberately increased his dependence on a small but immensely powerful clique of nobles.

One consequence was to drive a wedge between the favoured few and the rest of the peerage, most of whom withdrew from court. Moreover, the Stanleys and the other great lords were generally unchecked in their domains, and the administration of justice and the enforcement of law and order were subordinated to their own interests. Edward achieved a degree of political stability during his last years, but it was bought at the expense of his authority in the regions.

On the Saturday following the king's removal from the Tower, the earl of Worcester was arraigned in the White Hall at Westminster, and there indicted of treason, and on the ensuing Monday, ordered to go from there, on foot, to Tower Hill to have his head cut off.

In accordance with this judgement the sheriffs of London, on Monday, 7 October, received him at Temple Bar at three o'clock in the afternoon, intending to have him brought down that night to the place of execution. But so many people gathered around to gawp and gaze at him that it was nearly night when they brought him to Fleet Bridge, so they borrowed the prison of the warden of the Fleet, and lodged him there until the morning. The next day he was again delivered to the sheriffs, and from there led to Tower Hill where he was executed, upon whose soul may Christ Jesus have mercy. Amen.

The earl of Worcester was known to be cruel and merciless. He had put to death two sons of the earl of Desmond who were so tender of age that one of them, who had a boil on his neck, said to the executioner that was going to chop off his head, 'Gentle godfather, beware of the sore on my neck!' Also it was reported of the earl that he had had several men executed by hanging and after they were dead, he cut off their heads and hung them by their feet, after which he put a stake in each of their orifices and on the other end of the stake put their heads. For these reasons, and other similar cruelties, he was much hated by the common people, and reputed in some cases even worse than he deserved.

On 26 November a parliament began at Westminster which continued until Christmas. In this session King Edward was disinherited, and all his children, and proclaimed throughout the city as usurper of the crown. The duke of Gloucester, his younger brother, was pronounced a traitor, and both were attainted by the parliament.

A source very sympathetic to Edward, the History of the Arrival in England of Edward IV, *now tells how, in the following year, he returned and once again took possession of the throne.*

1471

Here follows the story of how the most noble and victorious prince Edward, by the grace of God king of England and France, lord of Ireland, in the year of grace 1471 in the month of March, departed from Zeeland, took to the sea, arrived in England, and by his strength and valour reconquered the realm from that traitorous rebel the earl of Warwick, who called himself lieutenant of England by pretended authority of the usurper Henry and his accomplices; and also from Edward who called himself prince of Wales, son of that Henry then wrongfully occupying the realm and crown of England; and from many other great and mighty lords, nobles and others with great followings.

In the year of grace 1471, on 2 March, the said most noble King Edward, with two thousand picked Englishmen, boarded ship at the harbour of Flushing in Zeeland with the intention of crossing the sea to re-enter and recover his realm.

When he and all his men were on board ship the wind turned against him, but he would not go back to land because of it; he remained aboard, and all his men likewise, for the space of nine days awaiting good wind and weather.

This they had on 11 March, and he set sail with all the ships that waited upon him, taking their course straight over towards the coast of Norfolk, and came before Cromer towards evening on Tuesday, 12 March.

It was not, however, safe for Edward to land in East Anglia, and he sailed north. Storms scattered his ships and he was driven ashore at Ravenspur. But he rallied his forces, proceeded through Yorkshire and then moved gradually south, gathering support as he went. By early April he had reached Northampton.

At Northampton, the king was well received. He then took the quickest way to London, always keeping a good band of spearmen and archers as a rearguard, to counter, if need be, such of Warwick's party as might have been sent to trouble him from behind.

Brave new world

A world map of 1489 shows a good understanding of western Europe, the Mediterranean and the Black and Caspian seas. The bulge of Africa is charted, the southern tip of the continent indicated, and the map shows awareness of the Indian Ocean. Europeans had known of the land routes to China since the 13th century, and reached India overland in the late 15th.

Scholars believed that the world was a globe, and there was mounting speculation that India and the Orient could be reached by sailing westward. Some people may even have conceived of the possibility of new land across the western ocean. In Scandinavia there were lingering memories of the Greenland settlement established by Eric the Red in the 980s, which had still been in contact with Norway in the 14th century. Somewhere in the papal archives lay the patchy records of the bishopric established there in about 1110. The Portuguese navigator João Vaz Corte Real (d. 1496) may have reached Greenland and, it has been suggested, touched the coast of North America (presumably Newfoundland) as early as 1472. In 1481, two ships, *Trinity* and *George*, were chartered out of Bristol 'to serche and fynde a certain isle called the Isle of Brasil'. Later in the decade John Cabot, the Genoese-born pioneer who was to open up Newfoundland, settled in Bristol and perhaps knew of this, unsuccessful, venture.

By 1450, shipbuilding in northern Europe had made important advances, inspired in part by Mediterranean examples. The traditional single-masted cog with its one square sail gave way to two-masted vessels with a second fore, or 'fukke', sail. Finally, a three-masted ship with a triangular lateen sail on a mizzen mast was introduced.

Navigation aids were also improved. A compass with a 32-point wind rose was used in the Mediterranean from the early 1300s, though northern navigators used the 'needle and stone', a suspended or floating iron needle which was magnetized, by rubbing with a loadstone, when the wind direction was to be checked. The permanently magnetized compass needle with a direction card (marked with the magnetic as well as the true north in some Mediterranean examples), housed in a binnacle, was a supplement to the basic tools of navigation: the sounding line and lead, and the hourglass to help calculate the longitude. In shallow-water navigation the 'lead' coated with wax was used not only to give depth soundings but also to take samples of the sea-bed – sandy, shingle, oozy, and so on, which indicated the ship's position to experienced seamen. In 1449 a Lisbon-bound Danziger, arrested at Plymouth, had her lead and line impounded to ensure she did not slip out of harbour.

From the mid 14th century a new type of navigation

Above *Prince Henry 'the Navigator'.*

aid used with the 'lead' enabled masters to sail unfamiliar waters: the Mediterranean 'portolan' book, listing depth soundings and currents along important sea-routes, with descriptions of how the sea-bed changed. The first English examples, from the middle of the 15th century, were called 'rutters' and covered routes like the Severn to Finisterre or Saint-Malo to Gibraltar along the Biscay coast.

From the early 1420s Prince Henry of Portugal, 'the Navigator', sponsored expeditions across the Atlantic and down the coast of Africa. They left from Sagres on Cape St Vincent where map-makers, captains and shipwrights all found patronage, and they searched for gold, for a route round the Islamic lands to the Indies and for opportunities to convert the heathen. Madeira was discovered and settled by 1425, the Azores by 1430. The first Portuguese *feitoria*, 'factory', was established on the African coast in 1445, trading horses, brassware and cloth for gold dust, ivory and slaves. When Prince Henry died in 1460 Portuguese ships had reached Sierra Leone and by 1475 they were 2° south of the equator. Twelve years later Bartholomew Diàz passed the Cape of Good Hope, so named by his patron, King John II.

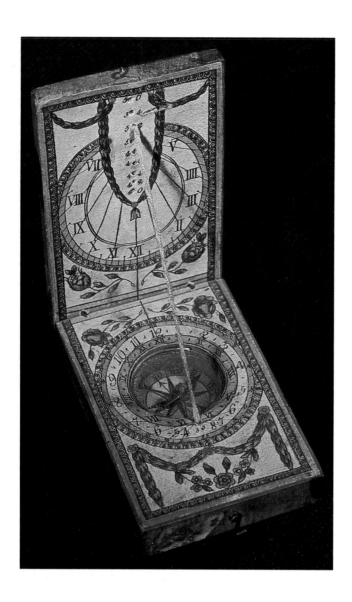

Above *A combined portable compass and sundial. Such devices enabled fifteenth-century mariners to navigate their improved vessels into new and uncharted waters.*

Right *Galleys at sea. By the 1480s the ships of Portugal were breaking out of the traditional European spheres of maritime commerce and pioneering routes for the great voyages of exploration that were to follow in the next century. Columbus himself crossed to America only a few years later, following João Vaz Corte Real's reputed voyage to Greenland and Newfoundland in 1472. The expansion of the known world at this time was one of the key factors that transformed the medieval world into that of the Renaissance and the Enlightenment.*

During the time that the king and his brother [and now ally] the duke of Clarence, were at Warwick, his opponents, Edmund who called himself duke of Somerset, John Beaufort, his brother, called marquis of Dorset, and Thomas Courtenay, who called himself earl of Devon, were at London, and had news from France that Queen Margaret and her son called the prince of Wales, the countess of Warwick, and many of their adherents were waiting by the sea with all the force they could raise, proposing to sail for the west country. So Somerset and the others left London and went to the west, and there tried to raise as many people as they could to receive them on their arrival, and accompany, fortify and assist them against the king and his party on the side of the so-called King Henry.

True it is that Queen Margaret, her son, the countess of Warwick, the lords and others set sail for England on 24 March and remained aboard until 13 April for lack of good winds, and because of great tempests at sea which lasted the space of twenty days.

But let us leave this, and return to the king's progress in his journey towards London, where he arrived on Tuesday, 9 April, meanwhile sending comforting messages to the queen at Westminster, and to his supporters and servants in London. Whereupon, as secretly as possible, they considered how he might be received and welcomed there.

The earl of Warwick, knowing King Edward's movements and his approach to London, sent letters to those in the city ordering them to resist Edward and not to receive him and his supporters. He also wrote to his brother, the archbishop of York, desiring him to do all he could to provoke the city against Edward and keep him out for two or three days, promising that he would then not fail to come up with great forces from behind, intending utterly to destroy Edward and his men.

So on 9 April the archbishop called together at St Paul's in the city of London such lords and gentlemen as were of that party, with as many of their armed men and servants as they could muster, who numbered in all no more than six or seven thousand. He caused Henry, called king, to mount a horse and ride from St Paul's down Cheapside and round to Walbrook, as the usual processional way of London runs, and so again to St Paul's, to the bishop's palace where Henry was then lodged; supposing that when he showed Henry in this array the Londoners would then be encouraged to stand by them and come on to their side.

In fact, the rulers of the city were in council and had set men at all the gates and wards; they, seeing that the power of Henry and his adherents was so feeble, could find no courage to join them and strengthen their party. Rather the opposite obtained, as they well saw that Henry's forces could not resist the king who was approaching the city, being at St Albans that night.

Thus, both for the love that many bore the king, and for the dread that many had that if the city were taken by force the citizens would sustain irreparable harm and loss, and for many other considerations, the mayor, aldermen and other worshipful men of the city determined among themselves to keep the city for the king, and to open it to him at his coming. So they sent to him that they would be guided as to his pleasure.

The archbishop of York, knowing the king was approaching the city, sent secretly to him, desiring to be admitted to his good grace and promising in return to give the king great pleasure for his well-being and security.

For his own good reasons the king agreed to take the archbishop into his good grace, and the archbishop, assured of this, was very well pleased and truly acquitted himself of his promise.

That night the Tower of London was taken for the king, whereby he had a clear entry into the city. On the morrow, Thursday 11 April, the king came, the city was opened to him, and he rode straight to St Paul's, and thence into the bishop's palace, where the archbishop of York presented himself to the king's good grace. He handed over the usurper King Henry; and there the king took possession of him and of divers rebels.

From St Paul's the king went to Westminster, and there prayed and gave thanks to God, St Peter and St Edward, and then went to the queen and comforted her. She had been in sanctuary at Westminster, securing her safety only by the great privileges of that holy place, in great trouble, sorrow and heaviness, which she bore with as much patience as belonged to any creature, and as constantly as anyone of such high estate has been seen at any time to endure. And while there she none the less had brought into this world, to the king's greatest joy, a fair son, a prince, whom she presented to him on his arrival, to his heart's singular comfort and gladness and to that of all them that truly loved and served him.

From thence the king returned that night to London, and the queen with him, and stayed at the lodging of my lady his mother, where they heard divine service that night and in the morning, Good Friday, when also the king took advice of the great lords of his blood and others of his council for the events that were likely to follow.

The earl of Warwick, who called himself lieutenant of England by the pretended authority of King Henry, was at Coventry. Realizing that the king would do much to be received in London, and not knowing whether he would be or not, he issued out of Coventry with a great force, and made his way through Northampton after the king. The earl thought he had the advantage of the king in one of two ways: either the city would keep the king out (which failed); or, if he were let in, he would there be keeping the solemnity of Easter, so that the earl could suddenly come upon him, take him and destroy him by surprise.

But the king, informed of this evil and malicious purpose, took pains to encounter him before he came near to the city, as far from it as possible. And therefore he went out of the city of London with a great army to meet him, on Saturday, 13 April, Easter Eve. With him he took King Henry; and so that afternoon he rode to Barnet, ten miles out of London, where his advance-guard found the advance-guard of the earl of Warwick's host and beat them and chased them out of the town more than half a mile where, under a hedge-side,

were ready assembled a great army in array of the earl of Warwick's men. The king coming up afterwards, and hearing this, would not suffer one man to stay in the town, but had them all to the field with him, and drew towards his enemies outside the town.

It was very dark and he could not well see where his enemies lay embattled, and he camped with all his host before them, much nearer than he supposed. Both sides had guns and ordnance, but the earl of Warwick had many more than the king and so the earl's army shot guns almost all night, thinking thereby to do great damage to the king and his host. But, thanked be God, it so happened that they always overshot the king's army and did them no harm, because the king's host lay much nearer than they thought.

Early in the morning between four and five o'clock, the king, knowing that the day approached, and notwithstanding there was a dense mist which prevented them from seeing each other, committed his case and cause to Almighty God, advanced banners, blew the trumpets, and set upon them, at first with shot; very soon they joined and came to hand-strokes, wherein his enemies manfully and courageously received them, as well in shot as in hand-strokes.

With the faithful, well-beloved and mighty assistance of his supporters, who did not desert him and were as devoted to him as they could be, King Edward vigorously, manfully and valiantly assailed his enemies in the centre and strongest part of their army, and with great violence beat and bore down before him all that stood in his way. Blessed be God, he thus won the field there and the perfect victory remained to him, and to his opponents the loss of thirty thousand men, as they themselves counted.

In this battle was slain the earl of Warwick, caught fleeing. He was reputed the chief of Edward's opponents in that he was called lieutenant of England, having been thus constituted by the pretended authority of King Henry. There also Lord Montague was slain in full battle, and many other knights, esquires and noblemen.

The victory was given to Edward by God through the mediation of the most Blessed Virgin, the glorious martyr George and all the saints of Heaven, because they held his cause to be true and righteous, and because of many good and continual prayers which many devout persons, monks, nuns and others, ceased not to offer unto God for his good speed.

The king refreshed himself and his host a little at Barnet, and then gathered his supporters together and returned with them to the city of London, where he was welcomed and received with much joy and gladness.

Edward IV was still in danger from another Lancastrian army under the command of the queen, Margaret of Anjou. The Crowland chronicle describes his vigorous and forceful reaction.

King Edward returned in triumph to London, in the afternoon, on Easter Day, accompanied by his two brothers, the duke of Clarence and the duke of Gloucester, and attended by an honourable retinue of a great many noblemen as well as common people.

However, worn down as he was by many different blows, he had but little time to refresh himself there. No sooner was he done with one battle in the east, as has been described, than he was faced with another in the western part of England, on account of Queen Margaret and her son, and had to prepare himself and his men to fight at full strength.

On leaving Flanders King Edward, against his will, had been driven by a terrible storm to Yorkshire. However, Queen Margaret and her attendants made a straight course from Normandy and landed in the region of Devon and Cornwall.

Daily, the ranks of the queen's army were swelled, for there were many in the west who favoured King Henry's cause above all others. Edmund, duke of Somerset, who of all the company after Prince Edward was foremost in rank (he had lived in exile since he was a boy), together with his brother John, who was called Beaufort,

Thomas, earl of Devon, John, Lord Wenlock, and Brother John Langstrother, prior of the Order of St John [the Hospitallers] in England, debated in council whether they might travel speedily up the west coast, perhaps through Bristol, Gloucester and Chester, and thus reach those parts of Lancashire where there was a large force of archers. They were certain that, in that region more than anywhere, the lords and the common people would support the house of Lancaster.

This plan might not have failed them, but for King Edward, who marched against them from London at great speed, though his troops were few, planning to intercept them and halt their progress, while they were still in Gloucestershire. And so it came to pass.

The battle commenced near Tewkesbury, when both sides were so footsore and thirsty that they could march no further. For some time it was not clear who would prevail. Finally, however, King Edward won a famous victory. Of the queen's forces, Prince Edward himself (King Henry's only son), the duke of Somerset, the earl of Devon, together with every one of the lords named above, met their deaths, either on the battlefield or afterwards at the hands of certain of their enemies.

Queen Margaret was captured and held prisoner, that she might ride in a carriage in front of the king in his triumphal procession in London. And so it came to pass.

While these events were taking place, the frenzy of the king's enemies was in no way quelled, particularly in Kent, and their numbers increased, in spite of the fact that King Edward's double victory seemed to all a clear sign of the justice of his cause.

Incited by the few men who remained of those who had been with the earl of Warwick as well as by the Calais regulars, sailors and pirates, such men assembled under the command of a certain Thomas, the Bastard of Fauconberg, and from the furthest corners of the county of Kent, they travelled to London, some by road, some by the River Thames.

The end of the house of Lancaster

WHEN Henry VI, a fugitive since the defeat of the Lancastrian remnant at Hexham in 1464, was captured while on the run at Bungerly Hippingstones in 1465 and paraded through London to the Tower 'on a small horse, a straw hat on his head and a rope tied round his body', the cause of Lancaster seemed lost. It was not. Margaret of Anjou and her son Edward, penurious exiles in France, were soon to win unlikely allies from the Yorkist side: Richard Neville, earl of Warwick, and George, duke of Clarence. For Edward IV had thwarted the ambitions of his 19 year old brother, the duke of Clarence, and alienated the earl of Warwick, with his marriage in 1464 to Elizabeth Woodville and later with her relatives' increasing influence at court. Their discontents spurred the two men into rebellion in 1469, a rebellion which almost succeeded when they captured the king in August. But their attempts to control Edward and his kingdom failed, and in April 1470 they fled to Louis XI in France.

The French king now brought together Warwick and his old adversary, Queen Margaret, Clarence being somewhat peripheral to the proceedings. With substantial French backing, Warwick prepared to return to England. Despite his contradictory behaviour and his political machinations, his popularity with contemporary Englishmen is unquestioned. He had either charisma or a cause which inspired them to follow him, as is shown when he landed at Plymouth in September 1470, and proclaimed Henry VI as king. Edward IV's authority crumbled away and it was now his turn to flee to France, to the duke of Burgundy.

When Warwick and Clarence entered London in October 1470, Henry VI was taken out of his dungeon in the Tower and, for a night or two, stayed in the room that had been redecorated for the queen's accouchement; Elizabeth had taken a barge to the sanctuary of Westminster Abbey where, in November, she gave birth to Edward's first son. Henry's restoration as king might have proved more long-lived had his own heir, Edward, a promising youth of 17, returned with him, but he remained in France with his mother Margaret. As lieutenant of the realm, and thus effective ruler, Warwick tried unsuccessfully to breathe life into new policies, but could not gain general support for war against Burgundy, which had valuable commercial connections with England.

Edward IV, with Burgundian support, now returned to England in March 1471 – before Margaret and Prince

Above *The battle of Tewkesbury, which marked the effective end of Lancastrian opposition to Edward. There was no more open warfare during his reign.*

Edward, who did not arrive until April. In a vigorous and decisive campaign, he moved from Yorkshire through the Midlands to London. His followers, both those who had shared his exile, like William, Lord Hastings, and those who now emerged from domestic exile, like John, Lord Howard, joined him in force.

At Barnet on Easter Sunday, 14 April 1471, the last battle between Edward and Warwick was fought, a battle in which Warwick was killed. Like the battle of Towton, almost exactly ten years earlier, it was tough: the contestants realized there would be no return bout. Edward won and marched rapidly into the west country to confront Margaret and Prince Edward who had landed at Weymouth from France. He pursued Margaret to Tewkesbury where, on 4 May, the two armies engaged. It was Edward's second fierce encounter in three weeks and his second victory. Many leading Lancastrian noblemen and gentlemen were killed in the battle and, afterwards, other diehard followers of Henry among the prisoners were executed. Prince Edward was the most important casualty; his death seemed to presage the end of the house of Lancaster. His father, Henry VI, did not long outlive him: when Edward IV returned to London on 21 May, the 50 year old king, more resilient in body than he had ever been of mind, was put to death in the Tower.

They surveyed all the ways in and out of London, to discover what forces would be necessary and how they might enter in order to pillage that most wealthy of cities. For this purpose, they sailed their ships almost into the port of London, ready to receive all the spoils.

But it was not God's will that this renowned city, the capital of the kingdom of England, should be the prey of those wicked pillagers, and so He gave stout hearts to the people of London, that they might stand firm in the battle. They dispatched all their assailants, killing some and putting the rest to flight. All this took place in the month of May, a short time before Ascension Day.

On 21 May, King Edward made his third entry into London, with a larger retinue than on the previous occasions, ordering his standards to be unfurled and borne before him and all the lords of his army.

Many who saw this were surprised and amazed, for no enemy remained to be dealt with. But this most prudent prince was familiar with the untrustworthy ways of the people of Kent and resolved not to lay down his arms until he had punished those rebellious men, as they deserved, on their own territory. So he rode into Kent, with his horsemen in battle array, and returned as a famed conqueror, a king whose praises echoed through all regions of his kingdom, for he had achieved such a great deal in so short a time.

I shall pass over at this point the discovery of the lifeless body of King Henry in the Tower of London. May God show mercy, and grant sufficient time to repent, to whomever it was who dared to raise a sacrilegious hand against the Lord's Anointed. Let the perpetrator, therefore, deserve to be called tyrant and the victim to be called glorious martyr.

For several days the body lay in state in St Paul's church in London, from where it was taken in a barge, suitably equipped with lamps, the fifteen miles up the Thames for burial at the monastic church at Chertsey, in the diocese of Winchester. The miracles which God worked in response to the prayers of those devoutly seeking his intercession are witness to his blameless life, the extent of his love of God and the Church, of his patience in adversity and of his other outstanding virtues.

The duke of Burgundy sent ambassadors to King Edward IV, not so much to congratulate him on his good fortune as to encourage His Majesty daily to plan and carry through his preparations for his march on France, with a view not only to avenging wrongs but also to claiming the lost rights of his ancestors. On this journey he would assuredly have the duke as companion through thick and thin.

One of the king's advisers, a doctor in canon law, was sent to determine more precisely what were the duke's intentions and to report back. He went via Boulogne, as Calais had still not been reduced to obedience. He met the duke at a large, well-fortified town on the River Somme, known as Abbeville, in the county of Ponthieu. This brief mission laid the foundations of the great expeditions in pursuit of the king's rights in France which will be described later.

I wish to mention here the dissension that arose during this Michaelmas term between the king's two brothers and which was difficult to settle. After the death of King Henry's son — he had married Anne Neville, the younger daughter of the earl of Warwick — in the battle of Tewkesbury, as has been related, Richard, duke of Gloucester sought to marry Anne himself. This aim did not suit the wishes of his brother, the duke of Clarence, for he had earlier married the earl's elder daughter, Isabel. He therefore arranged for the girl to be kept hidden so that his brother would not know her whereabouts, as he feared a division of the vast Warwick inheritance, which he desired to come to him alone through the rightful claim of his wife, rather than to divide it with another.

However, the cunning of the duke of Gloucester proved superior, for he discovered the girl in London disguised as a kitchen maid and he had her moved to the safety of St Martin's church. This provoked such strife between the two brothers and so many incisive arguments were put by both sides

Clarence

GEORGE, duke of Clarence (1449–78), was second in line to the throne after Edward seized power in 1460. 'Right witty and well visaged', charming and able, Clarence was also unstable, jealous and ambitious. Handsomely endowed with lands, he nevertheless came into conflict with Edward over his intention to marry Isabel Neville, daughter of Warwick the Kingmaker, with whom he sided in 1469 when the simmering hostility between Warwick and Edward came to a head. In July 1469, after his marriage to Isabel had been solemnized at Calais, he returned to England with his father-in-law in defiance of his brother, and connived with Warwick as he prepared to declare Edward a bastard and George king in his place. The plan came to nothing. However, Clarence abandoned the readeption of Henry VI only when it became obvious it was doomed.

Reunited with his brothers, the king and the duke of Gloucester, with 'right kind and loving language betwixt them', Clarence was indulgently treated by Edward. Then, late in 1471, a blazing row broke out between him and Richard of Gloucester over the heiress Anne Neville, George's sister-in-law. Richard wanted to marry her, but George was determined to keep her vast estates in his own family and, according to court gossip, had hidden her away in a London mansion disguised as a kitchen maid. That winter, the king ordered his brothers to argue their case before the royal council. After a scintillating debate Richard won his bride but surrendered part of her inheritance. Clarence next caused trouble over his share in the estates of Warwick, killed in the battle of Barnet in 1471, and seemed to be aiming once more at the throne itself.

Isabel died in December 1476 and in January of the following year the death of Charles, duke of Burgundy, at the battle of Nancy opened the possibility of a dazzling new match. Duke Charles left an heiress to his vast estates, his daughter Mary, who, through her grandmother Isabel of Portugal, herself the granddaughter of John of Gaunt, could show a claim to the English throne. Clarence proposed to marry her. Edward vetoed the very idea.

Rumours about Edward's legitimacy were circulating again, for the first time since Warwick's attempt to declare him a bastard in 1470, and it is likely that Clarence was behind them. In May, John Stacey, a noted Oxford astrologer who was arrested on a charge of using his science for evil purposes, implicated Thomas Burdett, a member of Clarence's household. Both were found guilty of 'having imagined and compassed' the death of the king, and, in addition, Burdett was convicted of circulating

Above *George, duke of Clarence.*

Below *The writ of attainder for Clarence.*

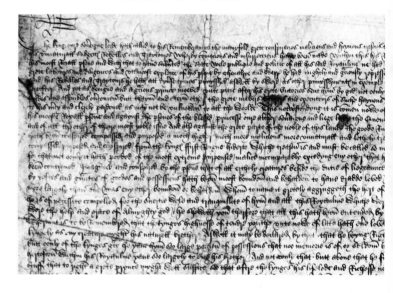

treasonable writings. Clarence himself was committed to the Tower in June, and in January 1478 he was tried for 'heinous unnatural and loathly treason'. Treason against a brother was remarkable even in 15th-century England, and Clarence had twice been guilty of the crime. Edward demanded his punishment for the safety of the realm and Clarence was sentenced in due form, but put to death secretly in the Tower on 19 February.

The rumour that he was drowned in a butt of malmsey is generally either discounted as a colourful fiction on the duke's drinking habits, or accepted as the literal truth. However, Hindley suggests that sawn-down wine butts were commonly used as baths at the time – one household inventory actually specifies 'ij vatis for the lords bathyng ymad of a bot of malmsely'. Clarence it seems was drowned – but in his bath.

before the king, sitting in judgement in the council chamber, that all present, even the lawyers, were astonished at the wealth of arguments that the brothers brought to their cases. The three brothers, the king and the dukes, possessed such outstanding intellect that, if they could have avoided disagreeing between themselves, the triple bond between them could not have been broken.

Finally King Edward intervened lest the disagreement should hinder his plans in France, and the entire dispute was resolved. After marrying Anne, the duke of Gloucester would possess such lands as was agreed between them through arbitration. All that remained was left in the possession of the duke of Clarence. Thus, little or nothing was left to the rightful owner and heir, the countess of Warwick, to whom the noble estates of Warwick and Despenser were due during her lifetime.

The king's major concern was to encourage his nobles and the people in the cause of the war in France. To this end many fine speeches were made in parliament by both foreign and English speakers, especially on behalf of the duke of Burgundy. Finally all approved the king's decision and praised his plan, and tithes and fifteenths were granted when the situation demanded in those assemblies of clergy and laymen concerned with making such grants. In addition, all heirs and owners of property freely granted a tenth of their possessions.

Since all these measures did not appear adequate for tasks of this magnitude, however, a new and unheard-of tax was introduced, by which each person was able freely to donate what he wished, or rather what he did not wish. The moneys raised by so many large donations amounted to sums the like of which had never been seen hitherto and are unlikely to be seen on any one occasion in the future. Furthermore, so that the king's enterprise should not be hindered by attacks from several directions, prudent measures were taken so that the Scots should not remain as enemies in the rear, and that the men of the Hanseatic League who were ill disposed to us and had for a long time made the seas off England unsafe would not use their fleet to attack us.

Europe's first economic community

THROUGHOUT the later Middle Ages two great trading zones met at the southern end of the North Sea in the Low Countries, particularly in the *entrepôt* of Bruges. The Venetian commercial fleet dominated the Mediterranean trade while the produce of Scandinavia and the Baltic was under the control of the Hanseatic League – a group of German cities of which the leading members were Danzig (Gdansk), Brunswick, Cologne and, above all, Lübeck. Their merchants had secured trading privileges and monopolies in Russia, Scandinavia, Germany, Flanders and England, and, broadly speaking, they dominated exchange between England and Flanders at one end of their great trade route and the Baltic at the other. To England they brought furs, pitch, rope, potash and softwoods from northern lands, salt from Brittany and the Bay of Bourgneuf, and above all fish (salt and fresh). On their return voyages they carried English raw materials, wool, hides, coal, tin and lead, and, from the later 14th century, increasing quantities of woollen cloth.

Hanseatic trading posts (kontors) were established along the east coast of England, in Hull, Boston, King's Lynn and Yarmouth, but the greatest was in London where the German merchants had a self-governing community and quay on the north bank of the Thames – the Steelyard. Their most valuable commercial concession was exemption from customs duties: loss of revenue to the crown was more than offset by the additional foreign trade they stimulated and the league's role in supplying vital raw materials over which they had monopolies.

As with most monopolists the Hanseatic merchants were widely unpopular. They clashed in particular with groups of English 'merchant adventurers' who also exported English cloth and wished to break into the Baltic and Rhineland markets. Throughout the century there was resentment that English merchants abroad did not enjoy privileges similar to those of the Germans. Flickering hostility became more serious when the breakdown of central government under Henry VI encouraged English captains to make piratical attacks on Hanseatic shipping. The English merchants received official backing in 1468 when Edward IV, thinking the English trade route to the Burgundian Low Countries secure, moved against London's Hanseatic colony.

His campaign was overtaken by events in England. When he was forced to flee to France in 1470 he found his brother-in-law Charles, duke of Burgundy, unwilling to help him regain his throne. Charles eventually relented, but the vessels in Edward's small invasion flotilla included

14 from the Hanseatic League. This alone was a good reason to make peace with the league, but, in addition, Edward intended to renew the war with France and it was vital to ensure safe passage across the Channel for his forces. In the treaty of Utrecht, in 1474, the privileges of the German merchants were restored and English traders were promised reciprocal rights in the Baltic – rights which the league ensured they never enjoyed.

Below *Hamburg, an important Hanse port.*

Accordingly, peace was made with two of our close neighbours by sending delegations, first to Utrecht and finally to Scotland.

1475

During May and June, Kind Edward transported his whole army to Calais in splendid and mighty fashion. There, Charles, duke of Burgundy, arrived with a few men to confer at length with the royal council about the route to be taken by each of the armies, the king's and his own, to enable them to join up in the most convenient place.

When the duke had again moved away towards his own towns, a proposal reached us from the enemy, the French, I know not how, to enter peace negotiations. The terms proposed should not be thought insulting or humiliating to us, as some have claimed. Amongst other things, they promised and offered the marriage of the dauphin to the king's eldest daughter with a most handsome dowry, an annual tribute of ten thousand pounds to offset the cost of going to war, together with a truce, or settlement, for seven years.

The duke of Burgundy, however, withdrew in displeasure, refusing to comply with the king's decision to make peace with the enemy, when he had agreed in private that their combined forces would continue the campaign against the common enemy. However, our representatives made peace with the enemy on the terms and to the effect stated above, and reported what had been achieved back to the king and his council.

For many reasons, the outcome was considered the right one in view of the state of the men at the time – they had spent all their wages – and it was accepted and welcomed by all, thus bringing the war to an end. At unbelievable cost and in spite of the unheard-of care and effort spent in preparation, it had never even got off the ground. Subsequently the two kings met at Picquigny to discuss strengthening the agreement that had already been made between them. There was not a single pledge, promise or public oath to which King Louis XI did not willingly assent in order to bring about what had been agreed.

The war that never was

THE Lancastrian revival of 1470–1, when Henry VI regained his throne for a few brief months, had shown that the Yorkist regime was not secure. After his restoration, it was essential that Edward IV do something to revive his credibility at home and abroad. He found the answer in war.

The ending of the Hundred Years War in 1453 had made little difference to the traditional enmity between England and France. Although Louis XI had originally been friendly to the Yorkists, he had thrown in his lot with Margaret of Anjou in 1470 and supported Henry VI. Edward began to build up a great anti-French coalition as soon as he was back on the throne, which included the rulers of Scotland, Denmark and Spain, the Hanseatic League and the duke of Brittany. Finally, in 1474, Edward persuaded Charles the Bold of Burgundy to join with him in carving up the kingdom of France. In diplomatic terms, all was ready for a major offensive.

Such an ambitious scheme demanded considerable financial outlay, and for three years Edward struggled to

get the English parliament to support his enterprise. In October 1472 he made an elaborate defence of his project, claiming that it would punish Louis XI for his pro-Lancastrian stance, eradicate piracy from the Channel, free new lands on the continent for English adventurers, offset civil disturbance at home and restore the French throne to the house of Plantagenet. The lords and commons were unimpressed, but eventually provided Edward with the £180,000 he needed to finance his campaign. The king assembled the largest army taken to France in the 15th century: 11,500 fighting men and almost as many non-combatants. They sailed for Calais in July 1475.

The campaign was a non-event. Edward marched south via Agincourt to Péronne, but, apart from a minor skirmish at Saint-Quentin, where they were taken unawares by a battery of cannon, the English made no move to fight. Many contemporaries believed the offensive was a bluff, intended to frighten the hard-pressed Louis XI into a truce. At the outset, however, Edward was more ambitious. He hoped to emulate the achievements of Edward III and Henry V, and even ordered the robes for his impending coronation as king of France. However, the failure of the dukes of Brittany and Burgundy to supply the promised military assistance forced him back to reality. Heavily outnumbered by Louis' troops, he soon realized that his best chances lay in a negotiated settlement.

The two kings met at Picquigny near Amiens. Security was tight, and the talks were conducted through a trellis to avoid assassination attempts. As in a modern summit conference, the heads of state paraded while the administrators worked. The result was the treaty of Picquigny of 29 August 1475.

A truce was established for seven years, and the English army agreed to withdraw from France on payment of 75,000 crowns (£15,000 sterling). In addition, Louis granted Edward an annual pension of 50,000 crowns (£10,000) and agreed to a marriage between the dauphin and the nine year old Elizabeth of York; this never actually happened. Reactions to the treaty were mixed, but it brought Edward considerable diplomatic and financial benefits, and kept the peace between England and France until the last year of his reign.

Below *A carving of the meeting at Picquigny.*

King Edward IV thus came back to England with honourable peace terms; for thus they were considered by the leaders of the royal army, although there is nothing so sacred or honourable that it cannot be distorted by evil rumour.

Indeed, some men immediately began to condemn the outcome and they paid the due penalty for their presumption. Others, when they got back home, gave themselves up to theft and pillage to the extent that no road in all England was safe for merchants or pilgrims.

The king was thus compelled to travel through his own kingdom with his justices, sparing no one, not even from his own household, from being hanged if they were arrested for theft or murder. Wherever it was enforced, this severe justice eliminated highway robbery for a long time to come. There is no doubting the depth of the king's concern at these events, nor his awareness of the state of mind of his people who could easily be drawn into insurrection and usurpation, if they were to find a leader.

He was aware that he had reached the position where he no longer dared demand subsidies from the English people even when in need and that for want of money – which was indeed very true – the French expedition had come to nothing in so short a time.

Accordingly, he devoted all his attention to how he might in future gather funds commensurate with his position as king from his own resources and by his own endeavour.

When parliament had been summoned, he took back almost all the royal patrimony from all those, whoever they were, on whom it had been conferred and devoted it entirely to bearing the crown's costs. He appointed as overseers of tolls at every port of the kingdom hand-picked men who were reputedly excessively hard on the merchants.

The king himself fitted out cargo ships and loaded them with fine wool, cloth, tin and other commodities of the kingdom and, like any other merchant, he traded goods for goods with both the

The unwritten law

ENGLISH law in the 15th century was as complex as, and a good deal more cumbersome than, it is today. Most important was common law, the unwritten custom of the land. Next came statute law, which was written down and arose mainly from complaints registered in parliament. Both systems were enforced in the same royal courts: King's Bench and Common Pleas (both of which normally sat at Westminster); circuit commissions such as the courts of assize; and local quarter sessions presided over by justices of the peace. Chancery dealt with cases for which there was no remedy in common or statute law.

Despite the royal courts' enormous powers, many cases did not fall within their jurisdiction. The Church, for instance, had tribunals which dealt with matters of family law such as paternity disputes, divorce proceedings and squabbles over wills. The lords of manors still claimed the right to hold private courts and judge the petty quarrels and offences of their tenants. And the whole country was dotted with 'liberties' where the king had given away his judicial rights to a local magnate, bishop or abbot.

Corruption and violence were endemic. There were two main reasons why the courts often failed to maintain law and order. First, procedures were protracted: a case could drag on for years, and many people preferred to resolve disputes by intimidation or private deals. Second, local landowners' power and influence made it virtually impossible for judges and juries to give impartial verdicts. The local magnate's support, not the sanctity of the law, offered the best insurance against enemies.

There had been an ominous increase in criminal activity throughout England during Henry VI's reign and in his first parliament Edward IV promised to halt this decline into anarchy. He undertook an ambitious programme of law enforcement: the council and court of chivalry were put to work to try cases of treason; and special commissions were appointed to tour the provinces and impose order on the king's subjects. Edward himself sometimes presided over these extraordinary sessions.

The number of convictions rose, but it is impossible to tell how many criminals still escaped justice. However, the campaign's superficiality raises doubts about its long-term impact. Edward made no attempt to overhaul the judicial system; his days on the bench look rather like public relations exercises. He was king by the goodwill of the nobility as well as by the grace of God, and any attempt to eradicate the magnates' influence from the courts would rebound on him. Ideals of justice would have to take second place to the cruder realities of politics.

Opposite *The Court of King's Bench.*

Italians and the Greeks through his agents. The income of vacant prelacies, which according to Magna Carta cannot be sold, he released from his possession for a sum fixed by himself and on no other terms.

He studied the Chancery registers and rolls and from those persons discovered to have trespassed on inheritances without observing due legal procedure he demanded heavy fines on what they had received in the mean time.

When added to the annual tribute of ten thousand pounds due from the French, and the frequent church tithes which the prelates and the clergy could not avoid, the income from these and similar snares — more than could be devised by someone inexperienced — made the king very rich over the next few years.

Indeed, in the collecting of gold and silver vessels, tapestries, valuable ornaments, both regal and religious, in the building of castles, colleges and other important places, in the acquisition of lands and estates, none of his predecessors could equal his outstanding achievements.

While Edward IV, as we have already related, had for several years been intent upon building up such great wealth, he spent a considerable part of it on the solemn service of reburial of his father, Richard, who had been duke of York.

The wise king, recalling the humble grave in the house of the Mendicant Friars at Pontefract, where the body of the great prince had been buried amid the disorders in which he died, transferred the bones both of his father and of his brother, Edmund, earl of Rutland, to the famous college of Fotheringhay in the diocese of York.

Recalling the splendour of peace and glory of Edward's reign after he had built up vast treasure from the French tribute and by the other means already described, let us consider something which was very true. For there then arose another disagreement with his brother, the duke of Clarence, which greatly disturbed the glory of this most prudent king. It was observed that the duke was gradually withdrawing from the king's presence, hardly speaking a word in council and eating and drinking with reluctance in the palace. Many were of the opinion that this shift from his earlier friendship had arisen in the duke's heart from the general taking back of grants that the king had recently enacted in parliament.

On that occasion the duke lost the noble lordship of Tutbury and many other lands which he had previously obtained by royal grant.

1477

Meanwhile Charles, duke of Burgundy, who, after leaving the king as I have related, had subjugated all Lorraine by force of arms, advanced courageously, nay rashly . . . as it is now generally called. He went into battle on 6 January and was defeated and killed on the battlefield in the year 1477, according to the Roman calendar.

I have inserted this event of foreign history here since it was widely known that after Charles's death the duchess, Lady Margaret, his widow, who had greater affection for her brother, the duke of Clarence, than for any other relative, put all her effort and attention into bringing about the marriage of Mary, the only daughter by an earlier marriage and heiress of the late Duke Charles, and the duke of Clarence whose wife had recently died.

The king was not pleased at the prospect of such an exalted future for an ungrateful brother. Accordingly, he put all the obstacles he could in the way of this marriage ever taking place; instead he favoured the heiress being given as wife to Maximilian, the son of the emperor, as indeed happened subsequently.

It is likely that this affair further increased the duke's anger. Each man thus began to regard the other in a far from brotherly way.

You would have seen — for such men are found in the palaces of all rulers — the fawning courtiers of both factions passing to and fro relaying the words of the two brothers even when they had been uttered in the most secret room.

The arrest of the duke, intended to compel him to answer charges against him, took place in the following manner. A certain Master John Stacey, known as the Astronomer although he had been a great necromancer, was accused among many other things of having made lead images and other items in order to bring about the death of Richard, Lord Beauchamp, at the request of his adulterous wife. This was done in league with a certain Thomas Burdett, an esquire in the service of the duke of Clarence. When closely interrogated about the practice of such an accursed art Stacey admitted many things against both himself and the aforesaid Thomas Burdett. The latter was thus also arrested.

Finally the death sentence was passed upon them both at Westminster in the court of King's Bench in the presence of almost all the lords temporal of the realm together with the justices. They were taken to the gallows at Tyburn and permitted to say briefly anything they wished before they died. They declared their innocence, Stacey in a low voice, but Burdett very forcefully and at length.

The following day the duke of Clarence brought with him to the council chamber at Westminster the famous Franciscan doctor, Master William Goddard, to read out before the lords assembled there in the council a statement of Clarence's innocence in the matter of Burdett. When he had done so, he withdrew.

At the time, the king was at Windsor. When he learnt of the incident, he was most displeased and, recalling certain facts against his brother which he had kept to himself for a long time, he summoned the duke to appear on a particular day in the royal palace of Westminster in the presence of the mayor and aldermen of the city of London. The king himself began to stress, among other things, the incident just described, as if it infringed the law of the land and were a great threat to the judges and officers of the kingdom.

What more need be said? The duke was arrested and from that day until his death was never again at liberty.

1478

The mind hesitates to relate the events that followed in the next parliament, for the dispute between two brothers of such stature was so sad a spectacle. No one argued against the duke except the king [who accused him of high treason], and no one replied to the king except the duke. Several persons, however, were brought forward and it was not clear to many whether they were appearing as accusers or witnesses. The two functions conflict when performed by the same person in the same case. The duke dismissed all the charges with a total denial, offering to defend his case in single combat if this was admissible.

Why dwell on all of this? The members of parliament considered that the information they had heard was sufficient, and they passed judgement against him. The sentence was pronounced by Henry, duke of Buckingham, who had been appointed steward of England for this occasion. The execution was postponed for a long time, until the speaker of the commons came with his colleagues to the house of lords to make a new request to finish the matter. As a result, whatever was the method of execution, it was indeed concluded — but would that this were the end of the misfortunes — in secret in the Tower of London within a few days.

Mancini, writing in 1483, alleged that 'it was decided that Clarence should die by being immersed in a butt of sweet wine'. This tradition, derived from the Burgundian Olivier de la Marche, has no contemporary confirmation, but was widely followed by Tudor chroniclers.

After this action, many people forsook King Edward who was convinced that he could rule at will throughout the country, now that all the idols had been removed to whom the populace used to turn its gaze in the past in the desire for something new. The earl of Warwick, the duke of Clarence and any other noble of the realm who withdrew from the royal court, were regarded as idols of this kind. The king — although, in my view, he often repented secretly of this action — subsequently discharged his office so grandly that he seemed to be feared by all the people and to fear no one himself. Having posted the more trustworthy of his servants in all parts of the kingdom to guard castles, manors, forests and parklands, no threat could be made anywhere in the land however secretly by any man, whatever his rank, without his being immediately confronted with it.

In 1478 Ivan III of Russia absorbed the prosperous city of Novgorod, his northern neighbour, which manufactured for and traded with the Hanseatic League. Among other luxury goods it exported to the west were furs.

1482

At this time, and for almost two years up to King Edward's death, King Louis XI of France failed to keep the promises he had made at Picquigny in 1475 concerning the truce with and the pension to King Edward. At the same time the capture of ships and men of both kingdoms began.

In addition to this unrest between the English and the French, the Scots, who had long been allies of the latter, flagrantly broke the thirty-year truce which we had made with them, in spite of the fact that King Edward had been paying a thousand marks every year as dowry for Cecily, one of his daughters, who, on the occasion of an official mission, had earlier been pledged to the eldest son of James III, king of the Scots.

Edward accordingly declared a fearful and deadly campaign against the Scots, led by his brother Richard of York, duke of Gloucester, who commanded the whole army. The outcome of this episode fully demonstrated how much money he fruitlessly spent. For, after reaching Edinburgh with the whole army without meeting any resistance, he left that most rich town untouched and returned via Berwick. Berwick Castle finally fell to the English, but not without slaughter and bloodshed. This small gain, or should I say loss (for garrisoning Berwick costs ten thousand marks a year) reduced the resources of the king and the kingdom by more than one hundred thousand pounds at the time. Such were the achievements of Richard, duke of Gloucester, during the summer.

Edward IV spent the ensuing Christmas at his palace at Westminster, often clad in very expensive clothes which were vastly different in style from those that were generally seen at the time. The sleeves of his cloaks were full and hung like a monk's habit, and had such sumptuous fur linings that when they were folded back over his shoulders the prince — whose most elegant figure overshadowed every one else — stood before the onlookers like some new and extraordinary spectacle.

In those days you would have seen a royal court worthy of a leading kingdom, full of riches and men from almost every nation, and above all with fine-looking and most delightful children, the offspring of his marriage to Elizabeth Woodville. They had ten children, of whom three had died and seven were living at the time. Of these latter, the two boys, Edward, prince of Wales, and Richard, duke of York and Norfolk, had not yet reached manhood.

There were five beautiful girls whose names in order of age were: first Elizabeth, second Cecily, third Anne, fourth Catherine, fifth Bridget. Although in earlier years solemn embassies and pledges of faith in the words of princes had been despatched, with letters of agreement drawn up in due form, concerning the marriage of each of the daughters, it was not now thought that any one of the marriages would materialize, for everything was susceptible to change given the unstable relations between England and France, Scotland, Burgundy and Spain.

The spirited King Edward was very worried and aggrieved when he saw how, in the end, he had been duped by King Louis XI, who not only defaulted on the promised tribute but also refused to allow the solemnly agreed marriage of the dauphin to the king's eldest daughter. Furthermore, Louis encouraged the Scots to break the truce and to reject the proposed marriage to our Cecily. In league with the men of Ghent he made a concerted effort to disrupt the territory of the king of England's friend, Maximilian of Austria, duke of Burgundy, and with all his cunning he used all kinds of malicious harassment on land and sea in order to ruin the kingdom of England.

Ivan III the first tsar of Russia

BORN in 1440, and grand duke of Moscow from 1462, Ivan III is regarded as the founder of the Russian state. For two centuries its principalities had been dependencies of the Golden Horde, part of the Mongol Empire; at his death in 1505 the imperial destiny which would culminate in the Soviet Union was in train.

The territories of the horde, with its capital at Sarayah at the mouth of the Volga river, included the once-powerful principalities of Kiev (overrun by the Mongols in 1260) and Ghernigov. The burgeoning principality of Lithuania lay to the west, and, to the north, a number of Russian states. The two most important were Tver and Vladimir, which included Moscow. North of these lay vast tracts of tundra and steppe, where scattered settlements owed allegiance to the princes of Great Novgorod.

The princes of Vladimir and Tver reigned by patents of authority conferred by the Mongol khan, and collected taxes and tribute for the horde.

The khans encouraged Russian rivalries and man-oeuvred to check the emergence of over-powerful princes. When the throne of Vladimir fell vacant in 1304 Prince Mikail of Tver received the patent. But when he proved a successful war leader and extended Vladimir's influence in Novgorod, the khan connived at his assassination and, in 1331, encouraged Ivan I, kalita of Moscow, in a decisive coup against the Tver dynasty. Moscow's rise also owed much to the Church. The metropolitan, who required the spiritual sanction of the patriarch of Constantinople, exercised authority under licence of the khan's patent or 'yarlik', also given to the lay princes.

In the 1360s the Golden Horde was torn by civil war. On its western frontier Prince Olgerd of Lithuania extended his frontiers into the Ukraine and parts of Greater Russia. Even the state of Vladimir rebelled when, in 1380, Grand Prince Dmitri Donskoi won the first Russian victory over a Tatar force.

In the 1390s crushing defeats by Tamerlane shook the khans' power. Under Vasilii II (1425–62) of Vladimir it was broken: by the end of his reign Tatar nobles were clients at his court. Russia, as Vladimir was now called, continued to accept patents sent by rival khans: by conforming to the fiction of Tatar suzerainty, Vasilii was able to stabilize his southern frontiers while he turned his attention to Russia's thriving northern neighbour, Novgorod. With a popula-tion of some 300,000, the city was a major factory for the Hanseatic League. A centre for the export of raw materials like honey, wax and, above all, furs, it was Russia's richest city, the site of international trade fairs.

Ivan III, Vasilii's successor in 1462, continued to put pressure on the city and in 1478 Novgorod and its hinter-land were absorbed into Russia. Hundreds of leading families were forcibly resettled in remote regions and two years later Ivan renounced allegiance to the Tatar khan.

Although minor states like Riazan on the south-west and the Tatar khanates remained independent, Russia was the greatest power east of Poland-Lithuania. Its pretensions were symbolized when Ivan adopted the imperial eagle emblem and married Sophie, niece of the last Byzantine emperor. For Orthodox Christians, Con-stantinople had been the home of the true faith and the emperor the thirteenth apostle. Although he was never crowned 'tsar' (caesar), Ivan was honoured with the title and Moscow was looked upon as the third Rome.

King Edward boldly considered any means of gaining revenge. He summoned parliament again and revealed the whole series of gross deceits; so he secured the willingness of all to assist him in obtaining revenge whenever opportunity or circumstances permitted.

He still did not dare seek any subsidy from the commons, but he did not conceal his needs from the prelates, persuasively demanding from them in advance the tithes which would soon be paid, as if whenever the bishops and clergy met in convocation they should do whatever the king asked. What a humiliating and damaging fate for the Church!

1483

Soon after these events had taken place, as I have narrated, and parliament had been dissolved, the king, although he was not afflicted by old age, or by any recognizable disease whose cure would not have seemed straightforward, took to his bed during Easter; and in his palace at Westminster surrendered his spirit to his Maker on 9 April. His body was brought for honourable and fitting burial at the new collegiate chapel at Windsor which he had reverently founded and built.

This prince, although at the time it was thought that he indulged his desires and passions to excess, was a Catholic of the truest faith and a most stern enemy of heretics, a most benevolent patron of learned men, scholars and clerics, a most devoted observer of the sacraments of the Church and most penitent of sinners.

Those who were present at his death bear witness to this. To them, especially to those whom he left as executors of his last will, he declared in an unambiguous and orthodox manner that it was his intention that satisfaction should be given to all those persons in whose debt he was, from his movable assets which he would leave behind him in great abundance.

This was the best of ends for a prince of this world.

Death of a king

ALTHOUGH Edward died on 9 April 1483, a mass was mistakenly sung for his soul three days earlier, in York, probably because his final illness took the form of a death-like paralysis or coma. Philippe de Commynes suggested that his early demise – he was only 40 years old – was caused by an apoplexy, the result of excessive eating and drinking and of debauchery; today we would call it a stroke.

The king was buried with proper ceremony at Windsor on 20 April. His funeral rites, which had started at Westminster on 17 April, cost £1,500, and some of his possessions had to be sold to cover the cost – at his death there was only £1,200 in cash in the treasury. Neither of the king's brothers was present: George, duke of Clarence, had been executed five years before, in 1478, and Richard, duke of Gloucester, was in the north.

Edward left a troubled legacy behind him. He had a pointless and expensive war on his hands against the French and Burgundians, who – to his fury – had allied at Arras in December 1482. The small clique of nobles to whom much authority had been delegated in the provinces was beset with rivalries: in particular Richard of York, duke of Gloucester, was bitterly opposed to the power and influence exercised by the Woodvilles. Edward's death made conflict between the two inevitable.

In the relatively stable conditions of the reign, government had made a recovery. The king's approach was not based on any abstract theories of monarchy but was pragmatic and practical; he raised new men to high offices and he put much energy into supervising routine functionings of the royal administration. To operate efficiently, his bureaucracy had to be solvent. An inner group of officials emerged who handled Edward's finances directly, largely by circumventing the cumbersome machinery of the exchequer, and by treating public revenues as if they

were his private finances. Much of the money raised went on schemes of personal and dynastic aggrandizement – the king's attempts to arrange suitable marriages for his children were a long-standing preoccupation. England's commercial interests concerned him, but largely for the revenues he reaped from them; and the strong emphasis he laid on law and order was not impartial, it aimed to benefit crown rather than people. Edward had restored the prestige of monarchy and had provided strong leadership, but he had created a personal regime which would be stable only as long as he survived. In April 1483 the English people therefore faced an uncertain future.

Above *Edward's tomb screen at Windsor.*

Below *Angels on Edward's chapel at Windsor.*

RICARDVS · III · ANG · REX ·

Part VI

Richard III
1483–1485

Edward V, the twelve year old eldest son and heir of Edward IV, ruled – in name only – for little more than two months. Real power was held by the protector, his uncle Richard of York, duke of Gloucester, who was crowned in his stead in July 1483.
Many contemporaries believed that Richard III ordered the murder of Edward V and his younger brother Richard – known to posterity as the princes in the Tower – and had thus earned his own subsequent death at the battle of Bosworth (1485), where his army was defeated by Henry Tudor. Although very little evidence survives for this matter, it is certainly the view held by John Rous, who describes the opening of the reign. The writings of John Russell, the Crowland chronicle continuator, and of the Italian humanist Dominic Mancini, are also critical of Richard III, but in a more measured way.
(Opposite: Richard III)

To King Edward IV succeeded, but for a lamentably short time, his son King Edward V, who was residing at Ludlow at the time of his father's death; the boy was thirteen and a half, or thereabouts. He was brought up virtuously by virtuous men, remarkably gifted, and very well advanced in learning for his years.

On the death of his father his father's friends flocked to him. On 24 April, after the accustomed service of the knights of the Garter had been solemnly celebrated at Ludlow, according to the English fashion, concluding with a splendid banquet, the young king departed for London.

Richard, duke of Gloucester, brother of the deceased king and by his ordinance protector of England, came upon him with a strong force at Stony Stratford and took the new king his nephew into his governance by right of his protectorship. The rest, namely Anthony, Earl Rivers, elder brother of the queen and the new king's uncle, Richard Grey, brother of the king on his mother's side, and Sir Thomas Vaughan were forthwith arrested, and imprisoned at Pontefract, where shortly afterwards they were unjustly put to death. And so the new king was separated from his loyal servants and was received like an innocent lamb into the hands of wolves. His special tutor and

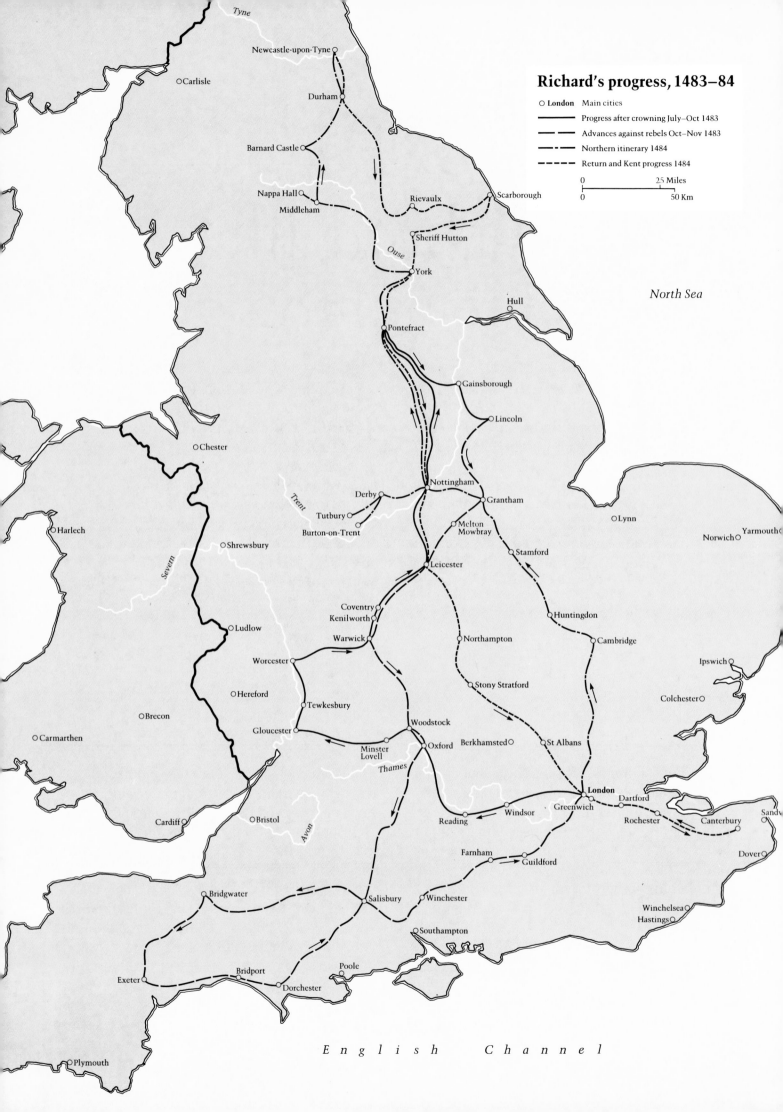

Richard's progress, 1483–84

○ **London**	Main cities
——	Progress after crowning July–Oct 1483
—·—	Advances against rebels Oct–Nov 1483
—··—	Northern itinerary 1484
- - -	Return and Kent progress 1484

0 ____ 25 Miles
0 ____ 50 Km

Tyne

○ Carlisle

Newcastle-upon-Tyne ○

Durham ○

Barnard Castle ○

Nappa Hall ○
Middleham ○

Rievaulx ○

Scarborough ○

Sheriff Hutton ○

Ouse

York ○

Hull ○

North Sea

Pontefract ○

Gainsborough ○

Lincoln ○

○ Chester

Trent

Derby ○
Tutbury ○
Burton-on-Trent ○

Nottingham ○

Grantham ○

Melton Mowbray ○

○ Lynn

Norwich ○   Yarmouth ○

○ Harlech

Shrewsbury ○

Stamford ○

Leicester ○

Huntingdon ○

Cambridge ○

Ipswich ○

○ Ludlow

Coventry ○
Kenilworth ○

Warwick ○

Northampton ○

Colchester ○

Worcester ○

○ Hereford

Stony Stratford ○

○ Brecon

Tewkesbury ○

Woodstock ○

Gloucester ○

Berkhamsted ○

St Albans ○

○ Carmarthen

Minster Lovell
Oxford ○

Thames

○ Bristol

Cardiff ○

Avon

Reading ○   Windsor ○

London   Dartford ○

Greenwich ○

Rochester ○   Canterbury ○   Sandw

Farnham ○   Guildford ○

Dover ○

Bridgwater ○

Salisbury ○   Winchester ○

Winchelsea ○

Hastings ○

Southampton ○

Bridport ○   Poole ○

Exeter ○
Dorchester ○

○ Plymouth

E n g l i s h   C h a n n e l

Richard III's progress 1483–85

During Richard III's short reign of two years and two months he was almost constantly on the move, a reflection of the problems and pressures he faced. The king, accompanied by his vast household of at least 200 people, probably covered as much as 3,000 miles altogether; at its fastest, on the march to subdue Buckingham in the autumn of 1483, his unwieldy company managed between 20 and 30 miles a day, where a smaller group might have achieved 45 miles.

In more settled times English sovereigns spent much of their time at London and Westminster coping with administrative and legal duties. Richard was there only for 10 months out of 26. On his travels the king visited such farflung but important places as Exeter, Worcester, Newcastle-upon-Tyne, and Dover, as he strove to retain crown and kingdom.

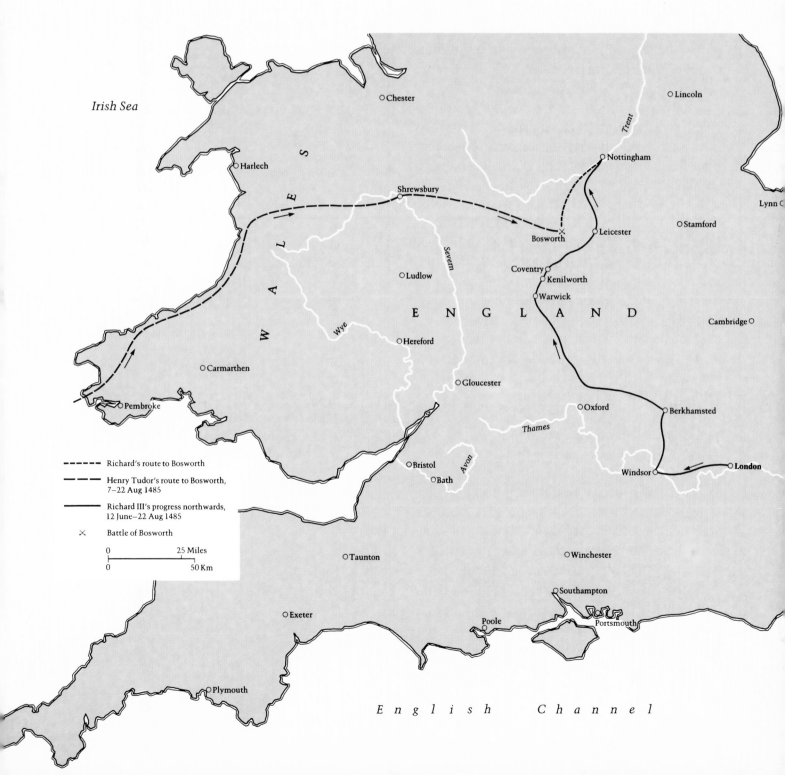

Irish Sea

○ Chester

○ Lincoln

Trent

○ Harlech

W A L E S

Shrewsbury ○

Nottingham ○

Lynn ○

Bosworth ✕   ○ Leicester

○ Stamford

Coventry ○

Kenilworth ○

Warwick ○

○ Ludlow

Severn

E N G L A N D

Cambridge ○

Wye

○ Carmarthen

○ Hereford

Gloucester ○

○ Oxford

○ Berkhamsted

Pembroke ○

Thames

Windsor ○

London

○ Bristol
○ Bath

Avon

- - - - -   Richard's route to Bosworth

– – – –   Henry Tudor's route to Bosworth, 7–22 Aug 1485

————   Richard III's progress northwards, 12 June–22 Aug 1485

✕   Battle of Bosworth

0	25 Miles
0	50 Km

○ Taunton

○ Winchester

○ Southampton

○ Exeter

○ Poole

Portsmouth

○ Plymouth

E n g l i s h   C h a n n e l

diligent mentor in *godly* ways, Master John Alcock, bishop of Worcester, was removed like the rest. What more? Edward V was taken to London and received with fitting honour by the mayor and citizens. In his name the laws of the kingdom were enforced at Westminster and throughout the realm in the accustomed way. Coins were struck in his name, and all royal honours were paid to him.

The young king was at that time staying in the palace of the bishop of London. The king's mother, Queen Elizabeth, hearing of the arrest of her brother and sons, fled with her possessions from the royal palace of Westminster to the abbey, to take shelter in the security of that privileged place. She kept with her her son, the boy Richard, duke of York, and her daughters.

Shortly after, Rivers, Grey and Vaughan were cruelly killed at Pontefract, lamented by almost all. Anthony Woodville, Earl Rivers, was found to be wearing, at the time of his death, the hair shirt which he had long been in the habit of wearing against his bare flesh. These lords were condemned to death by the earl of Northumberland on the false charge that they had in fact plotted the death of Richard, duke of Gloucester, at that time protector of the kingdom of England; and, for a thing they had never contemplated, the innocent humbly and peaceably submitted to a cruel fate from their enemies' butchers. The consecrated hair shirt of Earl Anthony was long after hung before the image of the Blessed Mary the Virgin at the Carmelite Friars at Doncaster.

Richard of York, the protector, was born on 21 October [1452] at Fotheringhay in Northamptonshire; he was retained within his mother's womb for two years, emerging with teeth and hair to his shoulders. At his nativity Scorpio was in the ascendant, which is the sign of a house of Mars. And like a scorpion he combined a smooth front with a stinging tail. He was small of stature, with a short face and unequal shoulders, the right higher and the left lower.

As the Crowland chronicler shows, Richard now set about eliminating more of the young Edward V's supporters.

Edward V

WHEN Edward IV died on 9 April 1483, his elder son was 12 years old and the king's demise raised the question of where power should lie during the prince's adolescence. The two men with the strongest claim to authority during a minority were away from court when the king died: Edward's only surviving brother, Richard, duke of Gloucester, was in Yorkshire; and the queen's eldest brother, Anthony Woodville, Earl Rivers, was at Ludlow with the prince of Wales, whose governor he was. Power therefore rested with the royal council, which started to organize the immediate coronation of the prince, a move which would have made a formal minority government unnecessary.

The general consensus is that the council's action was almost certainly in line with Edward's last wishes. However, the Italian observer Dominic Mancini believed that the king had wanted Richard to be protector until the prince came of age, and that the council deliberately ignored his wishes. He interpreted the council's preference for an immediate coronation as a cynical attempt to exclude Richard from power in favour of the Woodvilles; the family's closeness to the young Edward V would ensure they dominated any government nominally headed by him.

At the end of May, Richard and the prince's party, both *en route* to London, met at Stony Stratford. The duke seized the prince and arrested Rivers and his leading associates. When the news reached London the queen dowager, Elizabeth Woodville, tried to launch a counter-attack. However, she gained no support and took refuge in sanctuary with her daughters and her younger son, Richard, duke of York. Gloucester entered London unopposed on 4 May.

Richard's control of the prince left the council with little choice but to recognize his claims to be protector, and for the next six weeks Gloucester and the council ruled in Edward's name. On 10 June, however, Richard wrote privately to the city of York requesting military aid against a conspiracy led by the Woodvilles. The first public indication that anything was wrong came three days later, when William, Lord Hastings was executed at the Tower of London. Richard claimed that Hastings had been plotting against him, but the execution was probably a pre-emptive strike, intended to clear Gloucester's path to the throne. Hastings had been one of Edward's closest friends and is unlikely to have acquiesced in the deposition of his heir. Three days later, on 16 June, Richard persuaded the queen dowager to surrender the duke of York, on the grounds that he would be needed to attend Edward V's coronation later that month.

Above *Prince Edward with his father and mother as Earl Rivers presents a book to the king.*

Contemporaries were by now in no doubt that Richard intended to take the throne, and government business started to wind down as men tacitly waited for a new regime. However, Gloucester still needed to find justification for deposing his nephew. First he used the story, current in the 1470s, that Edward IV himself was illegitimate. Later he claimed that Edward's marriage to Elizabeth Woodville was bigamous because the king had been pre-contracted to Lady Eleanor Butler, who had died in 1468. If true, this would have rendered the children of the king's marriage illegitimate and barred from the succession. On 26 June Richard took the throne.

His motives are controversial. Tudor chroniclers ascribed his action to simple ambition. Recent writers, influenced by the rediscovery of Mancini's account earlier this century, have seen him as a victim of circumstance,

forced into increasingly extreme measures to protect his position. Mancini, who probably derived his version from sources close to Richard, believed the Woodvilles, not Gloucester, to be the aggressors. The truth is probably somewhere between these two extremes. Richard must have feared that the Woodvilles' closeness to the young king would diminish his own influence – and his earlier career shows him to have been a man who liked power. But domination by the Woodvilles would also have destroyed the political harmony established by Edward IV in his second reign. Richard presented himself to the people as the one hope of stability in a worsening political climate, and he himself may well have believed this view.

283

The day when the coronation of Edward V would definitely take place had been fixed as 24 June, and everyone was looking forward to the peace and prosperity of the kingdom. However, what prompted the greatest doubt was the imprisonment of relatives and servants of the young king, and the fact that the protector did not have sufficient regard for the honour and safety of the queen, Elizabeth, widow of Edward IV.

The powerful Lord Hastings, chamberlain of Edward IV, who seemed to oblige the dukes of Gloucester and Buckingham in every way and to have earned special favours from them, was overjoyed at this new world, declaring that nothing more had happened than the transfer of the rule of the kingdom from two of the queen's relatives to two of the king's. This had been achieved without any killing or any more spilling of blood than that from a cut finger.

However, a few days after making this remark, joy gave way entirely to grief. The previous day, the protector showed extraordinary cunning by dividing the council, so that in the morning part met at Westminster and part in the Tower of London where the king was.

On Friday, 13 June, Lord Hastings came to the council at the Tower where, on the orders of the protector, he was beheaded. Two senior churchmen, Thomas, archbishop of York, and John, bishop of Ely, were spared capital punishment out of respect for their status, and they were taken as prisoners to different castles in Wales.

Thus, without justice or trial, the three strongest supporters of the new king had been removed, while his remaining followers were fearing something similar. Thereafter, the two dukes did whatever they wished.

Dominic Mancini, who was in London in 1483, gives an elegant description of the protector's assumption of power. As a preliminary step, Richard procured the release of the younger prince, Richard, duke of York, from his Westminster sanctuary, and placed him in the Tower with his brother, Edward V.

Richard Crouchback

RICHARD, duke of Gloucester, was the youngest son of Richard, duke of York, and Cecily Neville. When his brother Edward took the throne in 1461 Richard was only nine and played little part in the early years of the reign. He came to prominence in the unrest of 1469–71 when, unlike his elder brother Clarence, he remained loyal to Edward. When the king returned to power in 1471, he created a major power base for Richard in the north of England.

Although Gloucester also had interests in East Anglia and Wales, and national responsibilities as admiral and constable of England, the heart of his power remained in the north, and after his accession he relied increasingly upon men from that region. The centrepiece of his northern power was the land formerly held by his cousin, Richard Neville, earl of Warwick, centred on Middleham and Sheriff Hutton in Yorkshire and Penrith in Cumberland. Richard was given the land by Edward but his claim on traditional Neville loyalties was strengthened by his marriage to Anne, one of Warwick's two daughters. Over the next ten years, with royal backing, Gloucester became the effective lord of the north. He built up a major following among the northern gentry, and also drew into his orbit the region's other noblemen, including the earl of Northumberland.

Richard's power came partly from his position as the king's brother, which allowed him to exploit royal influence on behalf of himself and his supporters, but it must also have owed something to his abilities and personality. He undoubtedly inspired considerable loyalty among his servants – loyalty which, in some cases, lasted beyond his death and is unlikely to have been entirely self-interested. Richard fulfilled contemporary expectations of a 'good lord'. He was in a position to be generous to his followers, and willing to be open-handed, both as duke and king. He upheld justice and brought to the north a

peace and stability which it had not known for several generations. Gloucester also conformed to the belief that a lord should be an effective war leader, and had an abiding interest in military matters. He shared the English kings' traditional commitment to war against the Scots and French, and, as king, dreamed of leading a crusade against the Turks. It was one of the ironies of his reign that he never led his country against a foreign enemy.

Richard enjoyed power and understood its demands. He also resented attempts to reduce it, and this resentment was probably one of the factors behind his coup of 1483. His seizure of power also reveals his preference for immediate, straightforward solutions to problems – which could result in actions of cynical brutality. He believed that the end justified the means, and his perception of himself as the best ruler to succeed his brother led to the central paradox of his reign: that a king committed to good government could so dramatically flout the conventions of acceptable political behaviour.

Above *A carving of Richard III from a choir stall. Impressions of his appearance vary with the source: many of those from before 1485 show a relatively upright kingly figure, while those which followed his death were coloured by the hunchback legend of Tudor propaganda.*

Opposite *Richard's boar badge. The subversive ballads of the time referred to Richard as 'the Hog'.*

In appearance Richard, unlike his brothers, apparently favoured his father's side of the family rather than his mother's. Contemporary references suggest that he was relatively short and slight; portraits show him with dark hair. His best-known characteristic, a hunch back, seems to have been a later literary invention, perhaps based on memories of a real, but slight, physical defect such as round shoulders.

Richard's actions up until now had given reason to think he was aiming for the crown. Yet some hope remained that this might not be his intention, for he had not yet gone so far as to lay claim to the throne itself. Indeed, he declared that he acted as he did only so that treason might be avenged and past wrongs righted. Moreover, all private deeds and official documents continued to bear the titles and name of Edward V.

However, after the removal of Hastings, the attendants who had previously ministered to the young king's needs were all kept from him. He and his brother were transferred to the inner chambers of the Tower proper.

Every day their appearances behind the bars and windows grew less frequent and eventually they ceased to appear altogether. The doctor, Argentine, was the only one of Edward's former retinue who still attended him. He told how the young king, like a victim prepared for sacrifice, sought remission of his sins by daily confession and penance, believing that death was close at hand.

It is fitting that I should here describe the young king's endowments. Yet they are so many that their enumeration would be a most arduous task. For it is recorded that, in word and in deed, he revealed the fruits of a liberal, indeed a scholarly, education, far in advance of his years. Thus is it permissible for me to spare myself this great labour.

One matter, however, I shall not pass over, and that is the young king's extensive knowledge of literature. For he was able to discourse most elegantly on literary matters. Indeed, whatever book, whether prose or verse, came into his hands (unless it were a work of one of the more abstruse authors) he was able to comprehend completely and declaim with clarity and feeling.

Such was the dignity of his person and charm of his visage that none who looked upon him was ever weary of the sight. And after he disappeared, I saw many men moved to weeping and lamentation at the mention of his name. However, I have not yet been able to establish whether he was done away with and, if so, by what means.

The princes in the Tower

THE fate of Richard III's nephews, Edward V and Richard, duke of York, is the most notorious issue of his reign. The two boys were in the Tower at the time of his accession and there is no evidence that they ever emerged again. Anxieties about their fate were current when Richard was crowned in July 1483. By the autumn it was generally believed that they were dead. By the end of September, Richard's opponents had turned to Henry Tudor as rival candidate for the throne, a choice which would have been inconceivable if the princes were thought to be still alive. In January 1484 the chancellor of France spoke of the crown of England being transferred to the murderer of Edward IV's children – the most plausible version of events, in spite of the vigorous counter-offensive launched by Richard's modern defenders.

As king, Richard was in the best position to order the princes' death. He also had the strongest motives for doing so. Although his coup had met with little overt opposition, his coronation was followed by conspiracies to

*Above **The two doomed princes, at left, praying with their father Edward IV.***

overthrow him and reinstate Edward V. In London there was a plot to start fires in the city and rescue the princes from the Tower under cover of the resulting confusion. The attempt failed, and four of the plotters were executed, but it proved that the princes were still a political threat. The claim that they were bastards did not bar them permanently from the succession since it could easily be repudiated.

By autumn 1483 Richard may have felt that his own security, and perhaps the peace of the realm, demanded the princes' death. The men most closely identified with his regime probably felt the same; two early accounts credit the duke of Buckingham with advising that the princes should be killed. This does not mean that Richard welcomed the necessity. A prayer composed for his use is to St Julian (a saint who achieved redemption even after murdering his own parents), and the tone of Richard's public pronouncements suggests that for the remainder of his reign he attempted to justify his action, spiritually and politically, through the quality of his government.

Previous usurpers had allowed deposed monarchs to live until a major rising demonstrated that they still commanded support, and the same was probably true of the princes. By killing his nephews Richard surely hoped to cut the ground from under his opponents' feet; and their choice of Henry Tudor, a political nonentity, as rival candidate suggests how nearly he succeeded. However, to be successful, the tactic required that the princes' death be publicized. Unlike previous deposed kings the princes had no public funeral – but there was a strong and widespread rumour that the princes had died violently.

The full story of their death is unlikely ever to be known. The version familiar from Sir Thomas More's history of the reign, which casts Sir James Tyrell as the murderer, is a later invention, which can be faulted on several points of detail. Tyrell, who is said to have confessed to his part in the murder before his own execution in 1502, was indeed one of Richard's closest allies and as such a plausible candidate. However, the responsibility was probably fastened on him because Henry VII at that time needed a scapegoat for dynastic reasons and Tyrell was the only one of Richard's inner circle still alive.

Once Richard felt secure, he put aside the mourning robes which he had worn constantly since the death of his brother, Edward IV. Instead, he wore robes of purple and often rode about the city accompanied by a thousand attendants.

He paraded himself with the intention that the people should see him and acclaim him – though he still pretended to no more than the title of protector. Every day he entertained large numbers of guests in his private apartments; yet, when he displayed himself in the streets of London, almost no one came to watch. Rather they cursed him, hoping he would be punished with a fate in accordance with his misdeeds, for his intentions were by now clear to all.

It was then that he took the chance to make his purpose quite plain. For he had so corrupted the preachers of God's word that they did not blush to say in their sermons to the people, without the slightest regard for decency or religion, that King Edward IV's offspring should be disposed of at once, since he had no right to be king, and no more had they. For they claimed that Edward was conceived in adultery and bore no resemblance to the late duke of York, though he had been passed off as his son. Rather, Richard, duke of Gloucester, who looked just like his father, should come to the throne as the rightful successor.

Meanwhile, Richard summoned all the peers of the realm to London. They supposed they were to hear the reasons for Hastings's execution and to reopen the discussion of the best time for Edward's coronation (for it seemed the coronation should be postponed after such a serious and unparalleled occurrence). Each man came, attended by the retinue that was appropriate to his title and station. However, they were advised by the duke to send all their retainers back home, excepting the few necessary for their personal requirements. As a pretext for this, Richard claimed that the people of London were afraid that such a vast gathering of men might turn to plundering the wealthy city, being too many for their masters to prevent them – this had happened in the past as the duke reminded them. The magnates complied with his request.

Then, when all was ready, Richard sent the duke of Buckingham to the house of lords. Buckingham was to submit to the decision of the peers the question of who was to be king, acting as if Richard knew nothing of his mission.

Buckingham argued that it was wrong for the boy to be crowned king since he was a bastard. For his father, King Edward IV, was betrothed to another woman, through the agency of the earl of Warwick, when he married Elizabeth.

Indeed, on Edward's instructions, Warwick had espoused this other lady by proxy, as they call it in her country. Besides this, Elizabeth herself had been married to another and had been rather ravished than wed by Edward. The children of such a marriage were not worthy of the throne.

As for the son of the duke of Clarence, Edward IV's brother, his father's crime had invalidated his claim to the crown. For Clarence, convicted of high treason, had forfeited not only his own but also his children's right of succession.

None was left of royal blood but Richard, duke of Gloucester, who was entitled to the crown according to the law and was, moreover, fitted by his many virtues to bear its burdens. Good government was assured by his record of distinguished service and by his excellence of character. If at first he declined the duties of kingship, he might yet be persuaded, if the magnates themselves were to ask him.

Hearing this speech, the lords were mindful of the fate which had befallen Hastings and were well aware that the alliance of these two dukes, of Gloucester and Buckingham, who had such vast armed forces at their disposal, would be difficult and dangerous to resist.

Fearing for their own safety, they decided to declare Richard king and request him to assume the duties of government.

The next day, all the lords assembled at the house of Richard's mother, for Richard himself had gone there so that this business might not be

The beginnings of portraiture

INTEREST in the precise representation of reality grew appreciably during the late 14th and the 15th centuries. In Italy, artists were obsessed with depicting calculable and tangible space. In Flanders, the development of oil as a painting medium and the strength of medieval manuscript traditions led painters to concentrate on the precise rendering of surfaces, their texture, and the way light fell on them. One aspect of this new realism was the development of the portrait.

In the 11th, 12th or 13th centuries, figures were identified by dress and accoutrements, which generally indicated their status – a king wore his crown, a bishop his mitre, a monk his habit – or by inscription. Donor portraits, in which the patron was depicted offering a building, or book, or reliquary, for which he had paid, to God, or perhaps the Virgin, were also standard.

Gradually, almost imperceptibly, however, identifiable individuals replaced idealized icons.

Tomb sculpture produced early attempts to achieve a recognizable likeness; as with Edward III's effigy in Westminster Abbey, death masks may have been used to help in this process.

A handful of official portraits have survived, portraits which put a stamp on the subject's status. The awe-inspiring, full-length, frontal painting of Richard II in Westminster Abbey is an example (p. 18): a unique survival, both an image of kingship and a representation of an individual as king. *The Arnolfini Wedding* by Jan van Eyck commemorates the wedding in 1434 of an Italian merchant trading in Bruges and seems to be another example of an 'official' painting. The artist painted a discreet self-portrait in the mirror in the centre of the panel, and signed it, as if he were a witness to the wedding, *'Jan van Eyck fuit hic'*.

As portraiture developed and devotional panel painting grew in popularity, donor portraits were given a new lease of life: it is clearly and specifically Richard II, not a generalized king, who is recommended to the Virgin in the Wilton Diptych. Federico de Montefeltro (1444–82) of Urbino had Piero della Francesca paint his famous tournament-scarred likeness at the feet of the Virgin. Van Eyck's Chancellor Rolin – serious, considering but confident – faces the Virgin firmly and on almost equal footing across his palatial hall. The Portinari family, who occupy the wings of van der Goes' *Adoration of the Shepherds*, are more grandly dressed than the Virgin, more fashionable than the angels and saints.

Portraits in which the subject appeared simply as

Above *A fifteenth-century French portrait of Philip the Bold, duke of Burgundy. The old-fashioned profile composition arose from donor portraits, where the donor was shown from one side offering items to the Virgin or Christ Child at centre stage.*

himself or herself were first painted in the mid 14th century. The earliest surviving example is also the earliest surviving French panel painting: the portrait of John II of France. Simone Martini's painting, now lost, of Petrarch's Laura, was made for purely private reasons and this concept of portraiture became increasingly popular in the 15th century.

The earliest surviving portraits usually show the subject in profile, and this viewpoint remained fashionable throughout the century. The pugnacious profile of Federico de Montefeltro – admittedly the right side of his face had been shattered in a tournament – is as familiar as the snub nose of John, duke of Berry, immortalized by the de Limbourg brothers in the *Très Riches Heures* in about 1413. However, by the early 15th century the more sophisticated three-quarter face was generally accepted as the one that best conveyed the subject's physical traits and personality. It has remained the standard approach in portraiture ever since.

Left *Van Eyck's* Arnolfini Wedding. *Oil
paint, which Jan van Eyck perfected, gives
the scene its rich luminosity. The bride is
not pregnant, merely posed in a
conventional attitude. Details such as the
chandelier and the oranges by the window
confirm the artist's remarkable sense of
space, far beyond the early perspective
experiments of his Italian contemporaries.*

Above *A donor portrait by Hans
Memling from the 1460s showing Sir John
Donne of Kidwelly and his family kneeling
before the Virgin and Child. Both Sir John
and his wife wear the Yorkist order of suns
and roses; signifying their allegiance.
Despite its perspective, the picture puts the
donors nearly in profile and Mary's throne
recalls old altarpiece frames.*

conducted in the Tower, where the young king, Edward V, was being held prisoner. There the business was transacted. Oaths of allegiance were pledged and all the other necessary acts were performed.

On the two subsequent days, the people of London and the higher clergy followed suit. For it is these three orders, which the English call the estates, who discuss all important matters and make all decrees law. Once these rituals had been duly performed, a day was chosen for the coronation. Then, acts which had been passed in the name of Edward V since the death of his father were rescinded or suspended. Seals and titles were changed. All matters were now guaranteed and confirmed in the name of Richard III.

In the mean time, as the day set for his coronation drew near, Richard summoned troops to London from his own estates and from those of the duke of Buckingham. In all, these numbered about six thousand, for he was afraid that the great gathering of people at his coronation might provide occasion for a demonstration against him.

He himself went out to meet the troops, as they approached the city. The soldiers were drawn up in a circle on a vast field and he went about their ranks bareheaded, thanking them. He returned thence to the city, accompanied by the troops.

When the day preceding the coronation dawned, according to English custom the king left the Tower of London, which is situated at the eastern edge of the city. Bareheaded, Richard passed through the centre of the town, accompanied by the entire nobility in a regal procession. The onlookers who stood along the streets acclaimed him as he greeted them. He rode on as far as the church they call Westminster, which stands at the other end of the city, towards the west – a distance of about two miles. For it is an English custom that sovereigns are crowned in this church.

So, on the following day [6 July], Richard was anointed and crowned King of England by the unwilling archbishop of Canterbury.

Now as we have so often had occasion to refer to the city of London, it seems only proper that we devote a little space to a description of its situation and resources. Indeed, London herself would have every right to complain of us, if we were to neglect her, for she is renowned throughout the world and has deserved well of us.

The city lies on the left bank of the River Thames – that is to say, north of the river, for the Thames flows from west to east into the ocean. The river is navigable for large vessels as well as rowing boats as far as London, since, besides boasting copious supplies of its own water, it is also replenished by the sea when the tide comes in (as happens twice a day).

Now, on the right bank, that is to say to the south of the river, is a splendid suburb whose many streets and buildings would make it worthy to be called a second city, were it surrounded by walls. This suburb is connected to the city itself by means of a most famous bridge which is built partly of wood and partly of stone. And on this bridge are houses and several gates, equipped with portcullises. Below the houses are workshops owned by artisans who ply a variety of different crafts.

The city on the opposite bank is built on a gentle incline towards the river; part is built on flat and even land, while to the north, open fields stretch out towards other suburbs.

To the east, London is protected by a great citadel on the river, which they call the Tower of London. From the Tower it is a distance of about two miles to Westminster, on the western side, which is also situated on the river. All along the banks of the Thames are vast warehouses for the storage of imported goods. There are also many cranes of enormous size which serve to unload the cargoes from the ships.

From the eastern part of the city, by the Tower, three paved streets lead towards the western walls and the western quarter of the town. Now these streets are the busiest in London and are virtually straight. The one nearest the river is on a level slightly lower than that of the other two. It is here

Resistance, politics and propaganda

RICHARD III's first – and only – parliament was summoned to meet in November 1483. It was, however, postponed when in the autumn of 1483 a series of risings broke out in the southern and western counties, expressing the dissatisfaction of former leading servants and councillors of Edward IV with his brother's regime. In particular their opposition focused on Richard's treatment of his brother's heirs, by this time presumed murdered. This dangerous threat was made worse when Henry, duke of Buckingham, emerged as the leader of the insurgents, promulgating a plan that Henry Tudor should marry Elizabeth of York and be placed on the throne in Richard's stead.

Richard put down the rebellion easily, but the defection of his supporters and the emergence of Henry Tudor as a serious rival were menacing signs. The king still felt vulnerable and was anxious to secure parliamentary approval for his seizure of the throne and to improve his image by introducing a series of legal and commercial reforms. He also had to obtain authority for the grants of land with which he had rewarded his supporters after the rebellion: the spoils had been distributed hastily and in disregard of the common law.

Richard therefore needed a compliant house of commons – and he probably 'packed' the parliament that assembled in January 1484 with yes men to get one. Although the names, and thus the affiliations, of only a few of the 300 or so members who assembled at Westminster are known, their choice of speaker is very revealing: the lawyer, William Catesby, sitting in his first parliament. One of Richard's favourites, he had been a notable beneficiary of the confiscations that followed the October uprisings and had a vested interest in pushing through the acts of attainder against the leading rebels. He was a skilful manager of a servile lower house: some English kings had been voted customs dues for life, but Richard was the first to receive them at the start of his reign. Within barely a month, his legislative programme passed on to the statute book. Measures were introduced to regulate the setting up of trusts, to allow bail to suspected felons, to establish property qualifications for jurors and to prevent fraudulent land sales. Although these enactments are sometimes given as evidence of Richard's enlightened approach to kingship, it is more likely that they were a calculated attempt to widen his dangerously narrow platform of support. Certainly, this was why he introduced protectionist legislation against foreign merchants, and promised to abandon Edward IV's

Above *William Catesby, Richard III's speaker.*

practice of extorting 'benevolences' or gifts from his wealthier subjects.

What mattered most to Richard was the confirmation of his royal title by the three estates (lords spiritual, lords temporal and commons) in parliament. His appeal for ratification, made through the chancellor, Bishop John Russell, in his opening sermon, has led some historians to describe him as the first 'constitutionally elected monarch'. Nothing could be further from the truth. He believed his claim to the throne had been endorsed by representatives of the three estates in June 1483, but hoped that parliament's formal sanction would check the spread of treasonous rumours more effectively. The events of the following year were to show that this hope was vain.

that liquid or heavy goods are stored, that is to say, all varieties of minerals, wines, honey, pitch, wax, flax, ropes, thread, grain, fish and other lowly commodities. Almost nothing but cloth is sold in the second of the three streets.

In the third street, which takes you to the middle of the town and runs on the level, men deal in far more costly goods – gold and silver cups, silks of purple and all other kinds, carpets, tapestries and many other foreign wares. You will find nothing lacking in any of these streets, but each provides best the sorts of goods I have described above.

Other quarters too of the city are thronged with many inhabitants and boast tradesmen of many kinds. Indeed, the whole city is in the hands of craftsmen and merchants. However, their houses, unlike those of merchants in other lands, are not cluttered up about the entrance with goods. Rather there lie great storerooms situated in the inner parts of the houses, where goods are laid up and stored, just as we see bees pack away honey in the cells of their hive. But no more of London.

Now I have told about the upheaval in England. But how Richard ruled and how he governs still, I have not been able to discover, since I was recalled from England to France, shortly after Richard came to the throne.

Farewell, then, and may my work, slight though it may be, find some little favour in your eyes. Once more farewell. This work was completed at Beaugency, in the county of Orléans, on the first day of December, 1483.

The Crowland chronicler describes Richard III's lavish progress to the north of England – his power base – to impress his new subjects with his royal power and status.

On 6 July, Richard, duke of Gloucester, received the gift of the royal unction and the crown in the conventual church of St Peter at Westminster. At the same time and in the same place his wife, Anne, received her crown as queen. Thereafter, for the rest of his life, this man was known as King Richard, the third after the Conquest.

Wishing, therefore, to show off the eminent royal rank that he had acquired for himself in this manner as widely as possible in the north, where previously he was best known, he set out from the city of London, passing through Windsor, Oxford and Coventry until he reached York.

There in the metropolitan church on the day appointed for the repetition of his coronation, he also introduced his only son Edward, whom that day he had invested as prince of Wales with the emblems of the golden staff and the wreath. He had organized splendidly lavish celebrations and banquets in order to win over the hearts and minds of many people. Nor was there a shortage of wealth with which to carry out the designs of his ambitious mind since, as soon as he considered usurping the throne, he seized all that his late brother, the most glorious King Edward IV, had amassed with great skill and effort during many years previously and which he had made available to his executors for them to carry out his last will.

While these events were taking place, Edward and Richard, King Edward IV's two sons, remained in the Tower of London under special guard.

However, people in the southern and western parts of the kingdom began to agitate for their liberation from captivity and to enter into societies and associations, many of which worked in secret, others openly, with this aim.

Finally the people living in the regions surrounding the city of London and several other southern counties of the kingdom, embarked upon avenging their grievances against Richard III.

It was publicly proclaimed that Henry, duke of Buckingham, who had supported Richard III and was then living in Wales at Brecon, was repentant of what had happened and was to lead the enterprise against the king. After this, it was widely believed that Edward's two sons must have met their fate by some unspecified act of violence.

Rous is more explicit about the end of the two princes. He alleges that Richard 'received his lord Edward V with embraces and kisses, yet within

Anne Neville

Above *Anne Neville shown with her royal husband and their son Edward. The bear at her feet is the Neville emblem.*

TWO of the greatest heiresses of the 15th century, Anne Neville and her elder sister Isabel were the daughters of Richard, earl of Warwick and Salisbury – the kingmaker – and Anne Beauchamp, an heiress in her own right. When Warwick broke with his cousin Edward IV, he married Isabel to George, duke of Clarence, the king's discontented younger brother, and then conspired with Queen Margaret, his old enemy, to restore Henry VI to the throne. To cement this fragile alliance, 14 year old Anne was married in December 1470 to Henry's only son, Edward, prince of Wales – and widowed when he was killed at the battle of Tewkesbury in 1471.

Warwick had died in the battle of Barnet earlier in 1471 and Anne's brother-in-law, Clarence, was reluctant to allow the sisters' inheritance to be split; he hoped to retain it all in Isabel's right. When his younger brother, Richard, duke of Gloucester, began to show an interest in the 15 year old widow and her share of the inheritance Clarence, according to one account, concealed Anne in London in the disguise of a kitchen maid. However, Richard found her and carried her off to sanctuary and they were married early in 1472. The great north country estates of the Nevilles that Anne inherited provided Richard with a power base from which he was able to launch his successful bid for the throne.

When Richard and Anne were crowned in 1483 they had one frail son, Edward, who became prince of Wales but who died in 1484. The king and queen were 'almost bordering on madness by reason of their sudden grief'. Anne died a year later from a wasting disease – probably tuberculosis – which had already claimed her sister Isabel.

Along with the Neville lands, the Yorkshire-bred queen had inherited the fierce loyalty of her father's northern followers. Richard, too, gained their support as a result of his marriage – and could ill afford to lose it. When rumours that he had poisoned Anne became rife, he was forced into the humiliating position of having to deny the accusation – and that he was contemplating marriage with his niece, Elizabeth of York – to the council. If he married Elizabeth, he was told, 'all the people of the north, in whom he placed the greatest reliance, would rise in rebellion against him and impute to him the death of his queen ... through whom he had gained his position'.

The first English heiress to become queen, Anne is a shadowy figure. Any significance she has is that she was the daughter and co-heir of Warwick the kingmaker.

about three months he killed him, together with his brother. [But] it was afterwards known only to very few what manner of death they suffered.'

The leaders of the opposition to Richard III realized that it would soon be the end of them all if they were unable to find a new candidate for the throne to lead their campaign. They remembered Henry Tudor, earl of Richmond, who for many years had been living in exile in Brittany. Accordingly, word was sent to him by the duke of Buckingham, urging him to hasten to England as quickly as he could in order to wed Elizabeth, the eldest daughter of the late king, and through her to take possession of the whole kingdom.

The whole plot was revealed by spies to Richard who as ever did not act sleepily, but swiftly and with the greatest vigilance. In both Wales and all the nearby Marches surrounding the duke of Buckingham, he arranged for armed men, encouraged by his considerable wealth which the king had transferred to them, to be ready to seize all the duke's household possessions.

The duke was meanwhile staying at Weobley at the house of Walter Devereux, Lord Ferrers, together with the bishop of Ely and his other advisers. When he realized that he was surrounded and could find no way out at any point, the duke secretly disguised himself and set out, leaving behind his followers. He was finally discovered hiding in the hut of a poor man, through the unusually abundant supply of food that had been brought there.

The duke was arrested and taken to the city of Salisbury, to where King Richard III had advanced with a large force. He was executed in the market square of that city on All Souls' Day, 2 November, even though that year it fell on a Sunday.

The following day, the king and all his army turned towards the west of the kingdom where all his enemies had taken up their positions, and he advanced as far as Exeter. Terrified by his arrival, Peter Courtenay, bishop of Exeter, Thomas, marquis of Dorset, and several other noblemen from the surrounding area who had conspired in the rebellion – those of them that could find ships ready and waiting at least – put to sea and finally landed on the welcoming shores of Brittany.

Others withdrew to temporary hiding-places, relying upon friends, and subsequently entrusted themselves to the protection of holy places.

While the king was still in Exeter, Henry Tudor, earl of Richmond, unaware of this unrest, was stationed with several ships beyond the mouth of Plymouth harbour, together with the followers he had brought over from Brittany, in order to find out what was actually going on.

When the news of the current situation reached him, both of the death of the duke of Buckingham and of the flight of his own faction, he hoisted his sails and put out to sea again.

After these events, the king gradually reduced the size of his army, discharging those whom he had summoned to the expedition from the distant northern Marches, and came to London having triumphed over his enemies without going to war, though at no less cost than if the two armies had fought it out hand-to-hand.

In this way all that very great treasure and wealth which King Edward had thought he was leaving behind him for very different purposes began rapidly to be used up.

1484

Passing over the Christmas celebrations, I come to the parliament which began on about 22 January. In this parliamentary session, the claim by which the king had ascended the throne the previous summer was confirmed.

Although that lay court could not legally pronounce on it since the validity of a marriage was in dispute, none the less it took it upon itself to do so because of the great fear that had struck the hearts even of the most resolute. In addition, so many great lords, nobles, other prominent figures and commoners, even three bishops, were proscribed, that we do not read of the like ever

Henry Tudor

ALTHOUGH Henry Tudor's descent was impeccably Lancastrian, it gave him a tenuous title, at best, to the crown. The circumstances of Richard III's reign, and not Henry's background, brought a Tudor to the throne in 1485.

After the Yorkist triumph of 1461 Henry, aged four, was put in the custody of an ally of the new king Edward IV, William Herbert of Raglan, who brought the boy up in his Yorkist household. When Herbert died in 1469, Henry was cared for by his uncle Jasper Tudor, who had remained unswervingly Lancastrian. After the collapse of Henry VI's regime in 1471, uncle and nephew fled into exile and spent the next 12 years, until Edward IV's death, in Brittany.

Margaret Beaufort, Henry's mother, forged links with Edward's court through her marriage in 1472 to the king's councillor and steward of the household, Thomas, Lord Stanley, and, by the time of Edward's death, the possibility of Henry's return to England had been canvassed, although nothing had come of it. Richard's accession changed the situation dramatically. His obvious insecurity gave Margaret the chance to arrange for her son's restoration as the price for supporting Richard's opponents and she was almost certainly involved in the plan to rescue the princes from the Tower.

As a result, Henry Tudor was in the public eye just when Richard's opponents were faced with finding a new figurehead after the princes' presumed death. Tudor sources credit Margaret Beaufort with persuading the rebels to accept her son's claims, and it is possible that one of her bargaining counters was the promise of help from her husband, Thomas, Lord Stanley, against Richard. Stanley had his own reasons for disliking Richard's regime, notably the intrusion of the duke of Buckingham, the king's leading ally, into Wales, where the Stanley brothers were influential. Ultimately, Buckingham joined the rebels, and Lord Stanley, unwilling to be allied with him, threw his support behind Richard.

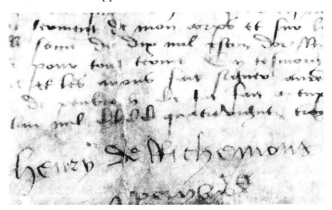

Above *A portrait of Henry Tudor.*

Left *Henry Tudor's signature on an IOU for a loan to finance the rebellion of 1483.*

Although the 1483 rebellion collapsed, it established Henry Tudor as Richard's rival for the throne. Almost completely unknown, he probably aroused little enthusiasm at first except as an alternative to Richard; but the tide turned slowly in his favour as the king's insecurity led him to rely increasingly on a small exclusive group of supporters. There were further outbreaks of unrest, several of which involved Richard's former allies.

Henry Tudor meanwhile strengthened his appeal to Edward's former servants by swearing to marry his daughter Elizabeth should he become king. Henry's credibility was increased further in autumn 1484 when the French king, Charles VIII, agreed to support him. Relations between France and England had been strained since shortly before Edward's death and Henry's campaign offered Charles the opportunity to put pressure on the English. Henry Tudor was a far more potent threat with this support: many Englishmen joined him in France, and French money made the 1485 invasion possible.

having taken place. How many estates and inheritances were gathered into the king's treasury as a result of these actions!

While this session of the supreme council of the realm continued, Queen Elizabeth, who had been harassed by repeated intercessions and dire threats, had sent all her daughters out of the safe sanctuary of Westminster to King Richard.

One afternoon in February almost all the lords spiritual and temporal of the realm and the most powerful knights and esquires of the king's household foregathered, at the king's specific command, in a downstairs room off the corridor leading to the queen's quarters.

Each man put his name to a new oath, drawn up by persons whose identity I know not, pledging their allegiance to Edward, King Richard III's only son, as their supreme lord, if anything should happen to his father.

Soon afterwards, however, it was made plain how fruitless are the plans of men when they wish to arrange their own affairs without God.

The following April, on a day close to the anniversary of King Edward IV's death, this only son on whom rested all hope of the royal succession, expressed in so many oaths, died in Middleham Castle after a brief illness.

Then you would have seen both the father and the mother, when they received the news in Nottingham where they were staying, go almost out of their minds for a time with sudden grief.

The father, however, still yet the king, looked to the defence of his territory, for there was then a report that the exiles and those who had been proscribed would soon reach England with their leader, Henry Tudor, earl of Richmond, to whom all these exiles had sworn allegiance as if to their king in the hope that a marriage could be arranged with King Edward IV's daughter. King Richard III was better prepared to resist that year than he would be at any time subsequently, partly because of the treasure which was to hand – for not all of

that left by King Edward IV had been spent – partly because of the personal grants that had been distributed throughout the kingdom.

Richard put into practice the new technique, introduced by King Edward during the last war in Scotland, of stationing one mounted courier every twenty miles.

These latter, riding hard but not crossing their own boundaries, were able to carry messages two hundred miles and always within two days by letters passed on from hand to hand. Nor was he without spies abroad whom he had hired at whatever price he could and from whom he learned nearly all his enemies' moves.

Furthermore, he had lost several ships and two of his boldest captains, Sir Thomas Everingham, and John Nesfield, at the hands of the French when he was occupied with maritime affairs at the outset of the second year of his reign. During that same period, none the less, Richard scored a notable triumph over the Scots using the same skills.

So notable a triumph was it indeed that they sent the most distinguished petitioners that they could find in the kingdom of Scotland as ambassadors to King Richard at the castle in the town of Nottingham on 7 September, who most respectfully requested peace and an end to the war in a lengthy and skilful speech.

This was in spite of the fact that the same summer they had suffered a great slaughter at our hands on land, but had inflicted no less a slaughter on our men in the same battle, for as well as many Englishmen captured in battle the fugitives from Scotland, Lord James Douglas, and many other of his fellow exiles, were taken prisoner by them at this time.

Thus, agreements were drawn up between the representatives of each kingdom in accord with the wishes of the king of England, concerning those topics which seemed to warrant most discussion. After the council had been dissolved, King Richard returned to London.

Shifting alliances

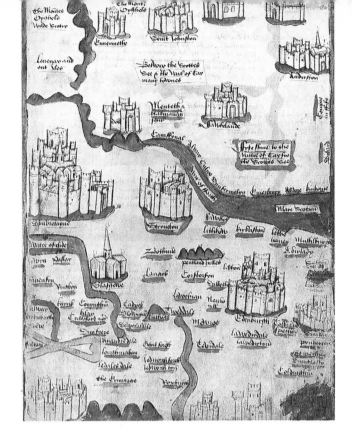

EDWARD IV had worked patiently to detach Scotland from the 'auld alliance' with France, and James III, the Scottish king, was responsive to his approaches. In 1474, the two men concluded a marriage alliance whereby James III's son and heir would marry Edward's daughter Cecily; a full peace treaty was promised.

In 1475, however, Edward sealed the treaty of Picquigny with Louis XI, isolating Scotland. It was the Scots who now made the running, but their negotiations with England bore little fruit. Despite a series of shaky truces, relations between the two countries deteriorated, and meanwhile Louis XI worked hard to sabotage *entente* and reactivate the 'auld alliance'. Edward joined with disaffected Scots to recapture Berwick (ceded by the Lancastrians in 1461) – and recover his daughter's dowry.

James III had many enemies, some inherited – notably men dispossessed by the political upheavals of the previous half-century – and some of his own making: an influential group was bitterly opposed to his pro-English policy, many of them border magnates whose way of life depended on perpetual hostility between the realms.

The former earl of Douglas, who had been in exile since his lands had been confiscated by James II in 1455, was one of the first group and had been recruited by Edward in the early 1460s. In Scotland he had little support: too many people had gained from the confiscations. Douglas's main use to Edward was to communicate with disaffected Scots north of the border.

James III's brother, the reckless and feckless Alexander, duke of Albany, was more directly useful to the English. In 1479 when he fled to France after escaping from prison and an impending treason trial, Edward promised him support in his attempt to gain the Scottish throne.

In April 1480, Richard, duke of Gloucester, was sent to wage war on the border strongholds. Hostilities intensified and in May 1482, the English king gave Richard 20,000 men and ordered him to recapture Berwick and set Albany on the Scottish throne as Edward's vassal. However, James III was captured by a small group of rebels led by his ambitious half-uncles, and the Scottish army was disbanded. Gloucester and Albany entered Edinburgh unopposed; James was being held, incommunicado, in the castle.

It soon became clear that no one in Scotland wanted Albany as King Alexander IV, while the duke himself was prepared to settle for the restitution of his lands and titles. Gloucester negotiated successfully on Albany's behalf with a handful of James's councillors, and with Edinburgh's representatives who, anxious to be rid of the English army on their doorstep, contracted to repay

Above **A map of Scotland**, *c. 1479–80.*

Cecily's dowry. Gloucester then returned home via Berwick, which he captured after a short siege.

James soon recovered his freedom and re-established his royal authority, and the alliance with the French was revived early in 1484. Albany's lands, titles, royal grace and public office were restored, but he continued to want more. When his intrigues became generally known in 1484, he fled to England, after handing over his castle of Dunbar to an English garrison. However, Edward IV had died, and his successors faced too many domestic problems to indulge in further kingmaking. Albany was paired with Douglas, and encouraged to make forays into Scotland. A border raid in July 1484 was defeated, and Douglas was captured and imprisoned for the rest of his life in Lindores Abbey in Fife. Albany fled to France, where he was fatally wounded while jousting.

James never forgave the Scots who had allied themselves with Richard as duke of Gloucester, but after 1483 he was quite prepared to open peace negotiations with him as king, for Richard's insecure hold on the south made him look favourably on a settlement in the north. In September 1484, at Nottingham, Scottish and English diplomats met and settled down to work out a lasting treaty. The stumbling-blocks were Berwick and Dunbar, whose return James demanded and Richard strenuously refused. Negotiations were still in progress when Richard died in August 1485.

A few months later, after a prolonged siege, Dunbar was recaptured by the Scots – and has been Scottish ever since. Berwick had changed hands for the last time and remained English.

1485

After the Christmas festival had been duly celebrated in the palace of Westminster, the king
entered on 6 January, wearing his crown, and,
while he was holding the feast in the great hall as
though back at his coronation, he was informed by
his spies on the coasts that, in spite of the power
and splendour of his rule, his enemies would
without doubt invade the kingdom early the following summer, or at least would attempt to do so.

Although nothing was more welcome to him, in
as much as it could be seen as putting an end to all
the doubt and misfortune, he realized none the
less that money – of which he was just beginning
to run very short – was the sinews of war. He
resorted to the demands of King Edward IV which
he had condemned in parliament – although he
spurned entirely the use of his brother's word
'benevolence' – sending out hand-picked men to
extract the greatest possible sums of money from
the coffers of almost all the estates of the kingdom
by pleas and threats, by fair means or foul.

O God, why should I spend more time prolong-
ing this account of so many improper actions that
they can scarcely be counted, and when these
examples are so damaging that it is inappropriate
for them to be imposed upon faithless minds?

There may be many other things that are not
written in this book and of which it is shameful to
speak, but let it not go unsaid that during this
Christmas festival, an excessive interest was displayed in singing and dancing and vain changing
of clothes by Queen Anne and Lady Elizabeth, the
eldest daughter of the late king, who were of
similar complexion and figure. The people spoke
out against this and the nobles and the bishops
were very astonished.

It was said by many that the king was concentrating all his attention on contracting marriage
with Elizabeth, either after the death of the queen
– for which he was waiting – or through a divorce
for which he considered he had sufficient grounds.
He could see no other way of confirming his
position as king nor of depriving his rival of hope.

A few days later, the queen fell seriously ill and
her weakness was considered to have worsened
because the king entirely forsook his consort's bed.
He considered it best to consult doctors.

What is there left to tell? Towards the middle of
March 1485, on a day when a major eclipse of the
sun took place, Queen Anne died.

She was buried at Westminster with all the
honours befitting the burial of a queen.

The king's intention and plan to marry his
niece, Elizabeth of York, was finally reported to
certain people who did not favour it and, after he
had summoned the council, the king was compelled to make a lengthy denial to the effect that
this idea had never entered his head.

There were those in the council who were quite
aware that this was not true. Those who objected
most strongly to this marriage, and whose opinion
the king himself rarely dared oppose, were Sir
Richard Ratcliffe and William Catesby, a member
of the royal bodyguard. They told the king to his
face that if he did not repudiate this plan and did
not respond in person before the mayor and
aldermen of the city of London the northerners,
on whom he principally relied, would all rise up
against him, accusing him of the death of the
queen, the daughter and one of the heirs of the
earl of Warwick, through whom he had obtained
his first honour, in order to satisfy his incestuous
desire for his close relative, in defiance of God.
Furthermore, they brought forward more than
twelve doctors of theology to state that the pope
could not grant a dispensation covering that
degree of consanguinity.

Shortly before Easter, therefore, the king stood
before the mayor and aldermen of London in the
great hall at St John's and in a loud, clear voice
followed entirely the advice to make such a denial;
more, in the opinion of many, in accord with the
wishes of his counsellors than with his own.

At length reports were increasing daily that
those in revolt against the king were finalizing and
speeding up preparations for their arrival in

Intelligence methods

THE essence of personal monarchy was for the king to be well informed, and the royal household provided the crucial link between the Yorkist kings and their subjects. Many household servants were only part-time courtiers. When they were not at court they lived on their estates or followed their careers, gaining knowledge and experience which could be useful to the king. The *Black Book*, Edward IV's household ordinances, recommended that royal servants should be chosen from the whole country so that they could keep the king informed. When Richard needed to raise a loan in 1485, he was well enough informed to be able to tell the collectors whom to approach and how much each man could lend.

Kings also exploited other sources of information. When the duke of Clarence became increasingly disaffected after his wife's death in 1476, tale-bearers ran between his household and Edward's with news of his latest outburst. Richard had advance warning of Buckingham's rebellion but concealed his knowledge until he had completed his preparations to defeat him. Betrayal of associates was a recognized way back to royal favour for men involved in treason. One of the conditions of Richard's pardon for Robert Clifford was that Clifford would keep him informed of conspiracies.

It was more difficult for English kings to obtain foreign information. Calais was a permanent listening-post – its lieutenant, John, Lord Dynham, sent Richard the first news of Louis XI's death – and merchants and travellers were questioned. Rulers exchanged embassies, who gathered information while they imparted it.

Kings were equally interested in publicizing their own points of view, at home and abroad. Parliament was one line of communication – the chancellor's speech at the opening of Edward V's parliament was intended to demonstrate the need for Richard to continue as protector – and the royal household was another; when Richard III repudiated rumours that he wished to marry his niece Elizabeth of York, he did so in front of an assembly which included men of his household. The Church could also be exploited: in 1483 Richard's claims to the throne were first aired in a public sermon.

For Richard III's parliament, in 1484, Chancellor Bishop Russell's opening address and some of the legislation were recorded in English, rather than the customary Latin or French: because it was spoken by the people, it was better suited for a government propaganda campaign. But this ploy exposes the limitations of such attempts: although levels of literacy were comparatively high, there was no uniform national language, and no common standard of usage, spelling or pronunciation.

Above *Spies were common at court.*

The Yorkshire knights who accompanied Richard to London had difficulty in making their 'rough northern dialect' understood in the south, and debates in the commons must sometimes have seemed incomprehensible, as members from opposite ends of the country were effectively addressing each other in different languages.

Information-gathering methods could be used against rulers as well as for them. Richard's plan to persuade the government of Brittany to hand Henry Tudor over to him in 1484 came to the ears of John Morton, bishop of Ely, then in exile in Flanders, who warned Henry in time for him to escape across the French border. In 1484 William Collingbourne, a Wiltshire gentleman, pinned 'bills and ballads of seditious rhyme' to the doors of St Paul's. They included the notorious attack on Richard's inner circle: 'The Cat, the Rat and Lovell our Dog/Rule all England under the Hog' (the Cat was William Catesby, speaker in the 1484 parliament and an esquire of the king's body; the Rat was Sir Richard Ratcliffe, a much-enriched royal knight; and Lovell our Dog was Francis, Viscount Lovell, the king's chamberlain). Richard's opponents may also have spread the story that the king had murdered his wife Anne in order to marry Elizabeth of York, while rumours of betrayal undermined his army's morale at Bosworth.

England. However, the king, uncertain as to the port where they planned to land – for none of his spies was able to give him reliable information – moved northwards shortly before Whitsun.

He left Lord Lovell, his chamberlain, near Southampton, where he was to station his fleet carefully in order to keep a close watch on the ports of the region and not to miss an opportunity of tackling the enemy with the combined forces of the area if they endeavoured to land there.

This unnecessary tactic wasted food supplies and money. In vain, since on 1 August, with a favourable wind, the earl of Richmond and his followers landed at the well-known port of Milford Haven near Pembroke in Wales, without encountering any resistance. The king was delighted – or pretended he was – when he learnt of their arrival, writing messages to all parts saying that the longed-for day had arrived when he would triumph easily over such a feeble company and that the benefits of certain peace would put new heart into his subjects. Meanwhile he despatched terrifying orders in a host of letters to all the counties of the kingdom, forbidding any of their men – at least none of those who were born into any inheritances in the kingdom – from absenting themselves from the forthcoming hostilities, with the threat that after the victory, anyone, anywhere in the kingdom, found not to have been present in person on the battlefield, could hope for nothing but the loss of all his goods, his estates and his life.

Shortly before these men landed, Thomas Stanley, steward of the king's household, had received permission to cross into his native Lancashire to see his home and family from whom he had been absent for a long time; but he was not permitted to stay there unless he sent his eldest son, George, Lord Lestrange, to the king at Nottingham in his place. This he did.

After the landing at Milford Haven in Wales, which we have described, the rebels advanced along difficult and out-of-the-way routes in the northern part of the province where William Stanley, brother of the steward, had sole command as chamberlain of North Wales.

The king sent word to Thomas, Lord Stanley that he should appear before him at Nottingham without delay. The king was afraid that the mother of the earl of Richmond, who in fact was married to Thomas Stanley, would persuade her husband to support her son's faction. However, Lord Stanley was unable to come, claiming the sweating sickness from which he was suffering as his excuse.

Meanwhile his son, George, who had secretly prepared his escape from the king, was discovered and taken in an ambush. After revealing a conspiracy to support the cause of the earl of Richmond involving himself, William Stanley, his uncle, and Sir John Savage, he asked for mercy and promised that his father Thomas would come to the king's aid as quickly as possible with all his forces. In addition, he wrote to his father informing him of the danger he was in, and of his wish that this help should be forthcoming.

Meanwhile, with the enemy advancing in haste towards the king by day and night, it was necessary to move the army from Nottingham, although it had not yet fully assembled, to Leicester. There, the number of men fighting on the king's side was found to be greater than had ever been seen on any one side in England.

On Sunday, 21 August, the king left Leicester amid great pomp and wearing his crown, together with John Howard, duke of Norfolk, and Henry Percy, earl of Northumberland, and other prominent lords, knights, esquires and an enormous throng of the common people. He was kept informed by scouts as to where the enemy was likely to spend the following night and he pitched camp [at Bosworth] eight miles from the town, near to Merevale Abbey.

The leaders of the opposing army were first and foremost Henry, earl of Richmond, whom his men called King Henry VII; John Vere, earl of Oxford; John, Lord Welles; Thomas, Lord Stanley, and his brother William; Edward Woodville, brother of Queen Elizabeth and a most courageous knight; and many other soldiers who had distinguished themselves before this uprising as well as at the outset of the present hostilities.

Perpendicular Gothic

Above *King's College chapel, whose construction spanned the reigns of five English monarchs.*

THREE buildings constructed late in the 15th century are examples of the Perpendicular style at its most refined.

In 1474 Edward IV began the reconstruction of St George's chapel, Windsor, built by Henry III and made a collegiate foundation by Edward III. Between about 1477 and 1483 more than £1,000 a year was devoted to the works, for Edward wanted to create not merely a castle chapel on the grand scale, or a church fit to house the Order of the Garter, but a shrine to the Yorkist monarchy. Unfinished when the king died, it was completed under Henry VII and Henry VIII to a modified design. The original architect, Henry Janys, and his Tudor successors created a vast aisled church, its depressed four-centred arches and its vault, which hovers between the lierne and the fan type, giving it a feeling of restrained elegance. Its focus was to have been a magnificent tomb for the king, fashioned from black marble and with a cadaver below and a silver-gilt effigy above, but Edward's successors made no attempt to complete this glorification of Yorkist kingship.

In a sense nothing became Perpendicular better than a plain box, and that is what the second and third grand buildings are. At Gloucester Abbey, burial place of Edward II and home of a still flourishing unofficial cult, the elegant glass lady chapel was tacked on to the choir where Perpendicular had first reached its full expression. The inclusion of Yorkist badges as ornamentation suggests the work was completed before 1485.

The chapel at King's College, Cambridge, is the same simple aisleless building on an enormously grand scale, with light pouring through the magnificent, largely original glass in the vast mullioned windows; and the whole box is closed by a panelled fan vault. Yet despite the feeling of homogeneity King's College chapel took a long time to build. It was begun in 1446 by the founder of the college, Henry VI. In his will of 1448 the king laid down careful and detailed instructions for the design, which was conceived by his master mason Robert Westerby. The octagonal turrets at the corners, although not mentioned by Henry, were probably a feature of the original design, and link the chapel with other royal foundations like St Stephen's chapel, Westminster.

In 1461 when Henry was deposed the work had cost £16,000 but was far from finished, and it was not until 1480 that it was resumed; both Edward IV and Richard III gave financial support. A second hiatus followed the overthrow of the Yorkists in 1485, but in 1506 Henry VII, who was taking an active interest in promoting the cult of Henry VI, the last Lancastrian king, and in having him canonized, began to take an interest in the chapel, and he had it finished at last.

At dawn on Monday morning the chaplains of King Richard's army were not ready to celebrate mass, nor was any breakfast ready which would restore the king's ailing spirit. That night, it was asserted, he had had a terrible dream, as indeed he confirmed in the morning when his face, which was always drawn, was deathly and drained of colour. He declared that the outcome of that day's battle, whichever side won the victory, would destroy the kingdom of England. He also declared that if he emerged victorious he intended to ruin all the adherents of the opposing side, predicting that his opponent would do just the same to the king's supporters if victory should be his.

Finally, as the enemy leader and his soldiers advanced steadily upon the king's army, still at Bosworth, Richard III ordered that Lord Lestrange should be beheaded forthwith.

However, those entrusted with the task, seeing that the situation was critical and more important than the execution of one man, did not comply with the king's order; they decided to let the man go, and returned to the thick of the fighting.

A most savage battle now began between the two sides. Henry Tudor, earl of Richmond, advanced with his troops directly upon the king, while the earl of Oxford, a most courageous knight and second to Henry in command of the entire army, with a force of both French and English troops, moved against the wing where the duke of Norfolk had taken up his position.

At last, a glorious victory, together with the most valuable crown which King Richard had previously worn, was granted by Heaven to the earl of Richmond, now the sole king.

King Richard, after receiving many mortal wounds, died a fearless and most courageous death, fighting on the battlefield, not in flight. His body was found among the other dead ... and after suffering many humiliations, it was taken to Leicester in an inhuman manner, with a rope around its neck, while the new king also proceeded to Leicester wearing the crown he had so conspicuously won.

Rous also extols Richard's courage, but his epitaph of the king is otherwise highly derogatory.

This King Richard, who was excessively cruel in his days, reigned for three years [*sic*] and a little more, in the way that Antichrist is to reign. And like the Antichrist to come, he was confounded at his moment of greatest pride. For having with him the crown itself, together with great quantities of treasure, he was unexpectedly destroyed in the midst of his army by an invading army, small by comparison, but furious in impetus, like a wretched creature.

For all that, let me say the truth to his credit: that he bore himself like a noble soldier and despite his little body and feeble strength, honourably defended himself to his last breath, shouting again and again that he was betrayed, and crying 'Treason! Treason! Treason!'

So, tasting what he had often administered to others, he concluded his life most miserably, and at last was buried in the choir of the Franciscan friars at Leicester.

Although Richard III's days were short, they were ended with no lamentation from his groaning subjects.

Bosworth

EARLY in June 1485 Richard III made his base at Nottingham, in the centre of England, to await Henry Tudor's invasion with some eagerness: a decisive victory would give him the security he needed to establish his regime on a sounder footing. It was 11 August before he received word that Henry had landed near Milford Haven on 7 August turning north into England near Shrewsbury.

The two armies met near Market Bosworth in Leicestershire on 22 August; the exact site of the battle is uncertain. Although Richard's army was almost certainly the larger, its morale was low. All previous opposition had been characterized by the defection of trusted royal allies, and Richard and his men must have been expecting further betrayals – even without an anonymous message left outside the duke of Norfolk's tent warning that the king was 'bought and sold'. Some of the men summoned to the king's army had already joined Henry Tudor, others had simply not turned up. The earl of Northumberland had been Richard's loyal ally in the north-east during Edward's reign, where he must have hoped for increased influence. The north, however, was crucial to the king's power and the earl's influence was, if anything, declining. No doubt Northumberland hoped that Henry Tudor, who

had little knowledge of the north, would give him a better role. His decision deprived the king of some of his most committed support.

But the *coup de grâce* was administered by the Stanleys. In 1483 they had supported Richard against Buckingham, but the relationship had subsequently cooled, and by the summer of 1485 Richard mistrusted them profoundly. He had kept Lord Stanley's heir George with the royal army, a precaution which seems to have deterred Thomas, Lord Stanley, from joining the battle. Instead, the family's forces were led by Thomas's brother William, who appears to have held aloof until the climax of the battle, when Richard and his bodyguard were committed to the charge against the troops around Henry Tudor. Stanley then threw in his men on Henry's side. The intervention was decisive; Richard's forces were overwhelmed and the king hacked to death. His body, stripped naked, was taken to Leicester, where it was buried in the Franciscan friary.

All assessments of Richard's reign have been distorted by his failure. Had he won – and his final charge came very close to success – he would almost certainly have been able to live down the circumstances of his accession and, as he hoped, justify himself by the quality of his rule.

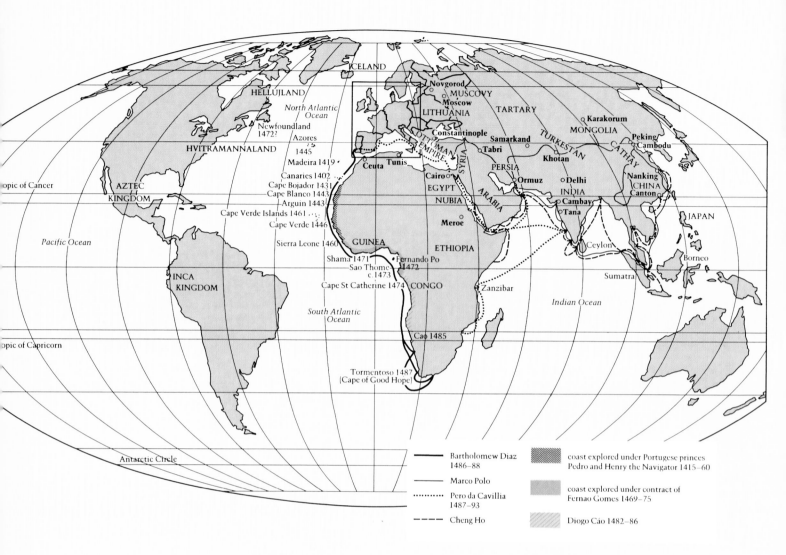

ICELAND

HELLULJLAND

*North Atlantic
Ocean*

Newfoundland
1472?

Azores
1445

HVITRAMANNALAND

Madeira 1419

Canaries 1402
Cape Bojador 1431
Cape Blanco 1443
Arguin 1443

Cape Verde Islands 1461
Cape Verde 1446

Sierra Leone 1460

Shama 1471
Sao Thome
c.1473

Cape St Catherine 1474

Tropic of Cancer

AZTEC
KINGDOM

Pacific Ocean

INCA
KINGDOM

*South Atlantic
Ocean*

Tropic of Capricorn

Cão 1485

Tormentoso 1487
(Cape of Good Hope)

Antarctic Circle

Novgorod
MUSCOVY
Moscow
LITHUANIA
TARTARY

Karakorum
MONGOLIA
Peking
Cambodu

Constantinople
Samarkand
Tabri
TURKESTAN
CATHAY
Khotan
Nanking
CHINA
Canton

OTTOMAN EMPIRE
Ceuta Tunis
SYRIA
PERSIA
Cairo
EGYPT
Ormuz
Delhi
INDIA
ARABIA
NUBIA
Cambay
Tana
Meroe
ETHIOPIA
JAPAN

GUINEA

Fernando Po
1472
CONGO
Zanzibar

Ceylon

Indian Ocean

Sumatra

Borneo

	Bartholomew Diaz 1486–88		coast explored under Portugese princes Pedro and Henry the Navigator 1415–60
	Marco Polo		coast explored under contract of Fernao Gomes 1469–75
	Pero da Cavillia 1487–93		
	Cheng Ho		Diogo Cão 1482–86

SCOTLAND
Edinburgh
UNION OF CALMAR
Baltic Sea
Copenhagen
IRELAND
Dublin
North Sea
ENGLAND
Hamburg
Warsaw
London
POLAND
Thames
Calais
THE EMPIRE
Atlantic Ocean
Paris
Seine
Vienna
Munich
Danube
FRANCE
HUNGARY
Rhone
Venice
Milan
Avignon
Genoa
BOSNIA
Florence
PAPAL STATES
Adriatic Sea
Corsica
Rome
PORTUGAL
SPAIN
Ebro
Tagus
Madrid
Naples
NAPLES
Lisbon
Sardinia
Balearic Islands
Granada
Mediterranean Sea
SICILY
Tunis

The world in 1485

In 1400 Europe was more isolated from China and India than a century before; and the trade in oriental luxuries as plied by Marco Polo and his family in the 13th century had dwindled away. But by 1485 Indian and Arab merchants were once more working the land and sea routes between Europe and Asia in greater numbers. European powers had moreover begun to explore unknown continents, as the Portuguese sailed the coast of Africa and, in the 1480s, reached the Cape of Good Hope and the Indian Ocean. Newfoundland known, like the eastern coast of North America, to the Vikings, may have been rediscovered as early as 1472. The great European expansion was about to begin.

Epilogue

In 1485, Europe's horizons were on the verge of a great expansion. Renaissance learning and culture were flowering and spreading ever further afield, men were increasingly questioning established views, and discontent with worldliness and corruption in the church was gathering momentum. Spain and Portugal were on the brink of establishing their vast maritime empires in the New World and of bringing untold wealth back to Europe. The Tudors replaced the Plantagenets at a time when a new world was dawning.

England, however, had come a long way since the middle of the twelfth century, and her fourteen Plantagenet kings, the male descendants of Henry II, had shaped her destiny. Some, like Richard the Lionheart and Henry V, gained an outstanding reputation on the battlefield; others, like Henry II and Edward I, earned the admiration of posterity for their legal and administrative reforms. Henry III and Henry VI both made a poor showing as politicians and warriors but supported the spiritual life of the kingdom, endowing religious foundations to intercede for their family and their people. The unhappy Richard II, inept as a ruler, was a noted patron of the arts. Many of the consorts of these kings, too, played a significant part in England's history. Eleanor of Aquitaine, the colourful and tempestuous wife of Henry II, fomented discord between his many sons so effectively that she had to be held prisoner by Henry. Isabella, 'the she-wolf of France', with her lover Roger Mortimer, focused opposition to her husband Edward II and was instrumental in his deposition. Margaret of Anjou was effectively in control of her weak and periodically insane spouse Henry VI for much of his reign.

Behind the high dramas of dynastic politics and war, the English kingdom saw many changes under its Plantagenet rulers. The lands it held in France were a link with continental Europe, but government had to function in the king's absence: England's administrative machine, largely set up in the twelfth century and developed thereafter, was long the most sophisticated in Europe. England's barons and parliament, too, were precocious in establishing the principle of opposition to tyrannical monarchy, but this notion allowed for the deposition of unsatisfactory rulers. Edward II's displacement and murder in 1327 was a precedent: it permitted Henry VI in his turn violently to be set aside in 1461 by the house of York, in the person of Edward IV. It was the start of the Wars of the Roses which ended in the downfall of the Plantagenets — on the battlefield — as they had begun six centuries earlier in Anjou. This greatest of families has had an enduring place in literature and history. Their most moving epitaph was spoken in the course of a dispute over a peerage claim in the early seventeenth century:

"And yet time has his revolutions; there must be a period and an end to all temporal things, finis rerum, an end of names and dignities and whatsoever is of this earth. Where is Bohun, where's Mowbray, where's Mortimer? Nay, which is more and most of all, where is Plantagenet? They are entombed in the urns and sepulchres of mortality."

Glossary

Attainder: An act of Parliament by which a traitor (or other offender) lost his lands, disinheriting his heirs.

Azure: The heraldic term for blue used in coats of arms.

Balinger: A light sea-going vessel often used as a warship.

Benevolence: A tax levied without the sanction of Parliament.

Blazon: In heraldry, the portrayal of a coat of arms.

Bull: A papal edict or decree.

Burgess: A citizen of a borough.

Bushel: A measure of 8 gallons (36 litres) volume.

Caparison: A cloth over horse trappings, often decorated.

Chantry: An endowment to pray for the benefactor's soul; a chapel set up privately with its own priests (chantry priests) to say masses for its benefactor's soul.

Chief: In heraldry, the top third of a shield.

Clarion: A shrill trumpet with a narrow tube.

Clerk: A man in religious orders, and by extension anyone learned.

Cloth of gold: Cloth part or wholly woven of gold thread.

Collar: An ornamental chain forming part of the insignia of an order of knighthood.

Crenellate: To add battlements, to fortify a building.

Eyre, justices in: Judges who travelled from county to county hearing cases on the king's behalf.

Florin: A Florentine gold coin famed for its unvarying weight and quality, long used as a standard for international trade.

Groat: A silver English coin worth four pence.

Gules: The heraldic term for red as used in coats of arms.

Hippocras: A medicinal drink made of wine and spices.

King-of-Arms: The official title of the three heralds of the College of Arms who decided heraldic issues.

Lists: The fenced-off area on a tournament field where the fighting took place.

Lollard: An English follower of John Wycliffe's heretical doctrines.

Malmsey: A strong sweet wine, deriving its name from its place of origin, Monemvasia in Greece.

Mark: A boundary, frontier limit, or area defined by frontier markers.

Noble: An English gold coin worth 6s 8d, first minted under Edward III: also called an angel-noble.

Or: The heraldic term for gold as used in coats of arms.

Palfrey: A riding horse, as distinct from a warhorse.

Palisade: A row of sharpened stakes fixed in the ground as a defence, as set up by English archers to defend themselves against horsemen.

Points: Tagged laces or cords for fastening clothing.

Pottage: A thick soup or vegetable stew.

Proctor: A deputy representing a diocese or church body in Convocation, the synod debating church affairs.

Provost: One assigned to superintend a city or area.

Recognizance: A bond recorded before a court, by which a person binds himself to some act or condition.

The Staple: A company of merchants based in Calais and holding a monopoly on the sale and export of English wool.

Surcoat: A coat worn over armour bearing heraldic arms.

Undercroft: A crypt or underground vault.

Yeomen of the Crown: Attendants of the royal household, ranking between a squire and a page.

Bibliography

This is not intended as a comprehensive bibliography of all relevant works, but is a selection of books relating to the topics discussed in the notes and the chronicles. Articles have not been included because they are more difficult for the general reader to obtain; most of the works cited here contain bibliographies which are a good starting point for more detailed reading on individual subjects.

Adair, J., *The Pilgrims' Way*, London, 1978

Aers, D., *Chaucer, Langland and the Creative Imagination*, London, 1980

Allmand, C., *Henry V*, London, 1968

Allmand, C., *The Hundred Years War*, Cambridge, 1988

Allmand, C., *Lancastrian Normandy, 1415–1450*, Oxford, 1983

Bagley, J. J., *Margaret of Anjou, Queen of England*, London 1948

Barber, R., *The Knight and Chivalry*, London, 1970

Barraclough, G., *The Medieval Papacy*, London, 1968

Barraclough, G., ed., *The Times Atlas of World History*, London, 1978

Bennett, J. M., *The Battle of Bosworth*, Gloucester, 1985

Blake, N. F., *Caxton and his World*, London, 1969

Boase, T. S. R., *Death in the Middle Ages: Mortality, Judgement and Remembrance*, London, 1972

Bolton, J. L., *The Medieval English Economy*, London, 1980

Brewer, D. S., *Chaucer in his Time*, London, 1973

Burne, A. H., *The Agincourt War*, London, 1956

Buxton, M., *Medieval Cooking Today*, Waddesdon, 1983

Carus-Wilson, E. M., *Medieval Merchant Venturers*, London, 1967

Chrimes, S. B., *Henry VII*, London, 1977

Chrimes, S. B., Rose, C. D., and Griffiths, R. A., eds., *Fifteenth-century England, 1399–1509*, Manchester, 1972

Clarke, B., *Mental illness in earlier Britain*, Cardiff, 1975

Cobban, A. B., *The Medieval Universities, Their Development and Organization*, London, 1975

Contamine, P., *War in the Middle Ages*, Oxford, 1984

Croft Dickinson, W., *Scotland from the earliest times to 1603*, 3rd ed., revised and ed., A. A. M. Duncan, Oxford, 1977

Crowder, C. M. D., *Unity, Heresy and Reform 1378–1460: the Conciliar Response to the Great Schism*, London, 1977

Davies, R. G., and Denton, J. H., eds. *The English Parliament in the Middle Ages*, Manchester, 1981

Deacon, R., *William Caxton, the First English Editor*, London, 1976

Dobson, R. B., ed., *The Peasants' Revolt of 1381*, 2nd ed., London, 1981

Donaldson, G., *Scottish Kings*, 2nd ed., *London*, 1977

Dufournet, J., *Nouvelles recherches sur Villon*, Paris, 1980

Evans, J., *English Art, 1307–1461*, Oxford, 1949

Evans, J., *A History of Jewellery, 1100–1870*, London, 1953, repr, 1970

Favier, J., *François Villon*, Paris, 1982

Fennell, J. L. I., *The Emergence of Moscow*, London, 1968

Finucane, R. C., *Miracles and Pilgrims*, London, 1977

Fox, J., *The Lyric Poetry of Charles d'Orléans*, Oxford, 1969

Fox, J., *The Poetry of Villon*, London, 1982

Fowler, K. A., *The Age of Plantagenet and Valois*, London, 1967

Fowler, K. A., ed., *The Hundred Years War*, London, 1971

Frankl, P., *Gothic Architecture*, London, 1962

Gentil, P. le, *Villon*, Paris, 1982

Given-Wilson, C., *The Royal Household and the King's Affinity; Service, politics and finance in England 1360–1413*, Newhaven, 1986

Goodman, A., *The Loyal Conspiracy: the Lords Appellant under Richard II*, London, 1971

Goodman, A., *The Wars of the Roses*, London, 1981

Gransden, A., *Historical Writing in England, II, c.1307 to the Early Sixteenth Century*, London, 1982

Grant, A., *Independence and Nationhood: Scotland 1306–1469*, London, 1984

Griffiths, R. A., *The Reign of King Henry VI*, London, 1981

Happe, P., ed., *English Mystery Plays*, Harmondsworth, 1975

Hargreaves-Mawdsley, W. N., *A History of Legal Dress in Europe until the End of the Eighteenth Century*, Oxford, 1963

Harris, G. L., ed., *Henry V: the practice of kingship*, Oxford, 1985

Hay, D., *Europe in the Fourteenth and Fifteenth Centuries*, London, 1966

Hayter, W., *William of Wykeham, Patron of the Arts*, London, 1970

Hibbert, C., *Agincourt*, London, 1968

Hibbert, C., *The Rise and Fall of the House of Medici*, London, 1977

Hicks, M. A., *False. Fleeting, Perjured Clarence*, Gloucester, 1980

Hillgarth, J. N., *The Spanish Kingdoms, 1250–1516, vol. II, Castilian Hegemony, 1410–1516*, Oxford, 1978

Hilton, R., *Bond Men Made Free*, London, 1973

Hilton, R. H., and Aston, T. H., eds., *The English Rising of 1381*, Cambridge, 1984

Hindley, G., *England in the Age of Caxton*, London, 1979

Hindley, G., *The Shaping of Europe*, London, 1969

Holmes, G. A., *Europe: Hierarchy and Revolt*, London, 1975

Horrox, R., ed., *Richard III and the North*, University of Hull, 1986

Howard, D. R., *The Idea of the Canterbury Tales*, Berkeley, 1976

Husa, V., *Traditional Crafts and Skills*, Prague, 1967

Jacob, E. F., *The Fifteenth Century*, Oxford, 1961

Jacob, E. F., *Henry V and the Invasion of France*, London, 1947

Johnson, P., and Leslie, S., eds., *The Miracles of King Henry VI*, Cambridge, 1923

Jusserand, J. A. A. J., *English Wayfaring Life in the Middle Ages*, London, 1920

Keen, M. H., *England in the Later Middle Ages*, London, 1972

Kemp, B., *English Church Monuments*, London, 1981

Kingsford, C. L., *English Historical Literature in the Fifteenth Century*, Oxford, 1915, repr. New York, 1962

Kirby, J. L., *Henry IV of England*, London, 1970

Lambert, M., *Medieval Heresy*, London, 1977

Lander, J. R., *Conflict and Stability in Fifteenth Century England*, London, 1969

Lander, J. R., *Crown and Nobility, 1450–1509*, London, 1976

Leff, G., *Heresy in the Later Middle Ages*, Manchester, 1967

Lewis, P. S., *Later Medieval France, the Polity*, London, 1968

Lindbergh, D. C., ed., *Science in the Middle Ages*, New York, 1978

Lloyd, J. E., *Owen Glendower*, Oxford, 1931

Loomis, L. R., *The Council of Constance*, London, 1962

Macdougall, N., *James III: a political study*, Edinburgh, 1982

McFarlane, K. B., *John Wycliffe and the Beginnings of English Nonconformity*, London, 1966

McFarlane, K. B., *Lancastrian Kings and Lollard Knights*, Oxford, 1972

McKay, A., *Spain in the Middle Ages, from Frontier to Empire, 1000–1500*, London, 1977

McKisack, M., *The Fourteenth Century*, Oxford, 1959

McNiven, P., *Heresy and Politics in the Reign of Henry IV*, Woodbridge, 1987

Marcus, C. J., *A Naval History of England*, London, 1961

Mead, W. E., *The English Medieval Feast*, London, 1967

Newhall, R. A., *The English Conquest of Normandy, 1416–1424*, London, repr., 1971

Nicholson, R., *Scotland: the Later Middle Ages*, Edinburgh, 1974

Nicol, D. M., *The End of the Byzantine Empire*, London, 1979

Ormrod, W. M., ed., *England in the Fourteenth Century*, Woodbridge, 1986

Pernoud, R., *Christine de Pisan*, Paris, 1982

Pernoud, R., ed., *The Retrial of Joan of Arc: The Evidence at the Trial for her Rehabilitation*, trans. J. M., Cohen, London, 1955

Perroy, E., *The Hundred Years War*, 1951

Platt, C., *The English Medieval Town, London*, 1976

Poirion, D., *Le Poète et le Prince: l'évolution du lyrisme courtois de Guillaume de Machaut à Charles d'Orléans*, Paris, 1965

Pollard, A. J., *The Wars of the Roses*, London, 1988

Poole, A. L., *Medieval England*, Oxford, 1958

Power, E. E., *Medieval Women*, M. M. Postan, ed., Cambridge, 1975

Power, E., and Postan, M. M., *Studies in English Trade in the Fifteenth Century*, London, 1933

René d'Anjou, *Le Cuer d'Amours Espris*, ed. S. Wharton, Paris, 1980.

Rickert, M., *Painting in England in the Middle Ages*, London, 1954

Ross, C., *Edward IV*, London, 1974

Ross, C., *Richard III*, London, 1981

Ross, C., *The Wars of the Roses*, London, 1976

Runciman, S., *The Fall of Constantinople*, Cambridge, 1965

Saltmarsh, J., *King Henry VI and the Royal Foundations*, Cambridge, 1972

Sass, L., *To the King's Taste*, London, 1976

Scammell, G. V., *The World Encompassed. The First European Maritime Empires, c.800–1650*, London, 1981

Scattergood, V. J., *Politics and Poetry in the Fifteenth Century*, London, 1971

Schramm, P. E., *A History of the English Coronation*, trans. L. G. W. Legg, Oxford, 1937

Scolfield, C. L., *The Life and Reign of Edward IV*, London, 1923, repr. 1967

Scott, M., *The History of Dress: late Gothic Europe, 1400–1500*, London, 1980

Scott, M., *A Visual History of Costume: the Fourteenth and Fifteenth Centuries*, London, 1986

Seward, D., *Henry V as Warlord*, London, 1987

Seymour, M. C., ed., *Sir John Mandeville's Travels*, London, 1968

Smith, J. H., *The Great Schism*, London, 1970

Steel, A., *Richard II*, Cambridge, 1941

Stone, L., *Sculpture in England, the Middle Ages*, London, 1954

Storey, R. L., *The End of the House of Lancaster*, London, 1966, repr. Gloucester, 1986

Talbot, C. H., *Medicine in Medieval England*, London, 1967

Thomson, J. A. F., *The Later Lollards, 1414–1520*, Oxford, 1967

Thomson, J. A. F., *The Transformation of Medieval England*, Harlow, 1983

Thrupp, S. L., *The Merchant Class of Medieval London*, Chicago, 1948

Tout, T. F., *Chapters in the Administrative History of Medieval England*, Manchester, 1920–33

Tuck, A., *Crown and Nobility, 1272–1461*, Oxford, 1985

Tuck, A., *Richard II and the English Nobility*, London, 1973

Vale, M. G. A., *Charles VII*, London, 1971

Vale, M., *War and Chivalry*, London, 1981

Vaughan, R., *Valois Burgundy*, London, 1975

Vickers, K. H., *Humphrey, duke of Gloucester*, London, 1907

Warner, M., *Joan of Arc, The Image of Female Heroism*, New York, 1981

Warren, F., ed., *The Dance of Death*, Oxford, 1981

Willard, C. C., *Christine de Pisan, her life and works*, New York, 1984

Williams, E. C., *My Lord of Bedford, 1389–1435*, London, 1963

Wilson, C. A., *Food and Drink in Britain*, Harmondsworth, 1984

Wolffe, B. P., *Henry VI*, London, 1981

Chronicles

Part I

Thomas Walsingham, *Historia Anglicana*, ed. T.H. Riley, 2 vols., Rolls Series, 1863–4; I, 329–382; II, 47–235. Extracts.

Froissart, *Chronicles*, ed. and trans. G. Brereton, Harmondsworth 1968; pp 210–408. Extracts.

Thomas Favent, *The Merciless Parliament of 1388*, in *English Historical Documents*, 1327–1485, London 1969; pp 161–2. Extracts.

Part II

Thomas Walsingham, op. cit.; II, 239–89. Extracts.

John Capgrave, *Liber de Illustribus Henrici*, ed. F.C. Hingeston, Rolls Series, 1858; pp 108–9. Extracts.

Chronique de la traison et mort de Richard Deux, ed. and trans. B Williams, in English Historical Society, 1846; pp 248–51. Extracts.

Robert Fabyan, *The New Chronicles of England and France in Two Parts*, London 1811. Extracts.

Part III

Tito Livio, *Vita Henrici Quinti*, ed. T. Hearne, Oxford 1716; pp 4–81. Extracts.

Thomas Walsingham, op. cit.; II, 302–45. Extracts.

John Streeche, *English Historical Documents*, op. cit.; ed. A.R. Myers. p 208.

Johannis de Fordun, *Scotichronicon*, ed. D.E.R. Watt, Aberdeen 1987, vol 8; pp 123–5. Extracts.

Part IV

The Brut or the Chronicles of England, part II, ed. F.W.D. Brie, Early English Text Society, London 1908; pp 431–73. Extracts.

Jean de Waurin, *Chroniques*, ed. W. Hardy and E. Hardy, Rolls Series, London 1884; pp 172–81, 242–53, 348–54. Extracts.

Journal d'un bourgeois de Paris, ed. A. Tuetey, Paris 1881; pp 266–70. Extracts.

Scotichronicon, op. cit.; pp 247–51. Extracts.

John Benet's *Chronicle*, ed. G.L. Harriss and M.A. Harriss, Camden Miscellany, XXIV, Camden 4th series, vol 9, Royal Historical Society, 1973; pp 187–230. Extracts.

The Paston Letters, ed. James Gairdner, repr. 1983; pp 272–3. Extracts.

John Hardyng, *Chronicle*, ed. C.L. Kingsford, English Historical Review, 27 (1912); pp 748–52. Extracts.

John Capgrave, op.cit.; pp 131–133. Extracts.

Part V

Jean de Waurin, op. cit.; pp 339–578. Extracts.

John Warkworth, *A Chronicle of the First Thirteen Years of Edward IV*, ed. J.O. Halliwell, Camden Society, 10, London, 1899; pp 1–13. Extracts.

The Great Chronicle of London, ed. I. Thornley and A.H. Thomas, London 1938; p 212. Extract.

The Crowland Chronicle Continuations, 1459–1486, ed. N. Pronay and J. Cox, London 1986; pp 128–151. Extracts.

Historie of the Arrival of Edward IV in England . . ., ed. J. Bruce, Camden Society, 1, London 1839; pp 1–30. Extracts.

Part VI

Dominic Mancini, *The Usurpation of Richard III*, ed. C.A.J. Armstrong, 2nd edn., Oxford, 1969; pp 59–105. Extracts.

The Crowland Chronicle Continuations, op. cit.; pp 156–84. Extracts.

John Rous, *Historia Regibus Angliae*, trans. A. Hanham in Richard III and his Early Historians, Oxford, 1975 from BL MS Cott, Vesp A XII; p 1. Extract.

John Rous, *The Rous Roll*, ed. C. Ross, London 1980; p 63. Extract.

Manuscripts

(b. = bottom; t. = top; c. = centre; r. = right; l. = left)

2 Elizabeth Woodville (*Book of the Fraternity of Our Lady's Assumption*. English, 15th century.
6 Gardeners disputing (*Cultivement des Terres*, English, 15th century. B[ritish] L[ibrary, London], MS Roy. 14 E VI, f.110).
23 t. The court of the young Richard II (Jean de Waurin, *Chronique d'Angleterre*, Flemish, 15th century. BL, MS Roy. 14 E IV, f.10).
25 The coronation of a king (*Liber Regalis*, English, 1380s. Westminster Abbey, London, MS 38, f.1v).
26 Fashionable group (*Romance of Guiron le Courtois*, French, c.1480. Bodleian Library, Oxford, MS Douce 383. f.1r).
27 b. Bridal couple. (*Histoire de Renaud de Montauban*, French, c.1462. Bibliothèque Royale Albert 1er, Brussels, MS 9967, f.39r).
29 Siege of Mortagne by Owen of Wales (Jean de Waurin, *op. cit.* BL, MS Roy. 14 E IV, f.23r).
31 Burning of heretical books (Netter's *Doctrinale*, book V ch.17, English, 1380s. Merton College, Oxford. MS 319, f.41r).
33 t. Coronation of Pope Boniface IX (Jean Froissart, *Chroniques de France et d'Angleterre*, Flemish, 15th century. BL, MS Harl. 4379, f.34r).
34 John Ball and Wat Tyler leading the rebels (Jean Froissart, *op. cit.* BL, MS Roy. 18 E I, f.165v).
35 t. Wat Tyler's death and Richard II addressing rebels (Jean Froissart, *op. cit.* BL, MS Roy. 18 E I, f.175r).
41 b. Fishmongers (Ulrich von Richental, *Constanzer Consilium*, German, 1450–75. New York Public Library, Spencer Collection, MS 32, p.51).
42 John of Gaunt taking leave of England (Jean de Waurin, *op. cit.* BL, MS Roy. 14 E IV, f.195r).
43 t. John of Gaunt arriving at Lisbon (Jean de Waurin, *op. cit.* BL, MS Roy. 14 E IV, f.195r).
43 b. John of Gaunt dining with the King of Portugal (Jean de Waurin, *op. cit.* BL, MS Roy. 14 E IV, f.244v).
45 t. Farming leeks (*Tacuinum Sanitatis*, Italian, 15th century. Osterreichischen Nationalbibliothek, Vienna, MS 2644, f.25r).
49 t. English chevauchée in France (*Chroniques de France*, French, late 14th century. BL, MS Roy. 20 C VII, f.214v).
51 Man killed by boar (Christine de Pisan, *Lepistre d'Othea*, French, 15th century. BL, MS Harl. 4431, f.124v).
55 Women spinning (*Les Evangelines des Quenouilles*, French, 15th century. Musée Condé, Chantilly, MS 654/1572, f.1r).
61 The Earl of Northumberland affirming loyalty to Richard II (*La traison et mort du Richard II, roy d'Angleterre*, English, mid-15th century. BL, MS Harl. 1319, f.41v).
63 t. New College courtyard (New College, Oxford, Chandler MS 288, f.3v).
64 St John of Bridlington (The Beaufort/Beauchamp Hours, English, mid-15th century. BL, MS Roy. 2 A XVII, f.7v).
67 Folio of sketches of birds (Pepysian sketchbook, English, 14th century. Magdalene College, Cambridge, Pepysian MS 1916, f.11v).
71 t. Geoffrey Chaucer (Thomas Hoccleve, *De Regimine Principum*, English, 15th century. BL, MS Harl. 4866, f.88r).
73 t. Froissart presents his book to Richard II (Jean Froissart, *op. cit.* BL, MS Harl. 4380, f.23v).
73 b. Contract for the tomb of Richard II and Anne of Bohemia (Exchequer KR Accounts Various, English, 1395. P[ublic] R[ecord] O[ffice, London], E101/473/7).
76–77 Richard II greets Isabella of France (Jean Froissart, *op. cit.* BL, MS Harl. 4380, f.89r).

79 Richard II yields the crown to Bolingbroke (Jean Froissart, *op. cit.* BL, MS Harl. 4380, f.184v).
83 Macmurrough riding to meet Gloucester (*La traison et mort, op. cit.* BL, MS Harl. 1319, f.9r).
89 Richard II put in the Tower by Bolingbroke (Jean Froissart, *op. cit.* BL, MS Harl. 4380, f.181r).
95 t. Henry IV cutting off Richard II's line (Genealogy and life of Edward IV, English, 15th century. BL, MS Harl. 7353).
95 b. The coronation of Henry IV (Jean Froissart, *op. cit.* BL, MS Harl. 4380, f.186v).
98 Selling jewellery (Louis de Bruges, *Des symples medichines*, Flemish, 15th century. B[ibliothèque] N[ationale, Paris], MS Fr. 9136, f.344r).
101 Blazing star appearing at the beginning of the Welsh wars (*The Pageant of the Birth, Life and Death of Richard Beauchamp*, English, 15th century. BL, MS Cotton Jul. E IV, art. 6, f.3v).
103 b. The coronation of Joan of Brittany (*The Pageant, op. cit.* BL, MS Cotton Jul. E IV, art. 6, f.2v).
105 b. Writing master's poster (MS fragments, English, early 14th century. Bodleian Library, Oxford, MS E. Mus. 198, f.8r).
107 Pillage and burning of a town (Jean Froissart, *Chroniques de France et d'Angleterre*, 15th century. BN, MS Fr. 2644, f.135r).
113 t. Reconciliation of a heretic (The Exeter Pontifical, English, 14th century. BL, MS Lansdowne 451, f.96r).
113 b. Burning heretics (*Chroniques de France ou de Saint Denis*, French, c.1487. BL, MS Roy. 20 E III, f.177v).
115 t. Charles VI of France with Pierre Salmon (*Demands of Charles VI*, French, 15th century. BN, MS Fr. 23279, f.4r).
115 b. The *Bal des Ardents* (Jean Froissart, *Chroniques de France*, 15th century. BN, MS Fr. 2646, f.176r).
123 Hoccleve presents his book to Prince Henry (Thomas Hoccleve, *De Regimine Principis*, English, 15th century. BL, MS Arundel 38, f.37r).
127 Pope John XXIII investing the abbot of Kreutzlingen (Ulrich von Richental, *op. cit.* New York Public Library, Spencer Collection, MS 32).
129 A sea fight (*The Pageant, op. cit.* BL, MS Cotton Jul. E IV, art. 6, f.18v).
131 The battle of Agincourt (St Albans Chronicle, English, 15th century. Lambeth Palace Library, London, MS 6, f.243r).
134 Crucifixion outside Paris with Charles d'Orléans (Poems of Charles d'Orléans, English, c.1500. BL, MS Roy. 16 F II, f.89r).
135 Christine de Pisan presents her book to Isabella of Bavaria (Collected works of Christine de Pisan, French, 15th century. BL, MS Harl. 4431, f.3r).
137 t. Fall of the Rebel Angels (Pol de Limbourg, *Très Riches Heures du duc de Berry*, French, 15th century. Musée Condé, Chantilly, MS 65, f.2v).
137 b. The month of February (Pol de Limbourg, *op. cit.* Musée Condé, Chantilly, MS 65).
138 Martyrdom of St Apollonia (Jean Fouquet, *Heures d'Etienne Chevalier*, 15th century. Musée Condé, Chantilly, MS 71, f.39).
143 Coronation order for a Holy Roman Emperor (Milanese, 15th century. Fitzwilliam Museum, Cambridge, MS 28, f.110v).
145 Henry V informed of a heretical conspiracy (*The Pageant, op. cit.* BL, MS Cotton Jul. E IV, art. 6, f.12r).
147 b. Building of the temple of Solomon (*Traité de droit coutumier*, French, 15th century. BN, MS Fr. 247, f.163r).

Index

Acknowledgements

Our grateful thanks to the many museums, libraries and individuals, including those listed below, who provided us with illustrations.

(b. = bottom; t. = top; r. = right; l. = left)

Arxiu Mas, Barcelona: 246, 247t., 247r., 250, 257, 258, 258/259.

Barnaby's Picture Library, London: 275.
Bayerische Verwaltung der staatlichen Schlösser, Gärten und Seen: 39t.
BBC Hulton Picture Library: 201.
The Beaufort Collection, Badminton: 47.
Centre Hospitalier de Beaune, Beaune: 179t.
Bibliothèque Nationale, Paris: 98, 107, 115t., 115b., 154/155, 177t., 183, 199t., 233b., 254.
Bibliothèque Royale Albert 1er, Brussels: 27b., 198.
Bodleian Library, Oxford: 26, 105b., 154t., 299.
Bridgeman Art Library, London: 103t., 122, 231, 297t.
British Library, London: 23, 29, 34, 35t., 42, 43t., 49t., 61, 64, 71t., 73t., 76/77, 79, 83, 89, 95t., 95b., 101, 103b., 113t., 113b., 123, 129, 133, 134, 135, 145, 149b., 151, 167t., 169t., 169b., 171l., 188, 190, 193, 206, 207, 209b., 214, 215, 217, 221, 223, 233t., 237, 240, 241, 245b., 253t., 265t., 284, 293, 295, 297b., 301.
British Museum, London: 66t., 99b., 171r., 177b.

Country Life Magazine, London: 81.

Edimages/Caubone, Paris: 147b., 209t., 211, 238, 239, 249t.
Edinburgh University Library, Edinburgh: 159r.

Fitzwilliam Museum, Cambridge: 143.

University of Ghent, Holland: 263.
Giraudon, Paris: 32, 39b., 125, 136, 137t., 137b., 138, 139, 149t., 154b., 175, 187, 196, 197, 213t., 248, 289.

Sonia Halliday: 181t., 286/287.
Staatsarchiv, Hamburg: 267.

King's College, Cambridge: 195b.

Lambeth Palace Library, London: 131, 283.

Museum of London: 71b.

Magdalene College, Cambridge: 67.
Marianne Majerus: 58/59, 60, 63b., 65t., 86, 87t., 87b., 109r., 117, 124/125, 147t., 161, 167b., 194, 195t., 222, 245t., 253b., 255, 268/269, 277t., 277b., 285, 303, 305.
Mansell Collection, London: 33b., 142, 186.
Merton College, Oxford: 31.

National Gallery, London: 22, 74/75, 290, 291.
National Library of Scotland: 185.
National Portrait Gallery, London: 118, 162, 226, 278.
New College, Oxford: 63t.
New York Public Library: 41b., 127.
Northampton Art Gallery: 235b.

Osterreichische Nationalbibliothek, Vienna: 45t., 199b.

L. Perugi, Florence: 111t.
Public Record Office, London: 73b., 189, 213b., 230, 265b.

Royal Academy of Arts, London: 54.
Royal Collections Department, London: 90 (reproduced by gracious permission of Her Majesty the Queen).
Rosgarten Museum, Constance: 158, 159t.

Société des Amis du Château de la Sarraz: 182.
Scala, Florence: 37, 45b., 65b., 110, 111b., 126, 191, 218, 219t., 219b., 243, 249b., 251.
Society of Antiquaries of London: 271.

Musée des Beaux-Arts, Troyes: 78.
Trinity College, Cambridge: 181b.

Victoria and Albert Museum, London: 200

Westminster Abbey, London: 18, 25.

The Worshipful Company of Fishmongers: 35b.
The Worshipful Company of Mercers, London: 109t., 179b.
The Worshipful Company of Skinners: 235t.